THE LION
OF MÜNSTER

THE LION
OF MÜNSTER

The Bishop Who Roared Against the Nazis

BY DANIEL UTRECHT
OF THE ORATORY

TAN Books

Charlotte, North Carolina

This work would not have been possible without the numerous lengthy extracts taken from Löffler, Peter (ed.). *Bischof Clemens August Graf von Galen: Akten, Briefe und Predigten 1933–1946*. Two volumes. 2nd ed. Paderborn: Ferdinand Schöningh, 1996. © Kommission für Zeitgeschichte. Used by permission.

Cover design by David Ferris

Cover images: *Bishop Clemens von Galen*, LizenzgebUhren inkl. 7 % MwSt Fotos of Kardinal von Galen from the Achieves of Anni Borgas Book by Daniel Utrecht and *Nazi Soldiers, 1939* UniversalImagesGroup / Getty Images

Back cover quote from Adolf Hitler as quoted in *Hitler's Table Talk 1941-1944*, Oxford University Press, 1988, p. 555. (Eng. trans. first published 1953 by Weidenfeld and Nicolson.)

ISBN: 978-1-61890-764-6

Published in the United States by
TAN Books
P. O. Box 410487
Charlotte, NC 28241
www.TANBooks.com

Printed and bound in the United States of America.

In memory of my parents

CONTENTS

Introduction: A Glorious Homecoming   ix

1   I and My House Will Serve the Lord   1
2   Priesthood   13
3   New Leader, New Bishop   33
4   Neither Praises nor Fear   41
5   Opening Shots Against the New Paganism   51
6   No Reflection on the Führer   63
7   The Great Procession   75
8   Battle Tactics   95
9   Fresh Graves in German Lands   103
10 Battle for the Cross   115
11 With Burning Anxiety   123
12 If *That* Is the National Socialist Worldview   135
13 Catholic Schools Under Attack   147
14 Nights of Broken Glass   171
15 To Be or Not to Be   179
16 Does the Führer Know?   187
17 "I Lift Up My Voice"   195
18 We Are the Anvil, Not the Hammer   215
19 The Destruction of "Worthless Lives"   229
20 Jesus Weeps   235
21 Revenge Is a Dish Best Served Cold   249

22	Finis Germaniae	261
23	Under Occupation	287
24	Cardinal	313
25	Two Homecomings	337
	Acknowledgments	359
	Appendix: On the Trail of a Mysterious Document	363
	Bibliography	385
	Index	389

A GLORIOUS HOMECOMING

March 16, 1946: a cold, late-winter day in Münster. As Bishop Clemens August Count von Galen's horse-drawn coach progressed through the old inner city, he told his secretary that he felt sorry for the crowds of people lining the streets to greet him: "The poor people are freezing to death this afternoon." Always a keen historian of his diocese, he told his secretary about the day when his predecessor, Bishop Johann Bernhard Brinkmann, had triumphantly returned to Münster sixty-two years ago after six years of exile in Holland—it was February, but it was so warm that many of the people who had come from out of town spent the following night sleeping in the open on the steps of the buildings.

This was another triumphant homecoming. Bishop von Galen had returned, not from exile but from Rome, and was wearing the red hat and robes of a cardinal of the Holy Roman Church. It was less than a year since Germany's defeat in the Second World War, and now Münster's own beloved bishop had been named by Pope Pius XII to the College of Cardinals. Some fifty thousand people had crowded into the city to rejoice.

There had not been much reason for rejoicing in Münster, or in the rest of Germany, for some time. Adolf Hitler's "Thousand-Year

Reich" had done untold damage during its twelve years of power. Germany was a pariah among nations. The horrors of the concentration camps and death camps had been discovered after the war, and they were infinitely worse than anyone could have imagined. Now the entire country was under foreign occupation, and all Germans were blamed for the crimes of their former leaders, even if they themselves had suffered under those leaders.

The people were poor. Many still did not know whether their husbands, sons, and fathers were alive or dead. Ten months after the war, hundreds of thousands of Germans still languished in prisoner-of-war camps, unable to contact their families.

Münster itself was still a city of ruins. Nearly 90 percent of the buildings in the inner city had been damaged by multiple Allied bombing raids. Most were unusable; many were totally destroyed. Very few people still lived in the inner city. By this time, nothing had been rebuilt. The rubble had at least been moved to the sides of the streets and piled up, and this provided elevated places where people could stand to see the festivities. Others climbed onto what remained of the walls of bombed-out buildings. The cathedral, with its roof and towers missing, was unusable for the reception of the new cardinal, but it would not have been big enough anyway. All the festivities were to be in the open air.

Despite everything, March 16, 1946, was a day of rejoicing in Münster. Münster was a staunchly, stubbornly Catholic city and one of the largest dioceses in Germany. The diocese had been founded by St. Ludger in 805, nearly eleven and a half centuries earlier. But it had always been a simple diocese, never an archdiocese, and never in all that time had there been a cardinal occupying its episcopal chair. Now Clemens August von Galen was returning to the city, his city, still its bishop but also a cardinal.

From the tower of the church of St. Lambert came the sound of a fanfare. Trumpeters from the city orchestra had a position there and began to play when the cardinal's coach came near. The coach had begun eight miles west of the city in the village of Telgte, where Cardinal von Galen had spent the morning at the shrine of the Sorrowful Virgin. He had a profound, childlike devotion to the Blessed Virgin Mary and had frequently visited that shrine during his twelve years as bishop, often going there on solitary pilgrimages on foot in the early mornings.

When the coach arrived at the Principal Market, Clemens August stood, blessing the crowd. He was an imposing figure in his scarlet robes, standing about six and a half feet tall. The people of his diocese had always held him in awe, partly because of the respect they would hold for any bishop, partly because of the respect they would hold for a man of noble blood, and partly because of his imposing bearing: He looked the part of a nobleman and a prince of the Church. But they also had a warm, loving affection for him. He was sure of his episcopal dignity and was physically prepossessing, but they knew his kindliness, his simplicity, his easy way with children, and his courage.

Slowly he came down from the coach. Two altar boys took hold of the train of the long red cape, the *cappa magna*, which came down from an ermine hood covering his shoulders. He ascended the steps to a balcony covered with evergreen branches, and the crowd cheered mightily. Ascending the balcony, the mayor came to a microphone and began to read a citation from the city council granting Cardinal von Galen the title of honored citizen of Münster: "Your Eminence: Faithful to your motto *Nec laudibus Nec timore*, you have fought for twelve years against the violations of justice and of conscience, making use of the spoken and written word, at the risk of your freedom and your life, to the wondering agreement of all right-thinking people throughout the world . . . You have consoled and comforted millions of Germans by your manly words."

Everyone knew exactly what the mayor was talking about. From the beginning of his time as bishop, shortly after Hitler took power,

Clemens August von Galen had attacked the Nazi racial theories. In the middle of 1941, when Germany's war successes were at their height, he openly reprimanded the Gestapo for confiscating the houses of religious orders. He had denounced the secret practice of deliberately putting sick and disabled people to death and, it seemed, had an influence in stopping it.

The cardinal spoke a few words of thanks. It was clear that he was deeply moved. He spoke only briefly, as the program of the day had planned for his address to come later.

After a procession to the cathedral, Cardinal von Galen took a seat on a throne that had been prepared before the ruined west portal. Across the large square packed with people, he had a clear view of what was left of his episcopal palace. He had been in the palace when it suffered several direct hits from American bombs in October 1943. When his secretary had come rushing back from the bomb shelter, he had seen the bishop standing high up in the ruins in the open air.

After several more speeches praising the cardinal's courage during the Nazi regime, he came to the microphone. Again and again, he was interrupted by shouts of applause as he thanked Pope Pius for the honor he had given him and the people of his diocese for standing behind him during those years:

> The dear God placed me in a position in which I had a duty to call black "black" and white "white" . . . I knew that many suffered more, much more than I personally had to suffer, from the attacks on truth and justice that we experienced. They could not speak. They could only suffer. . . . But it was my right and my duty to speak, and I spoke . . . and God gave it His blessing. And your love and your loyalty, my dear diocesans, also kept far from me what might have been my fate, but also might have been my greatest reward, the crown of martyrdom.

These were no empty words, and everyone knew it. Documents had been found and published after the war, showing that after Bishop von Galen's sermons in the summer of 1941, the local Gestapo leader had recommended that the bishop be publicly hanged. Berlin responded that "revenge is a dish best served cold." It would be better, thought Joseph Goebbels, to deal with the Bishop of Münster after the war had been won. Otherwise, his popularity in Münster and in all of Westphalia was so great that the government would have to reckon with losing all support for the war effort there.

Cardinal von Galen's voice broke with emotion as he spoke about having missed the crown of martyrdom. After a pause to gather himself, he continued, "It was your loyalty that prevented it. The fact that you stood behind me, and that those who were then in power knew that the people and Bishop in the Diocese of Münster were an unbreakable unity, and that if they struck the Bishop, all the people would feel as if they had been struck"—loud cheering from the crowd interrupted him at this remark. "That was what protected me from external harm; but also what gave me inner strength and confidence."

It was a glorious day for Münster. It was a glorious day for Clemens August Cardinal von Galen. It was Saturday, the sixteenth of March, 1946. It was his sixty-eighth birthday.

Six days later, he was dead.

I and My House Will Serve the Lord

In 1844, Count Matthias von Galen erected a new chapel on the family property at Castle Dinklage. The chapel, large enough to be a small village's parish church, had an inscription above the side entrance:

> I AND MY HOUSE WILL SERVE THE LORD. JOS[HUA] XXIV, 15
> MATHIAS VON GALEN AND ANNA VON KETTELER THE
> LADY OF HIS HOUSE BUILT THIS HOUSE OF GOD AND
> CELEBRATED ITS DEDICATION ON THE DAY OF
> ITS PATRON ST AUGUSTINE, 28 AUG. 1844

For Matthias and Anna von Galen, as members of old noble houses, it was self-evident that they should serve the Lord, live the life of the Catholic Church with deep piety and love, and conscientiously fulfill their obligations to Church and country. They were to pass these principles on to their children and grandchildren and beyond.

Anna was the sister of Wilhelm Emmanuel von Ketteler, the Bishop of Mainz from 1850 to 1877, who was a pioneer of Catholic social teaching and a great influence on Pope Leo XIII's encyclical

Rerum Novarum (1879). The second, fifth, and eleventh of Matthias and Anna's thirteen children became priests, and among their grandchildren are two who have been honored by the Church with the title Blessed. Maria Droste zu Vischering (1863–1899), in Religion Sister Maria of the Divine Heart, was superior of the Sisters of the Good Shepherd in Porto, Portugal. She strove for the rehabilitation of girls and young women driven into prostitution by poverty and urged Pope Leo XIII to consecrate the world to the Sacred Heart of Jesus, which he did two days after her death. Her younger cousin, Clemens August von Galen, the subject of this book, was chosen Bishop of Münster soon after the National Socialist German Workers' Party of Adolf Hitler took power in Germany in 1933. The "Lion of Münster," as he came to be called because of his courage in speaking out against Nazi injustices, outlived the Nazi regime by less than a year.

The fourth child of Matthias and Anna, Ferdinand Heribert von Galen, born in 1831, was to inherit his father's position as head of the family and hereditary chamberlain because his oldest brother, the second child, became a priest and the next son died as an infant. In 1861, Ferdinand Heribert married Imperial Countess Elisabeth von Spee. She also came from a staunchly Catholic noble family. Three of her half brothers became priests, and two of her half sisters became Dominican nuns. Ferdinand and Elisabeth also had thirteen children, of whom Clemens August was the eleventh.

Life at Burg Dinklage, in Lower Saxony (northwestern Germany), was full of love and joy and at the same time was strict and austere. The castle is not what we might think of as a castle. It could hold out against half a dozen knights on horseback in the Middle Ages, but it was really a large set of timber-and-brick farmhouses and barns surrounding a central courtyard, encircled by a moat. There was no running water and, in most of the rooms, no heat. On the ground floor of the left wing were stalls for horses. The children's rooms were above. As Clemens August grew to his full height of over six and a half feet, he not infrequently bumped his head on the ceiling beams of these rooms. An open gallery faced the interior courtyard. The windows on the opposite side looked over the moat to the chapel, to the house of the forester, and to the fields and woods where the children learned to hike, ride, and hunt.

Each day began with Mass at the chapel—a short walk from the front gate, over the moat, to the right, and to the right again. Punctuality was expected. If one of the sons was late for his service as an altar boy, he would get no butter for his bread at breakfast. Those who missed Mass altogether could expect no breakfast at all. Clemens, in later life, remembered a morning when he and his closest brother Franz overslept. "Strick," he cried, addressing Franz by his family nickname, "hurry, we're late for Mass." "Well then, Clau," replied his sleepy brother, using the nickname for Clemens August, "we may as well keep sleeping, because we're not going to get breakfast anyway!" In the evenings, the father led the Rosary in the chapel for the family and servants, followed by a meditation lasting half an hour.

Life in Castle Dinklage gave the von Galen children a love for their family; a sense of what it meant to be an aristocrat related to many of the noble houses of Europe; a keen awareness of the social responsibility that was expected of members of an old noble house; a love of their German fatherland; and a love for the people, landscape, customs, and dialect of the *Heimat*. The *Heimat* was the home territory, the particular part of Germany in which Dinklage was situated, known as Oldenburger Münsterland. In the complex history of the patchwork of kingdoms, principalities, duchies, counties, and cities that came to be modern Germany, the region of Vechta, which included Dinklage, ended up politically as part of Oldenburg in Lower Saxony, but ecclesiastically it remained part of the Diocese of Münster in Westphalia. To this day, the Oldenburger part of the

Münster Diocese is divided from the rest of the diocese by part of the Diocese of Osnabrück.

Above everything else, family life at Dinklage gave the von Galen children a love for the Catholic Church. Ferdinand Heribert and Elisabeth took great pains in the religious education of their children. The farmers and craftsmen of the village of Dinklage, as well as the family and servants at the castle, lived and loved their religion. Münster and Oldenburger Münsterland were staunchly Catholic areas. At roadsides and entrances to farms and businesses, on paths in the woods, one still sees countless shrines: images of the crucified Lord, the Blessed Virgin, and the sorrowful Mother holding her dead son and shrines displaying a prayer for the family or an expression of trust in the Lord's love and mercy. When Clemens August was at boarding school, later in the seminary, and still later as a priest serving in Berlin, his letters to his family constantly returned to the thought of the feasts they celebrated in the chapel built by his grandfather or the outdoor procession of the Blessed Sacrament on Corpus Christi. He sent greetings not only for birthdays but for name days and family anniversaries, and he always recalled with thanksgiving to God—and to his parents for passing on the gift of the Faith—the anniversaries of his own Baptism and first Holy Communion.

Family tradition and Catholic tradition were firmly bound together. In the long history of the Münster Diocese, a von Galen had been bishop before: Christoph Bernhard von Galen ruled the diocese from 1650 to 1678. In those days, when the bishop was also the secular ruler as prince-bishop, Christoph Bernhard was known for the quality of his army, especially his artillery, which won him the nicknames "Bomben Bernd" and "the Cannon Bishop." But he was also a deeply religious man and a good bishop. The ambulatory chapels that he added to the Cathedral of St. Paul in Münster became the place of his tomb and also that of his twentieth-century relative.

The nineteenth century brought a separation between civil and Church authority and frequent struggles over what influence the Church should have on civil and public life. When Clemens August was born in 1878, the *Kulturkampf*—culture war—waged by German Chancellor Otto von Bismarck was beginning to wind down. As the architect of the new German empire dominated by heavily Protestant Prussia, Bismarck had sought to reduce the influence of Catholicism on public life. Religious houses were closed, and priests who criticized the government from the pulpit were imprisoned. This persecution only succeeded in deepening the Catholic identity of Münster, a place with a strong Catholic history in what was a largely Protestant part of Germany. All Catholics of Münster honored their "Confessor Bishop," Johann Bernhard Brinkmann, who was imprisoned for forty days by the Prussian government in 1875. He spent the years 1876 to 1884 in exile in Holland after the government declared him deposed, only to return in triumph to finish his life as Bishop of Münster. Clemens August was proud of the fact that his father twice secretly visited Bishop Brinkmann in Holland and had previously visited him during his imprisonment in Warendorf.[1] In an earlier generation, Clemens August Droste zu Vischering, the Archbishop of Cologne, spent some time in prison in 1837 for refusing to allow priests to celebrate mixed marriages between Catholics and Protestants unless there was a guarantee that the children would be raised Catholic. At that time, Wilhelm Emmanuel von Ketteler, who would later become bishop, resigned his position in the civil service, refusing to serve a state that would require the sacrifice of his conscience.[2]

---

1   Clemens August von Galen, "Haus-und Familienchronik der Grafen von Galen auf Burg Dinklage und Haus Assen," in Joachim Kuropka (Hg.), *Streitfall Galen* (Münster: Aschendorff, 2007), 397.

2   Hubert Wolf, *Clemens August Graf von Galen: Gehorsam und Gewissen* (Freiburg: Herder, 2006), 28.

Clemens August von Galen grew up when these events were still a part of everyday life. Political discussion on the role of the Faith in the state, and the obligations of conscience of a citizen, was regular fare at Castle Dinklage. Count Ferdinand Heribert took an active part in the Centre Party and the Catholic political party and was a member of the Reichstag in Berlin for thirty years. All this contributed to Clemens August's outlook on life. "Father took life and his duties and responsibilities very seriously," he wrote years later in a family history that he produced for his young nephew when the latter became head of the family:

> He had a unique gift, and the regular practice, of considering all questions on the basis of principles, and seeking their solution from the fundamentals of the knowledge of natural and supernatural truth. He considered himself obliged to train us from our youth to think in this fundamental way. To strengthen this in us, he wanted his sons after secondary school to get a fundamental education in Christian philosophy. Through earnest private study, he was constantly working on improving his mind, so that it would serve him with strong logical thought and clear, certain decision. All of us were constantly learning from him. He let us take part in his studies: every morning after breakfast he read to Mother and the older children from a serious book, frequently a historical one. In my years we had Janssen's History of the German peoples, Brück's History of the Catholic Church in Germany, the biography of Fr Pfülf, S.J., Pastor's History of the Popes, as many volumes as had appeared by that time; also journals such as the "Historical-Political Paper" and "Voices from Maria-Laach." From this, in addition to the daily occurrences in the Church and the world, in the house and in the family, there was a great wealth of material for earnest discussion in the family circle. Mother followed these

discussions with great interest, but also took care that we were not lacking in beautiful literature: in the evening after prayers Father would read in the family circle the works of Catholic poets and novelists. In the Catholic newspapers—there were never any other papers in Dinklage—politics was followed assiduously.[3]

Elisabeth von Galen taught all her children their Catechism and gave them such a thorough and good foundation that Clemens later realized that he never learned anything new about the Faith until he began the study of theology. Personal service to the poor was practiced by both parents. The mother and daughters made clothes by hand for poor families and rosaries for the children of the village to receive when they made their First Communion.[4]

The inscription over the entrance of the chapel came from the Book of Joshua. Joshua had challenged the Israelites after their entry into the Promised Land to decide whom they would serve, the pagan gods of their ancestors or the pagan gods of the peoples now living around them. As for him and his house, they would serve the Lord: This motto perfectly expressed the essence of life at Castle Dinklage. When as Bishop of Münster, Clemens August was in constant struggle for the rights of the Church against Nazi totalitarianism, he once told a Jesuit priest, "We Galens aren't great-looking, and maybe we're not very smart; but we're Catholic to the marrow."[5] Among relatives, he used the same line but gave it a more pungent conclusion: "We

---

3   Kuropka, *Streitfall Galen*, 392.

4   Ibid., 397.

5   Günter Beaugrand, *Kardinal von Galen: Der Löwe von Münster*, Freundeskreis Heimathaus Münsterland, Telgte (Münster: Ardey-Verlag, 1996), 29, citing Friedrich Muckermann, *Im Kampf zwischen zwei Epochen*.
R. L. Sedgwick also recounts this in the introduction to his translation of Portmann's biography: Heinrich Portmann, *Cardinal von Galen*, trans. R. L. Sedgwick (London: Jarrolds, 1957), 16.

aren't great-looking and not very smart, but we're brutally Catholic [*aber wir sind brutal katholisch*]."[6]

Clemens August Joseph Emanuel Pius Antonius Hubertus Maria Count von Galen was born in Castle Dinklage on March 16, 1878, and baptized three days later in the temporary church that was serving the village while a new parish church was under construction. The long list of names he was given reflects a common practice among the nobility and was one more element that kept tradition in memory. The double name Clemens August began to be used among the nobility in the eighteenth century to honor Duke Clemens August von Bayern. This man was named Bishop of Regensburg in 1716 at the age of fifteen, resigned that post at eighteen, and managed to acquire and hold simultaneously the posts of Archbishop of Cologne and Bishop of Münster, Paderborn, Osnabrück, and Hildesheim from different dates beginning in 1719 until his death in 1761. In his younger days, Clemens August von Galen used only the single name Clemens but took the double name when he became a bishop, perhaps thinking not only of Clemens August von Bayern but also of Clemens August Droste zu Vischering, the bishop who was imprisoned in 1837 for his courage in defending the Catholic faith. Clemens von Galen was baptized on the feast of St. Joseph. That—and the fact that an older brother named Joseph had died two years earlier at the age of two and a half on March 16, the date on which Clemens was born—accounts for the name Joseph. The name Emanuel recalled Bishop Wilhelm Em[m]anuel von Ketteler, who had died the previous year, in 1877. Pope Pius IX, whom Count Ferdinand Heribert had served as honorary chamberlain during the (First) Vatican Council, had also recently died in February 1878. His name indicates the reverence the family had for him and for the papacy.

---

6   Conversation of the author with Christoph Bernhard von Galen, July 22, 1991.

For two generations, all the children of the family were given the names Antonius Hubertus or Antonia Huberta, and Maria was added at the end of all the boys' names and the beginning of all the girls' names. Adding the name of the Blessed Virgin to all the children's names indicates the family's great devotion to the Mother of God, which would be a constant feature in the life of Clemens August. The other two saints reflect the family's life as country aristocracy. St. Hubert is the patron saint of hunters. There are several saints named Anthony, but a good guess for the one in mind is St. Anthony of Egypt, a popular patron of farmers and of knights, well beloved in Münster.[7]

For his first twelve years, Clemens August was educated at home. His mother gave him his first religious instruction and prepared him for his first Confession. Beginning in 1886, he and his brother Franz had a tutor. At the age of twelve came the great day of his first Holy Communion. (This was before Pope St. Pius X lowered the age for First Communion.) Franz made his First Communion on the same day, and to mark the day, their father gave them a memorable gift: Each received a small linden tree, which they planted across the moat from the entrance to the castle, so that one still passes between them when approaching the bridge. Over fifty years later, Bishop Clemens August von Galen came to Oldenburg to celebrate the Sacrament of Confirmation in the area and brought his secretary to stay with him at Castle Dinklage. "Do you see the two linden trees on the right and left of the bridge?" he asked. "How long have they been there? I can tell you. On April 27, 1890, my brother and I made our First Communion in the parish church of Dinklage. The next morning, my father took us aside and said: 'Here are two small linden trees; you must plant them yourselves. Whenever you see them, you should remember the day of your First Communion.'"[8]

---

7   Other than the remarks on St. Anthony, all this is thanks to Clemens
     Heitmann, *Clemens August Kardinal von Galen 1878–1946* (Dinklage:
     B. Heimann, 2005), 58.
8   Portmann, 35.

Later that year, Clau and Strick were sent off to the boarding school Stella Matutina, run by the Jesuits in Feldkirch, Austria. It was a terrible separation from home and family, but they had each other to help deal with the homesickness, and their older brothers Friedrich and Augustinus had also studied there. Soon Clemens and Franz became accustomed to Stella Matutina, which was widely regarded as one of the best boarding schools in Europe. The Jesuit Fathers believed strongly in a solid education of the whole person. In the classroom, the boys studied Latin, Greek, and French in addition to their native German, along with the usual academic studies. Community life with schoolmates from at least ten nations and all parts of Germany broadened their understanding of the world and developed them in virtue. Music and drama were a regular part of school life. Clemens acted in school plays and played the French horn in the band. Mountain climbing and a variety of winter sports were wonderful new experiences.

Then as now, German students were required to undergo a rigorous examination, the *Abitur*, upon completing secondary school. The von Galens could not take this at Stella Matutina, for the Prussian government still had some of its anti-Jesuit laws on the books. The school was not recognized by the government. So Clau and Strick returned to their native Oldenburg and enrolled for two years at a Catholic school that the government did recognize and support, the Oldenburg Grand-ducal *Gymnasium* Antonianum in Vechta. Clemens would later study again under the Jesuits. He had already begun to have the great admiration for them that he would express so movingly in 1941, when denouncing the Gestapo for appropriating their houses in Münster.

Clemens successfully completed the *Abitur* in August 1896. His report card gave him marks of *good* for morals and industriousness and *satisfactory* in Physical Education. The academic marks are generally divided: a mark for work during the school term and a separate mark for the examination. More often than not, *satisfactory* is the mark given for school work in German, Latin, Greek, Religion, History, and Physics. For French, Mathematics, and Philosophical Propaedeutic, he was assessed as *good*. The examination marks were better, with only Greek and Physics still at the *satisfactory* level.[9]

Upon finishing secondary school, Clemens was eighteen years old and Franz just seventeen. Their father thought it best that they stay at Dinklage until the following spring before beginning university studies. The fundamental education in Christian philosophy, which Ferdinand Heribert considered so crucial for his sons, began in May 1897 at Fribourg in Switzerland. In the mornings, Clemens took courses in philosophy, literature, and history. Three evenings a week, he had lessons in French. He and Franz put order into their lives: Beginning each day with Mass at 7 a.m., they attended lectures until noon, took long walks after lunch, and played cards in the evening after French lessons. The fact that they began each day with Mass shows that the "brutally Catholic" upbringing in Dinklage, as well as the ordered life inculcated by the Jesuits at Feldkirch, had borne fruit. Clemens had become a young man of deep piety and devotion. The year in Fribourg was a crucial year of decision; he was feeling more and more strongly that the Lord was calling him to the priesthood, perhaps as a diocesan priest but perhaps in a religious order.[10] Not surprisingly, he was strongly attracted to the Jesuits.

His first visit to Rome—where he spent three months and was received in private audience by Pope Leo XIII, followed by a retreat in the Benedictine Monastery of Maria Laach—confirmed his decision. He would dedicate his life to God. He enrolled in the

9   Document reproduced in Joachim Kuropka, *Clemens August Graf von Galen: Sein Leben und Wirken in Bildern und Dokumenten*, 3rd ed. (Cloppenburg: Runge, 1997), 54–55. Possible marks were, from best to worst, *sehr gut, gut, genügend, ungenügend*.
10 Max Bierbaum, *Nicht Lob Nicht Furcht: Das Leben des Kardinals von Galen* (Münster: Regensberg, 1946), 53.

theological college run by the Jesuits at the University of Innsbruck. He arrived there in the fall of 1898, sporting a beard that he had allowed to grow during the previous summer in Dinklage because he couldn't be bothered to shave. It made him appear older than his twenty years. "I am Graf Galen," he announced to the rector on his arrival. "Oh," replied the rector, "how nice that you have accompanied your son here for the beginning of his studies." The young man and the priest had a good laugh when Clemens corrected the mistake.[11] The beard quickly disappeared, never to return. Soon, Clemens moved into the Jesuit residence for theology students, the Canisianum.

When he began his theology studies in Innsbruck, Clemens von Galen was, for the first time in his life, separated from his dear brother Franz. Throughout life, however, they remained one in mind and heart. The bishop frequently counted on the advice and support of his younger brother, and Franz, who became a soldier and then a politician, sought the counsel of Clemens in how best to approach the political and social issues of the day.

Clemens studied in Innsbruck until the end of 1902, when, at the insistence of Bishop Hermann Dingelstadt of Münster, he entered the seminary at Münster to prepare for the practical aspects of caring for souls. In the end, the diocesan priesthood won out. Bishop Dingelstadt desired this, and the Jesuits thought it would be good for him, at least for the time being, to get pastoral experience. As it turned out, this was not something temporary. On May 28, 1904, Clemens von Galen was ordained a priest for the Münster Diocese by Bishop Dingelstadt. He was to be a priest of that diocese, and later its bishop, until the end of his life.

---

11   Portmann, 43.

CHAPTER 2

Priesthood

On the day after his priestly ordination, Father Clemens von Galen, wearing vestments that had been made by his mother, celebrated his first Mass in one of the "Galen Chapels" built by Prince-Bishop Christoph Bernhard von Galen in the Münster Cathedral. On June 5, he had a celebratory "first Mass" in the parish church at Dinklage. His uncle, Max Gereon von Galen, who had long been auxiliary Bishop of Münster, preached the sermon. Afterward, Clemens posed for a photograph with his immediate family and a second photograph with his uncle, the bishop, and three priest relatives: his brother Wilhelm Emanuel, who was a Benedictine priest in Prague with the name Father Augustinus, and two of his mother's half brothers, Friedrich von Spee, a member of the Cathedral Chapter in Cologne, and Johannes, now Father Placidus von Spee, a Benedictine at Maria Laach.

On June 16, the new priest received his first assignment. The bishop named him cathedral vicar and assigned him to assist his bishop uncle as his secretary. This entailed accompanying Bishop Max Gereon on his pastoral visitations and Confirmation tours throughout the vast Diocese of Münster. For the young priest, this assignment was an ideal introduction to the pastoral ministry. His uncle lived a simple, ascetic, holy life, which was an example for Clemens to follow throughout his own life. Clemens observed how this holy man preached, conducted ceremonies, and interacted with people from all walks of life. Through his uncle's example, he deepened his love for the holy Mass and the liturgy of the Church. He became familiar with the different regions of the diocese. In this experience, he learned many things that would serve him well as a bishop.

There was one other gift he received indirectly from Bishop Max Gereon von Galen. The bishop was deeply devoted to the Blessed Virgin Mary and loved to visit the image of the Sorrowful Mother at the pilgrimage shrine of Telgte, eight miles from Münster. His nephew shared that devotion. When he became Bishop of Münster, he frequently went to Telgte on foot in the early morning hours. Toward the end of his life, Bishop Max Gereon left at the shrine as a gift to the Blessed Virgin a beautiful neo-Gothic pastoral staff, with the condition that, if there were to be a future bishop from the von Galen family, it should be handed over to him. Clemens August received it in 1933 and used it until it was destroyed in the Allied bombing of his episcopal palace ten years later.

Count Ferdinand Heribert von Galen died in the first days of 1906 after a brief illness. Visiting Elisabeth a few days later, the Count's sister was awestruck by her sister-in-law's attitude of Christian trust. "I cannot mourn," Elisabeth said. "He has reached the goal for which he has tirelessly striven his whole life, and the dear God has overwhelmed us with consolation and graces. I cannot mourn."[1]

In the meantime, Clemens was aware that plans were afoot for him to be sent to Berlin. Berlin was not part of the Diocese of Münster; at this time, it was not even its own diocese, being part of the Archdiocese

---

1   Max Bierbaum, *Nicht Lob, Nicht Furcht: Das Leben des Kardinals von Galen* (Münster: Regensberg, 1946), 104.

of Breslau. As part of the largely Protestant area of Prussia, Catholics considered it *diaspora*. Priests from elsewhere were needed to serve those Catholics that were there. By long custom, priests from the Diocese of Münster were lent to the Archbishop of Breslau to care for the parish of St. Matthias in Berlin. Father Clemens von Galen was sent there in the spring of 1906 as an assistant pastor.

Münster had been a part of Prussia since the Congress of Vienna in 1815, but her inhabitants considered themselves Westphalians or Münsterlanders, not Prussians. Berlin was the capital both of Prussia and of the German Empire, which was dominated by Prussia. Whereas Münster was largely Catholic, Berlin was predominantly Protestant among those who practiced religion at all. But with the growth of industrialization, more Catholics were heading to Berlin for work, and the need for spiritual care was great.

In obedience to his bishop and with a desire to serve Christ and His flock, Clemens threw himself with great energy into the pastoral work. There was plenty of it: Masses, Confessions, teaching school religion classes, home visits. For a man to whom the life of the Church was as natural as breathing, with a love of rural life and its changing seasons in rhythm with the seasons of the liturgical year, the change from the staunch Catholicism of the Münsterland to the spiritual wasteland of a modern, industrial, secularized city was a shock. It amazed him to visit the homes of born Catholics who simply had no interest in having their children baptized. The thought that socialists would go door-to-door urging people to renounce their membership in the Church was terribly disturbing.[2] He perceived a progressive loosening of morals in the fashions and attitudes and manners, especially of the young, and it was difficult for him

---

2   Ibid., 112. Church membership in Germany, then as now, was recorded by the government, because the main financial support of the Church was through Church taxes collected as part of the government's taxation system.

to adjust to it. He was criticized for not greeting women and girls when passing them on the street. He knew he was somewhat shy and awkward with women anyway, but he had learned from his youth that it was bad manners to greet a woman or a girl unless she greeted him. When it was made clear to him that people thought him cold and aloof, he strove to adapt his ways.[3] His love of the virtue of chastity also caused him problems. Once he refused to give Holy Communion to two girls who were dressed in a fashion that he considered immodest; after Mass he was shouted at by both fathers.[4]

His work with young men was more congenial but very difficult. Soon after his arrival at St. Matthias, he was appointed head of the young workers' club for the whole of Berlin. "Imagine this," he wrote to his sister on May 3: "Yesterday I gave my first address for the Founding Day feast of the Workers' St. Joseph's Club, and it was—be astonished and laugh—a toast to the women! Can you believe it? Just my luck! Fortunately it went over all right."[5]

Young Catholic working men came to Berlin for work from all over Germany. They needed a place to gather for social discussion, for entertainment and education, and for support in keeping their Catholic faith. From the work of his great-uncle Bishop Wilhelm Emmanuel von Ketteler, Father Clemens von Galen was a keen student of the social needs of his time and place. Adolph Kolping had taught the Church in Germany to be close to workers, to seek solutions to the problems of injustice facing them, and to protect them from the false solutions of Marxism and other forms of socialism. In addition to providing a Catholic gathering place for them, Kolping had seen that housing was also necessary: housing that would

3   Cf. Hubert Wolf, *Clemens August Graf von Galen: Gehorsam und Gewissen* (Freiburg: Herder, 2006), 45.
4   Heinrich Portmann, *Kardinal von Galen: Ein Gottesmann seiner Zeit*, 17th ed. (Münster: Aschendorff, 1981), 67–68.
5   Bierbaum, 110.

give them a way to live a decent human life, something better than overcrowded and soul-deadening apartment blocks. But the Kolping House in Berlin had become much too small for the needs. Clemens acquired a property near the Anhalter Bahnhof, the train station where newcomers to Berlin arrived. On that site, he arranged for the construction of a church, St. Clemens, and a house for the young workers, with rooms for meetings and social activities and living accommodations for over two hundred men. When the building was completed in 1911, the area surrounding it was designated as an independent part of the parish of St. Matthias, with Father von Galen in charge as curate of St. Clemens. He lived in simple rooms in the house, to be close to the workers.

When the plans for construction were being made, Clemens sought a license for a lottery to help pay for the buildings. When the application was not approved, he gave the whole of his inheritance from his father for the project. For the workers' house, he gave forty-five thousand gold marks.[6] In addition, he gave thirty-five thousand marks to the Church of St. Norbert and its hospital. The spirit of *noblesse oblige* that he had learned at Castle Dinklage applied to the enormous wealth that he inherited from his father. It was not for his use; he gave it to the Church.[7]

Father von Galen lived with the workers for eight very busy years, including the years of World War I. On the whole, they were happy and fulfilling years, even considering the shock of Germany's defeat in the war and the end of the monarchy. He was called again to St. Matthias in 1919, this time to be its pastor. He held that post until 1929.

---

6   The gold mark was on the gold standard: 2,790 marks = 1 kilogram of pure gold.

7   See Markus Trautmann, *Clemens August von Galen: Ich erhebe meine Stimme* (Kevelaer: Topos Plus [Lahn-Verlag], 2005), 19; Bierbaum, 119–22; also the website *St. Clemens Berlin*, http://www.st-clemens-berlin.de/kirche/geschichte.

This position gave him responsibility for the spiritual care of thirty thousand Catholics, a load he could not possibly shoulder alone. The assistant priests, however, presented him with more responsibility. It was his task to assign them their share of the work, to see that they were fulfilling their duty, to advise them in difficulties, and to set a good example for them. One of these priests later recalled:

> In the course of time I learned that our opinion of him was decidedly too one-sided. He was extraordinarily interested in all sorts of things. There was no area of the care of souls, the circumstances of the Church or of public life, that he had not seriously thought through and come to his own judgment on. Certainly he saw many things from a biased perspective, and often in a one-sided way; but he had from his inheritance and his upbringing a wonderful fine feeling for the exact Catholic line, which almost always by instinct led him to the right answer . . . Above all he had a burning love for the Church and for the salvation of souls. He took his responsibilities so seriously and so industriously in all their parts, was so selfless and ready to help, and was so well-formed interiorly through his deep piety and goodness, that one had to treasure and love him more and more. Whereas one could only with difficulty discuss issues of pastoral care with his predecessor, for Spruenken lived too much in his own projects and took interest in our work only when it went wrong, Galen took every question and concern that we brought to him as if it were his own, thought it over, and kept coming back to it until everything was clarified. On top of this, he had a heavenly patience with us young chaplains who were frequently very unruly, with our foul-ups and mistakes and our demands on his time. He bore with us with the most delicate love and friendship, which was not always easy for him. Later he told me once that I had often irritated

him. I had had no idea of that, but now I believe that my way
of doing things, often so contrary to his way, must have gotten
on his nerves.[8]

Father von Galen lived the same kind of Spartan—or perhaps better, monastic—simplicity in the parish house at St. Matthias as he
had in the workers' house at St. Clemens. He worked hard, prayed
much, and kept his rooms free of any luxury. He had, after all, not
been accustomed to luxury at Burg Dinklage, and he certainly did
not think that as a priest he should change that. His Lenten fasts
were strict, and when one of his fellow priests pointed out that he was
edgy when he was fasting, he worked all the harder at self-control. He
never completely gave up his beloved pipes during Lent, however:
He truly could not concentrate on work at his desk without one.[9]

His housekeeper, in a letter written to one of Father von Galen's
sisters just after Christmas 1921, gave evidence of his devotion to
his pastoral duty:

> On Christmas Eve night Herr Pastor did not go to bed at all. At
> midnight he had the Mass for the Sisters; the parish Mass was
> at 5 a.m. For almost the whole Mass Herr Pastor distributed
> Holy Communion; then he heard confessions until 10, and
> then he had the High Mass, and came to the house for break-
> fast at 11:30 . . . When I saw that again he had not touched
> his bed, I cried again, just like last year . . . Father Augustinus
> (von Galen, Clemens' brother) scolded him last year for going
> too late to bed. I cannot change anything, only pray for him.[10]

---

8   Memoir of Heinrich Holstein, reproduced in Joachim Kuropka, *Clemens
     August Graf von Galen: Sein Leben und Wirken in Bildern und Dokumenten*,
     3rd ed. (Cloppenburg: Runge, 1997), 87.
9   Portmann, 61.
10   Letter of Catharina Bussmann, in Kuropka, *Clemens August Graf von
     Galen*, 84–85.

The twenty-three years that Clemens von Galen spent in Berlin were critical years for Germany, Europe, and the world. The First World War, 1914–1918, saw more casualties and destruction than anything the world had ever experienced. There was scarcely a German family that did not lose at least one member. The oldest nephew of Clemens von Galen fell in France in 1918, leaving an eleven-year-old brother, Christoph Bernhard, to inherit the position as head of the family. The crushing blow of Germany's defeat led to a revolution, to the end of the monarchy, and to the founding of the Weimar Republic, which was to last less than fifteen years. The Treaty of Versailles placed all the blame for the war on Germany and submitted her to crushing reparations costs, severely hampering her chances of reconstructing her economy. Germans felt themselves unjustly blamed for the horrors of the war, and many believed that the humiliating treatment by the Allies was the fault of her politicians. The legend that her armies were still able to fight and win the war but were stabbed in the back by politicians back home fueled the unrest and instability that Adolf Hitler would eventually exploit in grabbing power in 1933.

During these years, von Galen occasionally wrote articles for the public press on issues of the day. They could be called political articles, provided that one does not think of politics in the partisan sense of supporting a particular political party or telling people how they should vote. They were political in a more fundamental sense, applications of a Catholic understanding of political philosophy on the origins and limits of state power. As such, they were the fruit of what he had learned from his father, the practice of "considering all questions on the basis of principles, and seeking their solution from the fundamentals of the knowledge of natural and supernatural truth."

An example of this is the article he published in the *Allgemeine Rundschau* for June 8, 1918, entitled "The Right to Vote—The

Duty to Vote."[11] Von Galen described two contrasting philosophies of the purpose of power. The first, illustrated by Louis XIV's "crass expression," as von Galen called it, "*L'Etat c'est moi!*" contends that the holders of power in society exercise that power to serve their own interests. The second, illustrated by the title of the pope as "Servant of the Servants of God," as well as by the axiom of the kings of Prussia that the king is "the First Servant of the State," stresses that the holders of power have a sacred duty to serve. The first conception he characterized as the "absolutistic pagan-egoistic philosophy of the state." The second is the "free, Christian-altruistic conception."

Either of these conceptions, von Galen argued, can characterize a monarchy or a democracy. In most European states, the power of governance and lawmaking was no longer in the hands of one man but was exercised by the people, either through referenda or plebiscites, or more often through the election of representatives. If a democratic system of government, he argued, is conceived of and practiced in such a way that the purpose of achieving power is to fulfill the interests of the majority, without concern for the common good and the just interests of the minority, "*it leads to the most awful tyranny* of the majority, and opens the way completely to demagoguery and corruption."[12] On the other hand, if "seen *as a sacred duty of service* for the good of the whole, it gives those elements of society who take part in the power of governance a lofty goal, a noble responsibility, and a wide-ranging opportunity to exercise those most beautiful Christian virtues, justice and charity, for the good of one's fellow citizens, *in the task of strengthening and preserving the social order.*"[13]

---

11   Clemens Graf von Galen, "Wahlrecht—Wahlpflicht," reprinted in Joachim Kuropka, *Streitfall Galen* (Münster: Aschendorff, 2007), 407–10.
12   Ibid., 409, emphasis in original.
13   Ibid., emphasis in original.

The constitutions of the German Empire (von Galen was writing before the fall of the monarchy) and of Prussia both expressed the concept of the power of governance as a sacred duty to the whole people and not as a power that one could exercise on behalf of one's own private interests or of the private interests of one's social group. Whether power is in the hands of princes or elected representatives, those who exercise that power must see it as a sacred responsibility, a public duty for which they are answerable not to man but to God and their conscience.

Father von Galen went on to argue that the same idea must be applied to the right to vote. It is not a private right that one may exercise or not as he sees fit, but a public duty. The right to vote implies a responsibility to vote. In the Christian conception, one who has the right to vote must see this as a duty to be exercised for the good of the whole community, for which one is answerable to God and one's conscience.

A year later, the political situation in Germany was drastically changed. After the defeat in the World War and the collapse of the monarchy, the most pressing issue facing Germany was the reconstruction of its political system. The monarchy was no more, and a national assembly was at work on a new constitution for Germany. Father von Galen was convinced that the revolution had been an injustice. But now the Emperor and the various princes had abdicated, and the German people had the right to specify what form of government they would have. Citing the teaching of Pope Leo XIII, von Galen taught that a variety of forms of government is possible. Whichever one is chosen, provided that its laws do not go against the commandments of God and the natural moral law, the laws that it makes are binding in conscience on the governed. Therefore, if the national assembly concludes that Germany is to be a republic, Catholics must accept this and give the new regime their loyalty and obedience: "*We Christians must therefore be prepared to give respect and obedience to the republican regime* 'for conscience's sake,' following the words of St. Paul: 'Everyone should obey the ruling authority; *for there is no authority apart from God; that which is in existence, has been put in place by God.* Whoever then sets himself against the ruling authority, sets himself against the ordinance of God; and he who sets himself against the ordinance of God calls down damnation upon himself.'"[14]

That the legitimate authority of a state comes from God and must in conscience be obeyed was a fundamental principle for von Galen. But it was a fundamental principle with crucial limits. The governing power itself must recognize that its authority derives from God and exercise that authority for the common good in accordance with the natural moral law.

It was on the basis of this fundamental principle that von Galen looked at the proposed Constitution that was being considered by the national assembly. Article I of the Constitution read: "The German Empire is a republic. The authority of the state comes from the people." Writing for Catholics in a Catholic newspaper, von Galen held that Catholics could accept the first sentence, even if they regretted the dissolution of the monarchy and hoped that the German people might one day decide in a just way to restore the monarchy. But the second sentence raised problems: "*We as Catholic Christians can accept the second sentence only if it is understood in this sense*: that 'those who have the positions of authority *will be elected* by the will and judgment *of the people.*'" Von Galen was again following the teaching of Pope Leo XIII.

To claim that the governing authority is grounded in the people rather than on God is to put that authority on the weak and

---

14   Clemens Graf von Galen, Kurat in Berlin: "Unsere Stellung zu Artikel I der Reichsverfassung," *Germania*, 9. Jg., Nr. 326 vom 20.7.1919, in Kuropka, *Streitfall Galen*, 410–14. The text quoted is on 411. The quotations from St. Paul are from Romans 13:5 and 13:1–2.

unstable foundation of a transient majority and to open the way to a permanent right to revolution. A state that consciously bases itself on such a foundation is giving away its right to command obedience of its citizens, for it no longer sees itself as God's representative. On the other hand, disobedience to an authority that is representative of God's authority is a sin, and so a community that acknowledges the true source of authority can bind the consciences of its citizens to obedience. If the regime consciously decides that it is based solely on the will of the people, von Galen wrote, "Woe then to our poor German people. Disorder and revolutionary convulsions will not come to an end until the battle of everyone against everyone has spent all its power." He ended with an appeal to Catholic representatives at the national assembly to "make clear our self-evident conception and to work for the truth about the origin of the authority of the state, *for freedom* against human arbitrariness, *for the rights of God, the King of Kings and Lord of Lords!*"[15]

Around the same time as this article appeared, von Galen wrote another in which he asked where the blame was to be found for Germany's military and political collapse in 1918.[16] He agreed with many that the German army was betrayed by leftist revolutionaries but argued that the real fault lay deeper: "How did it happen that the revolution succeeded, that many, maybe even the majority of the people, did not merely accept the revolution quietly, but saw it as something of a good fortune, as a salvation?" This could not have happened unless Germany was already sick within. The sickness was the sickness of an ideology:

> the idea of the State as God, the idea of an all-powerful, boundlessly mighty State owing no duties to anyone.

---

15   Ibid., 414, emphasis in original.
16   "Wo liegt die Schuld," discussed in Trautmann, 20–22.

Prussian Germany did not understand how to earn the inner loyalty of its citizens. The State was constantly putting itself first; that, above all else, was what alienated its citizens. The State is everything; the individual person is nothing; he has no freedom, no rights, no self-determination, other than what the State confers upon him; the State is the only source of rights . . . That is where the central point of the national blame is to be found. That is the sickness that brought down our German Empire despite its apparent splendor.[17]

The all-powerful state, what von Galen called state-absolutism (*Staatsabsolutismus*), was in his mind the enemy of true freedom. He expounded on this theme in a 1922 essay, "The Enemy of the German Community."[18] Here he explained his political philosophy in that fundamental way he had learned from his father—and, one can add, from his study of the writings of his great-uncle Bishop von Ketteler.

What, von Galen asked, makes for a good community—one in which people of different classes, professions, and social positions really consider themselves to be united and to which they can give their hearts, their loyalty, and their service? Why, he continued, did Germany not have such a community? For although it had the externals of a community—indeed, a self-governing community, since all power had been given to the people—in fact the people of different classes, professional standing, political parties, and religions felt themselves at odds with each other.

The fault, he argued, was egoism, disordered self-love, by which everyone seeks his own interests without concern for the good and

17   Ibid., 21.
18   Pfarrer Graf Clemens von Galen, Berlin, "Der Feind der deutschen Gemeinschaft," *Allgemeine Rundschau*, XIX Jg., Nr. 31 vom 5.8.1922, S. 363–65, reprinted in Kuropka, *Streitfall Galen*, 421–26.

the rights of his neighbor. To this disordered self-love, von Galen contrasted a correct understanding of self-love. This, he said, is the precondition and measure of true love of neighbor; indeed, without true self-love, love of neighbor is not possible:

> Love of neighbor demands that we respect, protect and pro-mote the rights and the good of the neighbor, and *that we do so the more, the nearer the neighbor is to us*. Now in fact one's self is the neighbor who is nearest to us, the one who has the first call to have his rights and happiness protected and promoted by us; *then* come the rights and good of the family members, *then* those of the neighbor *or* those of the same position in soci-ety, the community, the relatives, and so forth up to the rights and good of the people's community and from there eventually to the good of the whole human race.[19]

This order, von Galen insisted, is the primordial order given by nature. Another order can come from society, which can require exceptions to this order, but only in cases of necessity. For example, the proper love of self requires one to defend his own life against an unjust attack, even to the point, if necessary, of killing the attacker, who is nevertheless a neighbor. But when the good of the com-munity is threatened, one can have the duty of sacrificing his own good, even his own life, for the threatened people's community. This is heroic love of neighbor, which cannot be required of everyone, if only because self-sacrifice of everyone would defeat the goal: If everyone died for the Fatherland, there would be no one left to enjoy the good fortune that was earned by this heroic sacrifice. Similarly, proper love of self requires a person to protect his property for him-self and those who are close to him. Necessity may obligate him to give up some of this for the sake of the community. But he cannot be

---

19   Ibid., 422.

required to give up all of it, because the good of the whole community involves the good of each of its members, which includes that each member deserves to have his right to his property respected.

Based on this reasoning, von Galen saw the state as containing within itself smaller communities of various sizes, all grouped on the basis of ever-widening circles around the individual, grounded in correctly understood self-love. That self-love is primary, and the rights that belong to the individual or to the smaller group must be respected and promoted, unless the wider circle can show compelling reasons why, for the sake of a greater good, the narrower circle or the individual must renounce its rights.

"This," he wrote, "is a *truth*, which in my judgment is *misunderstood and ignored almost universally*." For socialism it is the state, not the individual, that is primary. The state "is the unlimited lord over all individual persons, over their rights and freedoms and their property, and correspondingly the lord over all natural associations of persons, the family (the school), the community, the tribe, the business enterprise, the professional organization, etc. According to this teaching, individuals, and also all communities within the State, *have only so many rights and so much freedom* as society (the State) grants and allocates to them, for *the State is the source of all rights!*"[20]

Von Galen's fundamental rejection of socialism and communism was based on this understanding of its nature; but the idea of the state as the foundation of all rights was not, he held, an invention of socialism. At the time of the Reformation, the independent rights of the Church were denied. In Protestant areas, the prince made the Church the slave of his power, and many Christians became accustomed to the idea that state power was the origin and lord not only of the church community but also of the rights of every other association within the state. This was worked out in theory by the

---

20   Ibid., 423.

positivist school of law, which held that the state is primary, and all rights are granted by the state and can be taken away by the state. People then felt themselves fortunate if they were on good terms with the holders of power. Socialism's only addition to this theory was to get rid of the previous holders of power and put the proletariat in charge. But, von Galen argued, many non-socialists, including Catholics, held to this theory in practice,

> inasmuch as they make the present majority, whether it be of the people or of the parliament, *into the absolute lords* of individuals, families, communities, tribes and all other natural associations within the State. To be sure, many are not aware of this: they strive in Parliament to defend the undeniable rights of the Church and many of the natural rights and freedoms of the individual and of associations; but it appears that the majority, even of Catholic politicians, hold to the opinion that every law that is passed by constitutional means is just, simply by virtue of the fact that the current state power has passed it and puts it into effect through the means of power which it employs, even if it encroaches upon or does violence to natural rights without compelling reasons.[21]

For von Galen, this *false* theory of the unlimited power of the state was the source of all the inner struggles that had kept Germany from developing a true sense of community. The correct order of self-love was not respected, and so egoism ruled in its place. Brother mistrusted brother; neighbor mistrusted neighbor. Each one sought to win the majority to his side, in order to use the power of the state to defend his own interests by attacking the rights and freedoms of the other. *Might makes right* is the motto of the modern state, according to von Galen. Why should it not be the motto of private life as well?

---

21   Ibid., 424.

People ask themselves, "If the might of the state, today the might of the majority, really makes right, then *why only this might*? Why not also the might of the stronger fist, why not the might of money, why not the might of craftiness and clever business dealings? The destruction that is introduced into the community by the working out of this fundamental principle should open people's eyes to the destructiveness of this principle itself,"[22] von Galen argued. But in fact, he saw something else happening. If the state is the creator of all rights and the all-powerful lord of all rights, then, many concluded, their rights and freedoms would be secure only if they themselves were the holders of state power.

"We will not come *to an inner people's community*," he concluded, "as long as State absolutism is the fundamental principle of our political life." Such absolutism leads inevitably to centralization and attacks on any persons or groupings that are independent of the state. That was the reason for the *Kulturkampf*, for the Prussian state saw the Catholic Church as the bulwark of freedom and the rights of individuals and small communities against arbitrary state power. Von Galen recalled Catholic politicians and thinkers of those days, including Bishop von Ketteler, whose names were still honored among Catholics but whose books were no longer being read and whose ideas were no longer known:

> I can think of *no more necessary reading for every Catholic politician* than the writings of the great Bishop of Mainz!
>
> Over and over again, and already more than fifty years ago, Ketteler pointed out that State absolutism and its development into centralization was the *worst* enemy of the German people's community. His thoughts were directed to opening the eyes of the German people to the deceitful system of State

---

22   Ibid.

omnipotence which has poisoned our public life for centuries, and to its *continuance and development in modern times.* For the forms of the State and the changes of structures of power make no difference to State absolutism; it knows how to adapt itself to all of them, monarchy as well as a republic, a so-called authoritarian State as well as a democracy.[23]

Not many years later, the Weimar Republic would be in ruins. Von Galen would confront a new form of state absolutism under Adolf Hitler.

After ten years as pastor of St. Matthias and a total of twenty-three years in Berlin, Clemens von Galen was called back to Münster in 1929 by Bishop Johannes Poggenburg, who named him pastor of St. Lambert. Now he was back home in the familiar Catholic milieu of the Münsterland, and in every way, he was at the center of things. Located just a couple of blocks from the cathedral in the historic old city, St. Lambert's has always been known in Münster as the City and Market Church. As the name implies, it is located at the Prinzipalmarkt, the main market of the city, and was parish church for the city center. In a place where the community organized its life around the Church, Father von Galen was now pastor of the most important church in Münster other than the cathedral. At the age of fifty-one, he had achieved a position of great respect and importance. He believed it would be his final position in the Church.

In addition to seeking a good priest to serve in that important parish, Bishop Poggenburg had one other crucial reason for calling von Galen back to Münster. In the chaotic political situation of the time, many of the Catholic nobility of Westphalia had left their traditional loyalty to the Catholic Centre Party and

---

23   Ibid., 425–26.

were finding themselves more at home with the National Socialist movement. The bishop hoped that von Galen, together with his brother Franz, would be able to keep the nobles loyal to the Centre Party and to the guidance of the bishops.[24]

Another pair of brothers were leading the pro-Nazi wing. Barons Hermann and Ferdinand von Lüninck were convinced that the Centre Party was leaning too far to the left by entering into coalition governments with the Social Democrats and Liberals. The Lünincks had led a growing faction in the Union of Catholic Nobles into the Protestant-dominated German National Party. Franz von Galen, president of the Union of Catholic Nobles since 1924, was regarded by the Lünincks as belonging to the left wing of the Centre Party. In 1928, as the Lüninck faction grew stronger and much more vocal in their attacks on the Centre Party, he felt compelled to resign the presidency of the Union.

Clemens von Galen was unsuccessful in bringing the Westphalian nobles back to loyalty to the Centre Party. Instead, the situation worsened. By 1931, the Lüninck brothers were convinced that the Nazi Party was in many ways the most compatible to Catholic ideals, whereas the Centre Party was accused of working hand in hand with the "deadly enemy of Christian culture"—namely, Marxism—which they characterized as dominated by Judaism and Freemasonry. They petitioned the Catholic bishops to retreat from their repeated condemnations of Nazism. In an attempted response to this, Father von Galen presented a motion that the members of the Union of Catholic Nobles make a solemn oath always to be loyally obedient to the bishops. It was self-evident, he argued at a tense meeting of the Union in August 1932, that the commands and warnings of the bishops should be obeyed, even by one who thinks he understands the situation better than they do. Obedience is a matter of the

---

24   Wolf, 65–68.

will, subjecting itself to lawful authority. One may communicate his concerns to the bishops but must follow their directions: "We are not responsible for ruling the Church, but for obedience in the Church," he said emphatically. Only if one is certain that, in a specific case, one is commanded to do something sinful, may he disobey the command on the principle that "God must be obeyed rather than man." In other cases, one may doubt the wisdom of the superior, but the principle of Catholic morality and the natural law stands: In doubtful cases, the presumption is with the superior, who is responsible for the common good. He may have reasons for his decision that the subject cannot know. Von Galen conceded that an extreme situation may arise in which one is convinced that obedience would be actually harmful: Then one may appeal to the superior, and above him to the pope, and withhold obedience pending his ruling, but one may certainly not strive to persuade others to disobedience.[25]

None of this satisfied Ferdinand von Lüninck and his group, who were convinced that their political wisdom was better than that of the bishops or of Father von Galen. The relationship of the nobles to the bishops, said Lüninck, should be likened to that of a grown son to his father. Now that he is independent, he owes him respect but not obedience. Hermann von Lüninck added that von Galen's proposal was playing into the hands of Moscow, a charge that was met with rousing applause. The von Lünincks had won. In the end, their position would win political power as well, and the brothers would achieve high positions in the Nazi regime. But the victory of Nazism was not a victory for Germany.

---

25   Horst Conrad, "Stand und Konfession. Der Verein der katholischen Edelleute. Teil 2: Die Jahre 1918–1949." *Westphälische Zeitschrift*, Band 159, Jahrgang 2009, 91ff., n. 295. Von Galen's argumentation from unpublished minutes of the meeting.

CHAPTER 3

New Leader, New Bishop

In the early months of 1933, parliamentary democracy in Germany died. On January 30, President Paul von Hindenburg appointed Adolf Hitler as chancellor of yet another coalition government. Most of the cabinet posts were given to non-Nazis. The hope was that this limited power would keep Hitler penned in and eventually lead to the Party's decline, which had already begun in the previous year. Instead, he managed by the middle of the summer to convert Germany into a one-party state, with himself as the dictator and a state-run propaganda machine spreading the cult promoting him as the leader (*Führer*) of a renewed Germany.

The Catholic Diocese of Münster was also looking for a new leader at this time. Archbishop Johannes Poggenburg (he had been given the personal title of archbishop, while Münster remained a simple diocese) died on January 5, 1933. It was clear that a strong and wise bishop would be needed to guide the faithful in the changing times. Where was such a bishop to be found?

In 1929, the Catholic Church had entered into a Concordat with the Prussian government in order to sort out Church-State relations. The Concordat stipulated how the election of a new bishop would take place. The Cathedral Chapter of the diocese needing a new bishop, and the other bishops of Prussia, would send lists of ideal candidates to the Holy See. Taking these lists into account, the Holy See would make its own list of three candidates from among whom the Cathedral Chapter would choose the new bishop in a free, secret ballot. After the election, the chosen candidate would also have to be regarded as "acceptable" by the Prussian government.

Spring passed into summer, and the Catholics of Münster prayed for a suitable bishop, but no news of a choice was forthcoming. The joke later went around that Father von Galen was giving a Catechism lesson to schoolchildren on the qualities desired in a bishop. To see whether he was making himself understood, he asked them whether it was possible that he could be a bishop. "No," replied one child. Why not? "Because my father says you totally can't preach."[1]

This was the first episcopal election in Prussia since the signing of the Concordat, and people expected that it might take some time to go through all the steps. But this dragged on month after month. With such a need for a good bishop, what was taking so long?

The details of the election are now known.[2] In addition to the chapter of the Münster Cathedral, nine bishops gave lists of candidates to the apostolic nuncio, Cesare Orsenigo. Adolf Donders, provost of the cathedral, was named most often on seven of the ten lists, five times as the first choice. Donders himself, together with two of his fellow chapter members, told Cardinal Schulte of Cologne that Father von Galen was their top choice, although the pastor of St. Lambert's was third on the list given by the chapter. Cardinal Schulte passed this information on to the nuncio along

---

1   Heinrich Portmann, *Kardinal von Galen: Ein Gottesmann seiner Zeit*, 17th ed. (Münster: Aschendorff, 1981), 81.

2   Hubert Wolf, *Clemens August Graf von Galen: Gehorsam und Gewissen* (Freiburg: Herder, 2006), 74–78.

with his own list, on which he placed Father von Galen second. Three other bishops also named von Galen, making him the second most frequently named.

Orsenigo took note of this fact when he sent his summary and recommendations to the secretary of state, Cardinal Eugenio Pacelli. He listed Donders first, then von Galen and four further possible candidates. Cardinal Pacelli, however, was well placed to have his own opinion, having served as nuncio to Bavaria and later to Germany from 1917 to 1929. The official terna, or list of three names, which he sent to the Cathedral Chapter in March, consisted of Auxiliary Bishop Antonius Moench of Trier, Provost Donders, and Heinrich Heufers of the Cathedral Chapter of Berlin. Heufers had not been named on any of the lists, but when the chapter met for the election on March 21, he was the choice.

Now came the delay. Heufers took a long time deciding whether to accept the post. Finally, in May he declared that for health reasons, he would decline the election. Early in June, Rome instructed the Cathedral Chapter to vote again, choosing between the two remaining candidates. Before this could take place, however, Donders also let it be known that he was unwilling to take the post if elected, as he surely would have been.

Now Cardinal Pacelli had another decision to make. The Cathedral Chapter could not hold a free election if there was only one candidate. Now Father von Galen's name was added to that of Bishop Moench, and from those two, the chapter elected von Galen on July 18.

The announcement could not be made yet. Still in confidentiality, the government had to be notified and asked if it had any objections; von Galen had to be informed of the election and asked if he would accept; and finally, the Holy Father was able announce on September 11 that a new bishop had been chosen for the Diocese of Münster. Clemens August Count von Galen was the first bishop chosen in Germany since the Nazi regime had taken power.

Much had taken place in the eight months since the death of Archbishop Poggenburg on January 5. Once it was a settled fact that Germany had become a one-party dictatorship, the bishops had to decide how to face the situation and what guidance to give to Catholics. Hitler had taken power by constitutional means. The Weimar Republic had been a total political failure. Not to give obedience to the lawfully constituted authority was contrary to Catholic teaching. As St. Paul wrote in his letter to the Romans, "Let every person be subject to the governing authorities. For there is no authority except from God, and those that exist have been instituted by God. Therefore he who resists the authorities resists what God has appointed, and those who resist will incur judgment" (Rom. 13:1–2). In Catholic teaching, the fourth commandment, "honor your father and mother," implies honor and obedience to every lawful authority. To be sure, there can be cases in which authority is abused, and even cases in which the abuse can justify rejection of the authority and rebellion, but among the conditions morally justifying such an extreme step is the requirement that there be a good chance of success. With Germans hungering for a stable government, there would have been no chance for a successful rebellion against the Nazis in 1933. If the Church were involved in such a step, it would have been attacked as it had been in the *Kulturkampf*. A rebellion would have been easily put down, or, if the opposition to the government were stronger, it would have led to a civil war, with the danger of Russian-style communism taking the place of Nazism. For the bishops, acceptance of the new regime was self-evident. This did not, however, mean the same thing as trusting the regime.

On March 23, the day the Enabling Act giving him dictatorial powers was passed, Hitler publicly softened his antireligious stance. He promised that Christianity would be a fundamental principle of the renewal of Germany that he was going to bring into effect, and he asserted that the two Christian Confessions that were always prominent in German life were most important factors in that renewal. Although that promise proved to be empty, like so many promises that he would make during the next twelve years, the bishops had no choice but to take him at his word. They dropped their prohibition against being part of the National Socialist movement.

During the fall of 1932, Franz von Galen, as a politician, and his priest brother, as an advisor and a writer of anonymous newspaper articles, had striven to prevent the Nazis from coming into power. Franz was a representative in the Prussian parliament as a member of the Centre Party. When the Enabling Act was proposed in March of 1933, he was unsuccessful in his attempts to have the Centre Party oppose it. Both in the national parliament and in the Prussian parliament, the Centre Party approved the act, and as Franz von Galen was the only member in the Prussian parliament to oppose it, he resigned his position before the vote took place.[3]

Soon the Centre Party, like all the other political parties in Germany except the Nazis, dissolved itself. A typical combination of brutality, threats, and promises brought this about. The Nazis had promised in return to finalize a Concordat with the Holy See, which they subsequently did. On paper, this guaranteed the independence of the Church and her rights to such important things as the direction of religious instruction in Catholic schools, which would continue to be financially supported by the state.

Many good people, Catholics and Protestants alike, thought that perhaps they should take positions in local or national government, with the aim of mitigating what they expected would be evil done by Hitler's regime. Clemens August von Galen did not blame anyone

---

3   Joachim Kuropka, Redaktion von B. Haunfelder, "Franz von Galen und das Ende der Zentrumspartei," "Auf Roter Erde." *Westfälische Nachrichten*, May 10, 2008.

who took this approach, although he had no illusions about it. When his nephew later asked for advice on whether to take that step, he replied, "What business do you want to have with those guys?"[4]

The Nazis did not veto von Galen's election as bishop, probably for a couple of reasons. They may have thought that as a patriot, he would be sympathetic to their program of a restoration of German national pride and glory. Somehow, despite his fundamental opposition to state absolutism and to Nazism, he had a reputation of being sympathetic to their goals. Many had the idea that as a "conservative," he was happier with an authoritarian regime than a parliamentary one. Almost from the start of his episcopate, however, Bishop von Galen would show his opposition to Nazi ideology.

A second reason was purely practical. It was in the interests of the regime to appear to be on good terms with the Church. To veto the very first bishop elected after they had taken power would not have been good public relations.

At least one committed Nazi was anxious about the choice of von Galen as Bishop of Münster. Adolf ten Hompel was a local lawyer, who therefore knew Münster better than Adolf Hitler and other leading Nazis. A few days before von Galen's episcopal ordination, he wrote a friend with the request that his thoughts be passed on to Hitler, that Münster, "not Cologne, Munich, or Breslau, is Rome's bastion in Germany. Now the decision has been made for Galen. The Chapter and the Jesuits are rubbing their hands together over this stunning victory over Hitler which, without their having done anything for it, has just fallen into their laps."[5]

---

4   "Was willst du bei den Kerls?" Christoph Bernhard von Galen interview in Günter Beaugrand, *Ein Leben im XX. Jahrhundert: Begegnungen und Gespräche mit Christoph Bernhard von Galen auf Haus Assen / Lippetal* (Werl: Börde-Verlag, 2004), 19.

5   Markus Trautmann, *Clemens August von Galen: Ich erhebe meine Stimme* (Kevelaer: Topos Plus [Lahn-Verlag], 2005), 48; Wolf, 83.

From the time of his election and nomination as bishop, Clemens von Galen began to use the double name Clemens August. As noted in chapter 1, the choice may have been made simply because that was a traditional name for bishops, but it may have been a symbolic choice. Archbishop Clemens August Droste zu Vischering had courageously opposed the Prussian government in the nineteenth-century controversy over mixed marriage. Bishop Clemens August von Galen, who could read well the signs of the times, expected that he would need similar courage in standing against the Nazi regime.[6]

Before the new bishop could be consecrated and take up his office, the new Concordat stipulated one more step: an oath of loyalty to the state. Since loyalty to the lawful authority was as natural to him as breathing, to swear such an oath was no problem for him. He made a request that he be able to swear the oath to President von Hindenburg, "whom the whole German people revere and love as the Father of the Fatherland,"[7] but it was decided that he should take the oath before Hermann Goering as minister president of Prussia. The brief ceremony took place in Berlin on October 18, followed by a polite exchange of greetings and a meal. The bishop-elect brought his own New Testament to use in taking the oath but asked if there was not a crucifix available. With apologies, he was assured that the next time a bishop came to take the oath, the ministry would have a crucifix on hand. Von Galen reassured his host that there was no need for anxiety on this occasion. He had brought his future pectoral cross with him—just in case.[8]

---

6   Wolf, 81–82.
7   Letter to Wilhelm Frick, in Peter Löffler, ed., *Bischof Clemens August Graf von Galen: Akten, Briefe und Predigten 1933–1946*, 2nd ed. (Paderborn: Ferdinand Schöningh, 1996), v. I, 13.
8   Portmann, 82.

CHAPTER 4

Neither Praises nor Fear

The consecration and enthronement of the new Bishop of Münster took place on October 28, 1933. In his sermon, Clemens August von Galen, now Bishop of Münster, spoke of the joy of the day. It was his wedding day. He had just come from the altar where he had pronounced his vows and received his ring, and now he was pledged to live, work, and die for the clergy and people of the Diocese of Münster. "I come to you," he told them, "with the truth on my lips, a blessing in my hand, and love in my heart." Preaching to them the truth of the gospel, blessing them with the consecrated hands of a bishop, he would love this bride faithfully until death, following the command given to husbands by St. Paul to love their wives as Christ loves His Church. The new bishop continued: "It is a wedding day, like that wedding day at Cana, with Jesus Christ our Lord and savior present in the Most Blessed Sacrament. May He, who then changed water into wine, now change our poor human desires and deeds through his miraculous power into pious thoughts and holy actions." In his view, the saints and angels were the wedding guests: the Blessed Virgin Mary; St. Paul and St. Joseph, patrons of the diocese; the apostles Simon and Jude, whose feast day it was;

St. Ludger, the first Bishop of Münster, and all his successors; and all the known and unknown saints of the diocese. The wedding guests also included the holy Archangel Michael and the guardian angels of the German people, Münsterland, and the city of Münster, as well as his own guardian angel, who had accompanied him into the cathedral. He prayed to all of them for their intercession, "so that the holy, lifelong covenant that I have entered into with you today may bear fruits of holiness for you and for me in time and in eternity!"

"Today," he concluded, "is a wedding day! As the Catholic Christian bridegroom, upon leaving the altar, traces the sign of the Cross with joyful emotion on the forehead of his bride as the first sign of his love, founded on God and faithful until death, so my episcopal blessing, which I now give to you with a heart overflowing with joy, shall also be the sign and pledge of my love as your shepherd, a love that with God's help will be faithful unto death. May almighty God bless you, the Father, the Son, and the Holy Spirit."[1]

On the same day, Bishop Clemens August issued his first pastoral letter, to be read at all the Sunday Masses in the diocese on the next day and published in the diocesan newsletter.[2] Recalling that first episcopal blessing that he gave after his installation, he remarked that in giving it, he was thinking not only of the faithful who were present in the cathedral but of all the Catholics throughout the vast Diocese of Münster. He asked God to give him grace and strength to be a bishop after His own heart, recalling that for months, they had been praying for God to give them just such a new bishop. He now expressed his trust that their prayer would not be in vain.

He said that when he had been asked by the nuncio of the Vicar of Christ to undertake this task, there was no hesitation: "In obedience

---

1   Peter Löffler, ed., *Bischof Clemens August Graf von Galen: Akten, Briefe und Predigten 1933–1946*, 2nd ed. (Paderborn: Ferdinand Schöningh, 1996), doc. 19, v. I, 25–28.

2   Ibid., doc. 20, v. I, 28–37.

to the Holy Father I declared myself ready. And I profess before all of you today, that for all the future, obedience to the Pope, full submission to the leadership of the holy Church and the instructions of the Holy See shall be the guiding star and the rule of conduct for my personal life and for my work among you. That was the lesson I learned in the house of my parents; that is what I will continue to practice until my last breath!"

Considering the call of the Holy Father to be the call of God Himself, he recognized that he was called from among them to serve them as their high priest. "You know me, and I know you," he told them:

> I don't know every single one of you, but I know in a general way the faithful Catholic people that I must lead; I know its religious situation, its strengths and its weaknesses, its needs and its perils. Not everyone knows me, but many know me, especially in Münster. You know also my weaknesses and mistakes, which now more than ever I must strive daily to fight against and root out, and for which I must daily make myself an offering to God in union with the offering on the altar. You know also, that in my awareness of my own weakness, I will have compassion for the ignorant and the erring. My constant concern will be to help sinners, to lead them back, to pray and sacrifice for them, with patience and love to bring the erring to the truth.

He begged his priestly brothers to help him in this task, "so that, insofar as it is up to us, no one is lost, so that we will be able one day to stand before Him who desires us to be 'the light of the world' and 'the salt of the earth.'"

A central part of the letter was dedicated to explaining the motto he had chosen for his episcopal coat of arms, *Nec laudibus Nec timore*—neither by praises nor by fear. It was taken from the text of the ordination liturgy. The prayer for the consecration of a bishop asserts that in his zeal, he should love humility and truth and be overcome neither by praises nor by fear—*aut laudibus aut timore superatus.* "This," he wrote, "shall be my motto, and shall be a signpost for all of us: *Neither the praises of men nor fear of men shall move us.* Rather, our glory will be to promote the praise of God, and our steadfast effort will be to walk always in a holy fear of God." His motto expressed perfectly his ministry for the next dozen years. Neither the praises nor the fear of men would hinder him from fulfilling his task of preaching the gospel of Christ, working tirelessly for the good of the flock entrusted to him, preaching the fullness of the truth revealed by God, and ensuring that the truth be taught in its fullness throughout his diocese.

The new bishop recognized that he had a sacred authority and responsibility. He cited the description of the bishop's tasks given in the rite of consecration: "to decide, to sanctify, to bless, to offer sacrifice, to baptize and to confirm." Recalling St. Paul's exhortation in the Acts of the Apostles (20:28) to the leaders of the church in Asia Minor to "take heed to yourselves and to all the flock," he promised to take heed to himself: to strive for holiness, to fight against his weaknesses and errors, and to live a simple, hardworking life. He begged for everyone's prayers to enable him to keep this pledge.

In promising to take heed to the flock of Christ, he thanked those who shared in the task of teaching the Faith, from the theological faculty at the University, to the seminary professors, to teachers in Catholic schools, to parents:

> You have, as the flock of Christ, the right to have the revealed truth preached to you fully, unchanged and unfalsified. In my promotion of teaching I will never swerve an iota from the truth of the one, holy, catholic and apostolic Church, which is "the pillar and ground of the truth" (1 Tim. 3:15). I will keep watch that no error insinuates itself into the faith and the teaching of the Church of Münster. "Neither the praise of

men nor the fear of men" will hinder me in this. And should I overlook such an insidious poison, and should I myself through human weakness be the cause of an error in matters of faith, then I hope that the Successor of Peter on the Bishop's Chair in Rome will correct me and protect you from the error.

He noted that Catholic teachers in the diocese had always been loyal in helping the parents and the priests pass on the Faith to the young, and he prayed that this would always remain the case.

The bishop's tasks, Clemens August continued, are not limited to the teaching of the Faith. He must take note of the signs of the times and, if necessary, give warnings and advice that will keep people on the narrow path that leads to heaven. The bishops, he assured the people, know what difficulties they face:

Do not think that they give orders or warnings lightly, without awareness of the facts and of the difficulties you will have in following them. And do not think that they are carelessly ignoring the situation when they are silent as you are longing for guidance. Be sure that their awareness of the responsibility they have for your souls is a very heavy one, and they know that they cannot save their own souls if they are silent or if they speak at the wrong time. I will gladly listen to information, expressed desires, and good advice from others, including from the laity and from well-meaning people of other faiths. But I know that the duty of "deciding" about necessary advice and warnings for my diocesans falls on me and my conscience alone, and cannot be taken from me by anyone. "Neither the praises of men nor fear of men" shall hinder me at any time from fulfilling this duty!

He added that corresponding to this duty, which God has given the bishops, is an obligation of obedience on the part of the faithful.[3]

---

3   Ibid.

No doubt this part of his letter was related to the task the bishops had frequently had in recent years to guide the faithful in matters related to the political situation in Germany. They had to warn against membership in the Nazi Party as well as against atheistic communism. They had spoken out on behalf of morals in a time when moral virtue seemed to be collapsing. Now, in the new situation, it was necessary to work with the Nazis because they were the de facto rulers of the country. Bishop von Galen gave thanks that, by the guarantees of the Concordat, they were taking a stand against the open propaganda for godlessness and immorality. He may have been more hopeful than the situation warranted. But his promises in this letter were fulfilled. When the Nazis systematically violated every provision of the Concordat, neither the praise of men nor fear of them hindered him from speaking out.

Franz von Galen undertook the task of organizing the festivities for the day of his brother's ordination and enthronement. As the plans were being made, Ferdinand von Lüninck, who was now Premier of Westphalia, let it be known that he wanted to give a brief address at the luncheon reception that was to follow the ceremony. It seemed an appropriate gesture, as Clemens August wrote to Franz: "I am neither surprised nor upset that Ferdinand Lüninck believes that he ought to say a few words at the meal as Premier. Let him do that without fuss. Besides, it seems quite right to me that he wants to end with a toast to the Pope. If he were not to speak, then I would have to finish my address with a toast to *both* of the highest powers. To me it seems totally appropriate that the political official speak about the highest church authority, and that I speak about the highest political authority."[4]

In the event, both addresses gave clues that the relationship between the Church and the new German state might not be a

---

4   Letter to Franz von Galen, October 5, 1933, in Löffler, doc. 9, v. I, 11.

smooth one. The new bishop spoke only briefly of Adolf Hitler but with great respect and even reverence for President Hindenburg. When in Berlin the previous week to take his oath of loyalty, he had taken the opportunity to call on the aged field marshal: "It was a great joy for me to bring my respects and best wishes to the venerable Field Marshal, for himself and for his first co-worker, the Imperial Chancellor. I promised him that we would also pray for him in his high office. He replied that he was grateful from the bottom of his heart. With this I will end by greetings to all of you and beg you to join with me in three cheers for our Imperial President von Hindenburg and our Imperial Chancellor Adolf Hitler."[5]

If von Galen's address indicated a certain coolness to Hitler as compared to his respect for Hindenburg, von Lüninck's, although it encouraged cooperation between Church and state, defined that cooperation purely in Nazi terms. After expressing best wishes for the new bishop and a desire for a good relationship between Church and state, he stressed that with a new Germany, with an authoritarian state under strong leadership, this relationship would now have a new basis. A renewal of Christian culture was now possible, thanks to the fact that Adolf Hitler had saved the West from what Lüninck called the "Asian plague."

"The Leader and Chancellor of our people, Adolf Hitler," von Lüninck asserted,

has now brought to fulfilment the principles that he has advocated and preached for ten, twelve years. And those who knew—at first there were only a few who knew how things stood—that we were right on the edge of the abyss, must realize that it is only thanks to the energy of the Leader and his followers that we were saved from the Asian plague. I believe

5 Löffler, doc. 21, v. I, 42.

that history will one day compare this deed, this battle of many years and final victory against the destructive Asian infection, with the great conflicts, the most important world-historical battles, that have been fought between the Christian West and the Asian Mongol hordes. History will one day show Adolf Hitler and no one else to have been the savior of the West. He truly brought about what he always promised, and today it is evident that the swastika, the symbol of German renewal, so far from being an opposite to or even an enemy of the Redeemer, has in fact become the best protection in the dangers of our times.[6]

It was a bizarre formulation, especially for a man who professed that he was a believing Catholic. In his excitement over Hitler's seizure of power and the signing of the Concordat, von Lüninck evidently was convinced that his support of Hitler had been correct. Now, in a fashion that was typical of Nazi ideology, he presented Adolf Hitler as the political savior of the West. Surely the listeners could have drawn the conclusion that for von Lüninck, Hitler was carrying forth the saving work of Jesus Christ. Like Christ, Hitler began with preaching and then fulfilled his preaching, bringing his prophecies to actuality. The swastika, which in German is *Hakenkreuz*, or "bent cross," was claimed to be the best protection for the West. Thus the Nazi bent cross was said to perform the same work as the Cross of Christ, only better. Calling it the best protection, "*vielmehr bester Schutz und Schirm*," von Lüninck parodied the ancient Christian prayer to the Blessed Virgin Mary, *Sub tuum praesidium*, which begins in German, "*Unter Deinen Schutz und Schirm fliehen wir . . .*" In Lüninck's formulation, the *Schutz und Schirm* was the swastika, implying that the Germany of 1933 would no longer seek the protection of Mary, the Mother of God,

---

6   Ibid., 43.

or of her divine Son, Jesus Christ—at least not exclusively; it would seek the protection of Adolf Hitler, the new leader and savior.

From this dizzying height of rhetoric, von Lüninck managed to come down to praise the ceremonies of the bishop's consecration as signs of a two-thousand-year-old tradition and so to introduce his remarks on Pope Pius XI. Lüninck praised the Holy Father's work for peace in the world. The German regime, he said, was also convinced that a peace with true justice would be the only cure for the ills of the world. This, he concluded, was the peace for which Germans must fight. He believed and hoped, he said, that the high spiritual power, the head of the Catholic Church, would stand by Germany's side, helping in this struggle. With that, he asked the assembled crowd to give three cheers for His Holiness, Pope Pius XI.[7]

The bishop and his fellow Catholics would have been happy to toast the pope, but their misgivings about the Nazis could not have been eased. "A Protestant would have done a better job of it," von Galen told a friend later.[8] Von Lüninck encouraged cooperation between Church and state, but that cooperation was to be governed by the great world-historical struggle being waged by the state under the leadership of its new messiah, Adolf Hitler. The Church was expected to do its part in that struggle, in cooperation with, but really under, that leader. But what would happen if the Church saw its mission as including tasks not subservient to the goals of the state?[9] The new Bishop of Münster did not have to wait long to find out.

---

7   Ibid., 43–44.

8   Heinrich Portmann, *Kardinal von Galen: Ein Gottesmann seiner Zeit*, 17th ed. (Münster: Aschendorff, 1981), 86.

9   The press report in the *Münsterischer Anzeiger* quoted the speeches in full. See Löffler, doc. 21, v. I, 38–45. Von Lüninck later came to oppose Nazism and was removed from office in July 1938. In July 1944, he was associated with the group that tried to assassinate Adolf Hitler. Subsequently, he was arrested and executed by the Nazis.

CHAPTER 5

Opening Shots Against the New Paganism

B ishop von Galen was consecrated and enthroned on October 28, 1933. Just over a week later, on November 6, he wrote a private letter to the superintendent of schools for Münster. Schools had received lesson plans "in connection with All Souls' Day" to teach "the theory of heredity and ethnology" in all subjects. The details leave no doubt as to what this phrase meant: hatred of the Jews. The lesson plans included the following:

- Religion: 5th Commandment. The people of Israel through the ages and their demoralizing effect on the host peoples.
- German: the concepts and words related to "Jew," explanation of the Jewish spirit, ruination of our literature.
- Arithmetic: on the horrible power of the banks and bourses (financial abuse).
- History: the Jews in Germany, the Middle Ages, financial support for wars.
- Geography: distribution of Jews in countries, particularly in Germany—places of residence, and so on.

- Biology: mixing of races through Judaism, physical characteristics of Jews, heredity.
- Sport: heroic and slavish peoples, importance of sports for the renewal of the people.
- Art: faces, masks.
- Singing: race and music, German romanticism.[1]

"I take it very seriously," Bishop von Galen wrote to the school superintendent,

> that your directive implies the intention of connecting the entire curriculum with the religious life of the children. Therefore I take the liberty of opining that the connection of the themes you have ordered with the month of the holy souls appears to be only a very loose, not to say totally artificial one. I am also convinced that it implies the danger of confusing the children, at least the less gifted ones, about the Catholic teaching on the mission of the Israelites in the history of salvation in pre-Christian times, and about the duty of love of neighbor. I believe that, as the one called to be guardian of the good of the Catholic faith, I have the duty to make these thoughts known to you.

The bishop went on to recall that, according to the Concordat, teaching materials for religion classes were to be made in agreement with the leaders of the Church. Since no new agreements had been made on the subject, the old teaching materials should still have been used, which had no place for an unsystematic treatment of the fifth commandment or a lesson on "the people of Israel through the ages and their demoralizing effect on the host peoples," a topic which, he remarked mildly, in no way belongs to Catholic religion lessons.

---

1   Peter Löffler, ed., *Bischof Clemens August Graf von Galen: Akten, Briefe und Predigten 1933–1946*, 2nd ed. (Paderborn: Ferdinand Schöningh, 1996), doc. 23, v. I, 46, n. 2; von Galen's letter, 46–47.

When pastor of St. Lambert's, von Galen continued, he had received friendly cooperation from the school superintendent when he had pointed out that a measure being undertaken went against the law. The hope that he would receive similar cooperation in regard to this violation of the legally guaranteed rights of the Church was his reason for writing a mild, private letter. This time, however, he received no reply.[2] There would be countless repetitions of this in the coming years.

Very clearly, the Nazis meant to convince everyone, especially the young, of German racial superiority. Many people could agree with the project of restoring Germany's national pride and building a strong national community. But the Bishop of Münster could not agree with the ideology of the superiority of the "Nordic" or "Aryan" race. Alfred Rosenberg, the leading proponent of the ideology being inculcated through massive propaganda, had promulgated his neo-pagan ideas of blood and race in his book *The Myth of the 20th Century*. For him and for many Nazis, the movement led by Adolf Hitler was more than a political movement. It was a religious movement based on a revival of ancient paganism. Germans needed to have a specifically German religion, based on German nationality and blood. A major problem with Christianity, of course, was that it was based on Judaism.

Bishop Clemens August von Galen indicated his disagreement with these racial and pagan theories in his private letter to the school superintendent just days after becoming bishop. He did so publicly and forcefully in his first Easter pastoral letter as bishop, which was read in all the churches of the diocese on Easter Sunday, April 1, 1934,

---

2   A complaint to the mayor led to a three-way conversation involving the mayor, the bishop, and the school superintendent and an assurance that the superintendent would not take it upon himself to dictate lesson plans for the Catholic religion classes. In July 1935, however, this promise was violated. See Löffler, doc. 24, v. I, 48–49, doc. 115, v. I, 254.

and published in the Catholic papers.[3] Recalling St. Paul's command to Timothy (2 Tim. 4:1–5) to preach the truth in season and out of season, "For the time is coming when people will not endure sound teaching, and having itching ears they will accumulate for themselves teachers to suit their own likings, and will turn away from listening to the truth and wander into myths" (vv. 3–4, RSV), he commented that "a Bishop dare not keep silent if false teachings and unbelief raise their head, if what is warned of in the letter to Titus comes to pass: 'They lead entire families into confusion.'" He continued, "A word of truth is so much more necessary when enemies of religion, such as we now see, are fighting not only against this or that teaching of the Church, but deny or falsify the very foundations of religion itself and the most holy mysteries of revelation."

He went on with "brutally Catholic" directness:

> Whoever undermines or destroys man's faith in God attacks the very foundations of religion and the whole of culture. According to Catholic teaching, as it was most recently expressed at the Vatican Council, God is the most pure Spirit, who was the beginning before all things. Today writings are distributed and recommended that say that God did not create the world and direct its development, but rather the idea of God is a result of this development. That is a new paganism. The Catholic Church teaches that God is really and essentially distinct from the world; the new paganism says rather that God is brought forth by the world and above all by blood. According to the teaching of the Catholic Church, God is eternal in His willing and His understanding. According to the neo-pagans God has will, understanding and personality only in men. God is no longer the Lord, but rather man, and from that step God directly becomes man's servant. . . .

---

3   Löffler, doc. 35, v. I, 67–72.

Anyone who seeks to destroy the moral law in man attacks the foundations of religion and of culture. But this is done by those who say that morality is valid for a people only insofar as it promotes the interests of the race. Clearly, this puts the race above morality, blood above the law. Indeed, this false teaching goes on to claim that the Ten Commandments were merely the expression of the morality of the Jewish people, and the commandments would be different for different peoples with different blood. In fact, the Ten Commandments, which were promulgated amid thunder and lightning on Mount Sinai, are obligatory for all peoples. The content of the Ten Commandments is written as the moral law on the hearts of all men, including the pagans, as the Apostle (Paul) teaches.

Quoting from an encyclical letter of Pope Pius XI, *Caritate Christi*, Bishop von Galen reminded the Catholics of his diocese that all social order depends on faith in God. Without it, the moral law becomes meaningless, and contracts and treaties have no binding force. What good are guarantees of conscience if there is no belief in God and no fear of God? Take away faith in God, and brute force tramples on all rights.

The new pagans of Germany, he continued, rejected not only the correct idea of God and the moral law but also the revelation that God gave to the world through Christ. What was worse, they sometimes gave the name "Christian" to this new religion they were inventing. In fact, it had nothing to do with Christ. They rejected the Old Testament completely. They accepted the New Testament only insofar as they could interpret it as an expression of Germanic blood. They claimed that for the Nordic race, there was no such thing as original sin or even a concept of sin. The morality of Christianity, they said, was a morality suited for slaves. There was no need for a redeemer who saved us by His blood. Why would we need salvation if there is no such thing as sin?

For von Galen, this entire ideology was not only a falsification of Christianity but also a falsification of German identity and an attack on the forefathers of the German people. It was "a radical break with the Christian past of the German people, whose culture has developed for more than a thousand years on the foundation of Christianity." Both his faith and his reverence for his ancestors were offended.

Recalling Hitler's public affirmation that the teachings of Christianity were the basis for the renovation of the German Reich, the bishop tried the tactic of dividing Rosenberg off from Hitler. Despite what Hitler said, he wrote,

> they dare, under the pretext of advancing the national rebirth of the German people, to insult Christianity and its teachings, to disparage Christian morality, to undermine our loyalty to the faith of our fathers. A deception from hell is here, that could lead even the good into error.
>
> Therefore I lift up my voice in warning as a German bishop, and I say to you: Hold fast to the faith of the one, holy, catholic and apostolic Church, as your fathers held to it and professed it. Arm yourselves against the traps of the one who has been our enemy from the beginning. You Christian parents, keep guard especially over the youth who are entrusted to you. Warn them against being led astray by having close relations with unbelievers and by reading things that "under the false appearance of the true and the good" spread the poison of neo-paganism.[4]

Thus from his first year as a bishop, Clemens August von Galen declared himself an enemy of Nazi ideology. This first Easter pastoral

---

4   Ibid.

letter of the Bishop of Münster made a huge impression on his diocese. Here were courageous words from a bishop who, as a relative wrote in a letter to him, called black "black" and white "white."[5] He taught the sheep of his flock with clarity what the true Catholic faith is and how to discern the errors in the new teachings. He encouraged them to stand firm in the Faith, even in the face of persecution, which he warned them was likely to come. Perhaps one should not say "warned." He reminded them that for faithful Christians, to suffer persecution and martyrdom would be a great blessing, and they would consider it a source of great joy if this were to be their lot.

From this time on, as a Jesuit opponent of the Nazis later reported, von Galen was the "*Liebling*"—the "darling" or "pet"—of his diocese.[6] The letter was greeted with surprise and then jubilation. The misgivings of the people about the Nazi ideology and program were put into clear words. The bishop's relative, in the letter just noted, passed on the comment of an acquaintance that it was a shame that Germans did not have the Italian practice of applauding in church.[7] A priest friend noted the profound silence that accompanied the reading of the letter at all four Masses in his church on Easter Sunday, after which the congregation sang with great gusto the hymn "*Fest soll mein Taufbund immer stehn*."[8] This hymn, "I shall keep firmly to my baptismal promises," written in the early nineteenth century by a priest from Münster, expresses one's desire to remain ever faithful to Christ and His Church. It had been a sign of Catholic fidelity and loyalty to the pope and the bishops during the *Kulturkampf*; it was to play the same role during the Nazi era.

---

5   Droste zu Vischering an v. Galen, Löffler, doc. 36, v. I, 72–73.
6   Muckermann, cited in Gunter Beaugrand, *Ein Leben im XX. Jahrhundert: Begegnungen und Gespräche mit Christoph Bernhard von Galen auf Haus Assen / Lippetal* (Werl: Boerde-Verlag, 2004), 29.
7   See above, note 6.
8   Janssen an v. Galen, Löffler, doc. 37, v. I, 73.

The bishop's pastoral letter showed that all the rhetoric and pro-paganda about national rebirth was united with an attack on Chris-tianity, an attack on morality, and a new racially based paganism in which the race took the place of God and defined good and evil in its own interests. There was a battle afoot between good and evil, and the souls of the young were a key battleground. The Nazis put special emphasis on winning the youth over to their ideology. The bishop therefore made strong efforts to educate them in the truth, strongly encouraging parents to keep a vigilant eye on what their children were being taught. When he visited the different regions of the vast diocese to administer the Sacrament of Confirmation, he was always received by exuberant crowds. The usual practice was for a horse-drawn carriage to meet his car when he came near to a town or village. The bishop would transfer to the carriage and enter the town in procession, with cheering crowds along the roads. He had a wonderful rapport with children and youth. It became proverbial in the diocese that the Bishop of Münster was a giant with the heart of a child.

When at home, he took an especial interest in his seminarians. Each day, a different seminarian would arrive early in the morning at the episcopal palace to serve his Mass and have breakfast with him. As the seminarians came one by one in alphabetical order, Bishop von Galen would get to know each one personally by having several breakfast conversations with him over the years of his seminary train-ing. The ways of thought of the younger generation were much dif-ferent from those of von Galen, but these conversations enabled him to overcome the gap. Father Heinrich Portmann, his secretary from 1938 until the end of von Galen's life, said that von Galen was able to overcome their shyness and put them at ease with his fatherly kind-ness. During Lent, it frequently happened that an anxious seminar-ian would want to imitate the abstinence of his bishop, who would breakfast on two pieces of dry bread put together like a sandwich but with nothing between them or spread on them, which he would dip into his black coffee. With a smile, von Galen would encourage the seminarian to eat more heartily, as the hardships of being a seminarian were penance enough. At all his meals, he himself kept to the simple farmer's fare of his childhood, eaten without ceremony. Sometimes a seminarian would wonder at the fact that he did not say grace before breakfast. "My mother didn't 'learn' me to do that," was his reply; "and anyway, we've just come from the chapel."

The Nazis quickly realized that they had an enemy in the episcopal palace of Münster. The area leader (*gauleiter*) of von Galen's *Heimat*, Oldenburg, a man named Carl Röver, wrote an anxious letter to the Chancellery in Berlin regarding his pastoral letter on neo-paganism. Other bishops also wrote similar letters, he noted,

> but it is clear that the Pastoral Letter of the Bishop of Münster goes far beyond the others in severity. Every sentence is dictated by hatred of National Socialism. Without using the name of National Socialism, the Bishop attacks all the fundamental principles of National Socialism, charging that it undermines the basis of religion, that it puts race ahead of morality and blood ahead of the law, and that it claims that the ten commandments are merely the expression of the morality of the Jewish people; that it openly attacks Revelation and Christendom; and that a series of ideas and concepts that came into men's heads through the godless movement of Bolshevism have come back again under national auspices.[9]

As a brief analysis of the key ideas of von Galen's letter, this was pretty good. The Catholic Church had long attacked godless

---

9   Letter of Carl Röver, reproduced in Joachim Kuropka, *Clemens August Graf von Galen: Sein Leben und Wirken in Bildern und Dokumenten*, 3rd ed. (Cloppenburg: Runge, 1997), 112.

communism. So had the Nazis, who wanted to present themselves as the bulwark against the system that had caused so much suffering in Russia and Ukraine. The area leader saw that Bishop von Galen was attacking Nazism for the same reason that the Church fought communism: It was a godless system that destroyed morality. Röver ended by saying that the pastoral letter had caused great distress among those Catholics of Oldenburg who had been sympathetic to National Socialism.[10] It would not be the last time that an action of Bishop von Galen's would cause distress to the gauleiter of Oldenburg.[11]

Nor was the bishop finished with Alfred Rosenberg or with the Nazi exaltation of paganism. Preaching at Billerbeck two weeks later to a crowd of nearly eighteen thousand men at a pilgrimage in honor of St. Ludger, the first Bishop of Münster, he reminded them that when their pagan ancestors converted to Christianity eleven centuries earlier, it was not, as the neo-pagans among the Nazis claimed, merely an external adherence to the religion of a conqueror but a joyful acceptance of the truth of the Christian revelation. "People speak today of a 'new faith,' of a 'myth of blood,'" he said:

> They want to persuade us "that the Nordic blood depicts the Mystery that has replaced and conquered the old Sacraments." We, however, hold firmly to the old faith, which our ancestors joyfully recognized and accepted as divine truth more than 1100 years ago, the faith in the divine mystery of that blood of which St Peter spoke: "You have been purchased, not with corruptible silver and gold, but with the Precious Blood of Christ, the Lamb without spot or stain." We believe in the old, holy Sacraments instituted by Christ, in the mysterious power of grace contained in holy Baptism, where we are saved, not by

10   Ibid., 113.
11   See chapter 10.

something like the inherited Nordic blood, but by the Precious
Blood of the God-man Jesus Christ, which He freely shed out
of love for us.[12]

In the same address, he exhibited a cleverness that made him
a tough opponent for his Nazi enemies. A newspaper article had
attacked his pastoral letter as an illicit mixing in party politics. He
sharply denied the charge. The Christian faith, he asserted, is not a
matter of party politics, and defending it is the holy duty of those
called to be religious leaders, and indeed, of every Catholic. Then
came the counterattack: "And when the same man says that the neo-
pagan teachings that have been attacked by the German Bishops
express the world view of National Socialism, he is setting himself
in opposition to the authoritative Leader (Führer) of the National
Socialist movement; for he, as Imperial Chancellor, declared on a
solemn occasion that he wanted to place the work of renewing our
people on the firm rock of the Christian faith. No one should dare
to shake one's trust in the solemnly given word of our Führer!"[13]

The bishop next recalled his own solemnly given word, in the
oath he had made before Hermann Goering: "In the dutiful care
for the good and the interests of the German State, I will, in performing the office entrusted to me, seek to ward off any dangers
that could threaten it."

Commenting on this oath in his address to the large crowd of
men, he continued:

> When people would seek to shake the inherited Christian faith
> of our People, that, in my most holy, most inward conviction,
> is the greatest danger that could threaten the German State.

---

12   Löffler, doc. 40, v. I, 78. The text contains in parentheses a page reference
      to Rosenberg's *Myth* for the quotation about Nordic blood and the refer-
      ence to 1 Pet. 1:18.

13   Ibid., 78–79.

And whoever would undermine trust in the solemn word of the Führer is introducing frightful dangers.

Therefore it is my duty, as a man who loves his fatherland, as a German Bishop, true to my oath, in performing the office entrusted to me, to ward off such dangers with all my strength. And therefore I repeat what I said to you in my Easter Greeting: Hold fast to the faith of the one, holy, catholic, and apostolic Church, as your fathers have held fast to it since the time of St. Ludger. Beware of false prophets, who want to proclaim a new faith to you. Guard yourselves and your children from writings which insult the true faith, the holy Catholic Church, and its leaders![14]

---

14   Ibid., 79.

CHAPTER 6

No Reflection on the Führer

The Bishop of Münster was preaching about family life. As usual, there were Nazi informers in the cathedral. This time, too, there was a heckler. "Celibates have no business talking about marriage and children!" came a shout from the congregation. The bishop slammed his fist on the pulpit and shouted back, "I will not tolerate any reflection upon the Führer in my cathedral!"[1]

The Führer, or leader, Adolf Hitler, had taken power in Germany by constitutional means. By the early 1930s, with Germany suffering terribly from the worldwide economic depression, the Weimar Republic was proving unable to deal with radical elements in the country on both left and right. The votes for the parliament, the Reichstag, were split among so many parties that governments kept collapsing. Police forces

---

1   Stories of this kind were widely circulated. R. L. Sedgwick heard this story and others when he worked for British propaganda during World War II. After the war, as Controller-General of Religious Affairs in Western Germany for the occupying government, he had frequent access to the Bishop of Münster and asked him if he could confirm the stories. Although the bishop denied most of them, this is one of those that he "let pass in modified form." See Sedgwick's introduction to his translation of Heinrich Portmann, *Cardinal von Galen* (London: Jarrolds, 1957), 16.

all over the country were useless at stopping the pitched battles fought in the streets between communists and Nazi brownshirts. Despite—or perhaps because of—the large numbers of fatalities, both parties were growing in electoral support. The results of the elections of November 1932 made them the two largest parties in the Reichstag, with the more moderate parties between them. Fear of communism, which had done so much harm in Russia and Ukraine, led many to support Hitler's promise of a strong, authoritarian government. Still, when President Paul von Hindenburg appointed Hitler as chancellor of a coalition government on January 30, 1933, the old politicians thought it would box him into a corner. He headed a large party, but it had lost two million votes in the November elections. Only two other Nazis were in the cabinet, with the rest of the posts in the hands of conservatives.

On February 28, a lone arsonist set a fire in the Reichstag. Hitler and his henchman Hermann Goering blamed the communists and persuaded the cabinet to suppress them. Richard J. Evans describes what followed:

> Four thousand Communists including virtually the entire party leadership were immediately arrested, beaten up, tortured, and thrown into newly created concentration camps. There was no let-up in the campaign of violence and brutality in the weeks that followed. By the end of March the Prussian police reported that 20,000 Communists were in prison. By the summer over 100,000 Communists, Social Democrats, trade unionists and others had been arrested, with even official estimates putting the number of deaths in custody at 600. All of this was sanctioned by an emergency decree signed by Hindenburg the night after the fire suspending civil liberties and allowing the cabinet to take any necessary measures to protect public safety.[2]

---

2   Richard J. Evans, *The Third Reich in Power* (New York: Penguin, 2005), 11–12.

Fresh elections on March 5 still did not give the Nazis enough seats in the Reichstag to change the Constitution, but by keeping up the violence, threatening civil war, and promising the Catholic Centre Party that they would enter into a Concordat with the Holy See guaranteeing the rights of Catholics, they were able to weaken and divide their opposition. On March 23, they pushed through the Enabling Act, which gave the cabinet the right to rule by decree without reference to the Reichstag or the president. This paved the way for the creation of a dictatorship.[3] Within six months of being named chancellor, Hitler was out of his corner and had managed to turn Germany into a one-party totalitarian dictatorship.

Once in power, the Nazis deliberately sought to build a totalitarian regime—that is, seeking to have the totality of human existence directed by the state, which meant by the Nazi Party. In November 1933, Joseph Goebbels, the minister of popular enlightenment and propaganda, stated: "The revolution we have made is a total one. It has encompassed every area of public life and fundamentally restructured them all. It has completely changed and reshaped people's relationship to each other, to the state, and questions of existence."[4]

The regime was in place by July 1933. Clemens August von Galen was named Bishop of Münster in September of that year and took office in October. As the anecdote above illustrates, von Galen, with his continued affirmations that there are aspects of human existence that are not subject to the state, was a problem for the Nazi regime. His popularity, built up by his clear teaching, was only enhanced by his clever quips. The Nazi propaganda machine specialized in gigantic public rallies, giving an impression of complete loyalty to the new National Socialist Germany. But Bishop von Galen was producing public relations successes of his own.

---

3   Ibid.
4   Cited in ibid., 120.

The Concordat concluded between the government and the Holy
See in July 1933 was supposed to guarantee the independence of
Catholic institutions, groups, and schools. For their part, the clergy
and those Catholic organizations were to stay out of party politics.
Thus the Church and the state were seen as partners in the revital-
ization of Germany. But from the start, the state kept up a many-
pronged attack on Catholic independence. Ferdinand von Lünincks
bizarre speech on the day of von Galen's consecration, the anti-
Jewish teaching materials being decreed for use in Catholic religion
classes, and the propaganda in favor of Rosenberg's paganism were
only parts of this attack.

In April 1934, the bishop gave his assessment of the situation at
a Conference of the Deans, the leading clergy of the many areas of
his large diocese.[5] Germans had lived through two revolutions, he
told them, first in 1918 and then in 1933. The 1918 revolution had
been a reaction against the abuse of authority, based on the motto
"freedom." After fifteen years, the people had now given up the ban-
ner of freedom, instead hoping for happiness from an authoritarian
regime. Would this bring happiness? It seemed not, he opined.

"Freedom and authority are both fundamental principles of
human communal life," he said. "Both find their foundation and
their ruling principle in God. When this foundation is misunderstood and misused, there will always be a misuse of freedom and
authority. During the war, authority was misused. Since 1918, freedom has been misused. This explains why the people have ecstati-
cally fallen into blind submission to the authority of a Führer."

When the new movement was growing, he continued, the bishops
had warned against Catholics taking part in it because some of its early

5   Peter Löffler, ed., *Bischof Clemens August Graf von Galen: Akten, Briefe und
      Predigten 1933–1946*, 2nd ed. (Paderborn: Ferdinand Schöningh, 1996),
      doc. 43, v. I, 82–87.

leaders had espoused a new German national religion in place of Christianity and an autonomous German morality in place of the divine moral law. But after the seizure of power, Hitler formally declared that Christianity would be the foundation of the newly constructed state. Trusting in his word, the bishops had rescinded their warning. Their trust was strengthened by the completion of the Concordat and by several positive measures of the new regime. "The Führer pledged his word and has not revoked it," von Galen told his priests:

> It is right and beneficial to call attention to this fact when appropriate. Catholics should not pessimistically put their hands in their pockets. It is our holy task to work especially for:
> - maintaining the purity of supernatural truth;
> - justice in all areas of human life;
> - freedom of the Church to fulfill her sacred tasks.

The bishop left his clergy in no doubt that attacks were being made against the Church and basic human rights in all three of these areas. Christian truth was being attacked by the propagation of Rosenberg's new paganism. In his opinion, he told his priests, "a positive presentation and convincing explanation is more fruitful than polemical battles with opponents of the truth." He added, however, that it would be necessary at times to point out that false teaching and even paganism were indeed being propagated. This would be done best by giving the positive presentation first and then explaining how this truth was denied by the false teaching.

He encouraged all who were seeking to defend the rights of the Church but cautioned his priests to resist only when truth, justice, and freedom were being endangered. He assured them that the bishops of Germany and his officials in the Diocese of Münster were not standing idly by. Much of what he called "The Battle of the German Episcopate for the Rights and Freedom of the Church" was deliberately kept out of the public eye. Out of respect for the authority of the government, the Church's tactic at this time was not to publicize violations of the Concordat, but to protest to the appropriate officials, reminding them of the provisions of the Concordat, which had the status of a treaty in international law.[6] Von Galen himself adopted this tactic, as shown clearly in the monumental collection of documents from his time as bishop, edited by historian Peter Löffler.[7] Again and again, von Galen wrote letters of complaint, often reminding the officials that he would have to bring the violation in question to the attention of the Holy See, the other partner in the Concordat. Occasionally, the protests received a positive response. More often, there was a non-committal reply, a defense of the step that had been taken by the government, a lengthy delay in responding, or simply no response at all. The Nazis soon became very proficient at bureaucratic delaying tactics.

In his meeting with his deans in April 1934, Bishop von Galen gave them a long list of topics on which the bishops were working. There was a constant struggle over the interpretation of Article 31 of the Concordat. This article guaranteed the continued existence of Catholic organizations that served purely religious, cultural, or charitable purposes. Organizations that served specific social groups or professions were also supported in their continued existence, provided that they refrained from working for a political party. The government also promised that any government-sponsored organizations for sporting or youth activities would allow their members to fulfill their religious obligations on Sundays and feast days and would not compel young people to participate in activities that conflicted with their religious and moral convictions. Both in Münster and throughout the country, the bishops were constantly protesting against violations of all aspects of this article. In numerous cases, Catholic organizations were simply closed down and

---

6   Ibid.
7   Ibid.

their property confiscated. The system of publicly supported Protestant and Catholic schools was also under attack, as well as religious instruction in trade and professional schools. Seminary students were being unlawfully required to take part in army training and work service. Within six months of this meeting, von Galen would deal with the first case in which a young man whom the diocese had approved for seminary studies, and whose academic grades met the standard for admission to the university, was informed by the government that he would not be permitted to study theology.

The bishops at this time protested against the imposition of a law inflicting compulsory sterilization on persons with mental illness and certain other conditions. This was well-known to his priests, so von Galen did not expand on it. Further, the freedom of the Catholic press was being attacked, while publications attacking the Church and the Faith were widely circulated. And by this time, less than a year since the Nazi seizure of power, nine priests of the Diocese of Münster had already been imprisoned.[8]

Shortly after this meeting of the bishop with his leading clergy, Catholic organizations suffered a new attack on their independence. Dr. Robert Ley, head of the German Labor Front, published a notice on April 27, 1934, that members of his organization could not simultaneously hold membership in any other professional or labor organizations. Catholic workers wanted to continue belonging to their Catholic Working Men's Clubs and hold memberships in the German Labor Front as well. This new ruling made such double membership impossible, putting Catholics in a difficult position. The propaganda of the German Labor Front already claimed that Catholics were unpatriotic and were not true Germans. Catholic workers wanted to defend the claim that a true Catholic was also a true German, but now it seemed they had to choose between patriotism

---

8   Ibid.

and faithfulness to their Catholic groups. If they remained in their Kolping groups and other Catholic clubs, they would be removed from the lists of the German Labor Front. Von Galen, with his background of living and working with the Catholic workers of Berlin, was so upset that he sent a telegram to Adolf Hitler himself. The topic was referred to a meeting between officials of the government and a group of bishops.

Like the Catholic workers' associations, Catholic youth groups were a special target. The Nazis wanted to have the souls of the young. Baldur von Schirach, head of the Hitler Youth, was virulently anti-Christian. Richard J. Evans gives a rough translation, with rather awkward rhymes, of a song that the Hitler Youth sang at the 1934 Nuremberg Party Rally:

> We are the jolly Hitler Youth,
> We don't need any Christian truth
> For Adolf Hitler, our Leader
> Always is our interceder.
>
> Whatever the Papist priests may try,
> We're Hitler's children until we die;
> We follow not Christ but Horst Wessel.
> Away with incense and holy water vessel!
>
> As sons of our forebears from times gone by
> We march as we sing with banners held high.
> I'm not a Christian, nor a Catholic,
> I go with the SA through thin and thick.[9]

This kind of propaganda easily led to the sort of behavior a Hitler Youth member exhibited in Munich in 1936. A witness watching him enter a classroom, "observed how his glance fell on the crucifix

---

9   Evans, 250–51.

hanging behind the teacher's desk, how in an instant his young and still soft face contorted in fury, how he ripped this symbol . . . off the wall and threw it out of the window into the street . . . with the cry, 'Lie there, you dirty Jew!'"[10]

No wonder Bishop von Galen frequently warned parents to keep a careful watch over the influences on their children.

"We are loyal Germans! We are also loyal Catholics!" he proclaimed to an audience of ten thousand people at a rally in Recklinghausen in September 1934.[11] These two statements, he insisted, were not and should not be in opposition to each other. True loyalty to the state was best preserved by living a serious Christian life and by insisting on the Christian foundations of Germany against the pagan ideology of Rosenberg. The propaganda in favor of Rosenberg's book tended in fact, he argued, to undermine the authority of the state. Fighting against it was, therefore, not only a Christian but a national duty. He told the crowd that Hitler had promised a group of bishops in June 1934 that the neo-pagan propaganda would cease. He trusted that this order would soon work its way through government and Party officials, which would be for the good of the Church and the nation.

In the same speech, von Galen spoke of St. Elizabeth of Thuringia, to whom he was going to dedicate a church on the following day. She was, he stressed, a great German woman, although only her mother was German, as her father was the king of Hungary. No one would dare to doubt, said von Galen, that she was the pride of the German people, a German saint, the model for all German women. "This should give us a warning," he continued,

> against overemphasizing the importance of one's blood; this has its natural importance, which is certainly not to be weighed lightly, but it ranks second in importance to her Christian, German

---

10   Ibid., 251.
11   Löffler, doc. 69, v. I, 124–30, here 127.

upbringing, and the Christian devotion and German loyalty by
which she was united in service with her German husband, her
German family, and her German people, and the nobility of
her soul, which did not come from a natural blood relationship but
from the Precious Blood of the Son of God, who has taken all of us
into the grace-filled blood relationship of the children of God by
His Incarnation and by the Blood He shed for us on the Cross.[12]

As the bishop regularly complained to government officials on
the ground that Hitler and the Concordat guaranteed a supposed
partnership between Church and state, so on their part, government officials sometimes made their own complaints to the bishop.
Minister of the Interior Wilhelm Frick wrote to him in July 1935 to
complain that priests and Catholic organizations were still engaging
in party politics, against the provisions of the Concordat.[13]

In his reply, von Galen respectfully noted that Frick's complaints
were without specifics. He would be happy to correct anyone violating the Concordat, if such violations came to his attention. But
he opined that Minister Frick was being led into error by his underlings. As an example, Frick had cited a case that had been publicized under the headline, "A Brave Girl." Claiming to be based on a
police report, the article stated that a priest in his sermon was criticizing the state when a young girl shouted, "Preach God's Word, not
politics." The priest, after recovering from his initial shock, asked the
girl to leave the church at once. She did so, according to the article,
and so did more than half the people in the church.[14]

This case, wrote von Galen to Frick, shows "that your Excellency
is in fact not always being told the truth." The event supposedly took
place in Bottrop, according to its first report in the newspaper there,

---

12   Ibid.
13   Löffler, doc. 114, v. I, 252–54.
14   Ibid., 253, n. 5.

but when that was found to be mistaken, a "correction" was printed, saying that it had happened in St. George's Church in Gelsenkirchen on May 12. "But that is also incorrect," the Bishop wrote:

> What is correct is that on April 7 in that church, a mentally ill woman caused a brief disturbance by shouting something out during a sermon which was not at all on a political topic. Immediately after the service, which she attended to the end, she went to the sacristy and begged the parish priest for forgiveness. It is also completely untrue that a great number of the congregation left the church because of this incident. The local police have long known the falsity of the original report and the truth of what really happened. It is very remarkable that they reported to you the fable of the "brave girl," which perhaps was originally believed and spread because of a garbled report, and did not tell you about the correction and clarification of the mistake and of the pointlessness and political meaninglessness of the actual events that were the basis of this fable.[15]

As this correspondence was taking place at the height of his battle with the neo-paganism of Alfred Rosenberg, von Galen did not finish his letter without a clarification for the minister. To defend the Catholic faith against the propagation of a new paganism, he maintained, is not a matter of party politics. Neither is defending the Church and her institutions against insult, nor is defending her teachings on faith and morals against distortion and abuse. The fact that, in the past, loyal Catholics who belonged to the Centre Party fought against unbelief, godlessness, and immorality and for the rights of God and the Church of Jesus Christ was not a matter of a specifically "Centre Spirit." "Such defense is the religious duty of every faithful Catholic of every age, regardless of membership in any political party. It was

---

15   Löffler, doc. 121, v. I, 263–67, here 265.

the acknowledged and exercised duty of German Catholics before there was a Centre Party; it continues to be an unchanging duty of German Catholics after the end of the system of political parties and after they have renounced membership in the Centre Party."[16]

Why would people confuse this purely religious duty with the spirit of a political party? Von Galen thought he had the answer: the widespread propaganda in favor of Rosenberg's theories. Rosenberg and his associates, the bishop told Frick, were insulting National Socialism by spreading the opinion that his theories were an essential part of the National Socialist worldview. But they were getting away with it, with the result that opposition to his theories was interpreted as opposition to the National Socialist state. No one, he continued, could really believe this without setting himself in opposition to the Führer, Adolf Hitler, who wrote in his *Mein Kampf* that anyone who would drag the people's movement into religious controversies was a worse enemy of the people than an international communist. The religious controversy affecting Germany had been caused not by the German bishops or the Catholic people but by Rosenberg's circle. Catholics, he concluded, could not make themselves believe that the Führer was aware of what was going on. "We believe that, if he knew, he would act in accordance with his words (also in *Mein Kampf*): 'It will always be the most important duty of the leadership of the National Socialist movement to stop in its tracks any attempt to drag the National Socialist movement into such battles, and immediately to expel from the ranks of the movement any propagandists of such a position.'"[17]

Truly Bishop von Galen was not tolerating any reflection on the Führer!

16　Ibid., 266.
17　Ibid., citing A. Hitler, *Mein Kampf* (Munich, 1934), 613f.

CHAPTER 7

The Great Procession

Late on a rainy Sunday afternoon in October 1934, Father Wilhelm Neuss, a professor of theology at Bonn, came to Münster with another professor friend. They called at the episcopal palace, for they urgently wished to see the bishop. But they were not expected, and the bishop was not there. Indeed, no one was there. They tried the home of the provost of the Cathedral Chapter, Adolf Donders. Again no one answered. At the house of one of the cathedral canons, they did find a housekeeper, who told them that the canon was out for a walk and would be back in a couple of hours. They telephoned the rector of the seminary—away until Thursday. Another telephone call was fruitless. Surely, they wondered, there must be some priest available in Münster on a Sunday afternoon who could tell them how they could reach the bishop. They tried the house of the provost again, and he was now back at home.

Professor Neuss explained the reason for their visit: Several professors had collaborated on a book detailing the errors and unscientific aspects of Rosenberg's *Myth*. The Archbishop of Cologne, Cardinal Schulte, was going to authorize it for publication but had changed his mind. Father Neuss and his friend hoped that Bishop von Galen would approve it. The provost told them that the bishop was visiting his brother-in-law for a few days of much-needed rest and was not to be disturbed. Anyway, how could he take over publication of a work by priests of the Archdiocese of Cologne, which their cardinal had decided against publishing?

The professors would not give up: "Then we must speak with your Vicar General. Please call him." Of course, he was not at home. A message was left for him to come as soon as he returned, and the two visitors were given a meal. The vicar general arrived at eight in the evening and agreed with Neuss: This was a matter for the bishop himself to decide. He telephoned the bishop: "Your Excellency, there are two gentlemen here, one from Bonn and one from Cologne, wishing to speak to you as soon as possible about a very important matter. Could they see you at eight o'clock tomorrow morning? They will tell you themselves what it's about."

"Certainly, I'll be expecting them. Just one thing, Herr Vicar General. What is your opinion of the matter?"

"I am completely in favour of it. There is just one difficulty, which the gentlemen themselves will explain to you." The difficulty, of course, had to do with the "cold feet" of Cardinal Schulte.

The Münster priests arranged for a car and the loan of some money, for their visitors had not counted on an extra journey and an extra day. At 7:30 the next morning, they arrived at the home of Baron von Wendt, the bishop's brother-in-law. They waited for a time while the bishop finished saying Mass, after which he rushed into the room, saying, "My God, what is it that's so important this early in the morning? Ah, Herr Professor, it's you! So what is it?" Neuss explained the situation. They had the corrected proofs with them; the book was ready to be printed; would he allow it to be printed under his authority? "Yes, that's good!" exclaimed the bishop, slapping himself on the knee gleefully. "Finally the theological faculty has moved itself to action. I've been critical of the professors in my thoughts: Why are they so quiet? Why don't they do anything? Now I take it all back. What do you want me to do?"

"Write a brief foreword."

"Gladly."

"Shall I take dictation?"

"I can't think any faster than I can write." The bishop wrote a few lines on the envelope containing the manuscript. "We hereby offer to the worthy clergy this text, in which learned German men give clarification about the content and sources of the book *The Myth of the Twentieth Century*. It is written with love for the German fatherland, the Holy Church, and the truth. May it bear fruit in the same sense." Then he asked, "What will the title be?"

"*Studies on The Myth of the Twentieth Century.*"

"Why so cautious? I'd prefer to blast the fellow."

"Perhaps a little caution is better. May we leave the title as it is?"

"Sure. Anything else? Oh yes, the good Lord Cardinal. Give him my warmest greetings. I hope he won't think badly of me for this."

In ten minutes, the interview was over.[1] Within days, the first three parts of *Studies on The Myth of the Twentieth Century* appeared as a supplement to Münster's diocesan newsletter. A fourth part came out in December, and a fifth in early 1935 responded to the attacks in a new book by Alfred Rosenberg entitled *Against the Obscurantists of Our Time*.

In March, the bishop completed another pastoral letter. To be read in all the parishes on April 7, it was a sixteen-page attack on the new paganism.[2] More than an attack, it was a heartfelt lament. Germany had been freed from the foolishness of paganism more

---

1   From the recollections of Wilhelm Neuss, reprinted in Peter Löffler, ed., *Bischof Clemens August Graf von Galen: Akten, Briefe und Predigten 1933–1946*, 2nd ed. (Paderborn: Ferdinand Schöningh, 1996), doc. 70, v. I, 130–33.

2   Löffler, doc. 85, v. I, 168–84.

than a thousand years earlier. It was a horrible thought that "once again there are pagans in Germany," that "today there are German men who call themselves pagans, who glory in the name of pagan."[3] To reject the one true God in favor of a self-invented paganism was a return to darkness, a terrible intellectual error that would also have grave moral consequences.

The new pagans were not going back to the old pagan gods. Their new gods were the nation, the race, the "eternal racial soul." Von Galen dismissed the eternal racial soul as a "nothing." For the German people to offer their service of body and soul to this "nothing," this "product of their phantasy," would be an irrational step backward from the intellectual and cultural advance their ancestors made more than a thousand years earlier.[4]

By the light of his natural reason, the bishop stated, man can be aware of the existence of the Creator and Lord of all things. This was in line with the teaching of the Catholic Church at the First Vatican Council, with the Old Testament Book of Wisdom, and with St. Paul's Letter to the Romans in the New Testament. Further, because there is an eternal, all-powerful, all-good Creator, there is also a moral order. The new pagans, argued von Galen, claimed that God is simply an idea created by human reason. One of the proponents of a German National Church had written: "The history of the world is the history of the emergence of God in men. God is nothing; God is becoming in men. And it is up to us whether he becomes real." Bishop von Galen dismissed this quotation with scorn: "This is what one can read in a book printed in Germany in 1933, whose author proudly claims that it contains a 'national socialist philosophy of culture'!"[5]

---

3   Ibid., 169.
4   Ibid., 174.
5   Ibid., 176. The quotation is from E. Bergmann: *Die deutsche Nationalkirche*.

Anyone who believes such doctrines, he wrote, is a pagan, an idol-
ater. The serpent in the garden of paradise had tempted Eve with the
phrase, "You shall be like God." The new pagans went further. Their
motto, von Galen said, could be: "You are more than God. God is
your product. God has not created you; you have created your own
god for yourself, and then bowed low to worship him."[6]

The bishop expressed compassion for those who had fallen under
the influence of these teachings. They were couched in noble phrases
and stressed the importance of making sacrifices for one's people—
even dying heroically for the good of the fatherland. But when one
follows a god of his own arbitrary creation, then his own will has
become the measure of moral right and wrong. The only limit to his
use of power against his fellow human beings is the power of someone stronger. "Anyone who thinks clearly," he wrote, "and honestly
accepts the witness of truth, must admit that turning away from the
one, transcendent, eternal God from whom all good comes, and a
universal conversion to gods 'that become in men,' gods whom each
one creates for himself out of the wishes and desires of his heart, will
infallibly undermine morality and destroy all justice; the doctrine of
the new paganism will lead to chaos, to the war of everyone against
everyone, to the bloody self-destruction of our German people."[7]

Ten years and tens of millions of deaths later, with Germany in
ruins, the bishop's words about Germany's bloody self-destruction
could be seen as prophetic.

He made it clear in his letter that he was far from being unpatriotic. To sacrifice, to fight when necessary, even to die for the
fatherland—all these, he said, were ideals that caused every noble
heart to beat higher. But to regard the nation as "the first and the last,
to which everything else must submit," would go against honor

6   Ibid., 177.
7   Ibid., 178.

and conscience. God is the first and the last. All must submit to Him, including nations and peoples. Von Galen insisted that acknowledging Him makes Catholics no less true and loyal children of the fatherland; such loyalty is demanded of the Christian conscience.[8] A constant theme of the Nazis had been for some time that committed Catholics could not be loyal Germans. "We are loyally German! We are also loyally Catholic!" had been a repeated refrain in the speech given by the bishop at Recklinghausen in September 1934.[9]

Now he raised the question, why did these modern pagans not leave Catholics the freedom to worship the one true God? They proclaimed their right to create their own "Myth." Why did they not leave Catholics their rights? Why the hatred of Christianity?

The answer was easy to find. Since they knew that their myth was their own creation, they believed that Christians were also following a self-created myth. The Christian "myth," however, acknowledged something higher than the German nation and people. From the national standpoint of the new pagans, belief in a God who is above the world and above all nations appeared to be disloyal. This, the bishop held, accounted for the mistrust of Christians, the belief that they were unwilling to cooperate with their fellow citizens in the rebuilding of their nation. That was why there were so many efforts to exclude Christianity from public life and the education of the young. That was why there were efforts to create a "German National Church" to overcome the differences between Catholics and Protestants. If it were true, the bishop wrote, "that our belief in the one true God and the truths revealed by Him were simply a 'myth,' then we could, perhaps we must, renounce these beliefs for the good of the unity of

8   Ibid., 178–79.
9   Löffler, doc. 69, v. I, 124–30.

our German people, and accept a newly-invented 'Myth of the Twentieth Century.' But as it is, we know that we are under an obligation to acknowledge, to worship and to serve the true, living God, the 'first and the last,' the origin and goal of all men."

Bishop Clemens August von Galen was not against a renewal of German society or a stronger national unity. But he was convinced that if it required a renunciation of the Christian faith and of the Catholic Church, investing the nation or the race with divine power, it would never lead to a true renewal of Germany.

In that spring of 1935, however, many leading Nazis held that the renewal of Germany did require attacks on the Church and rejection of the Christian faith in favor of Alfred Rosenberg's new paganism. One of those was the Reich Youth leader, Baldur von Schirach. The previous November, Schirach announced that "the way of Rosenberg is the way of the German youth." On March 31, he gave a speech in Essen attacking the Catholic youth organizations. This speech, broadcast by radio across the country, drew from the bishop a letter of protest to Adolf Hitler himself. Schirach said that the leaders of the Catholic youth organizations "are always against Germany," and that while claiming they are involved in the religious development of youth, "they actually serve no god other than their bellies." In saying this, von Galen noted, Schirach was attacking not only the lay leaders of Catholic youth groups, but also his priests and himself as the responsible leader of the youth groups of his diocese. He asked Hitler to order a public retraction from Schirach. Recalling the oath he had sworn before Hermann Goering to work for the good of the German state, the bishop argued that such public insults against honorable German men must not go unpunished. If such insults are made by a young man who is known to enjoy the especial trust of the leader of the nation and allowed to stand, this would undermine the people's respect for the reputations of others, their love of truth, and their sense of justice and thereby damage the moral foundations of the German state.[10]

A few days after the bishop's pastoral letter on the new paganism was read in the churches, the local gauleiter, Alfred Meyer, made a public address attacking those who claimed that the Nazis were neo-pagans. The leader, Adolf Hitler, had stated that the Party stood on the foundation of positive Christianity. It was bitter for Hitler, Meyer claimed, to have people calling them neo-pagans and thus casting doubt on his words. Bishop von Galen interpreted Meyer's address as referring, at least in part, to his own attacks on Rosenberg and his supporters, and took the opportunity to write Meyer a clarifying letter. Enclosing a copy of his pastoral letter, he pointed out the explicit texts of those Nazis who were claiming the title of pagan for themselves: "I have never had occasion, sir, to number you among these neo-pagans. It is my belief that you are an evangelical Christian, and therefore I presume that as such you believe in the eternal transcendent God and in our savior Jesus Christ. I know that I am at one in this belief with many of your fellow Party members, and I hope to see you on our side as a fellow citizen and fellow fighter against this 'neo-paganism.'"[11]

It was not the Catholics, he went on to say, who cast doubt on the Führer's words. It was those well-known members of the Nazi Party who openly called themselves pagans. No one could doubt, he continued, that there were men among the National Socialists who were pagans, many of whom had positions of high influence. It was no secret that Alfred Rosenberg was a bitter opponent of the Christian faith. How was it then that in the "most Christian State in the world," his book was compulsorily placed in the libraries of Christian schools? How was it that it was recommended for study

---

10   Löffler, doc. 88, v. I, 188–89.
11   Löffler, doc. 90, v. I, 193.

by Party members? How was it that in countless school courses and lectures, it was declared to be a handbook of the National Socialist viewpoint on the world?[12]

That put the issue clearly. It was no secret that Alfred Rosenberg hated Christianity. He had a high position in the Party. The leader of the Party and the nation claimed that his movement was based on Christianity, but Rosenberg was in charge of education in the National Socialist *Weltanschauung*. What should be believed: Hitler's words, or the actions of his followers? When Christians raised objections, the response was always given that Rosenberg's anti-Christian book was simply an expression of his private opinion. But in practice, the book was being touted as the official expression of the Nazi philosophy, and Rosenberg held the official position of the national instructor in the Nazi philosophy.[13]

The issue came to a head in Münster, when the newspapers announced a great Nazi Party rally to take place on July 6. Alfred Rosenberg was to be one of the featured speakers. The rally was set for the Saturday before the annual Great Procession through the streets of Münster. This event, also known as the Fire Procession, was a procession of the Blessed Sacrament through the streets that had been held on the second Monday of every July for hundreds of years. The town council began it as the result of a vow when the city was threatened by a plague in 1382 and a fire in 1383. With more than five hundred years of tradition behind it, the Great Procession was an act of thanksgiving to God and a celebration of the city's Catholic identity. In Bishop von Galen's first year as bishop, the celebration had included a remembrance of Bishop Johann Bernard Brinkmann's return to Münster from

---

12   Ibid., 194.
13   See also Löffler, docs. 94, 95, 97; *Osservatore Romano* editorial of August 4, 1935, cited in Max Bierbaum, *Nicht Lob Nicht Furcht: Das Leben des Kardinals von Galen* (Münster: Regensberg, 1946), 226.

exile fifty years earlier in 1884. Seeing that difficult times had once again come to the Catholics of Germany, von Galen had publicized the 1934 procession as a specific act of loyalty to the Savior, Jesus Christ, and His Church.

Now in late May of 1935, when he learned of the plans for Rosenberg to speak just before that year's procession, Bishop von Galen wrote to Premier Ferdinand von Lüninck asking him to use his influence to cancel the invitation to Rosenberg. Perhaps he was a bit naïve in thinking that this might be effective. Or was he seeking to have von Lüninck show his hand? A year earlier, during a visit to Rome, he argued in a letter to Cardinal Pacelli that the Church should press Hitler to make a *public* declaration either for or against Rosenberg. The regime should make it clear whether National Socialism was merely a political party or also a political *religion*. If, as it seemed, it was committed to producing a new religion, this was a directly religious issue and was more important for the Church to focus on than eventual violations of the Concordat.[14] Now von Galen's letter to von Lüninck was certainly aimed at having the Premier of Westphalia show his colors. But it was also a pastor's call to conversion. Was von Lüninck going to continue along the lines of his bizarre speech at the bishop's installation, or could he be called back to the Catholic faith that he still officially professed as a member of the league of Catholic nobles of Westphalia?

"I allow myself to remark," the bishop wrote him about the planned appearance of Rosenberg in Münster, "that the news of this plan has already caused strong negative reactions among the Christian, and especially the Catholic, population of Münster, and if it comes to pass, will without doubt lead to serious unrest." He went on to note that Rosenberg was well-known for fanatical attacks

---

14   Hubert Wolf, *Clemens August Graf von Galen: Gehorsam und Gewissen* (Freiburg: Herder, 2006), 87.

on the Catholic Church, the papacy, and the Christian past of the German people, attacks of the kind that were normally associated with liberal and socialist "freethinkers." In his view, serious Protestants as well as Catholics would regard Rosenberg's appearance as a deliberate provocation, especially considering its timing the weekend before the Great Procession. Thus he requested that it be cancelled and ended by suggesting that if that did not happen, he would have to consider seriously whether he should issue a decree encouraging Catholics to remain peaceful in the face of this provocation. "I am honestly doubtful," he concluded, "whether this step would be fully successful."[15]

The bishop sought to act in the name of civic peace. He wanted, if necessary, to encourage Catholics not to stir up trouble, such as in recent cases of fighting between Hitler Youth and Catholic youth. Perhaps not surprisingly, von Lüninck decided to read his letter not as a call for peace but as a veiled threat. Not only did he refuse to cancel Rosenberg's appearance—he also passed von Galen's letter on to Berlin. The result was an increased propaganda campaign not only against Catholicism but specifically against Bishop von Galen of Münster. A cartoon in a party magazine depicted him admiring instruments of torture supposedly used by the Inquisition and wishing that he could have at least a muzzle to keep Rosenberg silent.[16]

At the Nazi rally on July 6, speaker after speaker attacked the Church. One leading Nazi declared that the aim of the National Socialists was a complete separation of the churches from public life. Another argued that millions of Germans who had formerly had no faith now believed in the German people and their Führer. Hence

---

15   Löffler, doc. 98, v. I, 221–22.
16   Joachim Kuropka, *Clemens August Graf von Galen: Sein Leben und Wirken in Bildern und Dokumenten*, 3rd ed. (Cloppenburg: Runge, 1997), 105.

there was more faith than ever in Germany. A third stated that the National Socialists and they alone were the soul of Germany.[17]

There was no counterdemonstration by the Catholics. They saved their demonstration for the Great Procession two days later. Over nineteen thousand faithful came to the procession, an increase of six thousand over the previous year. The clergy had asked them to come, to bear witness to their Catholic faith, and to show their support to their beloved chief shepherd.[18]

There was also further motivation for a big turnout. Four hundred years earlier, Münster had suffered for sixteen months under a brutal self-proclaimed monarchy by a radical Protestant sect. Known as the Anabaptists or rebaptizers—because they did not believe in infant baptism and therefore rebaptized adult converts to their sect who had already been baptized as children—the leaders of this group practiced polygamy, enforced a complete collectivization of property, and desecrated churches. After a siege by the prince-bishop, Münster was freed on June 24, 1535.[19] From that time, the anniversary was celebrated as a religious day of thanksgiving. Jesus Christ, in His sacramental Presence in the Eucharist, had reentered His city and been restored to the tabernacles of the churches.[20]

Bishop von Galen and his clergy had planned for a procession in June, but it had to be called off when the government refused

---

17   Ibid., 98–99. The speakers were, respectively, Interior Minister Wilhelm Frick, Gauleiter Alfred Meyer, and Leader of the German Workers' Front, Robert Ley.
18   See Löffler, v. I, 259, n. 2.
19   Following the standards of a different age, three leaders of the sect, who had themselves practiced cruelty of various kinds, were tortured and killed, and their bodies hung in cages high on the tower of St. Lambert's Church. Replicas of those cages still hang there today.
20   See von Galen's sermon for the feast of Corpus Christi in Löffler, doc. 113, v. I, 246–52.

permission for it.[21] The bishop then combined the celebration of the end of the Anabaptist dictatorship with the Great Procession in July. Since their faith and their bishop were being attacked by a new form of totalitarianism, it was easy for Catholics to see parallels between the time of the Anabaptists and their own days.

After the procession, the bishop returned to his palace across the square from the entrance of the cathedral. Thousands of the faithful remained, filling the square, cheering their bishop, and singing hymns. As a counterpart to the rallies of the Nazis, it was an extremely moving experience for the people in the crowd, celebrating and expressing their Catholic identity in the face of the new threats posed by Nazism. Eventually, the bishop appeared at a window of the palace and thanked them for their loyalty, first of all to Jesus Christ and then to himself. He knew they were there to bring joy to their Savior by their expression of thanksgiving and loyalty to the Faith. "But I think," he said to rousing applause, "your presence here before the episcopal residence, and the cheers and shouts of loyalty with which you have just greeted me, were also intended to give me also a little bit of joy."[22]

The bishop continued: "A few days ago bitter charges were publicly made against me here in Münster. A step which I took with the best of intentions of preventing unrest and serving peace, was publicly portrayed in a way that was designed to cause unrest. Plans were attributed to me that were the farthest things from my intentions."

---

21   Bishop von Galen went to complain to a government official about this prohibition, taking one of his priests with him. At one point, as he was speaking rather vehemently, the official began angrily to rise from his chair, at which the bishop very calmly said, "Remain seated peaceably, Mr President. You do not need to stand up in my presence." Walter Adolph, *Geheime Aufzeichnungen aus dem nationalsozialistischen Kirchenkampf 1935–1943*, 2nd ed. (Mainz: Matthias-Grünewald Verlag, 1980), 21.

22   This and the following from Löffler, doc. 116, v. I, 255–58.

Noting that threatening words had been used against him, von Galen recalled the example of past Bishops of Münster who had stood firm against threats, including Bishop Johann Bernhard Brinkmann, who had suffered imprisonment and exile sixty years earlier. He raised the possibility that he himself might have to suffer—as he put it, that he might be worthy to suffer for the name of Jesus. In case Divine Providence had such plans for him, he trusted in God's help and in the love and prayers and loyalty of his people. Bishop Brinkmann sixty years earlier had been strengthened and encouraged by the people of the diocese:

> So I beg you: be imitators of your forefathers, as I desire to be an imitator of my predecessor. Keep up a loyal fulfilment of your duties according to the commands of a Christian-Catholic conscience; keep up your prayers for me, your Bishop, that God give him light and strength to know the true, the good, the necessary for our salvation, and to carry them out unswervingly and loyally, without fear or hesitation. Should God's Providence send us further tests, should it happen again that the shepherd be separated by force from the flock, then as in the days of our fathers, the loyalty to the faith, the zeal in the sacrificial fulfilment of duty, and the unremitting prayer of the faithful of the city of Münster and of the whole diocese must gain from God the Lord solace and help and the shortening of the time of such tribulation.
>
> Your participation in the Great Procession in such great numbers through the beautifully decorated streets of our city today, and now your declaration of loyalty to your Bishop, give me the confidence that this fidelity to the faith, this willingness to fulfill duties selflessly, this zeal for prayer to our Lord and savior, Who in the Blessed Sacrament is our oldest fellow citizen, still lives in you and in your children. We know, and are deeply convinced, that this attitude is the most certain foundation for

the loyal fulfillment of all the duties that we have as children of the German people; that its existence and preservation enables and inspires us to work together in generosity and loyalty for the rebuilding of our people, for a peaceful and happy future for our nation, our beloved German Fatherland.[23]

With these words, von Galen showed that he still believed in the possibility of peaceful cooperation between Church and state, working together for the rebuilding of German society. But proponents of a totalitarian state saw the entire demonstration as the assertion of an independent power within the state. The official rhetoric continued to be of cooperation between Church and state. The real aim was total control by the state and total submission of everyone and everything to the state. Civic officials were sent a secret order: When the bishop makes his journeys through the diocese, public officials should not take part in the welcoming ceremonies. But even Ferdinand von Lüninck recognized that this was a mistake; von Galen had become so extraordinarily popular that if at least the mayors did not take part in welcoming ceremonies for him, they would lose any support of the populace in their towns.[24] The Nazis would have liked to hem in the bishop's public appearances with restrictions, but a radical break with customary practice would have caused too much unrest among the people. They could not, however, have appreciated the results of a visit to a school the previous year. The schoolmaster, a very short gentleman, had greeted the bishop and led him into the school. They were photographed from the rear, the gigantic bishop in his cassock next to the tiny schoolmaster wearing a Nazi uniform. Some Catholics had copies of this photograph, labelled "Church and State."[25]

---

23   Ibid.
24   See Löffler, doc. 117 and n. 1, v. I, 258–59.
25   Nor were they amused in 1937 when the bishop was on a Confirmation visit in Coesfeld. A local Nazi leader led the crowd in a rousing three

What the Nazis could do was step up their propaganda campaign against the bishop and the Catholic Church and keep a careful eye on everything he did. Gestapo informants were in the crowd wherever he appeared. Sometimes their reports provide helpful information to the historian.

The Great Procession of 1935 had repercussions in the League of Catholic Nobles. Von Galen complained that Ferdinand von Lüninck was responsible for public attacks against him as Bishop of Münster. Hermann von Lüninck responded with a countercharge that von Galen broke the eighth commandment by bearing false witness against his brother, a charge which he eventually dropped. In the meantime, von Galen resigned his membership, remaining outside the league from April 1936 until early in 1939.

There were further repercussions when the day of the Great Procession came around again in July of 1936. By this time, the Reich minister for churches had ruled that public demonstrations—as opposed to purely religious events—were forbidden. A great crowd had gathered in the cathedral square in April 1936 after von Galen had consecrated an auxiliary bishop. The Münster Gestapo were shocked to report to their superiors in Berlin that the crowd was singing hymns *to Nazi melodies*. On June 10, the bishop had made appearances both at a youth rally in the pilgrimage town of Telgte and in Münster, and again Catholic hymns were sung to the melodies of songs of the Hitler Youth and the SS. The Gestapo asked Berlin whether they should, in the future, put a stop to such singing. At the June 10 rally in Münster, police barriers caused a dangerous situation when the crowd leaving the cathedral unknowingly forced the people ahead of them into

---

cheers for the bishop. It was not long before the Nazi was replaced. Ludger Grevelhörster, *Kardinal Clemens August Graf von Galen in seiner Zeit* (Münster: Aschendorff, 2005), 83.

the barriers. There was some shoving and throwing of punches, and a few people were arrested.[26]

So it was that when the Great Procession returned to the cathedral square on July 10, 1936, after winding through the streets of the old city, the police were erecting crowd-control barriers in the square between the cathedral entrance and the bishop's palace. As the *Te Deum* was sung inside the cathedral, the people waiting outside to cheer the bishop, as in the previous year, began to complain loudly about the police activity. It was clear that there was no desire on the part of the officials to have another public demonstration for Bishop von Galen outside his palace. Word began to spread through the crowd that they should enter the cathedral. The bishop decided, contrary to normal custom, to speak from the pulpit.

Noting that the police were claiming that the restrictive barriers were for public safety, he stressed that such a measure had never been used in the entire history of the Great Procession. The police, he asserted, wanted to prevent them from accompanying him to his palace. They were trying to separate the people from their bishop. He encouraged them nevertheless to stay behind the police lines and not to cause a disturbance by trying to accompany him back to his palace. But, he added, "if anyone thinks that by force, by barriers and by police measures he can separate you from me and me from you . . ." Shouts of "Nein, Clemens August! Heil! Heil! Heil!" came from the crowd.[27] When he was able to speak again, he reminded them of the ring that he had received at his episcopal consecration, a sign, like a marriage ring, of his connection to his diocese. "No one can break our connection to one another as long as we stay true to our following of

26   Löffler, docs. 169, 170, 171, 171, 186/III.
27   Heinrich Portmann, *Kardinal von Galen: Ein Gottesmann seiner Zeit*, 17th ed. (Münster: Aschendorff, 1981), 97.

Christ throughout life, as long as, like our forefathers for a thousand years, we love and worship our Lord and savior."[28]

The fact that it rained during the procession that morning gave rise to a further reflection from the bishop. It was a sign that the people of Münster must remain loyal to their savior not only in times of sunshine but also in times of rain, not only when following Christ seemed easy and honorable but also when it caused misunderstanding and insult, not only on Palm Sunday but also on Good Friday. He encouraged the people to continue in that spirit of loyalty not only on Sundays but also on workdays, not only in church but in every aspect of their lives. "And if it rains for hours," he continued,

> the sun is still there; just now I see through the open doors of the Cathedral that the sun's rays are breaking through the clouds. If we as disciples of Christ must walk through hardships and persecutions and sorrows, so long as we faithfully follow our savior, He, the light of the world, is still near! And we hope for the day in which even those who now mistrust us will come to realize that the truest disciple of Christ is also the best, most conscientious, most generous son of the German fatherland, the surest support for a happy future for our beloved homeland.[29]

The bishop returned to his palace, accompanied by his clergy and the Knights of Malta. The crowd for the most part stayed behind the barriers, but they stayed, cheering for the bishop and singing hymns for about half an hour, until he appeared at a window of the palace, blessed them again, and waved for them to go home.

For a second successive year, he had managed to turn the Great Procession into a public demonstration of loyalty to him and to the Catholic Church, and of dissatisfaction with the regime.

---

28   Löffler, doc. 178, v. I, 406–7.
29   Ibid., 408–10.

The local Gestapo and the governor of Münster, Kurt Klemm, complained to their superiors that the bishop deliberately misrepresented the purpose of the police barriers in order to stir up the crowd to fanatical opposition.[30] They noted that there had been no attempt by the police to separate the bishop from his flock. On the contrary, the police had cooperated in enabling the procession to wind its way through the streets for over two hours. Only when the bishop entered the cathedral were the barriers moved into place. The purpose was to prevent the crowd from following him across the square and uncontrollably gathering before the bishop's palace as they had in 1935. To make matters worse from the Nazi point of view, the diocesan newsletter printed an account of the day's events. This article was read from the pulpits of churches in various parts of the diocese. What the authorities regarded as merely a local matter in Münster thus became publicized far beyond the city, leading to widespread dissatisfaction with the regime. Klemm and the Gestapo recommended that the bishop be arrested and tried on a charge of abuse of the pulpit, a crime, inserted into the criminal code during the *Kulturkampf*, of using the pulpit for political purposes.

Ferdinand von Lüninck more astutely argued that to prosecute the bishop would do more harm than good. Why encourage his tendency to set himself up as some sort of martyr? Instead, give him a serious talking-to about his attitude so that nothing like this happens again; confiscate the offending issue of the diocesan newsletter, and from now on subject it to prior censorship. Lüninck wryly added his assessment that the police actions on the day of the Great Procession had shown an embarrassing lack of intelligence.[31]

---

30   Löffler, docs. 181 and 182, v. I, 415–20.
31   Löffler, doc. 184, v. I, 422–23. See also doc. 180, v. I, 414.

CHAPTER 8

Battle Tactics

I n October 1935, Bishop von Galen held another Deans' Conference.[1] In the conference of April 1934, he had raised the possibility that the government or its officials might misuse their authority.
Now he expanded on that theme. It was their duty as priests, he
told the deans, to support the regime, which had been recognized
by the Holy See. But this did not entail passive apathy about the
destiny of Germany and its people. He repeated his constant teaching that authority comes from God; therefore it was the duty of
priests to teach the virtues of piety and obedience but also to recognize that authority has limits against human arbitrariness. Sadly,
he noted, much arbitrariness had been observed and suffered. The
authoritarian state had taken a much greater interest than did the
previous liberal and democratic regime in being a spiritual influence
on its citizens, especially the young. Many violations of the Concordat had taken place because of this. Teachers had been forced
into unions that inculcated pagan ideology. Much of what they

1   For the following, see Peter Löffler, ed., *Bischof Clemens August Graf von
     Galen: Akten, Briefe und Predigten 1933–1946*, 2nd ed. (Paderborn:
     Ferdinand Schöningh, 1996), doc. 139, v. I, 301–13.

were taught in biology and "race education" was irreconcilable with Christianity. Priests had been carefully watched in the pulpit and in their school teaching and kept from visiting the schools on whatever pretexts could be found. Catholic youth organizations had been attacked and young people all but forced into the state-run organization, which constantly attacked Christianity. Although Catholic schools and organizations were allowed to remain in existence, the aim of all these measures was to raise an un-Christian—even an anti-Christian—generation of young people. Attacks on the Catholic workers' and professional groups, as well as pressure on parents to remove their children from the Catholic youth groups, were being promoted under the theme of "De-Confessionalizing Public Life."

The bishop recommended that his clergy be tolerant toward people who dropped out of Catholic groups under this pressure. Thank them for their past cooperation and stay close to them, he urged. Recommend that they join groups that have purely religious aims. He expressed his fear that if most people ended up in the state-run groups, many would not be strong enough in their faith to recognize false teaching for what it was.

Hitler had promised a delegation of three bishops that he would put a stop to the pagan propaganda. This promise had not been fulfilled, but neither had it been rescinded, and the bishops continued to urge him to fulfill it. A complete breach of the Concordat could lead to a much worse *Kulturkampf* than the one that had been so painful sixty years earlier, one that only those very strong in faith, courage, and the spirit of sacrifice could withstand. Von Galen urged his priests to strengthen their people in the Faith: "The time of conventional Christianity is past," he said. "Today, almost everyone will be personally put to the test . . . will he decide for Christ or against Him?"[2]

---

2   Ibid.

What means did the Church still have to support her people in the Faith? Von Galen suggested five areas in which the priests could work. First, the schools, where they still had the right to teach religion classes. Teach well, he urged, and build friendly relations with the teachers. Second, the pulpit, which must be used for a clear teaching of the Faith. If errors must be refuted, this should be done only *after* explaining the truth that was being attacked. Further, they should clarify what the *error* is but not attack the *person*. Third, priests should frequently visit the homes of their parishioners. Fourth, they should provide frequent days of recollection and retreats. Finally, he suggested the possibility of forming a variety of small groups to study dogma, moral questions, liturgy, Church history, and so forth.

There was yet one more recommendation. The priests, including himself, should pray and do penance. Eighteen months earlier, he had noted that nine priests of the diocese were in prison. At this time, there was a bishop, Peter Legge of Meissen, in jail for the crime of currency speculation, one of the favorite charges used in Nazi show trials. Bishop Legge had urged his priests to undertake prayer and penance, and Bishop von Galen echoed him, reminding his priests of the teaching of Christ that some kinds of demons can be driven out only by prayer and fasting.[3]

The guidance he gave to his clergy shows that von Galen thought long and hard about how to deal with a totalitarian regime. The diplomatic approach—lodging formal complaints when the rights of the Church were being attacked—was one aspect of this strategy. As a bishop of the Catholic Church, von Galen never hesitated to speak the truth to those in power. His first duty as a bishop, however, was to his diocese. As the chief shepherd of some two million Catholics spread over a huge area in northwestern Germany, he saw it as his task to support the Catholic people in their faith. He constantly

---

3   Ibid.

sought to bolster their courage in the face of pressures to renounce their faith and their membership in Catholic organizations. He had told his people, on the day of his installation as their bishop, that he knew that the duty of teaching and of making decisions fell upon him and that he would fulfill this duty without being moved by fear or flattery. The "positive presentation and convincing explanation" of the truth which he had recommended to his clergy was his own guiding principle. As he sought every opportunity to preach and to issue pastoral letters, the people of his diocese benefited from the habit he learned from his father, that of considering the day's questions on the basis of fundamental principles.

As for the specific problem of dealing with the regime, another factor needed consideration. Von Galen was convinced that the German bishops needed to speak with one voice and act in a unified way. The problem was that they were not united in their assessment of the Nazi regime. Historian Hubert Wolf describes the two "camps" in the German Episcopal Conference: "The first group, under the leadership of the Chairman, Cardinal Adolf Bertram, Prince-Bishop of Breslau, was fundamentally convinced of the possibility of friendly cooperation between the Catholic Church and the National Socialist State, and believed the bishops could successfully appeal to the Chancellor of the Reich in cases of encroachment on the rights of the Church." This group believed that these efforts of the bishops should *not* be made known to the public.

"On the other side was the group around the Bishop of Berlin, Count Konrad von Preysing." Preysing was, Wolf says, the trusted ally of Cardinal Eugenio Pacelli, the secretary of state, and later Pope Pius XII, who appointed him Bishop of Eichstätt and then of Berlin. Preysing "was profoundly convinced of the uselessness of the politics of petitioning, and pushed for a change of strategy: the bishops should consciously go public, openly denounce the regime's infringement of rights, and utilize the Catholic masses in support of their approach. The Bishop of Münster also favoured this position."[4]

Bishop von Galen knew, however, that the bishops needed to be united. Furthermore, he and his fellow nobleman, von Preysing, were fairly new as bishops, and younger men as well. Von Galen had grown up in Dinklage on stories of the Catholic struggle for religious freedom in the *Kulturkampf*. On the other hand, Cardinal Bertram, born nineteen years earlier than von Galen, had directly experienced those terrible times during his boyhood. Perhaps he was justified in hoping that by exercising secret diplomacy, another *Kulturkampf* could be avoided.

Still, as early as May 1934, von Galen recommended to Cardinal Secretary of State Pacelli the need for a "*public* protest against neo-paganism and immorality and a *public* appeal to Hitler to stand by his words about the new Germany being built upon 'the foundations of Christendom.'"[5] By March 1936, von Galen was more strongly convinced of the need to go public. In a lengthy memorandum for Cardinal Pacelli, he argued that a change of battle tactics was necessary.[6] Events of the last year showed that the propaganda campaign against the Church eased *only* when the Holy See and the bishops issued sharp protests and made them public through the press.

The systematic battle against the Church was continuing at all the lower levels of the Party, but the Führer himself had backed away from openly declaring himself as anti-Christian. Other high officials also took a more irenical tone and reopened negotiations regarding

---

4   Hubert Wolf, *Clemens August Graf von Galen: Gehorsam und Gewissen* (Freiburg: Herder, 2006), 100–101.
5   Letter in the Vatican Archives, quoted by Wolf, 102.
6   This memorial, discovered in the archives of Cardinal Faulhaber, was printed only in the second edition (1996) of Löffler's collection (doc. 569, v. II, 1438–45). Only more recently was the same document found in the Vatican Archives, proving that it was indeed both intended for and sent to Cardinal Pacelli. Wolf, 165, n. 208.

Article 31 of the Concordat. The phrases "political Christian" and "the De-Confessionalizing of Public Life" disappeared. It seemed, von Galen argued, that the higher authorities were taking "public opinion," both in Germany and abroad, into account. "They are afraid," he wrote, "of provoking further *public* protests from the Vatican, and perhaps also of an equally clear and sharp statement from the German bishops."[7]

But this did not mean that all was well. The Nazis, he argued, could prolong the discussions on the interpretation of the Concordat for years, while continuing to pull members away from Catholic organizations, bring the Catholic schools into de facto non-existence, force the young into the state youth movement, and alienate them from the Church through their leaders and writings. Thus by the time the negotiations concluded, the shepherds would have no more flock and the leaders of Catholic organizations no more followers.

The Catholic clergy and people, he wrote, knew that a cessation of the regime's battle of extermination against the Catholic Church was mere fiction. "But they know only a little bit," he continued,

> about the innumerable protests and petitions of the Chairman of the Bishops' Conference and the individual bishops to the Reich Regime and the other responsible government officials, almost all of which have been unsuccessful, indeed most of which have not even been answered. They also know nothing about the contents and progress of the resumed negotiations . . .
>
> Therefore it is not surprising that loyal Catholics and in part also the clergy are gradually losing their courage and their trust in their leaders . . . The fear is growing that the bishops have been satisfied with the small success of greater temperance in the Führer's speeches, and that they don't see that the struggle to

---

7   Ibid.

exterminate the Catholic Church is still being carried on by his underlings. Such thoughts are unjustified and dangerous. But do we dare to ignore the fact that they are growing and spreading, that they paralyze courage and trust, that they are paving the way to an attitude of tired resignation in the Catholic people? . . .

The tactic of negotiating behind closed doors and of unpublicized petitions and protests to officials of the regime was the correct one, as long as one could hope to find a real desire for peace and concern for justice in those officials. Surely there is no more reason for such hope. Such tactics were and would be justified if we could hope that within a foreseeable time the authorities would come to see that the battle against Christians and against the Church is not only unjust, but also bad for the German people and the Fatherland, and would give it up of their own accord. If we dared to hope that this change of mind and policy would come about before the destructive work of the enemies of the Church destroyed the loyalty of the Catholic people, poisoned souls, and seduced the youth, then we would have to accept a temporary "crisis of trust" and the corresponding casualties as the lesser evil in comparison with an open *Kulturkampf.* I do not doubt that eventually time will bring about such a change of mind. But in my opinion that might take a long time, so long that by the time it comes there will be only ruins left of what was once a flourishing Catholic life in Germany. Can we dare to take this risk?

The other tactic, that of going public last summer . . . had a two-fold success: it gave the faithful courage and deep gratitude and the hope for clear decisions. It also brought about a backing away on the anti-Christian front, at least in the form of a greater circumspection in the highest leadership, and so it showed that the leadership at present is hesitant to be known *to the public* as a persecutor of the Church.

Whoever sees the battlefront in this way must ask himself
if it is not necessary to follow that old rule of battle tactics:
chase the retreating enemy, and exploit his known weaknesses.
In our case that means: at every opportunity go *public*; *publicly*
denounce every violation of the Church's right to live or of the
Concordat; *publicly* protest every new attack on the rights and
freedom of the Church.

Here von Galen laid down a crucial condition. "Such a change in
battle tactics cannot be undertaken by an individual bishop. In
today's situation of a muzzled press the word of a single man will
not spread widely enough. But above all the action of a single bishop
would give new nourishment to the appearance and the rumors of
a lack of unity among the German episcopate and would be used in
that sense by our enemy."[8]

Surely von Galen was right that the bishops needed to act in uni-
son, and for this change in tactics, they needed, as he stated at the
end of his memorandum, the encouragement or at least the approval
of the Holy See. Unfortunately, neither at this time nor in the nearly
nine years remaining until the Third Reich was destroyed was he able
to win Cardinal Bertram's faction to his point of view. In the meantime, he continued to do his share of complaining to the authorities
while instructing and encouraging his flock.

---

8   Ibid.

CHAPTER 9

Fresh Graves in German Lands

The town of Xanten, on the west side of the Rhine near the Dutch border, takes its name from the Latin *ad Sanctos*, meaning "the place of the saints." St. Victor and his companions—Roman legionaries martyred in the fourth century for refusing to sacrifice to pagan gods—had been venerated there for centuries. In 1933, archaeologists from the Provincial Museum of Bonn discovered, beneath the cathedral, a series of earlier churches and, far beneath, a double grave.[1] The condition of the bodies indicated that they had been tortured and killed. Because of this admittedly inconclusive evidence that martyrs had been venerated on this site since the fourth century, an altar was erected in the crypt of the cathedral. On February 9, 1936, Bishop von Galen came to consecrate the new altar and offer the first Mass on it. His sermon on that occasion naturally took the

---

1   In addition to Peter Löffler, ed., *Bischof Clemens August Graf von Galen: Akten, Briefe und Predigten 1933–1946*, 2nd ed. (Paderborn: Ferdinand Schöningh, 1996), doc. 150, see Ralph Trost, *Eine gänzlich zerstörte Stadt: Nationalsozialismus, Krieg und Kriegsende in Xanten* (Münster: Waxmann Verlag, 2004), 181–99. The church has long had the honorary title of a cathedral, although it is not the site of an episcopal see.

theme of martyrdom. But he did more than praise fourth-century martyrs. He compared their struggles with the situation of Catholics in Germany in 1936.

With clear logic, he reached what may have seemed a paradoxical conclusion: that the martyrdom of those Roman saints was a patriotic act and an act of obedience to rightful authority. They disobeyed the emperor when commanded to sacrifice to pagan gods, but that was out of obedience to a higher authority. If, von Galen said, we were able to go back and ask their judges and executioners whether these men had done good or evil, we would receive the answer "that by command of the Emperor they must die, because they stubbornly refused to honor and pray to the gods acknowledged by men and recognized by the State; because they were guilty of acknowledging only a transcendent God who rules all peoples with fatherly love."[2]

Perhaps, he continued, it was feared that these men would not fight against the enemies of the Roman Empire because they would see the enemies as made in the image of God. "Foolish fear! For true Christians are always the most loyal citizens, the most conscientious officials, and the bravest soldiers of their people." This is the case, he argued, because their obedience to the state is grounded in something higher than a desire for earthly honor. They know that even when no man sees their actions to honor them, the almighty God will give them a heavenly reward.

This, Bishop von Galen said, has been the attitude of many Christian soldiers who, like St. Victor and his companions, have suffered martyrdom for their faith in Christ. He made this argument to show that their martyrdom was an act of obedience and patriotism:

> They let themselves be cut down by their pagan comrades, without defending themselves or resisting. The sword, which they had

---

2   Löffler, doc. 150, v. I, 341. The sermon is on pages 339–44.

heroically wielded in fierce battles for their Emperor and their Fatherland, they refused to draw against their own comrades, when these comrades attacked them as enemies by command of the Emperor in order to strike them down. They saw these comrades not as enemies, but as friends who had been led astray. They did not fight against the Emperor. Rather, even in dying they obeyed the Emperor. The Emperor had commanded, either sacrifice to the gods or die. Since they could not offer sacrifice without sinning, they chose death, in order not to sin. Is that not loyalty? Is that not heroic courage? Is that not bravery in the service of the Emperor and in the service of God even unto death?[3]

Because they did not resist their comrades who were obeying the order of the emperor, they too were showing proper obedience to him, but obedience to God first. Thus Bishop von Galen used these saints' example to teach the demands of conscience, urging his listeners to act likewise: "Yes, follow their example! For the sake of your souls, for the sake of your children, for the sake of our people. We also are called and obligated to serve God and the Kingdom of God on earth, to serve our fellow men, to serve our people and our State, by loyal fulfillment of our duties in our families, occupations and communities, by loyalty grounded in the fear and the love of God, as the holy martyrs did . . . And if, as we do so, we are misunderstood, insulted, slandered, reviled, even persecuted, tortured and killed"—here the bishop cited Christ's words in the Sermon on the Mount—"'Blessed are you when men revile you and persecute you and utter all kinds of evil against you falsely on my account. Rejoice and be glad, for your reward is great in heaven'" (Matt. 5:11).

"Yes," he continued,

---

3   Ibid.

rejoice and be glad! You know that the time has come when such is the lot of not a few of us. How the holy Church, the Pope, the bishops, the priests, the members of religious Orders, how true children of the Church are today openly and with impunity calumniated, slandered, and defamed in Germany! How many Catholics, priests and laity, are attacked and insulted in newspapers and public meetings, are forced out of their jobs and positions, and are put into prison and mistreated without trial. The head of the Bishops' Information Service in Berlin, Dr. Banasch of the Cathedral Chapter, has been in prison for months, and his employers, the Bishops, have been given no indication of what wrong he is thought to have done. Monsignor Wolker, who has been appointed head of the Catholic Young Men's Association by the Bishops, has been in jail for three days, and no one can guess how long it will be before he appears before an independent German court. There are in German lands fresh graves, in which rest the ashes of men whom the Catholic people regard as martyrs, because they see in their lives the witness of a most loyal fulfillment of duty to God and Fatherland, to people and Church, and because the darkness that surrounds their deaths causes great unrest. And how frequently are officials and bureaucrats, parents and teachers, placed under strong pressures of conscience, when they are forced to choose between loyalty to God and their Christian conscience, and the good opinion and favour of those on whom they depend for their positions and indeed their living![4]

The bishop's listeners knew exactly what he was talking about. On June 30, 1934, the so-called Night of the Long Knives, when Hitler acted against Ernst Röhm, the leader of the Nazi brownshirts who

---

4   Ibid.

was becoming a political liability, numerous other potential opponents to his power were arrested or summarily shot. Among them
was Erich Klausener, the former leader of Catholic Action, who had
become a senior civil servant. Von Galen considered him a martyr
and felt honored that Klausener had been a member of his parish
in Berlin.[5] Klausener's murder, writes Richard J. Evans, "sent a clear
message to Catholics that a revival of independent Catholic political
activity would not be tolerated."[6] Among other notable Catholics
who were killed in the Röhm affair was Adalbert Probst, head of the
Catholic Youth Sports Association. It was reported that Probst was
shot while "fleeing from arrest."[7] A more recent death was that of
the Dominican priest Titus Horten, who died in prison after being
charged with currency speculation.[8]

It should not surprise them, von Galen told his listeners, that
God would allow them to undergo hardships and persecution—
even martyrdom. "Our holy Church is the Church of martyrs." He
recalled words of Christ in St. John's Gospel: "If the world hates
you, know that it has hated me before it hated you. If you were of
the world, the world would love its own; but because you are not
of the world, but I chose you out of the world, therefore the world
hates you. Remember the word that I said to you, 'A servant is not
greater than his master.' If they persecuted Me, they will persecute
you . . . The hour is coming when whoever kills you will think he is
offering service to God" (John 15:18–19; 16:2).

5   Löffler, doc. 55, v. I, 103.
6   Richard J. Evans, *The Third Reich in Power* (New York: Penguin, 2005),
      34.
7   John S. Conway, *The Nazi Persecution of the Churches 1933–1945* (Van-
      couver: Regent College Publishing, 1997), 92, listing other prominent
      Catholics killed in the bloodbath.
8   Löffler, v. I, 343, n. 8.

The answer to the question of how suffering and persecution come upon Christian people, von Galen continued, is the death of Jesus Christ. The bishop portrayed this death as a sacrificial death, a martyr's death, a hero's death. Christ placed Himself under the authority of an earthly judge, while reminding that judge that all authority derives from God. He died for the truth of His claim to be the Son of God and King of all creation. Von Galen reminded his listeners that every Mass was the memorial and the unbloody re-presentation of Christ's sacrifice, offered on an altar containing relics of a martyr or martyrs:

> Like Christ, like the Apostles, like the holy martyrs, we are obedient to authority, loyal to our people, conscientious in our professions, in our work, in our families, in our communities, willing to sacrifice even to the risk of our lives, like St. Victor and all holy soldiers, like our brave soldiers who risked and gave their lives for our German fatherland in the thousands in the World War. But if, like those saints, we are put to the test, and made to choose between earthly success and the confession of our faith, between the service of idols and death, then we want, like those brave models we seek to emulate, to stay firm in the faith with the help of God's grace; we want, like them, to die rather than to sin. May today's celebration and the memory of the holy heroes of faith whose remains are in this house of God, and the power of the holy sacrifice of the Cross which we have just devoutly celebrated together, strengthen all of us in a holy resolve, so that what Christ promised to His disciples who follow Him on the glorious way of the Cross will one day be true of us: "Blessed are you when men revile you and persecute you . . . Rejoice and be glad, for your reward will be great in heaven."[9]

Death rather than sin. The bishop, as chief teacher of the Faith in his diocese, reminded his people of what they had learned from

---

9   Löffler, doc. 150, v. I, 339–44.

their Catechism: Obedience to lawful authority is commanded by the fourth commandment, "Honor your father and your mother." This obedience is regulated, however, by obedience to God. If the authority commands something that is sinful, that command is not to be obeyed, even at the cost of one's life.

The consecration of the new altar after the discovery of the relics in Xanten was a notable public occasion, covered by newspapers and magazines. Thus the bishop's words received wide circulation. It was customary in those days for newspapers to give the complete text of public speeches. This time, two paragraphs were blacked out by the censors. The bishop's words about fresh graves in German lands could not be read in the newspapers, but the many people who heard them kept them in their hearts and reported them to their friends.

Two weeks later, on February 22, 1936, von Galen issued the following decree to his diocese:

Clemens August
by the grace of God and the favor of the Apostolic See
Bishop of Münster
wishes the worthy Priests and all the faithful of the diocese
greetings and blessings in the Lord!
Since it has been the case in recent months that not a few
priests have been forcibly hindered from exercising their
sacred responsibilities under a variety of pretexts and charges,
some by being forced to leave the area in which the Church
has placed them, others by being arrested and held for a
long time in prison, I must reckon with the possibility that
I too may be subjected to such injustice. Should God permit
that I be forcibly hindered from exercising my episcopal
responsibilities in the Diocese of Münster, I hereby order, by
my power as the chief shepherd, that in this case and for as
long as this hindrance continues, the following measures. . . .

The first measure was a clarification of who would be in charge of making decisions in the diocese in his absence. The next two measures had to do with church bells. As soon as the news was received of an action against the bishop, the largest bell of each church in the diocese was to be tolled in mourning for one hour. This was to be repeated the next day from twelve noon to one p.m. From then on and until his restoration, all use of church bells was forbidden. There were only three exceptions: By a tradition going back to the Middle Ages, church bells have been rung at morning, midday, and evening for the Angelus. Three triple strokes are rung, at each of which a verse recalling the announcement of the Angel Gabriel to the Blessed Virgin Mary is recited, followed by a Hail Mary. Bishop von Galen ordered that this custom could continue, but in a curtailed form. The customary pealing of bells after the third Hail Mary was not to be done. The Angelus would be marked by only a simple three-times-three stroke on one bell. "From the heart," he continued, "I beg all the faithful who hear the bell and thus greet the beloved Mother of God in the customary way, to add each time a reverent 'Ave Maria' as a prayer for the Bishop." The other exceptions to the ban on the ringing of bells would also be to encourage prayer: for the sick, "on the occasion of a priest's visit to administer the Sacraments to the dying," and for the dead at the time of their burial.[10]

Unknown to the bishop, on the day that he issued this decree, the Gestapo in Münster sent a report on the sermon at Xanten to Ferdinand von Lüninck, who subsequently passed it on to Wilhelm Frick, the minister of the interior in Berlin. Von Galen was certainly being carefully watched. On March 23, Hans Kerrl, the government minister in charge of church affairs, gave a speech in Xanten attacking von Galen and the Catholic Church. Nine days earlier, Kerrl had written von Galen to complain about the bishop's Xanten

---

10   Löffler, doc. 153, v. I, 348–49.

sermon: "According to reliable reports, you thought it was fitting, in a sermon before a large congregation, to call to mind a most serious political event of a year and a half ago. I have to assume that you were fully aware of the far-reaching political implications of your action, which has also found an echo in the anti-German foreign press. I have to see this sermon of yours as evidence that in your role as spiritual head of a large diocese you are not inclined to cooperate with my attempts to produce a real peace with the Churches."[11]

It was a sign of how far Germany had gone down the road of lawlessness that a minister of the government could refer to a night of widespread murder as a "political event." In his reply, von Galen wrote to Kerrl that he was far from opposing attempts to build a peaceful relationship between Church and state. He had spoken the words of his sermon at Xanten about the "events of a year and a half ago" with precisely that goal in mind. The memory of those events stood in the way of such peace. People were disturbed because of the widespread opinion that innocent people had been killed along with the guilty and that this crime had not been punished.[12] Shortly after the Night of the Long Knives, the Führer had designated a specific group of persons who had been punished for endangering the safety of the people. Because of his authoritative statement, the death of those members of the National Socialist German Workers' Party, although painful, had not caused unrest. But many people had been killed who were not mentioned by the Führer and perhaps whose deaths were unknown to him. Until a definitive judgment was given that they had justly received such a heavy punishment, their fate continued to be considered an unrectified injustice. The bishop continued with an example: "I knew Ministerial Director Klausener personally, for he belonged to my parish when I was a pastor in

---

11   Löffler, doc. 161, v. I, 364.
12   Löffler, doc. 168, v. I, 380–84.

Berlin. I can attest, as can many others who knew him well, that his life was [here the bishop quoted from his sermon at Xanten] 'the witness of a most loyal fulfillment of duty to God and Fatherland, to people and Church.'" Von Galen reminded Kerrl that General Kurt von Schleicher, the last chancellor before Hitler, was among those shot on the Night of the Long Knives (along with his wife) and that his honor had subsequently been publicly vindicated. Von Galen expressed the hope that Klausener's killers would be brought to justice and his honor also restored. That would be to promote justice, he said, a task to which he was bound as a bishop and which was necessary for the inner peace of the German people. It was only for this reason, and not for some political motive, that he had spoken as he did. He continued: "As for 'political implications' of my action and an 'echo in the anti-German foreign press' whose positions I have neither opportunity nor time to follow, I know nothing."[13]

Kerrl also said in his March 23 speech at Xanten: "How can anyone claim that we want to take you away from the faith of your fathers, when for fourteen years we have been the only ones in Germany who believed, and who have taught the people to believe again!" Von Galen told Kerrl that this "would be an almost unbearable insult, not only to believing Catholics, but also to countless Protestant believers in Christ, if not for the fact that in earlier speeches you have made it clear, Herr Minister, that you use the word 'belief' (or 'faith') in a completely different sense from the Christian Gospel." He continued by noting that he had clarified the ambiguities and equivocations in the use of the word "faith" in his Lenten pastoral letter of February 1936, and he enclosed a copy of this letter for the minister's benefit.[14]

On September 6, Bishop von Galen was again in Xanten for a festival and procession in honor of St. Victor, which drew a huge

---

13   Ibid.
14   Ibid.

crowd of twenty-five to thirty thousand people. Again he spoke on the virtue of obedience to authority, which, he stressed, is an obligation of conscience: "How, then," he asked, "can Christians honor as martyrs men who disobeyed their emperor? Did St. Victor not know that those in legitimate authority are God's servants, and must be obeyed?"

Yes, he did, but he also knew that authority has its limits: "He who has the earthly power to give commands to others also has a sacred responsibility, to subject his commands to the holy will of God." This is why Christian kings and princes are often called such "by the grace of God." Only as a servant of God, he continued, can someone claim the authority to make commands that would bind the conscience of another. To rule others merely because one is stronger than they are is to destroy justice and to offend human dignity. The bishop recalled the teaching of St. Augustine that governments that rule unjustly are, in reality, bands of robbers.

Thus if the authority commands what God has forbidden, or forbids what God has commanded, it has overstepped its bounds and must be disobeyed. "One must obey God rather than men" was the straightforward phrase of St. Peter and the other apostles (Acts 5:29), which Bishop von Galen urged his listeners to take up as a motto. He added three other memorable phrases on the same theme: "Better dead than a slave" was an ancient Frisian saying. "Death rather than sin" was a motto of Christian saints. The third came from a story involving Frederick the Great, the Prussian king Frederick II. The king commanded one of his ministers to do something unjust, reminding the minister that he could be beheaded for disobeying. The minister replied, "My head stands at your Majesty's pleasure, but not my conscience."[15] With these colorful and memorable phrases, von Galen hoped to guide his people as to the decisions of conscience that might face them in the days ahead.

---

15   Löffler, doc. 189, v. I, 439–47.

CHAPTER 10

Battle for the Cross

In November 1936, a protest in Clemens August von Galen's "brutally Catholic" home territory of Oldenburg resulted in something rare in Nazi Germany: the reversal of a government decision. On November 4, Julius Pauly, minister of the interior and for churches and schools, issued a decree that religious symbols should be removed from all public buildings. Oldenburg, as was typical for Germany, had publicly funded denominational schools, and the decree applied specifically to them. As they were regarded as public buildings, crucifixes were to be removed from the Catholic schools and pictures of Martin Luther from the Protestant schools.

The decree was secret, but within a week, its contents came to the attention of Monsignor Franz Vorwerk, the episcopal official for Oldenburg. Since Oldenburg had become a part of the Diocese of Münster, the position of the episcopal official, a curiosity in canon law, was that of the bishop's representative for that part of the diocese.

When he learned of Pauly's decree, Monsignor Vorwerk acted immediately. On Saturday, November 13, he sent an announcement to all the parish priests, which was read at every Mass the next day. The faithful were shocked. At all the churches, a special sermon about the meaning of the cross was preached on Wednesday, November 18. A novena was called for and begun that evening.

In his report to the bishop, Vorwerk said:

> In the urban communities this took place each evening in the church at eight o'clock. In farm country, it was held in the houses, in this form: the father of the family led the praying of the Sorrowful Mysteries of the Rosary before a crucifix with two lighted candles, kneeling with the whole family. Almost one hundred per cent of the families did this. The public fury increased day by day. The mayors refused to pick up their mail. Large numbers of Party members resigned their posts. In many communities, the Party Organizations, particularly youth and women's organizations, were dissolved because all the members quit.[1]

Despite the fear of concentration camps, Vorwerk reported, protests grew from day to day, with even longtime Nazi Party members defending the cross.

Pauly, however, refused to rescind his decree and suggested a compromise: The cross could stay in the school buildings but not on the walls. It could be brought out as a "visual aid" during religion classes. Vorwerk rejected the suggestion.

The gauleiter, Carl Röver, decided that something had to be done. This was the man who had complained to Berlin about the "hatred of National Socialism" in Bishop von Galen's 1934 pastoral letter on the new paganism. Posters went up announcing that Röver would speak in the Münsterland Hall in Cloppenburg on

---

1   Peter Löffler, ed., *Bischof Clemens August Graf von Galen: Akten, Briefe und Predigten 1933–1946*, 2nd ed. (Paderborn: Ferdinand Schöningh, 1996), doc. 197, v. I, 464–65, n. 2.

Wednesday, November 25. The theme would be: "What does the Gauleiter and Representative of the Reich have to say to you, Münsterlanders? It will deal with matters that are agitating all of us at the moment, so everyone should come."

On the appointed day, seven thousand people packed the hall. Thousands more listened outside to loudspeakers. Röver entered the hall to a chilling silence. He began his speech with standard themes of Nazi propaganda, discussing colonies, race, and industry. A farmer named Heinrich Götting interrupted him with a shout from the rear of the hall: "To the point! The cross!" Röver tried to continue, and more people took up Götting's cry as a chant: "To the point! The cross!" Röver lost his composure. Shouting, "We old fighters for the cause will not be intimidated!" he unsuccessfully commanded the crowd to keep quiet. Brownshirts were unable to restore order. Röver then pleaded for silence, which helped for a few minutes. But when he started to speak again of the great spiritual revolution of National Socialism, the crowd resumed its chant: "To the point! We don't want this! The cross!"

The gauleiter tried a conciliatory tone: "If only we spend an hour here together, surely we will understand each other better." Some of the farmers of Oldenburg responded with cynical laughter. Angrily, Röver called for the "cowards" to show themselves, but this only led to greater commotion in the hall. He tried again, citing alleged anti-Party actions by priests. "What has that to do with the cross?" shouted the crowd. "To the point!"

Shaken, Röver pulled a piece of paper from his pocket and held it up before the crowd. "A wise government knows how to correct itself when it has made a mistake . . . The crosses stay in the schools." A wild cheer went up, and the crowd began streaming to the exits. The gauleiter tried to continue speaking, then sank to his chair. The parish priest of Dinklage later reported that he was convinced there was nothing at all written on the paper. Rumors circulated that Röver had collapsed, weeping, when he returned to his hotel room.[2]

Upon learning of this victory in what came to be called the *Oldenburger Kreuzkampf*—the Battle for the Cross in Oldenburg—Bishop von Galen immediately sent a jubilant pastoral letter to the Catholics in Oldenburg.[3] They had suffered a terrible shock, he said, when they heard that the crosses were to be banned from the schools. Rosenberg and the neo-pagans of the "German Faith Movement" had already stated that the crucifix must gradually be replaced, even in churches, by a more "heroic" German symbol. Now this seemed to be taking place. "Was the first step in this process to take place in Oldenburg?" the bishop asked. "Should it be here, with us, in our beloved *Heimat*, that the demand of the propaganda magazine of the German Faith Movement, 'The cross must fall!' should be put into operation? Should it happen here, what many neo-pagans urge: 'The cross is falling; tear it all the way down'? Should our teachers be required to take down the cross, before which, up to now, they have daily prayed with their children?"[4]

Rosenberg had stated that the cross must be replaced "little by little." "We understood that!" wrote the bishop:

> And should it begin now? "The cross must fall," first in the schools, so that the children "Say farewell to the image of Christ." "Out of sight, out of mind!" is the hope of the enemies of the cross of Christ. How long would it be before we would hear, "The cross must fall in the village streets and public highways!" "Out of sight, out of mind!" And finally, says

---

2   Löffler, doc. 197, v. I, 465–66, n. 2, and Günter Beaugrand, *Kardinal von Galen: Der Löwe von Münster*, Freundeskreis Heimathaus Münsterland, Telgte (Münster: Ardey-Verlag, 1996), 31, citing Joachim Kuropka, *Zur Sache! Das Kreuz!*

3   Löffler, doc. 197, v. I, 462–67.

4   Ibid.

Rosenberg, the cross must fall even in the churches, which will be taken from the Christians and handed over to a so-called German Church! "Out of sight, out of mind!" And should this plan be put into execution here, among us? Little by little? Beginning with the banning of the crosses from the schools?

Von Galen urged his "dear fellow children of the *Heimat*" to give thanks to God that He had opened their eyes to the danger. Echoing his episcopal motto, he praised their courage in bearing witness to their faith without fear of men. In what must have been infuriating to Gauleiter Röver, von Galen thanked God for giving Röver the wisdom and courage to annul the decree banning the crucifixes, a decree which, the bishop said, "appeared to all of us as an insult to God and a calamity for our people and our *Heimat*." He continued:

When the Head of State for Oldenburg realized, in the gathering of more than 7,000 people in Cloppenburg, that all of you stood for the cross as one man, that our Münsterland will not abandon the Cross, that you want to raise your children and your children's children to be German men and women in the shadow of the cross, in reverence for the cross, in love of the crucified savior, he publicly proclaimed the fundamental maxim, "A wise government knows how to correct itself when it has made a mistake." Then, loudly and solemnly he declared: "The decree of November 4, 1936 has been rescinded. The crosses stay in the schools!"[5]

The bishop took up this phrase of the gauleiter's as a jubilant cry:

The crosses stay in the schools! That should be a sentence that we take up with rejoicing and thanksgiving! The crosses stay in the schools! The crosses stay on our village streets and

---

5   Ibid.

highways! The crosses stay in our homes and our churches! The cross stays—this is the most important thing—in our hearts! Nothing dares, nothing should, nothing will separate us, tear us, our youth, our people, our *Heimat*, from the cross! We will shun any community that is an enemy of the cross of Christ! We will read no books or magazines, nor tolerate them in our houses, in showcases, in shop windows, that insult the cross! And should it be our fate to suffer insult and persecution for the sake of the cross, in union with the crucified Christ, we will not be cowardly and without courage. We will think of Him who by dying on the cross won for us the victory of everlasting life! We will think of that day that is promised to us at the end of all times, that great day when the cross, the sign of the Son of Man, appears in heaven: on that day everyone, even the enemies of the cross, will see the Crucified One coming on the clouds of heaven! Then will be fulfilled what St Paul says to us in the Epistle for the Feast of the Triumph of the Cross: "In the Name of Jesus every knee shall bow, in heaven, on earth and under the earth; and every tongue proclaim that Jesus Christ is Lord to the glory of God the Father" (Phil. 2:10–11).

He finished the pastoral letter with the customary bishop's blessing and signature, marking the page with the triple sign of the cross. In this case, there was a fitting variation in the formula of blessing:

May He bless you in the sign of the cross, which you have so courageously defended and honored, God the + Father, the + Son, and the + Holy Spirit.

+ Clemens August
Bishop of Münster[6]

---

6   Ibid.

The Battle for the Cross had been won. It was one of the rare occasions that the Nazi government backed down from a declared plan of action. Pauly, the minister who issued the original decree, wrote to Episcopal Official Vorwerk that he rescinded the decree in consideration of the feelings of the people once he became convinced that the cross was seen by them as a most important religious symbol. He expressly denied, however, that his original decree had been in violation of the Concordat, on the grounds that it had nothing to do with the content of classroom instruction.

The victory in the Battle for the Cross would be a pyrrhic one. For a time, the crosses remained in the Catholic schools. But the propaganda campaign was already mounting for an end to denominational schools in Germany. In February 1937, the farmer Heinrich Götting would be arrested and sent first to prison and then to the Oranienburg Concentration Camp, where he would remain until the end of May. In July 1938, Episcopal Official Vorwerk would be forcibly expelled from Oldenburg. And by 1939, Catholic schools would have almost completely disappeared from Germany.

CHAPTER 11

With Burning Anxiety

The bishops of Germany disagreed about the tactics to use in dealing with the Nazi regime. But they kept their disagreements behind closed doors, agreeing that it was essential to keep a united front and to coordinate their activities with Rome. In addition to keeping one another updated by letter about their various protests to government officials, the German Bishops' Conference continued to meet annually at Fulda, the burial place of St. Boniface, the great Englishman honored as the Apostle of Germany. Bishop von Galen was also instrumental in the formation of a conference of the bishops of western Germany.

In January 1937, Pope Pius XI invited five bishops to discussions in Rome. They included, naturally, the three German cardinals: Bertram of Breslau, Schulte of Cologne, and von Faulhaber of Munich. In addition, two bishops were invited: the outspoken Bishop of Berlin, Konrad von Preysing, and Clemens August von Galen, Bishop of Münster. The recent discovery that von Galen's memorandum of March 1936 had been sent to Cardinal Pacelli clarifies why he was given an invitation. His arguments had struck a positive chord with the cardinal secretary of state.

During the time in Rome, Bishop von Preysing complained to Cardinal Pacelli about Cardinal Bertram's domineering attitude and diplomatic approach. He also remarked to an assistant that Bertram treated von Galen badly during those days. Von Preysing and von Galen took advantage of the visit to make long walks through the Eternal City, once, on von Galen's suggestion, making the pilgrimage to the seven churches.[1]

Cardinal Bertram still supported the policy of written appeals and negotiations behind closed doors. He recommended to Cardinal Pacelli that Pope Pius should write a personal letter to Adolf Hitler. Pacelli disagreed.[2] Clearly, von Galen's memorandum had made an impression on him. The decision was made to go public. The Holy Father would write an encyclical letter "On the Situation of the Catholic Church in the German Reich." For the first time ever, an encyclical was written in the German language, so that its popular title, taken, as is customary for encyclicals, from its first words, is in German rather than Latin: *Mit brennender Sorge*—*"With Burning Anxiety."*

Sorge could also be translated as grief, care, worry, apprehension, uneasiness, concern, or sorrow. Any one of these or all of them together could express the sense that Pope Pius wanted to convey. He was deeply concerned for the situation of Catholics in Germany, which he could see growing more desperate almost daily. When the new regime had come into power, he wrote, he had agreed to a Concordat, which had been in the works for a long time before the Nazis came to power. This should have secured the freedom of the Church for her mission of saving souls and also the peaceful development and well-being of the German people. But the results had not lived

---

1   Walter Adolph, *Geheime Aufzeichnungen aus dem nationalsozialistischen Kirchenkampf 1935–1943*, 2nd ed. (Mainz: Matthias-Grünewald-Verlag, 1980), 39, 40.

2   Ludger Grevelhörster, *Kardinal Clemens August Graf von Galen in seiner Zeit* (Münster: Aschendorff, 2005), 77.

up to those hopes. Many powerful Germans seemed set on a campaign to destroy the Catholic Church. Violations of the Concordat were common. No one could doubt which party to the treaty sought peaceful cooperation and which did not.

All his actions, the pope said, had been inspired by the binding law of treaties. Not so those of the "other contracting party," which "emasculated the terms of the treaty, distorted their meaning, and eventually considered its more or less official violation as a normal policy."[3] Yet even with the campaign for the destruction of Catholic schools in full swing, he hoped that the German government would return to fidelity to treaties.

The pope saw his encyclical as giving fatherly encouragement to his children suffering hardship and guiding them so that they would not be confused by Nazi propaganda. In this regard, his task was to clarify the correct meaning of religious terms and concepts. The pagan ideology and the Hitler personality cult had falsified these. Thus the pope wrote:

> The believer in God is not he who utters the name in his speech, but he for whom this sacred word stands for a true and worthy concept of the Divinity. Whoever identifies, by pantheistic confusion, God and the universe, by either lowering God to the dimensions of the world, or raising the world to the dimensions of God, is not a believer in God. Whoever follows that so-called pre-Christian Germanic conception of substituting a dark and impersonal destiny for the personal God, denies thereby the Wisdom and Providence of God who "Reacheth from end to end mightily, and ordereth all things sweetly" (Wisdom viii, 1). Neither is he a believer in God.

---

3   Pope Pius XI, *Mit brennender Sorge*, no. 5. Vatican translation. http://w2.vatican.va/content/pius-xi/en/encyclicals/documents/ hf_p-xi_enc_14031937_mit-brennender-sorge.html.

Whoever exalts race, or the people, or the State, or a particular form of State, or the depositories of power, or any other
fundamental value of the human community—however necessary and honorable be their function in worldly things—
whoever raises these notions above their standard value and
divinizes them to an idolatrous level, distorts and perverts an
order of the world planned and created by God; he is far from
the true faith in God and from the concept of life which that
faith upholds . . .[4]

True faith, he insisted, also upholds a correct ethical order. The
true God, the pope wrote,

has issued commandments whose value is independent of time
and place, country and race. As God's sun shines on every
human face so His law knows neither privilege nor exception.
Rulers and subjects, crowned and uncrowned, rich and poor
are equally subject to His word . . . None but superficial minds
could stumble into concepts of a national God, of a national
religion; or attempt to lock within the frontiers of a single people, within the narrow limits of a single race, God, the Creator
of the universe, King and Legislator of all nations before whose
immensity they are "as a drop in a bucket" (Isaiah xi, 15).[5]

Further on in the letter was this passage: "Should any man dare,
in sacrilegious disregard of the essential differences between God
and His creature, between the God-man and the children of man,
to place a mortal, were he the greatest of all times, by the side of, or
over, or against, Christ, he would deserve to be called prophet of
nothingness, to whom the terrifying words of Scripture would

---

4   Ibid., nos. 7–8.
5   Ibid., nos. 10–11.

Castle Dinklage in Lower Saxony. Family home of Clemens August von Galen.

Count Ferdinand Heribert von Galen.

Countess Elisabeth von Galen, born Countess von Spee.

Clemens August von Galen at age 20 (1898) with his sister Agnes.

Father von Galen (standing, sixth from left) with his family on the occasion of his solemn "first" Mass at the parish church in Dinklage, June 5, 1904. Next to him, fifth from left, is his brother Franz.

Father von Galen with his bishop and priest relatives at the time of his first Mass.

"Church and State." Bishop von Galen with a schoolmaster in Emmerich in 1934.

Bishop von Galen was at his best with children.

During a Confirmation visit in Lüdinghausen in July 1936.

be applicable: 'He that dwelleth in heaven shall laugh at them' (Psalm ii, 3)."[6]

Themes that Bishop von Galen stressed in his preaching and teaching abound in the pope's searing encyclical. Pius clarified the misuse of religious terms such as revelation, faith, original sin, and immortality. He stressed the divine origins of the Old Testament and denounced as blasphemers those who would banish it from schools and church. He encouraged parents whose right to Catholic schools for their children was being infringed: "Parents who are earnest and conscious of their educative duties," he wrote, "have a primary right to the education of the children God has given them in the spirit of their faith, and according to its prescriptions. Laws and measures, which in school questions fail to respect this freedom of the parents, go against natural law, and are immoral. The Church, whose mission it is to preserve and explain the natural law, as it is divine in its origin, cannot but declare that the recent enrollment into schools organized without a semblance of freedom, is the result of unjust pressure, and is a violation of every common right."[7]

In parts of Germany, there had been a recent vote in favor of non-denominational schools, but the voters did not have the opportunity to cast their ballots in secret. The pope was convinced that a free and secret ballot, rather than one under pressure, would have produced a different result.

He made it clear that he was not against national youth organizations: "What We object to," he wrote, "is the voluntary and systematic antagonism raised between national education and religious duty. That is why we tell the young: Sing your hymns to freedom, but do not forget the freedom of the children of God. Do not drag the nobility of that freedom in the mud of sin and

---

6   Ibid., no. 17.
7   Ibid., no. 31.

sensuality. He who sings hymns of loyalty to this terrestrial country should not, for that reason, become unfaithful to God and His Church, or a deserter and traitor to his heavenly country."[8]

Preparations for the encyclical's publication took place in complete secrecy. The Holy See and the bishops wanted to ensure that the Nazis would not learn of its existence until their spies heard it being read in all the pulpits of the country and saw it in print everywhere. It was to be read in all the parishes of the country on Palm Sunday, March 21, 1937.

The first copies of the text were delivered by hand to the bishops from the Nunciature in Berlin. On Monday, March 15, Bishop von Galen sent one of his priests, with a copy of the letter, to see Dr. Bernhard Lucas, the proprietor of the Regensberg printing house in Münster. Using the telephone for any discussions about the encyclical was out of the question; one never knew who might be listening. The priest told Dr. Lucas to read the pope's letter carefully and asked him, on behalf of the bishop, if his firm would be willing to print it. The bishop wanted Dr. Lucas to understand the risks involved in printing the encyclical and made it clear through his representative that no one would blame him if he refused the job. Could Regensberg print it in the usual form, as an insert in the church newsletter, and later perhaps in a special print run? After consulting with a technical assistant, Dr. Lucas announced his decision:

> We have never let the Bishop down. Nor did my predecessors in the time of the *Kulturkampf.* We will print this week—provided that the Bishop decides quickly—not only the insert to the church newsletter, but also as many additional copies as our staff and our machines can handle. We believe we can guarantee discretion, also on behalf of our employees. We will

---

8   Ibid., no. 34.

print by day and night, using moonlight that comes in through our windows. First, we will print the 2,200 copies of the insert; then, up until Saturday noon, the special printing, at least 100,000 copies, 12 × 17 centimeters, 32 pages, bound.

From Thursday morning, March 18, until Saturday at noon, about a third of the thirty-two workers in the firm remained on the job day and night, taking only short breaks. In the end, they managed to produce 120,000 booklets, roughly half of the total copies printed in all of Germany.[9]

Dr. Lucas paid for his loyalty to the Church. The Regensberg printing house had been owned by the Lucas family and had served the Diocese of Münster for over three hundred years. On Holy Saturday, 1937, six days after *Mit brennender Sorge* appeared, the printing house was closed by the Gestapo. Dr. Lucas did not recover his property until 1950.[10] A similar fate befell the eleven other publishing houses in the country that printed the papal encyclical.

The pamphlets were delivered to the more than five hundred diocesan parishes in time for distribution on Palm Sunday. The print run meant that there was one copy of the encyclical for every twenty Catholics, with an additional twenty thousand copies for the city of Münster. Bishop von Galen recommended that the pope's letter be read to every congregation while the priest at the altar silently read the long Palm Sunday gospel of the Lord's Passion.

The government was taken completely by surprise. In the Münster Diocese, there was only one case of a disturbance. A police

---

9   Peter Löffler, ed., *Bischof Clemens August Graf von Galen: Akten, Briefe und Predigten 1933–1946*, 2nd ed. (Paderborn: Ferdinand Schöningh, 1996), doc. 209, v. I, 496–97, n. 2, where it is stated that more than half of all the copies in German dioceses were produced by Regensberg. Cf. Grevelhörster, 77, who says there were three hundred thousand copies in the whole country, so the total from Münster was slightly less than half.

10   Löffler, doc. 221, v. I, 536, n. 14.

official in the village of Hauenhorst interrupted the pastor as he
was reading the encyclical, saying it was forbidden to read it. The
pastor replied, "The police forbid, and the bishop commands.
Whom shall I follow? I follow my bishop!" He continued reading,
but to the shock of the congregation, the policeman came to the
pulpit and tore the letter from his hands. Two weeks later, the pastor announced to his people, "Because the Pope's letter was forcibly
torn from my hands on Palm Sunday, I went to the Bishop and the
Vicar General on the following Monday to make a personal report
as to what had happened. The Bishop gave me another copy of the
letter and forcefully gave me the command that I must make use of
my right to read the Pope's letter. Thus as I begin to read the letter
again today, I am doing this only at the command of my bishop."
Meanwhile, Bishop von Galen protested to the government, and
this time he received a letter of apology.[11] But his complaints about
the closing of the Regensberg printing house, taking all the responsibility for the printing of the encyclical on himself, went unheard.

The bishops of northwestern Germany met soon after and produced a draft of a common pastoral letter, which they hoped the Fulda
Bishops' Conference would issue. Cardinal Schulte sent the proposed draft to Cardinal Bertram. A few days later, hoping to explain
the reasons for recommending a common pastoral letter, Bishop
von Galen sent Cardinal Bertram a memorandum.[12] He argued
that the government seemed to be hoping to kill the encyclical
by silence. Almost no references were made to it in the press. Von
Galen feared that if this policy of ignoring the encyclical caused it
to be forgotten, the Holy Father's effort to help the Church and the
German people would be wasted. In his opinion, it was the task
of the bishops to break the wall of silence by frequent references

11   Löffler, doc. 210, v. I, 498, n. 1.
12   Löffler, doc. 211, v. I, 500–505.

to the teaching of the encyclical not only in church but also before the public.

Subsequent events had proved, he wrote, that the pope's letter had impressed both Catholic and non-Catholic Christians. The letter was "a call to all Germans who still stand for God, for Christ, for the Christian past and culture of the German people." It had "strengthened the front of the defenders of Christianity, but also broadened that front." As Bishop von Galen saw it, if the message of the encyclical were forgotten, the enemies of the Church would attack again and make use of the old anti-Catholic prejudices. They would attack at a moment of their choosing, but then it would be too late for the Church to act. It was important to act *now*, to keep the words of Pope Pius in the public eye, so that people would clearly understand that his encyclical was written not as an attack on Germany but in a holy concern for the spiritual well-being of the German people. "The Holy Father has given us extraordinary help by taking an unusual step," he wrote:

> He has strengthened our unity and at the same time broadened the front of the defenders of Christianity. It appears that a strong and fearsome impression has been made upon our opponents, who seem to have no counter-attack except the effort to build up a "wall of silence." But behind this wall a counterstrike will be prepared. At a given time it will begin, with the familiar old battle cry of the danger of "ultramontanism." Can we take the chance of timidly waiting for this without doing anything, perhaps without hope?
>
> The Holy Father can and should expect from us that we prepare for this, and that we make use of the chance of defending and spreading Christian truth that he has given us![13]

---

13   Ibid.

For his part, Cardinal Bertram still thought the Bishop of Münster lacked political tact. He complained privately that von Galen
seemed to think that he could command the bishops as if they were
Westphalian peasants.[14] By the end of July, von Galen pressed his
argument in a memorandum to Cardinal Faulhaber.[15] The Holy
Father's encyclical, he wrote, struck the enemies of Christianity at
a weak point, as shown by the fact that they had not attempted
to refute its specific points but were trying to kill it by a policy of
silence. In addition to that tactic, they were increasing their propaganda attacks on the pope, the bishops, the clergy, and loyal Catholics as enemies of the German state, the German race, and the
German "essence." The reaction of the enemies of Christianity, as
well as the positive reaction of Catholics and Protestants, showed
that the pope's decision to "go public" was the right tactic.

Von Galen, aware that a meeting of the conference of bishops was
slated for late August, pressed his case to Faulhaber for a common
pastoral letter taking up themes of the papal encyclical. He thought
that a particular focus should be placed on the topics of morality and
natural law, topics on which Catholics, Protestants, and "all upright
and normal-thinking German citizens" can agree:

> I cannot believe it is true that the majority of the German peo-
> ple, that all of those who march in the lines of the new "move-
> ment," are so far from normal sound thinking today that they
> are not troubled by the denial and violation of all rights of
> persons, all rights of parents, all rights to property, all laws of
> contracts and all individual freedom! The Church has always
> been the proponent and defender, not only of revealed truth,

---

14   Stefania Falasca, *Un vescovo contro Hitler: Von Galen, Pio XII e la resistenza
      al nazismo* (Milan: Edizioni San Paolo, 2006), 123, n. 41, citing
      W. Adolph, 130.
15   Löffler, doc. 225, v. I, 552–56.

but also of the God-given natural rights and freedoms of the
human person. The recent popes have been exceptional in this
regard. Today, when these rights and freedoms are denied in
theory and violated in practice, there could be a response going
far beyond the margins of the believers in revelation and the
loyal members of the Church if we came out loudly and solemnly for justice and freedom, in union with the Pope and
following his example.[16]

In this regard, von Galen made reference to the positive response
that a recent pastoral letter of Preysing's had received, but this letter
was known only in limited circles. A joint pastoral letter on the foundations of the moral order and the natural law seemed to von Galen
to be the only area in which there could be hope for success, even
among people who were far from the Church. In his view, nothing
like this approach had been tried since the Nazis had seized power.

16   Ibid.

CHAPTER 12

If *That* Is the National Socialist Worldview

During the period of tension surrounding the Nazi Party rally and the Great Procession of July 1935, a propaganda poster was posted widely in Westphalia with the heading, "German people, listen!" The poster bore Gauleiter Alfred Meyer's name on behalf of the National Socialist party and claimed that Catholics were trying to stir up the fear of a new *Kulturkampf*. Vandalism of Catholic churches and the singing of insulting songs against the Bishop of Münster, the poster claimed, were actually undertaken by Catholics but blamed on members of the Nazi Party: "That is to sabotage the inner peace of the nation!" shouted the poster.[1] Catholics, of course, found the posters offensive, but they had to remain in place. In one case, a priest who tore down a poster on church property was sent to a concentration camp.

Truth was one of the first casualties of Nazi rule. In August 1936, Bishop Clemens August preached in the Cathedral of Münster about a pastoral letter the German bishops issued concerning the

---

1   Joachim Kuropka, *Clemens August Graf von Galen: Sein Leben und Wirken in Bildern und Dokumenten*, 3rd ed. (Cloppenburg: Runge, 1997), 154.

Spanish Civil War.[2] This was one matter about which the Church could agree with the government, though not always for the same reasons. Both agreed about the dangers of communism and saw the Republican government in Spain as bringing to western Europe the inhumane policies and practices of the Soviet Union. A further concern of the bishops was with the anticlerical, anti-Catholic policies of that government and with reports of atrocities on the Republican side, including the murders of large numbers of priests and nuns.

Von Galen's sermon focused on the official press reaction to the pastoral letter of the bishops. The Essen National Newspaper had praised it for its attack on communism. But in doing so, the paper acted as if this were a surprising new development. The Vatican and the German bishops, it claimed, had stood idly by for years before finally fighting the evils of communism. This statement was so blatantly untrue that it must have seemed embarrassing even to have to refute it. All the popes since Leo XIII, von Galen reminded his listeners, had condemned communism and socialism. The bishops of Germany had warned against communism and socialism three times during the period of the Weimar Republic, in 1921, 1924, and 1931. Von Galen noted that this had taken courage, considering that, during the Weimar years, parties of the Left often received a majority of the votes in German elections.

He was particularly concerned that young people were being misled by the magazine of the Hitler Youth. It was constantly filled with lies about the pope, but its young readers might not have enough historical knowledge to recognize the falsehoods. Bishop von Galen suggested that the young men who wrote for and edited this magazine seemed to be too self-sure to learn their history from impartial

---

2   Peter Löffler, ed., *Bischof Clemens August Graf von Galen: Akten, Briefe und Predigten 1933–1946*, 2nd ed. (Paderborn: Ferdinand Schöningh, 1996), doc. 188, v. I, 436–38.

sources. If they did, they would have known that throughout the years, thanks to the Catholic workers' associations, communist propaganda had been least influential among Catholics.

At any rate, he asked, if Nazi propaganda was correct in its claim that communism was now completely dead in Germany, why should it be necessary for the German bishops to warn against the errors of a system no one any longer believed in?

Finally, he said, if the Essen National Newspaper really thought the bishops' letter had something good to say, one would assume that the government and the secret state police—the dreaded *Geheim Staatspolizei*, or "Gestapo"—would allow it to be printed in regular newspapers as well as in church papers. The diocesan newsletter, von Galen noted, had the honor of being under prior censorship by the Gestapo. With that in mind, he had arranged for a small pamphlet to be printed containing the text of the bishops' letter. "Under these circumstances," he told the congregation, "and after the praise of the pastoral letter by the official party paper, the Essen National Newspaper, I am sure you will be surprised, as I am, at the fact that yesterday the Secret State Police in Münster confiscated all the remaining copies of the pamphlet at the printing house!" The congregation indeed was surprised, and the Gestapo informers reported that loud cries of disapproval were heard in the cathedral.[3]

It was no secret that the official press was full of lies and that attempts at publishing alternatives met censorship and confiscation. By early 1937, von Galen had numerous occasions to protest on behalf of the rights of the Catholic press. The Gestapo frequently confiscated issues of the diocesan newsletter. The bishop protested that he was thus prevented from communicating his pastoral letters to the people, or that they had been censored, contrary to the provisions of the Concordat that communications between the bishops

---

3   Ibid.

and their people could continue in the customary forms. On the occasions when he received an answer to his protests, it was to the effect that although pastoral letters could be read from the pulpit, there was no guarantee that a printed version could be distributed, despite the fact that printed versions of pastoral letters, both in Catholic newspapers and in the secular press, had long been customary.

Things came to a head just before the publication of Pius XI's encyclical, *Mit brennender Sorge*. The propaganda apparatus of the regime frequently used charges of sexual immorality against clerics and Catholic leaders in order to blacken the Church's reputation. Some of the charges contained an element of truth, but certainly not all. Even in cases that were true, they were, as often as not, distorted to attack the Church.

Such was the case of a nineteen-year-old young man convicted of committing incest with his two younger half sisters. The press reports claimed that he was a leader in a Catholic youth organization and a theology student and that the Diocese of Freiburg had allowed him to continue in these activities after being aware of his crimes. In fact, as the diocese had made clear in early January 1937, his time as a leader in the Catholic youth organization had ended two years earlier; he was *not* a student of theology; and the diocese knew nothing of his crimes until he was arrested.

Nevertheless, in March of that year, the Westphalian branch of the Reich Ministry for People's Enlightenment and Propaganda ordered the regional diocesan newsletters to print an article about the case containing the false attacks on the Catholic Church. Bishop von Galen intervened, advising the papers *not* to print the article, because it did not come from a church source and so would mislead the readers. Only one newsletter printed the article, and it was the only regional paper that was permitted to continue in existence.[4]

4   Löffler, doc. 207 and notes, v. I, 492–93.

In a lengthy sermon in the cathedral on May 30, the bishop detailed for the congregation his correspondence with Joseph Goebbels, head of the Ministry for People's Enlightenment and Propaganda.[5] Goebbels had given a condition for allowing the diocesan newsletters to be printed again: a written declaration by the bishop that the newsletters would no longer act against measures undertaken by the state. Von Galen replied, "I gladly give the assurance that I reject in principle actions against commands of the State, and I will not tolerate such by anyone under my authority, for example the editors of my diocesan newsletters, under the self-evident exception that would be granted to any German man, of something that would go against his conscience or his honor." Goebbels would not grant this exception unless von Galen *explicitly* clarified that it did not include cases such as the article that he had rejected in the first place.

The congregation cheered when he boldly told them that he could not give such an assertion. He told them that if he did so, "I would be ashamed to wear my episcopal ring."[6]

The main diocesan newsletter, he told them, was also under a three-month prohibition because of the printing of *Mit brennender Sorge*. He had received a letter from the Gestapo stating that the pope's letter contained "highly treasonous attacks against the National Socialist State and thereby aims at endangering the peaceful order and security of the State." His appeal against this order, made on Easter more than two months earlier, had not received a reply.

It was a complete misreading of the pope's letter, he said, to regard it as an attack on the German state or people. It was a friendly, fatherly warning to those who believed in Christ to be careful to maintain their faith in the face of attacks and falsifications of religious words and concepts. Only recently, the government's minister

---

5   Löffler, doc. 221, v. I, 526–42.
6   Ibid.

for relations with churches stated that "positive Christianity" was not based on belief in the divinity of Christ; indeed, the minister had added, such a claim made him laugh. Thus, von Galen pointed out, the word "Christianity" was now being used in Germany for a teaching that denied Christ. "Christianity without Christ, the Son of God! Truly, in a time when people can change well-known words into such new and erroneous meanings, it is the right and the duty of the highest defender of truth to give us a warning."

When the pope spoke about the many violations of the Concordat—after four patient years of vainly sending notes of protest—this too was the action of a friend, warning another friend who is on the slippery slope of danger. The bishop cited several examples of widely known systematic violations of the Concordat, including the closing of the Regensberg printing house because it printed the pope's encyclical. But he clarified that he was not trying to stir up a revolution:

"My Christians," he cried,

> if I say all this publicly; if I publicly protest against the attempt to silence the voice of the Vicar of Christ in Germany; if I publicly bear witness against the disregarding of the holy rights of the majesty of Christ our King in our Fatherland; against the infringements of the freedom of the Church; against so many measures by which priests and lay people are punished without being accused of crimes and without the possibility of juridical defense; this is not done in order to ask for your help or to call you to resistance against the power of the State. "Our help is in the Name of the Lord, who made heaven and earth."

The bishop urged his listeners to call on God's help: help to change the hearts of those in power or, if such not be His holy will, help to the Christians of Germany to bear hardships patiently. To those Catholics of his diocese who might feel tempted to take violent measures, he recommended the words of St. Thomas Becket: "The Church of Christ is not to be defended like an earthly fortress! I am gladly ready to suffer death for the freedom of the Church!" He added words of the same holy bishop for those who would punish Catholics for circulating the papal encyclical or the pastoral letters of the bishops: "I am the one responsible; I am the one you wish to strike! Why are you persecuting my loyal followers? In the name of God I say to you: do not dare to harm one of those who belong to me!"[7]

Cardinal Bertram had defended the pope's encyclical against the charge that it was damaging the interests of the German state both at home and abroad. Bishop von Galen quoted from his letter:

> If anything damages the interests of the German State both at home and abroad, it is the fact that an uninterrupted battle against Christianity has been tolerated in Germany for years . . . that newspapers and magazines with circulations in the millions appear daily and also go into foreign countries, in which unrestrained and disgraceful attacks are made on Christianity . . . with shameful pictures such as we never had to endure in the worst of the communist times. Can anyone really believe that such symptoms are not noticed in foreign countries, and do not lead people to the conclusion that the aim is to destroy Christianity in Germany? What the Pope has now publicly said has long been the bitter conviction of all believing Christians in Germany and perhaps even more abroad![8]

There was a large crowd in the cathedral that day. Two days earlier, Joseph Goebbels had made a well-publicized attack on the Church in a speech in Berlin, and the word had spread that Bishop von Galen's sermon would reply to this. The sermon led to another great

---

7   Ibid.
8   Ibid.

demonstration of loyalty to the bishop and the Church. This time, the Gestapo noted, von Galen left the cathedral by a side entrance, so that his path back to his palace took him through the midst of the cheering crowd.

However, his sermon had no positive effect on the regime. Attacks on the Church continued.

The next week, while preaching at a Catholic youth rally in the Rhineland, Bishop von Galen made a humorous reference to the fact that several leading Nazi propagandists were not, in fact, born in Germany. Alfred Rosenberg was born in Latvia, Rudolf Hess in Alexandria, Egypt, and Richard Walther Darré in Argentina. Von Galen told the young people that their forefathers had built a German culture on the foundations of Christianity. Now people were telling them that in order to be true Germans, they had to deny their Christian faith. "We do not need to be taught by others," he thundered, "what the 'essence' of being German is, no matter whether they come from Riga, Reval, or Cairo, or Chile."[9]

The Church went to great lengths to show that Catholics were good German citizens. On public holidays and days of patriotic demonstrations, church buildings would fly flags at government request and even did so when it was simply the case of a Nazi Party celebration, such as happened in mid-October 1937. Despite this, when the Nazi parade was passing the bishop's palace, the participants sang a particularly horrible song with the refrain, "Hang the Jews; put the priests"—using a derogatory slang term—"against the wall." Von Galen wrote a letter of complaint to Ferdinand von Lüninck. A reply finally came two months later: an expression of sincere regret for the incident and a claim that it had been impossible to find out who was responsible.[10]

---

9   Löffler, doc. 222, v. I, 543.
10   Löffler, doc. 229, v. I, 562.

On November 17, 1937, Bishop von Galen was in Vreden, which had a Catholic history dating back to 839. The Church there had been founded by the son and grandson of the Saxon king Widukind, who was converted from paganism to Christianity and baptized in 785. With this history in mind, von Galen attacked the claim that Christianity was foreign to the German spirit.[11]

He rehearsed for his congregation the standard arguments they had heard and read so often: that the Catholic Church had invented the ideas of sin and punishment for sin, and of heaven and hell, in order to keep men enslaved under the yoke of priests; that the Nordic men, and especially the Germans, knew nothing of sin and of divine justice until the Frankish king Charlemagne, by the power of the sword, forced the old Saxons to accept these foreign ideas of sin, punishment, atonement, and a Redeemer.

The people of Vreden listened with glee as their bishop, of whom they had heard so much but who had never visited them before, exposed the nonsense of that position. "Think a bit," he exhorted them. "Isn't the difference between good and evil, between truth and lies, between justice and injustice, a completely undeniable fact for any normal thinking man, and also for us Nordic men? Did Christianity have to come here before our ancestors knew that it is unjust, dishonorable, and mean to cheat, to rob, to murder?"

Surely their pagan ancestors knew about good and evil. Surely they had a sense of divine justice, of reward and punishment after death—after all, what was Valhalla? To say that they did not recognize these truths was more than nonsensical. "It is an insult," von Galen said, "to our German forefathers." Their pagan ancestors had an inkling of those truths. What they did not know was the true, eternal, Trinitarian God. They did not know about the original sin of Adam and Eve. They did not know that our eternal Father has sent His coeternal Son

11   Löffler, doc. 232, v. I, 579–86.

into the world to redeem mankind from sin. This was the gospel that Widukind accepted as "good news" late in the eighth century.

So then, von Galen asked, are we to say,

> Widukind was a traitor to German blood, when he accepted Christian Baptism and received the means of grace of the Catholic Church, when he proved himself to be Christian in his faith and in his life? And Wigbert, his son, and Walbert his grandson, who built monasteries and churches here, who erected here an altar for the sacrifice of the New Covenant over the relics of the Roman Saint Felicity—are we to say that they were degenerate idiots, or cowards and traitors to their people, to their race, to the German essence? And your ancestors, the ancestors of you men and women of Vreden, who were squires and companions-in-arms with these noble Saxon dukes, . . . who have prayed and lived here, who have bravely borne the toil and trouble of this earthly life in the "blessed hope of the coming of the great God and Savior," who have died here courageous and strong in their trust in the blood and the salvation of Christ; all people of Vreden who have been buried in your cemetery for the last eleven hundred years—that they betrayed their German blood, their German essence, by giving themselves over to an alien faith in their life and death?
>
> Truly, my fellow Christians, a holy anger boils up in me, a holy anger must boil up in all of you, in every honor-loving German person, when day after day he has to read and put up with such insults and slanders aimed at his fathers and his ancestors![12]

He called to mind his own ancestry:

> It galls me that people malign my ancestors, my father, my mother, and insult their faith, their Christian life, as un-German, as alien!

---

12   Ibid.

They say that German blood is supposed to speak through a person and his assertions. If that is the case, I know and will not let it be denied that what they call the "voice of German blood" also speaks through me, and through my—without exception—loyal Catholic ancestors from the Galen family, who have honorably borne their German nobility for more than seven hundred years!

What Widukind, the brave Saxon duke, received as the Good News of salvation; what he and his sons and grandchildren left to you people of Vreden, the squires and companions-in-arms of these loyal German men, through their pious Christian lives and their unforgettable benefactions to the Catholic faith; *that* has become the best German inheritance, that is the true German essence. We will not let our heroes and saints, our forefathers and ancestors, our fathers and mothers, be insulted!

And if we cannot hinder it and bring the insults to silence, then let it, one time, be said openly: a so-called worldview that would make us slanderers and despisers of our loyal German forerunners, our parents and ancestors; that would have us declare that our forerunners betrayed the German essence and disavowed German blood: we reject such a worldview. And if *that* is the National Socialist worldview, then we reject the National Socialist worldview!

Let them advertise elsewhere for followers and parrots. We Westphalians, we Münsterlanders and German people from the lower Rhine, will stay loyal to the blood and the best intentions of our Christian forerunners, true to the Roman Catholic Faith, which we have experienced in the words and example of a God-fearing father, which we have drunk with mothers' milk, which we have learned at the knees of our mother! Shame on those who would make their Christian-German ancestors into traitors![13]

---

13   Ibid.

CHAPTER 13

Catholic Schools Under Attack

A dolf Hitler's aim was to build a unified German people's community. To accomplish this, Nazi propaganda claimed, required overcoming the divisions created by different religious denominations and certainly those created by the denominational schools. In Oldenburg, the Party had lost the Battle for the Cross, but throughout the country, the plan to remove Christianity from the schools was in full swing. In one area of Germany after another, the denominational schools were being replaced by the "German Community School." At first, to give the change an aura of legitimacy, parents were pressured to sign documents claiming they preferred the community school. When a town's denominational schools were subsequently amalgamated into one community school, the claim was made that this was what the public wanted.

Just before Christmas in 1936, only a month after the victory in the Battle for the Cross in Oldenburg, Bishop von Galen sent a report to his priests on the topic of the Catholic schools.[1] This was

---

1   Peter Löffler, ed., *Bischof Clemens August Graf von Galen: Akten, Briefe und Predigten 1933–1946*, 2nd ed. (Paderborn: Ferdinand Schöningh, 1996), doc. 200, v. I, 470–78.

the first of many communications with priests and with people, to keep them aware of what was happening and to encourage support for Catholic schools.

A pastoral letter in February 1937 was directed primarily to parents.[2] A few days earlier, the priests in the city of Münster had given a warning about the need to defend Catholic schools. Teachers had asked their pupils to vote on whether, when they became parents, they would send their own children to the community school. Clearly, the bishop said, this was a step in seeking to destroy the Catholic schools. It was designed to cause children to mistrust their parents and must also have caused great conflicts of conscience for the Catholic teachers who were ordered to take these votes.

Attacks on the Catholic schools, the bishop now told parents, were attacks on their most sacred right and duty. They as parents were the first educators of their children. The school existed to assist them in their fulfillment of this sacred duty. "Therefore," he said, "it is your obligation to send your children to such schools as will instruct and educate them in accord with God's truth and commandments. That is the task and goal of the Catholic school. Therefore every attack on the Catholic schools is a threat to the most sacred rights of Catholic parents."

"A Catholic confessional school," the letter clarified, "is a school in which Catholic children are taught by believing Catholic teachers, in accordance with the principles of the Catholic Church. Religion influences every aspect of the education." The duty of Catholic parents to see to the Catholic education of their children was enshrined in canon law and guaranteed by the law of the land. The letter quoted the relevant school laws for Prussia and Oldenburg and the articles of the Concordat guaranteeing Catholic schools and requiring that the teachers in those schools be Catholics who would support the principles of a Catholic school.

---

2   Löffler, doc. 204, v. I, 483–89.

It urged parents not to be fooled by the different names that might be used in the propaganda for the new schools, whether it be "the community school," "the German school," or "the German confessional school." "Demand instead: the Catholic confessional school." Then it gave clear, simple, straightforward answers to the standard arguments in favor of the new community schools. Perhaps, it said, parents would be told that in Catholic areas, everything would remain the same in the new schools. "That is not true," was the response. "If all were to remain the same, then why all the pressure and advertising for a new school? Will all remain the same if teachers can be assigned to your schools who are not Catholic, or who have left the Catholic Church, or who deny the articles of her faith? If everything is supposed to remain the same, then why are people trying to remove the cross from the school, or at least from its place of honor in the schoolroom?"[3]

To the claim that the new schools would still have religious instruction, the bishop replied that a brief class on religion each day does not constitute a Catholic education, if for the rest of the day, the educational philosophy was based on a non-Christian spirit and if there were no more prayer and celebrations of feast days. He reminded parents that already, teachers who no longer believed in the Catholic faith were teaching in Catholic schools.

The slogan "One people, one Reich, one school" was frequently used, claiming that confessional schools hindered the desired national unity. In response, the bishop's letter noted that Germany could not be united in religious faith as long as there were Catholics, Protestants, and pagans in the country. But unity of people and Reich, loyalty and love for the fatherland, had always been supported by Catholic schools, as was proved by, among other things, the participation of Catholics in the 1914–1918 World War. He urged parents

---

3   Ibid.

to respond with fiery indignation if they heard the charge that proponents of Catholic confessional schools were traitors to their country:
"You are not traitors to your country when you make use of your
right, protected by law and the Concordat, to insist on the Catholic
confessional school." To all the slogans, they should make the reply:
"We want to keep the Catholic confessional school."[4]

In a separate note to the clergy, he encouraged them to keep in
close contact with parents and keep them informed of the tactics
being used by the promoters of community schools. Pressure and
terror tactics were being used to promote those schools and to
get Catholic teachers to promote them. If the teachers supported
the new schools, the parents could be led into error because of the
trust that they naturally placed in the teachers. The priests were
warned that in many localities, advertising for the new schools
would suddenly appear, sometimes followed very soon afterward
by petition forms for them to sign in favor of the new schools. The
priests would need to act quickly to remind parents to support
only the Catholic confessional school. Should advertising for the
community school begin in their parishes, they should also inform
the general vicariate of the diocese right away.[5]

In late April, Bishop von Galen was in Oldenburg to administer the Sacrament of Confirmation in the Deanery of Friesoythe. A
shock came to him when he arrived on the evening of the twenty-
first, which he related to the congregation in the church the next
morning. The superintendent of schools in Cloppenburg forbade
him to visit the Catholic schools.[6] The bishop had always visited
Catholic schools during his Confirmation visits in order to verify
that the children were well instructed in religion. From the time of

---

4   Ibid.
5   Löffler, doc. 205, v. I, 489–91.
6   Löffler, doc. 214, v. I, 509–11.

his appointment as bishop, he had done this on all his Confirmation tours, whether in Westphalia, the Rhineland, or Oldenburg. He allowed full rein to his indignation:

> This is an unheard-of ill-treatment, which has never befallen a bishop of Münster in the Oldenburger Münsterland. The bishops of Münster founded the schools in Münsterland. Just a few days ago I was reading that my forerunner Christoph Bernhard (von Galen) had given the order for the construction of the schools in Friesoythe! And now the bishop may no longer visit the schools? This has never happened in all of Germany, except for one case in the time of the Weimar Republic in Saxony, when the Social Democrats and the Marxists were governing there. It is certainly interesting that a superintendent of schools in today's State permits himself to do the same thing that the Social Democrats and Marxists did!

He told the congregation he had sent a telegram to the minister president of Oldenburg, to which he had not yet received a reply. He still hoped that the prohibition would be overturned. If not, he would not put the teachers into the position of having to shut their own bishop out of the school:

> I know how your brave teachers shared my anxiety and prayed with me half a year ago, when people wanted to exclude from the schoolrooms the image of the One who has sent the Bishop, the Cross of Christ the Son of God . . . I do not want to put these teachers into the qualm of conscience that would come if they, as officials of the State, would be required to prevent their Bishop from entering the Catholic school . . . But I will let it be known everywhere that it is against my will, and only under the constraint of power, that I omit the school visit on this occasion. Today the Bishop is

kept out of the school; who doubts that there are influential men who want by and by to put the priests, the religion teachers, religious instruction, and finally all Christianity out of the school?

He added that this was a clear example of a breach of the Concordat by state officials. It confirmed the complaint made by the Holy Father in his encyclical letter that the Concordat was not being honored.[7]

Three days later, he was able to give further information. It was not the school superintendent who was responsible for keeping him out of the schools. The superintendent was only passing on the order he had received from the minister for churches and schools in Oldenburg, the same Julius Pauly who had originally ordered the crosses to be removed from the schools the previous November. Pauly would not reverse his ruling. As justification for keeping the bishop out of the schools, he cited a pact dating back to 1830, which regulated the relations between the Duchy of Oldenburg and the Diocese of Münster. According to the pact, claimed Pauly, the church official who had the right to visit the Catholic schools was not the bishop but only the episcopal official.

Von Galen fundamentally rejected this claim. Since the official was the representative of the bishop, it was ridiculous to say that the official had the right to inspect the schools but the bishop did not. In any case, that point had to do with a regular inspection to determine that religious instruction was being properly done. The visits of the bishop during a Confirmation tour had been regularly undertaken for more than a hundred years since 1830 and after the signing of the Concordat in 1933. No one ever thought that this was a violation of the pact of 1830. Now suddenly, in 1937, when the question of Catholic schools was being raised in Oldenburg, Minister Pauly

---

7   Ibid.

thought that it was illegal for the bishop to visit the schools, although the same minister had not objected to the bishop's visits in 1935 and 1936. "Why now, in 1937?" the bishop asked. "Everyone can answer that question himself!" He expressed his protest against the minister's action and also against the unfriendly and inconsiderate way it was done, being communicated to him only by word of mouth and only the evening before the visits were to begin.[8]

On May 18, Bishop von Galen wrote a brief message for parents on the occasion of "School and Education Sunday."[9] The note was filled with brief exhortations on the theme of the role of the parents within the family as teacher, priest, and shepherd. As teachers, their first lesson to their children should be their example. No school could make up for parents' neglect in their children's religious education. They should be sure to keep good religious writings in the home and to watch carefully the teaching their children received in school. The Bible and the Catechism should be read in the house by the parents and children.

The message continued: "Consecrate your family by means of your priestly office so that it will be an acceptable offering to God! Be conscientious about the divine service of communal prayer in your houses! The father as the head of the family should be its delegate and its representative before God. Plant the spirit of fear of God and reverence for the saints in the hearts of your children! The cross should have the place of honor in a Christian home!"

As shepherds, the parents were urged to keep a careful eye on the influence that spoken or written words, whether within or outside the home, could have on their children:

> Guard your authority! Give your children healthy spiritual nourishment and genuine joy! Do not tolerate any poisoning

8   Löffler, doc. 215, v. I, 512–14.
9   Löffler, doc. 218, v. I, 516–17.

of their loyalty to the Church or disparaging of the Faith by
slanders against priests and bishops! Also, keep good connec-
tions with your children who are far from home!

Above all, safeguard the Catholic school for your children!

He reminded parents that one of the leading propaganda magazines stated quite openly that community schools with religious
instruction were only a step toward community schools without
religious instruction. As parents, it was their duty before God, and
also their right in regard to the state, to stand up for Catholic
schools: "What does the Concordat say? 'The maintenance and
new erection of Catholic confessional schools remains guaranteed.'
Therefore learn this sentence by heart: 'As long as there is German
loyalty, as long as a word given by the Chancellor has value, as long
as covenants are sacred, for so long there remains a right to Catholic schools in Germany.' Use this sentence in reply to anyone who
tries to undermine your fidelity to the Catholic school!"[10]

God had given them a sacred responsibility, he told fathers and
mothers, a responsibility for which they were consecrated by the
Sacrament of Matrimony. The great importance of this sacrament
was becoming ever more clear in their own days. Neither the
Church nor the state could absolve them of their duty as educators of their children, nor could the school take this responsibility
from them. He urged them to recall the words of St. Peter: "He
who has an office, let him fulfill it in the strength that God supplies" (1 Pet. 4:11).[11]

In April 1937, the minister of education set out the curriculum guidelines for the coming school year. Among the provisions,
which were communicated to the schools during the summer, was a

---

10   Ibid.
11   Ibid.

reduction of the number of hours for religion classes for the younger grades, from four hours per week to three. Bishop von Galen was convinced that this would not be sufficient and called on all priests to set up additional religion classes outside of school hours.[12]

The attack on the Catholic schools was stepped up when the new term began in September. Suddenly, as von Galen had predicted was likely to happen, priests were excluded from coming into the schools to teach Catechism. This measure, he wrote in a pastoral letter, showed a mistrust of the Church on the part of the regime and was contrary to a good working relationship that had long been in place, whereby the priests taught Catechism lessons and the regular classroom teachers gave the lessons on biblical history.[13] Cardinal Bertram had sent an appeal on behalf of the bishops, he noted, but it was necessary to prepare for the likelihood that the appeal would be unsuccessful. Von Galen encouraged teachers to continue to fulfill their tasks in conformity with the teachings of the Church and praised those who maintained their faithfulness in spite of extreme pressure. He reminded them that Catholic teachers should be good practicing Catholics and that Catholics who no longer believed should have the integrity to say so and transfer to a position in a non-Catholic school. Parents were again reminded of their sacred responsibility. More than ever, they needed to watch what was being taught to their children and to see that the full content of the Catholic lesson plans was being given to them.[14]

The Catholic schools were not alone in facing an escalation of opposition in the autumn of 1937. In a coordinated move on October 27, the Gestapo closed down all the young men's associations throughout the diocese, as well as the confraternities and sodalities

---

12 Löffler, doc. 226, v. I, 556–57.
13 Löffler, doc. 228, v. I, 558–61.
14 Ibid.

dedicated to the Blessed Virgin Mary. Their meeting places were closed and all their property confiscated—even the banners that had been blessed by the Church, which the young men would carry in processions or display on feast days in the churches. This was done, the bishop stated in a sermon in the cathedral on October 31,[15] without any law being passed and without any judicial proceedings. The pretext was the decree signed by Hindenburg after the Reichstag fire in 1933. This decree, suspending civil liberties and allowing the cabinet to take whatever measures it deemed necessary for protecting the public safety, was originally aimed at suppressing the Communist Party. Now it was being used against Catholic groups on the claimed ground that they endangered the state. With his chivalrous concern for honor, Bishop Clemens August strongly expressed his dismay at the attack on the reputation of the members and leaders of the Catholic youth groups. The leaders, including the bishops and priests, had aimed only at inculcating in young Catholics loyalty to Christ and love for the fatherland. It was a bitter injustice to accuse them of plotting the same kind of violent acts against public order that the communists engaged in. He told the congregation that he had sent a telegram of protest to the Führer and Chancellor of the Reich, Adolf Hitler. In the hope of a positive response, he would say no more on that subject.

He had much more to say that day about the schools. Priests had by then been excluded from teaching the religion classes in the vocational schools, which generally they had taught without pay. Religion classes would now be taught by lay teachers. Von Galen noted that Article 22 of the Concordat required that religion teachers be appointed in agreement with the bishop. He formally declared that any teachers taking over those religion classes, even if they had formerly been religion teachers at the elementary school level, did not

---

15   Löffler, doc. 230, v. I, 563–72.

have a canonical mission to teach religion in schools at other levels. He warned parents and students that he could not guarantee that such teachers would give their lessons in accord with the teachings of the Catholic Church. He did not wish to call into question the good will of teachers whose names he did not know, but there was no question that some formerly Catholic teachers had lost their faith. He pointed out that, a few days earlier, an education official from Berlin had given a lecture to teachers and educators in Münster, in which he had made fun of the Christian faith and asserted that heaven and hell were fairy tales. Some of the teachers present at the lecture had applauded these remarks. "God protect your children from such teachers!" von Galen proclaimed. "God protect German young people from such teachers! And if teachers who have lost the faith dare nevertheless to teach so-called Catholic religion classes, woe to the poor children who fall into the hands of such traitors. Better no religion classes in the schools than religion classes that destroy rather than build up, that poison rather than heal! Keep watch, Christian parents, and observe carefully whether your children are learning the true faith in the school, and are being directed in the truly Christian way of life!"[16]

He urged them especially to be on their guard if their children would not discuss with them what they were learning in school. When teachers tell children not to discuss what they are learning, he said, then you can be sure "that something is happening in the school that they want to keep secret from you and that will alienate the hearts of your children from you. In that case you will have the right, indeed the duty, to complain about that teacher to his superiors, and through petitions and written complaints and all legal means to bring it about that such destroyers of a child's trust in his parents and of orderly family life are removed from a position that

---

16   Ibid.

can be worthily fulfilled only in trusting cooperation with the parents of their pupils!"[17]

Although he pointed out that it was the Church that had created the educational system at all levels in Germany, his attempts to protect both the schools and the Catholic organizations proved fruitless. He kept up a steady stream of protests to government officials and a steady stream of sermons and pastoral letters to keep his priests and people informed and to give them guidance. A lengthy sermon in March 1938 gave the most up-to-date information.[18] New community schools were being established in various parts of Germany. In some places, they were begun without even a show of community support; without warning and simply by a decision of the mayors and city councilors, the denominational schools were merged into a community school. Once again, he warned parents that these new schools would inculcate a worldview completely opposed to their Christian faith. In addition, a great number of private schools run by religious orders were being forcibly closed. Religious sisters, brothers, and priests who had dedicated their lives to teaching and who had all the professional qualifications for their positions were left with no possibility of teaching. He noted the irony that, in some cases, the closing of schools for girls run by religious sisters led to the requirement that the girls attend mixed schools with boys, despite the fact that only in January, the Reich education minister had declared that mixed schools with boys and girls together were contrary to National Socialist principles of education. The Church in Germany at that time held to the same principle as the government, but the government made an exception when it wanted to close the schools run by sisters. The situation, von Galen said, called to mind the sad days of the *Kulturkampf*, when large numbers of

---

17   Ibid.
18   Löffler, doc. 237, v. I, 603–14.

religious had to give up their educational work in Germany and leave the country.

He then addressed the situation of the young men's associations. The telegram that he had sent to Adolf Hitler, he told the congregation, had been forwarded to the minister for church affairs on November 1. When no reply had been received by the middle of November, and thus there had been no opportunity for the leaders of the youth organizations to know what the charges were against them and to defend themselves before a proper court, he had issued a pastoral letter on the subject. In early January, he had sent a further letter of complaint. Finally, on February 11, 1938, the minister sent a letter rejecting all his claims. Von Galen read the minister's letter to the congregation:

> The Bishop of Münster saw fit to bring public attention to the measures under dispute in the sharpest way in his Pastoral Letter on the Pastoral Care of Youth of November 11 and in the sermon that he preached in the Cathedral of Münster on November 14, even though his telegram directed to the Führer and Chancellor of the Reich of October 30, 1937—as the Bishop knew—had been forwarded to me for consideration, and that no decision had yet been reached regarding his petition of the same date to the Office of the State Police in Münster. This fact, as well as the tone and contents of these utterances, which could not contribute to a positive solution to the situation, naturally make it impossible for me to recommend a rescinding of the Order of the Secret State Police of October 27, 1937.[19]

Thus the bishop's actions in defense of his young men's associations were used against those associations. The event well illustrates

---

19   Ibid.

the difficulty facing the bishops, or anyone else, in deciding what tactics to use in dealing with the regime. The kind of behind-the-scenes appeals favored by Cardinal Bertram generally had no effect. But adding a public protest to the appeal, such as Bishop von Galen did, resulted only in giving the minister a convenient excuse to deny the appeal. Nevertheless, von Galen's public protests were clearly not the reason for the closing of the young men's associations. This was a planned operation throughout the country. Von Galen pointed out that the associations had also been closed down in all of Bavaria and in the dioceses of Cologne, Trier, Aachen, Limburg, and Paderborn. What caused greater pain to all Catholics was the implication that the groups were involved in communist activities. He asked, "How can they accuse our Catholic youth of mixing themselves up with Communist subversion? How can one account for the fact that in many circles, there is a fear that we Catholics are somehow making common cause with Communism?" He cited an example:

A few days ago the newspapers reported that somewhere in Poland a horrible sacrilege took place in a church: during the celebration of the holy Mass a Communist fired a shot at the celebrating priest and mortally wounded him. The murder was said to have been planned and decided upon by a Communist organization because the priest was known to have been a staunch opponent of Communism. I do not know the priest. But if he was a true son of the Catholic Church, then it is self-evident that he was an opponent of Communism. Communism and its teachings have been refuted and condemned countless times by the Catholic Church.

How then, he asked, was it possible for people to think that Catholics were making common cause with communism? In short, because of propaganda and censorship. The statements of the Holy Father against communism were not allowed to appear in the newspapers, and the police confiscated church newspapers containing his pastoral letters on the subject. Meanwhile, as Bishop von Galen showed at great length, the propaganda in German newspapers sought to convince people that the highest authorities in the Catholic Church were making common cause with communism, even while communists were murdering priests in Poland and Spain.[20]

Bishop Clemens August wanted his hearers to grasp clearly the goal of this propaganda campaign. Someone once said, he noted, that if you repeat a story often enough, whether it is true or not, people will believe it. The propaganda of falsehood and hatred against Catholicism was designed to provoke mistrust of the Church among all non-Catholic Germans. This, he added, was how the bloody persecution of the Church in Spain had its beginnings. It was prepared by banning religious instruction from the schools and by years of slanderous attacks on the Church in newspapers and public meetings. "It could be," he continued,

> that there (in Spain) the fearfully earnest prophetic words of the savior are being fulfilled: "The time will come when whoever kills you will think that he is serving God. I have said this to you, so that when the hour comes, you will remember that I have said it to you" (Jn. 16:2). Will this hour also come to Germany? Will we have to experience and suffer this hour?
>
> Dear Catholics of Münster! In humble prayer and serious penance we will beg our Lord and Savior to keep far from us and our beloved German fatherland such a terrible fate. We will stretch out our hands in heartfelt brotherly love to all our fellow Germans, including those who mistrust and mistreat us; not in order to go over with them into the camp of the opponents of truth, but rather to draw them to us, into

---

20   Ibid.

the kingdom of divine truth and grace. If we ourselves remain firm in this truth, and if we fulfill all of our duties loyally, aided by grace, then we can take confidence in the promise of the Lord, "In the world you will have persecutions. But have confidence, for I have conquered the world."

"And now," he concluded, "let us pray for our Führer, for our people and our fatherland."[21]

By this point, these prayers seemed to have no effect on the policy of attacks on the Church. In April, rumors were spreading that the Bishop of Rottenburg, Joannes Baptista Sproll, had to flee his diocese after the Nazis organized public demonstrations outside his episcopal palace. Demonstrators had broken into the palace, set a fire, broken windows, and caused other damage. On April 10, 1938, the outspoken Bishop Sproll had refused on grounds of conscience to vote in the plebiscite designed to show unanimous public approval of the annexation of Austria and of Hitler's list of deputies for the Reichstag. The two questions were combined into one—the only one—on the ballot paper, and the circle in which to mark a *Ja* vote was considerably larger than the circle for a *Nein*. Bishop Sproll had no objections to the annexation of Austria, which had already taken place. But not wanting to express approval of men such as Rosenberg for public office, he stayed away from the polling station.

By late April, von Galen knew only rumors about Bishop Sproll, and he wrote Cardinal Bertram asking for an improved system of communications and more frequent meetings of bishops in the light of the further developments in the "war of destruction" against the Catholic Church.[22] In the same letter, he encouraged a previously mooted proposal for regular meetings of the metropolitan

21   Ibid.
22   Löffler, doc. 239, v. I, 617–19; Bertram's reply, doc. 241, v. I, 620–22.

archbishops but with a special request that all bishops be invited to take part. "This request," he said, "comes from the awareness of the responsibility for his own diocese, which each Ordinary personally bears, and which neither his own metropolitan nor a majority decision of the Bishops' Conference can take from him." "I myself," he continued, in words of criticism to which Cardinal Bertram took strong offense, "am happily ready, as I am sure every other German bishop is, to coordinate my positions and actions with the decisions of the other most worthy men, who most certainly outstrip me in virtue and pastoral wisdom, in age and experience. But I can do this with a peaceful conscience in important questions only when I have had the opportunity or at least the possibility, when decisions are being prepared, to present freely for discussion what may appear to me to be reasons against those decisions."

He added his own opinion, already forcibly expressed to Cardinal Pacelli in 1934 and 1936, that the bishops needed to become more vocal:

> In my opinion almost the only way of trying to stop outrageous infringements of rights, getting the enemy to fear to undertake further violent deeds and making the regime willing to deal with us fairly, is by making the deeds and practices that infringe on rights publicly known . . . The only way of doing this is by announcements made from all the pulpits at the command of the bishops. Thus, for example, to speak only of events of the past few months, the following should have been made known from all pulpits: the unlawful establishment of a community school in Trier-Koblenz, the closing of the main office of the episcopal conference in Düsseldorf, the actions against the bishop of Rottenburg, among others. These are things which have more than a local importance, which all the Catholic people, indeed all the German people should know

about, but which can be made known effectively only if all
the bishops make them known in an authentic way from all the
pulpits. Such announcements must be discussed, formulated
and approved of at regular meetings of bishops from all parts
of the country.[23]

Within a week, Bishop von Galen had more attacks of the regime
against the Church to deal with. In late April, the school issue
emerged again in the Diocese of Münster and once again in Oldenburg. The regime simply started opening community schools. As
in the case of the threatened removal of the crosses a year and a
half earlier, the stubborn farmers and the stubborn episcopal official,
Monsignor Vorwerk, were vehement in their protests. In the town
of Goldenstedt, both Protestant and Catholic parents participated
in a school strike. Fourteen men were arrested, twelve of whom
spent some time in concentration camps before being released in
late August. During the night of May 1, 1938, and again on the
eighth, crowds demonstrated outside his episcopal palace, singing
filthy, insulting songs, with no response from the police.

On May 10, the bishop was in Velen to confer the Sacrament of
Confirmation. He was heartily greeted by large crowds who knew
of the insults to which he had been subjected the previous week.
In his remarks to the crowd, he informed them of the situation of
Bishop Sproll of Rottenburg.[24] Those who are proud to call them-
selves pagans, he said,

> had made use of the fact that Bishop Sproll, as a free Ger-
> man man, exercising his rights, had declined to vote in the last
> Reichstag election. He had made no secret of his reasons of
> conscience, that he could not support the one list of candidates

---

23   Ibid.
24   Löffler, doc. 243, v. I, 627–29.

because on that list stood a large number of names of men who are open enemies of Christianity. There is in Germany no law obliging people to vote. It was always claimed that there was full freedom, that everyone could act according to his conscience . . . This is what the Bishop of Rottenburg did. This is what was used as a reason to force him out of his episcopal city of Rottenburg . . . It was officially declared that no one was able to protect the Bishop from harm, and now the head of state for Württemberg has told the Vicar General that he desires the bishop not to return to the diocese, as he can give no guarantee of the bishop's personal safety; in the event the bishop did return, he would take steps that no government official would have any communication with the bishop.

Thus has the Bishop of Rottenburg been in fact expelled from his episcopal city and his diocese; thus is a German bishop in fact given exactly so much respect that he cannot have dealings with any official of the State!

Does this not make us recall with fear the words of Christ: "He who rejects you, rejects me! He who does not receive you and refuses to listen to your words . . . truly, I say to you, it will go better with Sodom and Gomorrah on the day of judgment than with that city"? God preserve Rottenburg, God preserve Münster, God preserve our German people from the righteous judgment of God that is indicated in these words. Sodom and Gomorrah were reduced to empty deserts and have remained thus up to the present day![25]

Later that same month of May 1938, a decree from Münster's chief of police appeared in the newspapers, announcing that flags, banners, and ribbons in "church colors" could not be displayed

---

25   Ibid.

during church festivals on outdoor altars, private houses, or triumphal arches. Nor could flags in those colors fly from flagpoles, even if these were on church property. Decrees about the colors of banners, flags, and ribbons that could be displayed during processions would appear less threatening than angry mobs trying to break into episcopal palaces, but they only added to the anxiety of Catholics about the direction of the new Germany and their place in it. This was one more move in trying to make Catholicism invisible so that Nazism would be the only social force in Germany.

With the feast of Corpus Christi approaching on June 16, Bishop von Galen wrote to the government on May 27, asking for clarification as to what color combinations were forbidden. On festival days, people were accustomed to using a variety of colors to decorate their homes and streets and outdoor altars. The term "church colors," the bishop proposed, presumably applied to the yellow and white of the papal flag and the gold-red-gold combination of the flag of the Diocese of Münster. Could he assure people that they would not be arrested by the police if they used any other combination of colors?[26]

No reply came until the day before Corpus Christi, and this was not a direct reply to von Galen's question. Instead, it was a copy of a government order to the police, telling them to act firmly against any attempts to violate the flag laws. Von Galen objected in a further letter to Kurt Klemm, head of the regional government. If this order to the police was intended as the answer to his question, he said, he took strong offense. He had no intention of violating the laws or of allowing his priests and people to do so. The question was the interpretation of those laws. The chief of police in Cologne had indicated in writing to the Bishop of Osnabrück that there was no problem at all with decorating homes and procession routes with church colors,

---

26   Löffler, doc. 244, v. I, 629–30. See also documents 246, 247, 250, 253.

as long as the decorations were not so large as to have the character of flags. In Münster, on the other hand, church colors were forbidden without an indication as to what colors were intended. Further, church flags were permitted on church offices, but on the day of Corpus Christi, clearly a new interpretation was being implemented as to what properties were understood to be church offices. Police were visiting the houses of priests and of the auxiliary bishop to ask whether these were truly church offices; they were ordering flags to be removed and, in one case, were confiscating these flags.[27]

On June 22, another declaration from the local chief of police appeared in the newspaper. Claiming that many people had violated the flag rules on Corpus Christi but may have done so in ignorance, the decree went further than the previous one, now threatening punishment for floral arrangements in church colors and warning against attempts to circumvent the laws by displaying church colors in new combinations. Again, the bishop pressed for clarification. He would be glad to make a public declaration as to what colors were permitted, provided that he could be sure that his declaration would be recognized and respected by the police.[28] Klemm's reply came only after the Great Procession, which fell on July 4 that year.[29] Any colors, he stated, which were used in the past on flags and banners on the occasion of church festivals were now forbidden. Von Galen noted in reply that in the past, a great variety of colors had been used for decoration on both church and secular festivals. He protested that Klemm's interpretation outlawing all such combinations was not in accord with the interpretation in other regions of Germany.[30] There the matter lay. The major processions for the year had taken place. In the meantime, a new crisis had arisen.

27   Löffler, doc. 246, v. I, 631–33.
28   Löffler, doc. 247, v. I, 634–35.
29   Löffler, doc. 250, v. I, 640–41.
30   Löffler, doc. 244, v. I, 629–30.

After the Battle for the Cross in 1936 and the school strikes earlier in 1938, the regime had had enough of Episcopal Official Franz Vorwerk. On June 27, 1938, he was informed that, by orders of the Gestapo in Berlin, he was no longer permitted to reside in Oldenburg. Vorwerk replied that he could not leave his post by his own choice, as he was in Oldenburg at the command of his bishop. On the thirtieth, two policemen took Vorwerk by car to Münster and dropped him off in the cathedral square.

On the same day, the bishop sent a letter to the Catholics of Oldenburg:[31] "We are," he told them,

> in the presence of the disturbing fact that the official representative of the Bishop of Münster in the Land of Oldenburg, the spiritual leader of the Catholics in the Land of Oldenburg, has been forcibly removed from his post, and that thus his fulfillment of his duties, so important for the religious life of our *Heimat*, has been made impossible. I do not know what he is thought to be guilty of. No legal proceedings have been taken against him; no court has accused him of any punishable offense against any law. He has been sentenced and punished, without being given any opportunity to defend himself before a court and to prove that he has done nothing illegal.

Von Galen added that twelve men from Goldenstedt and Lutten had been incarcerated since May and that in recent weeks, four other priests had been exiled from Oldenburg. All these men had been punished without any proper legal proceedings or the possibility to defend themselves. "We are under authority," he told his people, "and we submit to authority, even if we cannot acknowledge that its actions are correct. We will follow the teaching of our savior, who has taught us by His example and His word: 'I say to you: do not resist evil' (Matt. 5:39). 'Do

31   Löffler, doc. 249. See also docs. 248, 251, 252, 254, 256.

not return evil for evil, or reviling for reviling' (1 Pet. 3:9). 'Do not be overcome by evil, but overcome evil through goodness' (Rom. 12:21)."[32]

For the Bishop of Münster, revolution against the regime was not an option. Instead, he adapted the plans he had made two years earlier in case he were to be rendered unable to fulfill his duties. Monsignor Vorwerk was the bishop's representative in Oldenburg, so the bishop ordered that church bells should not be rung in Oldenburg until the time of Vorwerk's return. The measure was fruitless. Nearly two years later, in May 1940, von Galen finally appointed a new episcopal official for Oldenburg, but the new official had nothing but trouble with the local government. Questions were raised as to whether the new official's appointment was properly done and therefore whether the government would recognize him. He was made to evacuate his offices and had difficulty negotiating for a suitable new space. In addition, the regime in Oldenburg refused to pay the traditional government subsidy for his salary and the expenses of his office. Eventually Julius Pauly, Oldenburg's minister of churches and schools, blamed all these problems on Vorwerk's opposition to Pauly's decree on crosses in the schools and to the new non-denominational schools. By such opposition, the Church had, wrote Pauly, violated its obligations and thus voided the treaty regulating relations between the Church and the Oldenburg government. Thus only in 1940 did von Galen first receive a statement as to what Vorwerk's supposed offenses had been.[33] Prior to naming a new official, the bishop had named Monsignor Vorwerk a residential canon of the Cathedral of Münster; this fact was seen as a provocation and would lead to more troubles with the government.

---

32   Ibid.
33   See Löffler, docs. 294–96, 298–305, 307, 309–13, 315–17, 321–24, 326–27, 371 (in v. II).

CHAPTER 14

Nights of Broken Glass

C atholics, of course, were not the only people who had troubles with the Nazi state, nor were their problems the worst. On the night of November 9–10, 1938, Hitler and his closest associates unleashed a wave of violence, the greatest yet, against the Jews. Hundreds of synagogues were set afire all over the country, while fire departments stood by and did nothing except make sure that the flames did not spread to adjacent so-called German buildings. So many windows were broken at Jewish-owned businesses and homes that the night became known as *Kristallnacht*, or "night of broken glass." Many Jews were killed or seriously injured, and within a week, thirty thousand Jewish men were sent to concentration camps.[1]

Nazi propaganda justified the violence on the basis of the murder of a German diplomat in Paris. Of course, that was a pretext, and another pretext would have been invented if that murder had not taken place. The aim was, in the words of Richard Evans, "the final,

---

1   Richard J. Evans, *The Third Reich in Power* (New York: Penguin, 2005), 580–91.

total expropriation of Germany's Jews and their complete segrega-
tion from the rest of German economy, society, and culture."[2]

It is easy for those in the present who know about the Holocaust
to say that here was a moment for morally upright Germans to speak
out. Those living within the events were not able to be so clear-
sighted. Nor is it easy for us to know whether Church leaders such
as Bishop von Galen contemplated speaking out. Certainly, people
had reason to fear danger to themselves for a protest that would
accomplish nothing and perhaps make things worse for the Jews.
Could speaking out accomplish anything without the support of a
large coalition of leaders willing to risk civil war to overthrow the
regime? Richard Evans summarizes the tragic situation:

> The Third Reich had passed a milestone in the persecution
> of the Jews. It had unleashed a massive outbreak of unbri-
> dled destructive fury against them without encountering any
> meaningful opposition. Whether people's sensibilities had
> been dulled by five years of incessant antisemitic propaganda,
> or whether their human instincts were inhibited by the clear
> threat of violence to themselves should they express open con-
> demnation of the pogrom, the result was the same: the Nazis
> knew that they could take whatever further steps against the
> Jews they liked, and nobody was going to try to stop them.[3]

Beth A. Griech-Polelle has criticized Bishop von Galen for not
speaking out publicly on behalf of the Jews after *Kristallnacht*. She
summarizes her criticisms:

> As an entity, the church leadership chose to focus on main-
> taining or saving Catholic institutional structures on Ger-
> man soil while losing sight of the larger, ultimate, and more

---

2   Ibid., 581.
3   Ibid., 589.

humane questions involved. Narrowing their protests to strictly "religious questions," they implied that governments rose and fell, but the church was to be eternal in its existence on German soil if not universal in its concerns. *Religious* came to mean not supporting the universal values of brotherly love and equality but rather keeping Catholic confessional schools, organizations, and associations alive. . . . In the end it was this focus on the tactical, short-term needs of the church, rather than on the long-term moral legacy, that opens the Church and von Galen to the severest critique. In short, the tragedy I focus on is how little of the immense cultural and spiritual capital of the Church was risked in combating a fundamentally anti-Christian regime.[4]

One might ask whether Griech-Polelle's charge makes too facile a distinction between Catholic institutional structures and larger, ultimate concerns—between tactical, short-term needs of the Church and the long-term moral legacy.[5] How was the Church to teach moral truth for the long term if she could not keep her schools and associations operating? Von Galen saw initially an anti-Christian and antihuman ideology at the heart of the regime. His aim was not just to keep Catholic schools and other institutions alive but to do so precisely in order that Catholic youth be inoculated against that ideology. The aim was to keep a Christian spirit alive in the younger generation of Germans. Surely that was a long-term, not a short-term goal. It should not be forgotten that his first protest to a government official after becoming Bishop of Münster was in regard to a change in the school curriculum that demonized the Jews. Nor

---

4   Beth A. Griech-Polelle, *Bishop von Galen: German Catholicism and National Socialism* (New Haven: Yale University Press, 2002), 7.

5   See the review of Griech-Polelle's book by John Jay Hughes, *Catholic Historical Review* 89, no. 2 (April 2003): 321–25.

should it be forgotten that he struggled with Rosenberg against a racist ideology. He knew well that Nazism had been founded on racism and paganism. But he also knew that politicians sometimes say one thing when they are out of power and do something else when they have power. Hitler, once he had taken power, had backed away from the overt anti-Christian and anti-Catholic positions that he and the Nazi Party had taken before 1933. It seemed a practical move, in the years between 1934 and 1936, to try to divide the Rosenberg faction off from Hitler and insist that Party officials live up to the word of the Führer. Keeping a space for a moral and Christian voice in the new Germany would have been more than a tactical victory for the Catholic Church. It would have moved the regime toward justice or at least blunted the effects of its injustices.

Von Galen's sermons and pastoral letters frequently included the theme of the equal dignity of every human being, no matter what that person's race or nation. His Easter pastoral letter of 1934 attacked the racism of Rosenberg's new paganism. His sermon at Xanten in February 1936 stressed that the martyrs were killed because they acknowledged "a transcendent God who rules all peoples with a fatherly love."

He had also used his wit to ridicule Nazi racism. When the Gestapo ordered that non-Aryans had to leave churches before the beginning of the sermons, he frequently mocked them, and in the presence of Nazi officials, by saying, "We can expect to hear a Child's voice from the crib, 'Come along, Mummy, we're not wanted here.'"[6]

Clemens August von Galen had nineteen centuries of Catholic history to reflect on, not to mention another two millennia of Jewish history, when considering how believers in a transcendent God should deal with an unjust regime. Not many regimes in history have been

---

6   Sedgwick, in Heinrich Portmann, *Cardinal von Galen*, trans. R. L. Sedgwick (London: Jarrolds, 1957), 16–17.

particularly just, but the Church has consistently taught the duty to obey the legitimate authorities—except when they command something sinful—and to pray for their rulers. Jesus taught His followers to render to Caesar the things that are Caesar's, and St. Peter taught the early Christians to honor the emperor, when the emperors were not particularly just and not particularly friendly to Jewish or Christian believers. But where is the line crossed between being a leaven in a society that is never going to be particularly just and deciding that an attempt must be made to overthrow an unjust regime? If one is too late in coming to that judgment, effective steps to overthrow the regime are often impossible. Could that be the real tragedy of the Church's attempts at coexistence with the Nazi regime?

Part of the tragedy, too, was that the Germans were accustomed to political thuggery and murder—by Nazis as well as by communists and others—for years before the Nazis took power. It was normal for people to get beaten and murdered, with no one brought to justice for it. To protest seemed pointless as well as dangerous. As is typical of a state that has become violent and lawless, citizens might hope that the perpetrators would be brought to justice but learned to expect nothing. To protest could not help those who had been killed and might bring others as well as oneself into danger. When the Nazis took power, brutality and intimidation became officially sanctioned. What good was asking for the police to find the criminals when government-sponsored propaganda made it clear that in the government's eyes, the victims deserved their fate? All one could do was hope that the violence would stop, urge friends who might be in danger to be on their guard, and do the same oneself. Thus there was no great public outcry after the "Night of the Long Knives" in 1934. Von Galen's reference to this event in the Xanten sermon— the section about "fresh graves in German lands"—came only a year and a half after the event. It was valuable as a moral statement but useless as a practical measure.

Kristallnacht was a huge step forward in Nazi brutality toward the Jews, but von Galen was convinced that no statement of his would be a help to the Jews and might well make their lot harder. When things got still worse, he advised a Jewish friend to leave Germany: "Leo, get out of Germany as quickly as possible! The political situation is reaching a crisis point. Today it's you they're after; tomorrow it will be me."[7] Catholics had not yet been subjected to the degree of brutality that had affected the Jews, but they were struggling in many ways. Priests and laity were in concentration camps. The Bishop of Rottenburg was exiled from his diocese and Bishop von Galen's episcopal official for Oldenburg exiled from his post. Nazi propaganda frequently coupled Jews and Catholics as enemies of the Nazi movement, as in the case of the mobs singing, "Hang the Jews, put the priests up against the wall." Catholic youth organizations were closed and their leaders denounced as enemies of the state, and the bishop's public protests were only used against them.

Bishop von Galen was away from Münster when the attacks on the Jews took place. After his return, a delegation from the Jewish community asked him if he would be willing to make a protest from the pulpit. He expressed his willingness to do so but asked whether a protest from him would only make things worse for the Jews. It was a serious question. Von Galen was willing to risk personal danger in standing up to Nazi injustice, but he had to take into account that

---

7   "Heute bist Du, morgen bin ich dran. Kardinal von Galen warnt die jüdische Familie Jonas aus Borken—Emigration in die USA." *Borkener Zeitung*, September 11, 2005. The story was related by the son of Leo Jonas in 2005 when he learned of the beatification of Cardinal von Galen. It bears the evidence of confused childhood memories—for example, he thought that his father and von Galen had been military comrades in World War I, which could not have happened, as von Galen was never a soldier—but it surely contains a kernel of truth. The father must have expressed to his family his gratitude for the timeliness of the warning and the bishop's bravery in speaking to him.

even if the Nazis did not touch him, other people could be brought into danger by his words. In the end, the rabbi and his associates decided it would be better if Bishop von Galen did not make a public protest at that time.[8]

Nor did he make a public statement about the fact that on November 11, 1938, two nights after *Kristallnacht*, the episcopal palace of Cardinal Faulhaber in Munich was damaged by demonstrators. The attack was closely connected with the attacks on synagogues and Jewish businesses two nights earlier and only reinforced the sense that Jews and Catholics together were under attack by an unjust regime. Von Galen wrote a brief letter to Faulhaber expressing his condolences, but nothing was said publicly.[9]

Bishop von Galen's own turn came in December. In May, his episcopal palace had been the scene of noisy demonstrations, and since then, the singing of offensive songs frequently took place about midnight. At about 4:30 on the morning of December 10, a new element was added. A group of hooligans threw bricks at the palace, breaking eight windows. With the bishop's popularity, this backfired on the Nazis. The policeman who responded to the call of the bishop's secretary, Father Portmann, was a devout Catholic. He agreed with all of von Galen's sarcastic complaints about the inadequacy of the police and agreed to repeat the complaints to his superiors. Meanwhile, crowds of sorrowful people stopped by on their way to the market or after morning Mass. "They looked at the holes in the windows, the splinters of glass and the stones on the floors," Father Portmann

8   Max Bierbaum, *Nicht Lob, Nicht Furcht: Das Leben des Kardinals von Galen* (Münster: Regensberg, 1946), 394–95; fuller discussion of differing accounts of the event in Hubert Wolf, *Clemens August Graf von Galen: Gehorsam und Gewissen* (Freiburg: Herder, 2006), 122–24.
9   Peter Löffler, ed., *Bischof Clemens August Graf von Galen: Akten, Briefe und Predigten 1933–1946*, 2nd ed. (Paderborn: Ferdinand Schöningh, 1996), doc. 264, v. I, 661.

later wrote. "Thus the incident acquired the notoriety of a public event. It had been suggested to the Bishop earlier that, as a gesture of protest, the broken window-panes might be ostentatiously replaced by wooden shutters or sheets of cardboard. He put that aside with a smile and the comment: 'We won't rub it in. They've got the worst of it anyhow.'" Later, an officer called on behalf of the chief of police and promised stronger police patrols and stern punishments for the offenders. The threat of a strong statement from the pulpit was not something the Nazis wanted to face at that time.[10] But in the end, to no one's surprise, no one was punished for the brick-throwing.

As the attack on Cardinal Faulhaber's palace indicated, leading Nazis connected the increased offensive against the Jews with an increased offensive against Catholicism. This affected the school issue. On November 11, 1938, the leadership of the National Socialist Teachers' League told their members to stop teaching religion "because we can no longer tolerate any glorification of the criminal Jewish people in German schools." The move, however, caused too great a reaction for the education minister, Bernhard Rust. When religious instruction completely disappeared from many schools, even the officially Catholic ones, so many protests came in that Rust issued an order urging the teachers to reconsider.[11] But he did so declaring that teachers had no need to fear that the religion curriculum approved by his ministry would oppose National Socialist principles, particularly in its presentation of Judaism. In various places, religion teachers were told to remove Old Testament history from their lessons as much as possible and to present the life of Jesus as "the heroic battle of the founder of Christianity against the destructive spirit of Judaism."[12]

---

10   Löffler, doc. 266, v. I, 662–63; Portmann, 163–64 (Eng. trans., 89–90).
11   Löffler, doc. 268, v. I, 665–69, esp. 665–66, n. 2.
12   Ibid., 667, n. 5.

CHAPTER 15

To Be or Not to Be

Bishop von Galen kept careful track of the attacks on the Catholic schools. On January 22, 1939, he summarized the situation in a letter to Cardinal Bertram, expressing his conviction that "the war of destruction against the Catholic Church has come to a decisive point, so that it is truly a question of 'to be or not to be.'"[1] As he saw it, the old dictum *Cuius regio, illius et religio* ("whose realm, his religion") was being introduced with potentially disastrous consequences. He insisted that the bishops' continued silence as the government decided the content of religious instruction would gradually lead to a triumph of Rosenberg's ideology.

Von Galen pointed out to Cardinal Bertram that Rosenberg had already boasted of success in establishing an "anti-Christian-Jewish" educational curriculum "in order to save the coming generation from the black swindle."[2] If things were to continue in this way,

---

1   Peter Löffler, ed., *Bischof Clemens August Graf von Galen: Akten, Briefe und Predigten 1933–1946*, 2nd ed. (Paderborn: Ferdinand Schöningh, 1996), doc. 268 and notes, v. I, 665–69.

2   In fact, Rosenberg had not used these words in the speech to which von Galen referred: Ibid., v. I, 668, n. 6.

von Galen warned, "Christian parents will eventually be obliged in conscience to keep their children away from school in order to protect them from a loss of faith," even in the hours of a so-called Catholic religion class. He called again for a public warning from the bishops: "We could manage to come to terms with the suppression of our organizations, with prohibition of processions and pilgrimages, even with an end of State financial support for the Church. But with a compulsory State school that makes our children into pagans? In my opinion, we must give our utmost in battle against this. And the necessity of this battle must be so clear to our Catholic people and remain so pressing in their sight that thousands will leap into the breach if the first leaders fall in the battle!"

Furthermore, von Galen said, "I do not have precisely formulated and comprehensive proposals to make. I must say openly that I have no hope for success from petitions to Berlin . . . And, as Bishop Berning recently told me, officials there in face-to-face meetings always end by acknowledging that our complaints are justified, but that they are hindered by the Party, and cannot count on our complaints being accepted by the Party."[3]

Despite his lack of hope in petitions, von Galen would make one more effort in the next month. This was preceded by one more stirring homily, given in the Münster Cathedral four days after the death of Pope Pius XI on February 10, 1939.[4]

The bishop spoke of the great respect with which Pope Pius was being praised in the press of the whole world, with the exception of the press in Russia and in Germany. He eschewed any attempt to give a complete picture of the pope's life, actions, and virtues. "My fellow Christians," he said, "I cannot do that, and I will not." He regarded such an attempt as a violation of filial piety. Just as it

3   Löffler, doc. 268, v. I, 665–69.
4   Löffler, doc. 272, v. I, 684–97.

is nearly impossible for a child to speak with justice of the goodness of his father or mother in front of others, so he had such love and respect and gratitude to Pius XI that he could not bring himself to describe in detail the life of this great man in public.

When one has such a father, he continued, one can overlook the fact that outsiders might not understand him. But to see one's noble and honored father publicly defamed requires a different response: "It is extremely bitter to me to have to speak of this today. I owe it to our beloved Holy Father Pius XI. I owe it to my own honor and nobility. I owe it to you, my diocesans, as the one called to represent you and speak for you, and I owe it to the honor of all Catholics in Germany and the world, to raise a protest and accusation against the treatment, the mistreatment, to which our beloved Holy Father has been publicly subjected in Germany even to the present day!"

Von Galen then detailed some of what he called the lies that were being retailed about the late pope in newspapers and in public speeches. What offended him most was the repeated claim that, out of hatred for Germany's renewed strength, Pius XI had entered into secret agreements against Germany with Soviet Russia and with Russian agents in other countries. This falsehood could only be supported by suppressing the truth about the countless speeches and actions the pope had taken against communism. "For example," stated the bishop,

> no German newspaper reported the major speech the Pope gave to thousands of pilgrims on May 31, 1936 on the occasion of his 80th birthday . . . as he warned the French Catholics against the invasion of Bolshevistic ideas and against cooperation with the proponents of those ideas. No German newspaper reported the touching words that Pope Pius XI spoke to the Spanish refugees who had fled the murderous Communist scoundrels in Spain. No German newspaper gave its readers the text of the great encyclical letter Pius XI issued on March 19, 1937,

in which he solemnly condemned godless Communism, warned the peoples of the world against it, and condemned and forbade even tactical cooperation with it. Indeed, printed translations of this most solemn denunciation by the Pope of godless Communism were confiscated by the police![5]

Why, he asked, should the truth about what Pius's stance on communism be hidden from the German people? Why should only those who claimed that Pius was a political enemy of Germany and entered into political alliances with Bolshevism have a free hand?

This, he said scornfully, was the pope who showed by word and deed that he did not engage in worldly politics. Although in times past, the popes were also worldly rulers, this was the pope who entered into a treaty with Italy whereby the popes gave up all their earthly power over the old Papal States. By the Lateran Treaty of 1929, Pope Pius kept only Vatican City, the smallest sovereign state in Europe, consisting of forty-four hectares and 930 inhabitants: "This was done only to ensure that the Pope would not be under a political leader to whom he would owe obedience. This frees the Pope from the suspicion of taking a party position in some eventual political conflict or war. But the deployment of worldly-political power is now out of the question and expressly rejected."

"Nevertheless," Clemens August continued, "it is claimed by German newspapers that Pope Pius XI, the leader who voluntarily shrank his worldly regime to an area of 44 hectares with 930 subjects, is carrying on a worldly struggle, a political power struggle, against a Reich of 80 million!"

The attacks against the pope were designed, the bishop asserted, to remove all influence of religion from public life, but in doing so, they caused great pain to the hearts of German Catholics. Rather than

---

5   Ibid.

serving the unity of the German people, the proponents of such propaganda put mistrust between them and all honor-loving people.

The claim that the pope was exercising political power also influenced the way people were looking on the upcoming election of a
new pope. "We are certain," said von Galen, "popes die, but the
Pope does not die!" Catholics, he added, were amused at the world's
speculations as to whether the next pope would be a religious or a
political pope. Of course, like Pius XI, he would be a religious pope.
But he would not fail to speak up if politics infringed on the realm
of religion, and for that, he would be attacked just as Pius XI was
attacked. Catholics in Germany would stand by him, and because
they had no newspapers or speakers' podiums from which to publicize their defense of the pope, they would often have to bear those
attacks with silence. "Today, however," the bishop concluded,

> I will speak loudly; in memory of Pope Pius XI, I will greet
> his successor the future Pope; in my name, in the name of all
> my diocesans, and united in spirit with all the millions of loyal
> German Catholics, I will publicly profess our conviction and
> our unrenounceable decision, in the words of our Westphalian
> fellow-countryman Baron Burghard von Schorlemer-Alst . . . On
> April 16, 1875, he replied as follows to those who at that time
> were insulting the Holy Father: "You can kill us! You can tear the
> hearts out of our bodies! But I say this to you: You can never tear
> these Catholic hearts away from the Vicar of Jesus Christ!"[6]

That sermon was on February 14, 1939. Within a week, the
bishop's plans for a final effort to save the Catholic schools were
in place. Priests were told to keep complete secrecy over the plans,
which involved reading a pastoral letter at all Masses on the twenty-
sixth of the month, followed by a show of hands by all the adults in

---

6   Ibid.

each church as to whether they desired to keep Catholic confessional schools.

Bishop von Galen's pastoral letter explained the legitimacy of and rationale for Catholic schools.[7] He reminded his people that a universal legal requirement to send children to state schools was a relatively recent historical development. Originally and by nature, the education of children is the parents' responsibility. Simultaneous classroom instruction was an invention of the Catholic Church, which founded schools from the elementary level through universities. In Germany, after the Protestant Reformation and the Peace of Westphalia that ended the Thirty Years' War, both the Protestants and the Catholics remained convinced that schools should be tied to the Church. Thus there were both Catholic and Evangelical Christian schools.

Over time, the state took on more responsibility for education, as was right in fulfilling its obligation to promote the common good. Quoting from Pius XI's 1929 encyclical letter *Divini Illius Magistri*, von Galen stressed that in its support for public and private schools, the state must always respect the natural right of the Church and of the parents to see that their children receive a Christian education. This, he noted, had been generally respected in the past in Germany and elsewhere in the world:

> In all modern States of the old and new world there is now a legal obligation to attend school. In connection with this, almost everywhere the rights of parents have been acknowledged and supported. They can decide freely whether to entrust their children to the state schools or to private schools . . . Thus, for example, in Italy, in France, in England, in Holland, in North and South America, in Japan, in addition to the state schools

---

7   Löffler, doc. 274, v. II, 699–705.

which in some countries are not religious, there is a richly developed Catholic school system, from elementary school up to vocational schools and universities. Everywhere, including in Germany, the Catholic religious orders have undertaken the greatest service.

With this historical and philosophical background, von Galen recalled and quoted the guarantees in the Concordat for a Catholic school system and private Catholic schools run by religious orders. Then he outlined how these guarantees were being violated. Among others,

- the private schools of the religious orders were being closed;
- teachers who had left the Catholic Church were being placed in Catholic schools;
- religious services were removed from the school day;
- teachers were forbidden to tell the children that they should attend divine worship and receive the Blessed Sacrament;
- teachers were forbidden to take part with their classes in church festivities such as processions;
- school books were introduced in which the Christian spirit was absent;
- the hours for religious instruction were curtailed;
- state officials made changes to the religious instructional materials without seeking or getting the approval of Church authorities;
- and now, after the Catholic schools had been weakened, their very existence was being fundamentally attacked with the move to require all children to attend the new "German community school."

This new school, according to the Nazi official in charge of teaching Party members the National Socialist worldview, was to be a confessional school. Just as much as the old church schools, it was to have a guiding principle of its entire program, but its formal principle was the National Socialist worldview. Its aim was to make the students firm believers in the ideas of Adolf Hitler. Von Galen wanted his people to have no doubt that in the express words of the Nazi leaders themselves, the new community schools intended to replace Christianity in the souls of the children with an alien ideology.

After the reading of the letter, all the adults in the churches were asked to stand. In the meantime, they had been carefully counted. All who wished to maintain Catholic confessional schools were asked to raise their right hands.[8]

On February 26, the reading of the pastoral letter and the survey of churchgoers took place as planned. After the totals had been communicated to his chancery, the bishop wrote letters to various government officials, including Adolf Hitler himself. In his letter to Hitler dated March 8, 1939, he stressed his duty to work against any danger to the German state. The closing of confessional schools against the wishes of loyal German citizens was such a danger. He informed Hitler of the opportunity he had given to his people to indicate their wishes on the question of Catholic schools, as Cardinal Schulte of Cologne had done earlier. Then he gave the results: "On Sunday, the 26th of February 1939, 824,122 adults were in church for the morning Masses in the Diocese of Münster. Of these, 813,471 indicated their support for Catholic confessional schools for the education of the young by raising their hand: expressed as a percentage, that comes to 98.70% of those in church."[9]

Von Galen never learned whether Hitler ever saw this letter. Certainly, it had no effect in saving the Catholic schools. In 1939, Hitler had other thoughts on his mind. He was preparing for war.

---

8   Ibid.
9   Löffler, doc. 277, v. II, 709–10.

CHAPTER 16

Does the Führer Know?

Despite the calls of bishops such as von Galen of Münster and von Preysing of Berlin for a more aggressive public stance, the German bishops continued Cardinal Bertram's policy of private protests supported by ever more extravagant public expressions of patriotism. When, in the autumn of 1938, Hitler stirred up a crisis over the Sudetenland and won from the western powers the partitioning of Czechoslovakia, Cardinal Bertram sent a telegram of congratulations to Hitler. This did nothing to stop the closing of the Catholic schools or to soften the anti-Catholic attitude of the Party-controlled press. Hitler's reply to the telegram was perfunctory, and there was no praise in the newspapers for the Church's patriotism.

Von Galen took note of this in April 1939 when Cardinal Bertram informed the bishops that the German cardinals intended to send a congratulatory telegram to Hitler on behalf of all the German bishops for his fiftieth birthday on April 20. Bertram had asked the bishops for approval of this intention, adding that he would take silence for consent. Von Galen, considering the fruitlessness of the telegram over the Sudeten crisis and the continuing introduction of the community schools, wrote that although he presumed that the cardinal and the other bishops understood things better than he did, his personal opinion was that such a gesture would be better omitted and might be seen by some as a scandal. Von Preysing was more cutting; it did not seem wise to him that such a message should be sent in the name of *all* the diocesan bishops, including the exiled Bishop of Rottenburg.[1] (This was a preliminary to a dispute that broke out during the Bishops' Conference in 1940, when von Preysing objected that Cardinal Bertram had sent birthday wishes to Hitler in the name of all the bishops; these wishes should not have included his name, he insisted, because he had not been asked beforehand.)[2]

On December 31, 1939, Bishop von Galen preached an end-of-the-year sermon in the Cathedral of Münster.[3] War was once again upon Germany and Europe. He had called for prayers for a just and lasting peace during the Sudetenland crisis of 1938 and again as Germany was about to invade Poland in 1939, but now the world faced, once again, the prospect of terrible bloodshed.

How was he able to persuade himself that this war fit the conditions traditionally accepted by the Catholic Church for a just war? He seems not to have found this too difficult. The traditional teaching on the conditions for a just war holds that a state has the right to defend itself against aggression and that it is the responsibility of the legitimate government to assess whether the conditions apply for the use of military force. Regardless of his thoughts about the regime, von Galen did hold that it was the legitimate government. Further, like many Germans who were not Nazis, he was convinced

---

1   Peter Löffler, ed., *Bischof Clemens August Graf von Galen: Akten, Briefe und Predigten 1933–1946*, 2nd ed. (Paderborn: Ferdinand Schöningh, 1996), doc. 280 and notes, v. II, 715–16.

2   Hubert Wolf, *Clemens August Graf von Galen: Gehorsam und Gewissen* (Freiburg: Herder, 2006), 104.

3   Löffler, doc. 292, v. II, 752–60.

that Germany had been a victim of an unjust peace at the end of the First World War. In his opinion, many of the nations of the world had fought the 1914–1918 war with the intention of destroying the German people and fatherland.[4] In a letter to his priests in September 1939, after war had been declared, he stated that this new war was in fact a renewal of the war that had been interrupted by an enforced peace some twenty years earlier. Although he was far from being a Nazi, he was pleased with the renewal of national pride that resulted from the foreign policy of the Hitler regime, and he may well have believed the propaganda that blamed the hostilities on foreigners' hatred of Germany and Germans. Joseph Goebbels's propaganda campaign against the Poles was particularly pernicious and effective in that regard. He had prayed for a peaceful resolution of the crises, and now he prayed for a true peace that would end the hostilities quickly. At the same time, he taught that German citizens in good conscience should support the war effort as a duty of patriotism and obedience to their fatherland. For the nearly six years of the war, much of his thought and action as a pastor and father was aimed at supporting those who were putting their lives at risk for the sake of their country and supporting their families on the home front, nearly every one of which had a father, brother, husband, or son serving in the military.

But it was one thing to support a nation's war effort and something else to support everything done by the nation's government. In his 1939 end-of-year sermon, von Galen brought forth a further argument for a better treatment for the nation's Catholics. A policy that alienates a great percentage of the nation's most loyal and obedient citizens, he argued, is not calculated to help that nation focus on the war effort. He reminded his listeners that Hitler, when he took power, had solemnly stated that Christianity would be the

---

4   See Löffler, doc. 279, v. II, 713.

foundation of the new Germany. In fact, however, this declaration was frequently denied in practice and by persons in high places, as evidenced by the widespread Party propaganda in favor of suicide and extramarital sexual relations. He reviewed many of the actions against the Catholic Church in the year just ending, particularly the closing of Catholic schools and the suppression of Catholic organizations. Even since the beginning of the war, the Nazis had closed down an organization of women dedicated to supporting young men studying for the priesthood, the central offices of the young women's organization, and the national Catholic organization of wives and mothers. All these actions contradicted the provisions of the Concordat of 1933, and in each case was done without right of appeal.

"My Christians!" he said. "I have frequently been asked: Does the Führer and Chancellor of the Reich Adolf Hitler know about these things? Does he know how blatantly the assurances which he gave when he took power have been ignored? Does he know about the improper way we have been treated by certain powerful officials, against whose prohibitions and punishments there is no appeal and no possibility of the restoration of justice by means of an independent court? Does the Führer know all this, and does he approve of it? This people have often asked."

He paused, then:

> My Christians, I do not know. I can only say, that in full awareness of my obligation under the oath I swore at the time of my ordination as a bishop, to fight against any danger that can damage the German people, I have personally written at length several times, and also in the year just ending, to the Führer and Chancellor of the Reich Adolf Hitler, to express our complaints and our concerns for the inner peace of our people, to put before him in a pressing way our concern for justice and freedom. Whether my appeals have reached the Führer,

I do not know. True, each time I have written I have received confirmation from the Reich Chancellory that my letters have been received there. But whether they have been placed on the Führer's desk, I have not been able to discover. In no case have I received an answer to the topics in my letter. And so I have to fear that it hasn't been possible to break through the wall that hinders the Führer from coming to know the complaints and concerns of the Catholics of Germany, concerns that we bring forward because the foundation given by God for all secure buildings, Jesus Christ and His truth and grace, are forgotten and rejected.[5]

Did Bishop von Galen really think that Hitler did not know what was going on? One suspects that the bishop was engaging in pious dissimulation, both in order to encourage his people to respect lawful authority and for the benefit of the Gestapo spies present in the cathedral. They could report to their superiors, as they frequently did, that the Bishop of Münster was hostile to Nazism, but as long as he blamed the injustices against Catholics on lower officials, frequently unnamed, they could not report a single word that he spoke in criticism of Hitler himself.

Did the Führer know? He had to know in general if not in detail. But it was his practice to leave details to his subordinates and only to rein them in when it was expedient to do so. Von Galen always tried to leave him room for such moves. If Hitler wanted a better relationship with the churches, which he did at times when he needed public support, he could curtail the activities of the more aggressive of his followers and let them take the blame for their unjust actions. Despite the general anti-Christian character of the Nazi movement, it was known that there were divisions of opinion in the Party as to

5   Löffler, doc. 292, v. II, 758.

how far the churches should be attacked and how far they should be conciliated.

Bishop von Galen saw these differences firsthand during 1940. This was the year when he finally appointed a new episcopal official for Oldenburg to replace the banished Monsignor Franz Vorwerk. During the eight months of ultimately fruitless negotiations and appeals that followed, which sought official recognition of the new episcopal official, the return of his office and house, and payment of his salary from the government,[6] von Galen learned that there was division among officials in Berlin, who were fulfilling Hitler's wish at that time to conciliate the Church, and officials in Oldenburg: notably Gauleiter Röver, still smarting over his public humiliation at the time of the Battle for the Cross, and Minister Pauly, who was the author of the decree to remove crosses from the schoolrooms and the main agent of the introduction of the new non-denominational schools. In this case, the officials in Oldenburg won.

In January 1941, the bishop announced in a pastoral letter his intention to renew the dedication of the diocese to the Sacred Heart of Jesus.[7] By this religious act, which he desired each parish and each family to undertake in a solemn way and to renew on the first Friday

6   The final note from the apostolic nuncio to von Galen indicating that there was no point in continuing was in fact another twenty months later, in August 1942. See Löffler, docs. 294–96, 298–305, 307, 309–13, 315–17, 321–24, 326–27, 371 (in v. II). These provisions, which may seem outlandish to Catholics accustomed to paying for the support of their clergy, had a history behind them that makes them easier to understand. After an immense amount of Church property was expropriated by secular governments in the nineteenth century, the restoration of peace between Church and state involved at least a partial restitution. In Oldenburg, that involved setting up a fund from the sale of certain of those properties, from which the support payments were to be made for the episcopal official and his office.

7   Löffler, doc. 325, v. II, 816–26.

of each month, he hoped to keep all the faithful of the Diocese of Münster firm in their Catholic faith:

> Where parents and children, those in authority and those under authority, take conscientiously their vow to offer all their thoughts, desires, and actions to the Most Sacred Heart of Jesus, the result will be a mutual understanding and a peace in the house and family greater and more perfect than could have been imagined. An atmosphere will rule there, which will not allow discord and quarrelling to arise. If the parents always look to Jesus in order to learn from Him, then they will find the way to act and the words to say, that will enable them to teach and build up their children in the fear of God and in loyalty to the Faith. If the young accustom themselves from an early age to the holy practice of examining all the desires of their hearts, all their projects and plans, in the presence of the Most Sacred Heart of Jesus, in order to form them according to that model, then they will build a sturdy approach to life that will enable them to hold firmly to a genuinely Catholic way of life, even after they have left their parents' home and have to live in a different atmosphere.[8]

The lengthy letter contained a full explanation of devotion to the Sacred Heart and expressed the strong and tender piety that von Galen had learned as a child at Castle Dinklage. Yet the Nazis saw it as a document aimed at spreading unrest among the people and discontent against the state.[9] The bishop was renewing a dedication of the diocese first made by his predecessor Johann Bernhard Brinkmann after his return from exile during Bismarck's *Kulturkampf.* Von Galen's letter gave at length the history of Bismarck's attempts

---

8   Ibid., 824.
9   Ibid., 826–27, n. 5.

to unite the German people in religion by suppressing Catholicism, a history which included Brinkmann's arrest, exile in Holland, and eventual triumphant return. The Nazis read the letter correctly when they saw it as inviting its readers to compare that situation with their own under the Nazi regime. As with the question, "Does the Führer know?" he was reminding his people that powerful forces sought to draw them away from their Catholic faith. They would need his combination of simple piety and "brutal Catholicism" if they were not to lose their bearings in the times through which they were living.

Chapter 17

"I Lift Up My Voice"

The war continued, with success after success for the German forces. But the British would not quit. Nor did the Nazis cease their injustices on the home front. People deemed dangerous to the regime or of the wrong racial type found themselves in concentration camps. Propaganda was growing that would justify the killing of the mentally disabled. Rumors were spreading that in parts of Germany, the Gestapo were confiscating the houses of religious orders. In Münster, poor Monsignor Vorwerk again found himself a subject of the attentions of the Gestapo. Since being exiled from Oldenburg in 1938, he had resided in Münster. Now, on May 4, 1941, he was arrested at his house and taken to the home of a family in Mecklenburg, a Protestant area far from Münster, and told that he must reside there and not return to Münster.

On May 26, Bishop von Galen wrote a letter to Bishop Berning of Osnabrück: "We see again the blind hatred and arbitrary abuse of power that we have to deal with," he wrote. Detailing many of the infringements of the Church's liberty, he wondered whether the bishops could justify their policy of defending the Church "in the almost completely passive way" they had followed up to this point. Bishops

such as St. Thomas Becket and St. Stanislaus suffered martyrdom
for the sake of the Church's freedom. He asked Berning, who was
chairman of the meetings of the western German bishops, to raise
the question whether the time had not come for them to take similar
risks. The war held them back from taking a stronger line, he noted,
but the regime had only seen this as weakness. Refraining from public protests had been his policy also:

> I have always quieted my conscience by saying to myself, "If
> Cardinal Bertram and so many other bishops, who are above me
> in age, experience, and virtue, can remain quiet in the face of
> all this, and be satisfied with the ineffective paper protests, com-
> pletely unknown to the public, of the Chairman of the Fulda
> Bishops' Conference, it would be presumptuous and insulting
> to the other bishops, and perhaps even foolish and wrong, if
> I were to force myself to come out into the open and perhaps
> even make things worse by provoking even more brutal mea-
> sures against the Church."

"But," he added, "I am coming to the point at which I can no longer
bring my conscience to rest with such 'arguments from authority.'"[1]

A couple of weeks later, a Dominican priest named Father Braun
visited him. In his memoirs, Father Braun wrote that he showed
Bishop von Galen lists of religious houses that had been confiscated.
Von Galen replied that no such things had happened in the Münster
Diocese.

"Your Excellency," Father Braun replied, "one should pick up a
hose when his neighbor's house is on fire. One mustn't wait until his
own roof timbers are burning."

---

1   Peter Löffler, ed., *Bischof Clemens August Graf von Galen: Akten, Briefe und
      Predigten 1933–1946*, 2nd ed. (Paderborn: Ferdinand Schöningh, 1996),
      doc. 330, v. II, 837–38.

"Yes, then what should I do? A pastoral letter?"

"Not a pastoral letter. When a bishop fires off an entire sermon from the hip, then we're getting somewhere."

"Yes, then we will be forbidden to preach."

"If I were a bishop, that wouldn't stop me."

"Then we'd be imprisoned."

"Then we would be a step forward, if a bishop were imprisoned," said the Dominican. According to his account, the bishop ended the interview with the words, "Trust in God and the Holy Spirit and the prudence of the bishops."[2]

It was not long before the bishop took the risk.

On Saturday, July 5, 1941, the Royal Air Force launched its first massive air raid over the city of Münster. The annual diocesan pilgrimage to the Marian Shrine of Telgte for the feast of the Visitation was scheduled for the next day. Only when they learned that the trains to Telgte were not running did people realize the severity of the bomb damage. Many of the faithful, however, had already planned to travel to Telgte on foot. Thus a great crowd was present to seek the aid of the sorrowful Mother. During the pontifical Mass, the bishop read out a joint pastoral letter of the German bishops against the euthanasia of the mentally ill. The bishops were alarmed that the government was now involved in the killing of persons with psychological ailments, a practice that Nazi propaganda had been justifying for some time. Bishop von Galen elaborated on some of the points in the joint pastoral letter at great length.[3] In four weeks, he would devote the third of his great sermons to this topic.

During the next few days, he visited the home of some relatives to take part in the celebration of a golden wedding anniversary. He kept

---

2   Hubert Wolf, *Clemens August Graf von Galen: Gehorsam und Gewissen* (Freiburg: Herder, 2006), 105–6.

3   Heinrich Portmann, *Cardinal von Galen*, trans. R. L. Sedgwick (London: Jarrolds, 1957), 99.

in touch with news in Münster as even more bombing raids took place. In four nighttime raids between the sixth and the tenth, the Royal Air Force dropped 890 high-explosive bombs and 10,000 incendiary bombs on the historic inner city. Forty-seven people were killed.[4] In the absence of bomb shelters, many people took to the countryside to sleep in the fields, rushing back afterward to see if their homes were on fire or still there. The bishop returned on July 10 and visited the most gravely damaged areas, offering his consolation to those affected. That night, the air raid sirens wailed again, but this time no bombs fell. Bishop von Galen could not be persuaded to take shelter in the cellar of his episcopal palace, even though during one of the air raids earlier in the week, the palace had been struck by an incendiary bomb. The fire it caused had been extinguished before causing much damage.

This was the moment the Gestapo chose to introduce in Münster the measure that had already been used in many other parts of Germany, that of expropriating the property of religious houses. They must have thought that the necessity of finding shelter for the homeless and wounded would provide a good excuse for this attack on the Church. They did not reckon on the Bishop of Münster.

On Saturday, July 12, he heard the news that two of the Jesuit houses were being expropriated and the Jesuits evicted. Furious, he rushed to both houses and for the first time confronted Gestapo men face to face, shouting that they were thieves and robbers. On his way home he said, "Now I can be silent no longer."

Father Portmann, the bishop's secretary, recalled that when von Galen came to supper that evening, he had already been working at his typewriter for an hour:

> Leaning forward with his elbows on the table, he rested his head on both hands; what he then said about the events of that

---

4   Löffler, v. II, 841, n. 1, with reference to Stadtmuseum Münster, *Bomben auf Münster* (1983), 35.

afternoon was the agonized cry of a man shaken to the depths of his soul. In the course of years I never saw the Bishop so distressed; neither before nor afterwards did he moan; only on that evening. Silent and oppressive, the hours of night brooded over the palace. Doors and windows were wide open. One heard only the slow tapping of the typewriter; now and then the Bishop coughed or cleared his throat. Only once he rose and came upstairs to the floor under the roof, where a servant named Rüsenberg and I, owing to a threatening thunderstorm, were busy spreading a tarpaulin to stop the rain from pouring in through holes made in the bombardment. Half-jokingly, he warned us to take care not to get a bad fall and advised us to pray to our guardian angel. With his long pipe in his hand, he walked slowly back to his room. In that night he wrote the words which in the eyes of the world have indissolubly bound up his personality with the city of Münster. He was firmly convinced that the enemies of the Church would soon put an end to his life here on earth. Looking death in the face, he trod the way of conscience and faithfulness fully ready to receive at God's hands the grace of martyrdom. On the day of his consecration as bishop, as a token that he was wedded to his bishopric, the golden ring had been bestowed on him. The ring should never be broken, so he had then vowed. The good shepherd giveth his life for his sheep. Priests of his diocese were suffering in the camps and dungeons of the Gestapo, or, driven from their homes, were pining in loneliness. For them he wrote in that night the words of righteousness.[5]

The next day, Sunday, July 13, 1941, Clemens August Count von Galen, the Bishop of Münster, mounted the pulpit in the nave of the church of St. Lambert, near the cathedral. It had been announced

---

5   Portmann (Eng. trans.), 102.

that the bishop would preach in the Lambertikirche, his former parish church, as the cathedral had been damaged by bombs and was unusable. The Catholics of Münster packed the church, eager to hear consoling words after the horrible bombing raids.

He indeed spoke words of fatherly consolation.[6] What most of the congregation did not know was that his sermon would not focus on the bombing. In a few moments, he was going to take his life in his hands by making an outspoken protest against the Gestapo, the Nazi secret state police. It was the first of what came to be known as the three great sermons of the summer of 1941.

He began, of course, by speaking of the bombing and expressing his hope that the efforts of the state and municipal authorities, as well as the brotherly love of his listeners and their donations to a special collection on that day, would help those who were most affected by it. Then he hinted that the subject of his sermon would be something else: "I had intended," he said, "to add a few words about the meaning of divine afflictions: how through them God seeks to call us back to Himself." The German word for an affliction or a divine visitation is *Heimsuchung*, built on the word for home, *Heim*, and the word for a search or a seeking, *Suchung*. Through the visitation, the *Heimsuchung* of the bombing raids, the bishop said, "God wants to call Münster back home to Himself." He recalled that their forefathers in Münster were always *at home* with God, always *at home* in His holy Church, in their public life as well as in their family life and in business. "Has it always been the same in our days?" he asked, then repeated, "God wants to call Münster back home to Himself!"

Thus the bishop considered the bombings as a call for repentance. This, he continued, was the subject he had planned to elaborate on in this sermon:

6   Löffler, doc. 333, v. II, 843–51.

But for today I must leave this aside, because I find myself compelled to speak out publicly on something else: a shocking event which happened to us yesterday, at the end of this week of horror.

All Münster still feels the effects of the awful devastation that the foreign enemy inflicted on us during this week. Then yesterday, at the end of the week, yesterday, on the 12th of July, the Secret State Police confiscated both establishments of the Society of Jesus, the Jesuit Order, in our city: House Sentmaring on the Weselerstrasse and the Ignatius House on Königstrasse; threw the inhabitants out of their homes; and ordered the fathers and brothers immediately, on the same day, yesterday, to leave not only their houses, not only our city, but the Province of Westphalia and the entire Rhine Province. And the same hard fate was inflicted, also yesterday, on the Missionary Sisters of the Immaculate Conception in Wilkinghege, on Steinfurterstrasse. Their house too was confiscated; the sisters have been ordered out of Westphalia and must leave Münster by six o'clock this evening.

Father Portmann reported that for the first ten sentences or so of the sermon, the bishop's voice quavered a bit. After that, "a wonderful strength and serenity came over him. That tall pastoral figure stood forth full of solemn dignity; his voice had a sound of thunder as the words fell on the ranks of the spellbound hearers, some trembling, some gazing up at him with tears in their eyes. Protest, indignation, fiery enthusiasm followed each other in successive waves."[7]

The attack on the religious orders had come to Westphalia, he told his hearers. It had already come to other parts of Germany and occupied lands. He predicted that more such horrific news could be expected in the days to come:

---

7   Portmann (Eng. trans.), 104.

That here also one convent after another will be confiscated, its occupants, our brothers and sisters, children of our families, true fellow Germans, will be thrown out into the streets like helots with no rights, chased out of the country like vermin.

And all this takes place at this moment! When everything shakes and trembles at the prospect of more nightly air raids that could kill us all, that could make any one of us into a homeless refugee! This is the moment that they drive innocent, indeed most worthy men and women, highly-esteemed by countless people, out of their humble homes; that they make fellow Germans, our fellow citizens of Münster, into homeless refugees.

"Why?" the bishop asked. He had been given no explanation except "state police reasons." None of the fathers, brothers, or sisters had been accused of any crime, and if so, they should be brought before a court. The innocent should not be punished along with the guilty.

In normal situations, Catholic priests or bishops in Westphalia would not encourage shouts or applause from the congregation during their sermons, but this was not a normal situation. "I ask you," Bishop von Galen cried out to the congregation, "before whose eyes the Jesuit Fathers and the Sisters of the Immaculate Conception have for years led their religious life dedicated solely to the glory of God and the salvation of their fellow men, I ask you: Who holds these men and women guilty of a crime deserving punishment?" The Gestapo informants in the church reported to their leaders that shouts of "No one!" came from the congregation. "Who presumes to make an accusation against them?" the bishop continued, and again came cries of "No one!" "If anyone does," he added, "then let him make his testimony! Not once has the Secret State Police produced such a witness, to say nothing of a court or the public prosecutor!" Now loud jeers came from the people.[8] Clemens August continued:

> I bear witness here as the bishop, who has responsibility of watching over the religious orders, that I have the highest esteem for the silent, humble Missionary Sisters of Wilkinghege, who have been driven out today. They were founded by my honored episcopal friend and fellow countryman, Bishop P. Amandus Bahlmann, primarily for the missions in Brazil, where he himself, highly-respected among the Germans in Brazil, worked tirelessly and successfully until his death three years ago.
>
> I bear witness as a German man and as bishop, that I have the greatest respect and reverence for the Jesuit Order, which I have known by close observation since my early youth, for fifty years; that I will remain bound in love and gratitude to the Society of Jesus, my teachers, guides, and friends, until my last breath. And that today I cherish that much more reverence for them; today, in the very moment that the prophecy of Christ to His disciples is once more fulfilled: "As they have persecuted me, so they will persecute you also. If you were of the world, the world would love its own. Because you are not of the world, but I have chosen you out of the world, therefore the world hates you."
>
> Thus I salute them today from this place; and also in the name of the true Catholics of the city of Münster and the diocese of Münster, I salute in heartfelt love these men and women, chosen by Christ and hated by the world, as they go off in their undeserved exile.
>
> May God reward them for all the good they have done for us; may God not punish us and our city that such an unjust mistreatment and banishment was visited here upon his true

---

8   Löffler, doc. 333, v. II, 843–51.

disciples! May God's omnipotence return to us these dear victims of exile, our brothers and sisters, as soon as possible.

My dear diocesans! Because of the terrible afflictions caused by the bombing raids, I had wanted to keep silent in public about other recent measures of the Secret State Police that also called for my public protest. But if the Secret State Police takes no consideration for the events which have rendered hundreds of our fellow citizens homeless, if just at this moment they throw innocent fellow citizens into the streets and drive them from their native place, then I dare not hesitate to make my justified protest—and to utter my earnest warning.

Frequently in recent times and at short notice we have seen innocent, well-respected Germans imprisoned without sentence and without opportunity for defence, robbed of their freedom, thrown out of their home province and interned somewhere, all at the hands of the Secret State Police.

In the last few weeks, two of my closest advisers, members of the Chapter of our Cathedral, were suddenly taken from their homes by the Secret State Police, taken away from Münster, banished to distant places, where they were told to remain. My protests to the Imperial Minister of Religion in the past weeks have not received a single answer. This much was able to be established by telephoning the Secret State Police: there is no accusation or charge of an act deserving punishment against either of the two members of the Cathedral Chapter. They have been sentenced to banishment without any guilt, without any accusation, and without any opportunity to defend themselves.

Christians! Listen carefully to this: It has been officially confirmed to us that the chapter members Vorwerk and Echelmeyer will not be charged with a punishable offence. They have done nothing deserving of punishment! And nevertheless they are punished by banishment!

And why? Because *I* did something that the regime did not like. In three of the four cases of vacancies in the Cathedral Chapter in the last two years, the regime informed me that they were not pleased with the person I nominated to fill the post. Since the Prussian Concordat of 1929 expressly excludes a right of veto on the part of the regime, in two of those four cases I nevertheless went ahead with the nomination. I did no wrong in doing this; I merely made use of my documented right. I can prove that in every case. Let them bring me before a court if they think that I have acted illegally. I am certain that no independent German court will convict me of any wrong-doing in regard to the appointment of the chapter members!

Is this the reason that they haven't used a court, but rather the one institution in the German Reich that unfortunately is not subject to review by any court?[9]

Now Bishop von Galen's attack on the Gestapo came to full force:

In the face of the physical superiority of the Secret State Police every German citizen is completely defenceless and unprotected. Completely defenceless and unprotected! This has been the experience of many Germans in the last several years: such as our dear religion teacher Friedrichs, who was incarcerated without a trial and without a sentence of a court; and also of the two members of the Cathedral Chapter, who languish in exile; and so today is it the experience of the members of our religious orders, who yesterday and today have been suddenly expelled from their homes, from the city, and from the province.

None of us is certain, no matter whether he knows himself to be the most loyal, conscientious citizen, no matter that he be

---

9   Ibid.

completely certain of his innocence, that he won't one day be taken from his home, robbed of his freedom, and thrown into the cells and concentration camps of the Secret State Police.

I am certain about this in my own case: that could happen to me, today, or any day. Since I will then no longer be able to speak openly, today I will speak openly. I want to give a public warning against continuing along a path that, I am strongly convinced, calls down God's punishment on man and must lead to unhappiness and ruin for our people and our fatherland.[10]

With these strong words, von Galen directly attacked not only the Gestapo but the unjust system that allowed it to operate without the oversight of an independent judiciary. Now he called a leading Nazi legal theorist to his support. In an article earlier that year in the *Journal of the Academy for German Law*, Dr. Hans Frank, the governor general of occupied Poland, stressed that it was essential for the accused in a criminal proceeding not to be condemned by the arbitrary power of the state but always to have the right to defend himself. Dr. Frank argued that the Nazis should be just as loud and clear as others in defending courageously the authority of justice in an enduring social order. Bishop von Galen then asserted his claim as a bishop to speak on behalf of justice and declared himself in full accord with the argument of that leading Nazi legal theorist:

I am conscious that as a bishop, as a proclaimer and guardian of the order of justice and morality willed by God, the order that gives to everyone his fundamental rights and freedoms before which, by God's will, every human claim must come to a stop, I am called, just as Minister Frank is, to plead courageously for the authority of justice and to condemn the condemnation of

10   Ibid.

the innocent without the opportunity of defence as an injustice crying out to heaven!

Christians! The imprisonment of many persons of good reputation without the possibility of defence and the judgement of a court, the deprivation of the freedom of the two chapter members, the dissolution of the monasteries and the banishment of innocent religious, our brothers and sisters, compel me to recall publicly the ancient, never-to-be-shaken truth: *"Justitia est fundamentum regnorum!"* Justice is the one solid foundation of every political system!

The right to life, to inviolability, to freedom, is an indispensable part of any moral social order. Certainly the State has the authority to curtail these rights by way of punishment, but only in regard to law-breakers whose guilt has been established by an impartial legal proceeding. The State which oversteps this divinely willed limit and imposes or permits the punishment of the innocent, undermines its own authority and the respect for its sovereignty in the minds of the citizens.

Sadly, in recent years we have had to witness over and over again, that punishments of more or less severity, mostly deprivations of freedom, have been imposed without any crime being proved against the victims by a proper legal procedure, and without their being given an opportunity to defend their rights or to make known their innocence. How many Germans have languished in prison or in concentration camps, have been banished from their home territories, without ever having been sentenced by a regular court; or, after having been acquitted by a court or having completed the sentence imposed by a court have again been taken into custody and imprisoned by the Secret State Police. How many have been expelled from their homes and from the place of their work! I recall again the honorable Bishop of Rottenburg, Joann Baptist Sproll, a venerable man

70 years of age, who recently had to celebrate his 25th anniversary as a bishop far from his diocese, because three years ago the Secret State Police exiled him from his diocese. I mention again our two Cathedral Chapter members, the worthy Fathers Vorwerk and Echelmeyer. I think of our honored Religion Teacher Friedrichs, who languishes in a concentration camp. I will forego mentioning other names. The name of a Protestant man who risked his life for Germany in the [First] World War as an officer and submarine commander, and subsequently worked as a Protestant minister in Münster, and whose freedom was stolen from him several years ago, is known to all of you, and we all have the highest respect for the valor and courageous faith of this noble German man.[11]

From this example, my Christians, you see that I am not dealing with a concern specifically of the Catholic Church, but a Christian, yes, a universal human and national, religious concern.

"Justice is the foundation of states!" We grieve, we see with the greatest sorrow, how that foundation is being shaken today, how justice, that natural and Christian virtue, indispensable for the orderly stability of every human community, is not being unequivocally recognized and esteemed for everyone. Not only on account of the rights of the Church, not only on account of the rights of the human person, but also out of love for our people and earnest concern for our fatherland, we beg, we insist upon, we demand: Justice! Who could fail to have anxiety for the stability of a house when he sees that the foundations are being undermined?

"Justice is the foundation of states!" If the holders of power in a state wish to fight against the illegal use of force by those

---

11   The bishop was referring to Martin Niemöller.

who happen to be stronger, against the oppression of the weak and their reduction to an unworthy servitude, they can do this with a hope of lasting success only if the holders of state power themselves bow before the royal majesty of Justice and use the sword of retribution only in the service of Justice. The only holder of power who can count on a noble success and the free service of honorable men will be the one whose actions and punishments are seen by the light of independent judgment to be free of all arbitrariness and measured by the impartial scales of Justice. For this reason the practice of condemnation and punishment without the possibility of defence, without legal proceedings, produces what Imperial Minister Dr. Frank calls "the condemnation without trial of those considered guilty from the start," a feeling of having lost all rights and a sense of anxious fear and servile cowardice, which must in the long run lead to a destruction of the national character and tear the community apart.

"This is the conviction and the concern of all right thinking German people," the bishop continued. Once again, he was able to quote from a legal article by a judge on the importance of independent courts to review decisions of the authorities. This is all the more important, the judge argued, the greater the power those authorities hold. Such independent reviews, von Galen continued, were not possible in regard to the actions of the Gestapo: "Since none of us knows a way for an independent review of the measures of the Secret State Police, of their restrictions on liberty, their prohibitions of residence, their arrests, their imprisonment of German citizens in concentration camps, there is already a feeling of a lack of rights, indeed, of a cowardly fear, in large sectors of the German people, which has seriously damaged the community." Here the bishop paused to give the next sentence the effect of a formal proclamation:

The duty of my episcopal rank, the duty of my oath, according to which I swore before God and before the representative of the Regime of the Reich to use my energies "to ward off any danger that may threaten the German people," force me to make this public warning in the light of the deeds of the Secret State Police.

Christians! Perhaps someone will charge me with weakening the home front of the German people during a time of war by these frank words. Against such a charge let me declare: It is not I who am the cause of any possible weakening of the home front; it is those who, despite the war situation, despite our present necessity, yes, here in Münster at the end of a horrifying week of terrifying enemy attacks, subject innocent people to hard punishments without trial, without possibility of defence, rob our Religious, our brothers and sisters, of their property, put them on the streets, hunt them out of the province! They destroy the security of rights; they undermine trust in the law; they destroy our trust in the leadership of our country. And so in the name of all upright German people, in the name of the majesty of justice and in the interests of peace and the solidarity of the home front I lift up my voice in protest, I proclaim loudly as a German man, as an honorable citizen, as a minister of the Christian religion, as a Catholic bishop: "We demand justice!"

If this call remains unheard and unanswered, if the rule of the queen Justice is not restored, then despite the heroism of our soldiers and their glorious victories, our German people and fatherland will perish through inner rottenness and decay!

Let us pray for all who are in need, especially for our exiled Religious; for our city of Münster, that God preserve us from further hardships; for our German people and fatherland and its Leader: Our Father, who art in heaven . . .[12]

---

12   Löffler, doc. 333, v. II, 843–51.

These lengthy quotations from the sermon show the force of von Galen's rhetoric and his argument. Repeating and stressing the suddenness and arbitrariness of the eviction of the religious fathers and sisters, as well as the other acts of the Gestapo and the innocence and honorable status of the victims, he brought his audience to a state of high emotional indignation. But he was aiming at much more than arousing emotions. He sincerely loved his country. He honestly believed that a state not founded on justice was bound to perish. In speaking on behalf of the majesty of justice, he voiced a real concern for the peace and well-being of his country and its people. As had been his tactic through the years in making appeals to government authorities, he supported his argument with quotations from high Nazi officials, who themselves argued against arbitrary arrests and convictions without process of law. This supported his point that Germany was a house divided against itself, a house built, to use his metaphor, on foundations that were being undermined. He forestalled the charge that he was weakening the home front by stating that the real cause of any weakening of the home front was the injustice of the Gestapo. Against the claim that he was an "internal enemy" of Germany during its war effort, he was laying the groundwork for what he would state explicitly in his next sermon. Germany was fighting against an external enemy *and* an internal enemy. The internal enemy was Germany's own security apparatus with its secret police and concentration camps. In defending his duty to speak out, von Galen even cited the oath he had sworn before Hermann Goering in 1933 upon accepting his nomination as a bishop. The oath of loyalty required by the Concordat between the Holy See and Nazi Germany did not merely give him a right to speak out; it demanded that he do so as a loyal German citizen.

The Gestapo report on the sermon claimed that the bishop delivered his sermon with tears rolling down his face. Both Nazis and anti-Nazis agreed that the sermon had a profound effect on its hearers, who left the church in a state of great agitation. Bishop von Galen was met in the sacristy by an enthusiastic throng of clergy, including many members of the Cathedral Chapter, one of whom asked Portmann for the typescript. At this point, however, the secretary held on to it. After they returned to the episcopal palace, von Galen told him that if the Gestapo came asking for it, he was quietly to hand it over. As the bishop had every reason to expect that the Gestapo would come for him, he had already hidden away two carbon copies. But the Gestapo never came.[13]

That evening, Portmann handed the original to a priest, who copied it and returned it, and then to another priest who did the same. The next morning, it was in the hands of Father Uppenkamp, and a process of copying and recopying began. Portmann wrote:

> On the Monday evening the office of the Caritas sent attache-cases full of [copies of the sermon] to the railway-station; thence they were scattered in smaller packets into the pillar-boxes of several Westphalian towns. Copies were sent off specially to all the leading clergy in Germany and also the chief personages in the Army, among others to Field Marshal von Kluge, who then commanded an Army Group on the Eastern Front. All that had happened while the Party and the Gestapo were rejoicing over their supposed successful suppression of the document. When they awoke, it was too late. No Gestapo could any longer hold back the flood which was pouring through the broken dam. There had been no planning beforehand; God Himself in His mysterious wisdom had done all.[14]

On that same Monday, the bishop was busy sending telegrams to various public officials—including the head of the chancellery

---

13   Portmann (Eng. trans.), 104.
14   Ibid., 105.

Hans Lammers, the Prussian prime minister Hermann Goering, the minister of public worship, the minister of justice and home affairs, and the supreme command of the army—asking them to rectify the injustices done by the Gestapo. To Lammers he wrote as follows:

> After the horrifying nighttime air raids by which the enemy has sought to destroy the city of Münster since July 6, the Secret State Police began on the 12th of July to confiscate monasteries and religious houses in the city and its surrounding area, and hand them over with all their contents to the administration of the province. The residents of these houses, innocent German men and women, honorable members of German families, some of whose members are fighting for Germany as soldiers, have been robbed of their homes, thrown into the streets, banned from their home province. I ask the Führer and Chancellor of the Reich, in the interest of justice and the solidarity of the home front, to secure the freedom and property of these honorable Germans against the arbitrary measures of the Secret State Police and against robbery on behalf of the provincial administration.[15]

Later that week, Lammers replied that he had forwarded the message to the head of the SS, Heinrich Himmler. As Himmler was responsible for the Gestapo, Bishop von Galen saw this as equivalent to making a man judge in his own case. His furious response to Lammers was composed the following week,[16] after the second of what became his three famous sermons.

Meanwhile, von Galen learned that the Gestapo were at work in confiscating two more convents. He sent his auxiliary bishop to one convent, and he himself went to the one on the Frauenstrasse, where

---

15   Löffler, doc. 334, v. II, 852.
16   Löffler, doc. 337, v. II, 864–66.

the Gestapo official in charge asked him who he was. "I am the Bishop of Münster, in case you don't know."[17] He went on to castigate the Gestapo men: "Shame on you, putting defenseless German women out on the street, women whose brothers are fighting at the front." Their leader called for his secretary to put the bishop's words on record, whereupon von Galen, standing up to his full six and a half feet, said forcefully, "And I *demand* that you put my words on the record."

---

17   Portmann (Eng. trans.), 106.

CHAPTER 18

We Are the Anvil, Not the Hammer

The following Sunday found Bishop Clemens August in another of Münster's central and historically important churches: the Church of Our Lady, also known locally as the Überwasserkirche. What further news would he have for his people about the attack on the religious orders?

After expressing his hope for the success of a collection to help those affected by the air raids, he came straight to the point: "Thanks be to God: over the last several days there have been no new attacks on our city by the war enemy. Sadly, however, I must say this: the attacks of our enemy within the country, the beginning of which I spoke about last Sunday at St. Lambert's, have continued during the past week, unhindered by our protests, unhindered by the sorrow that they have brought to the victims and their relatives."[1]

Thus the bishop made an explicit comparison between the British air raids and the attacks of the Gestapo. The Catholics of Westphalia

---

1   Peter Löffler, ed., *Bischof Clemens August Graf von Galen: Akten, Briefe und Predigten 1933–1946*, 2nd ed. (Paderborn: Ferdinand Schöningh, 1996), doc. 336, v. II, 855–63.

were dealing with two enemies: the external, foreign enemy and the enemy within.

He recalled the protests he had made the previous Sunday against the "injustice crying out to heaven" done by the Gestapo. Now he added to the list of religious houses that had been taken over by the Gestapo: the convent of the Sisters of Our Lady of Lourdes, the college of the Camillians in St. Mauritz-Sudmühle, the Benedictine Abbey in Gerleve, the convent of the Benedictine Sisters of Perpetual Adoration in Vinnenberg, and the convent of the Sisters of the Cross in Haus Aspel near Rees. Several of these had been expropriated on the previous Sunday. Then he came to the most recent one of which he had cognizance:

> A few hours ago I received the mournful news that yesterday, on the 19th of July, at the close of this second week of horror for our Münster, the Secret State Police also occupied, seized, and expropriated the Provincial House of the Missionaries of the Most Sacred Heart of Jesus, the large Missionary Convent in Hiltrup, well-known to you all. The fathers and brothers presently living there had to leave their home and belongings by yesterday evening at 8 o'clock. They also have been expelled from Westphalia and, further, from the Rhine Province.
>
> The fathers and brothers *presently living there*. I say this with special emphasis: because from the ranks of the Hiltrup Missionaries there are at present, as I have been reliably informed, 161 men serving as German soldiers in the field, some of them directly in the face of the enemy! Fifty-three fathers from Hiltrup are serving wounded soldiers in the medical service; forty-two theology students and sixty-six brothers serve the fatherland as armed soldiers; some of them have already been decorated with the Iron Cross, the Assault Badge and other insignia. It is

similar with the Camillian Fathers from Sudmühle, the Jesuits of Sentmaring and the Benedictines of St. Joseph in Gerleve! While these German men, obedient to their duty, fight for their homeland at the risk of their lives, in loyal comradeship with the other German brothers, back in their fatherland their home is ruthlessly taken away without any just cause; their monastic fatherhouse is destroyed. If they, as we hope, return victorious, they will find their monastic family dispersed from house and property, their home occupied by strangers, by enemies!

What does this mean? How will it end? This is not about finding temporary housing for homeless residents of Münster. The religious orders were prepared and settled upon cutting down their own living space to the bare minimum in order to provide space for and to look after others who were homeless. But it is not about this: as I hear it, the Convent of the Immaculate in Wilkinghege is being made into the provincial film studio. I have been told that the Benedictine Abbey of St. Joseph will become a home for unwed mothers. What is planned for Sentmaring and Sudmühle and Vinnenberg, I have not yet learned. In fact, I have been given absolutely no official notifications. And so far, no newspaper has reported on the danger-less victories of the officials of the Secret State Police over unarmed German men and defenceless German women, and of the conquests that the Provincial Administration has made of the property of German citizens in our homeland![2]

This sarcastic jibe was followed by a report of the official protests that Bishop von Galen had made. He had made a personal visit to the office of the president of the provincial administration, who had told him that he could not interfere in actions of the Gestapo, as it

---

2   Ibid.

was a fully independent agency not under his jurisdiction, but that he would forward the bishop's protests and requests to the gauleiter. "It was to no avail!" von Galen exclaimed.

He then quoted the telegram he had written to Hans Lammers in Berlin and named the other officials to whom he sent telegrams. He had hoped that, if considerations of justice meant nothing, at least the interests of solidarity on the home front during time of war would move someone in authority to put a stop to the actions of the Gestapo, "and innocent German women would not be denied chivalric protection." Again, it was useless:

> The actions continued, and what I have long foreseen and last Sunday predicted is coming to pass: we are standing before the ruins of the national community, which has been recklessly destroyed in these days!
>
> I forcefully explained to the President of the Administration, the Ministers, the Head of the Army, how the acts of force against respected German men, how this harshness to defenseless German women—which is a mockery of all chivalry and can only spring from a hatred of the Christian religion and of the Catholic Church—how these machinations have the same effect on the national community as sabotage and bombs.
>
> National community? With the men who hound our religious, our brothers and sisters, out of the province like wild animals, without any legal basis, without an inquiry into the facts, without an opportunity of defence or the judgment of a court? No! With them, and with all those responsible, a community of feeling and thought is no longer possible for me!
>
> I will not hate them. I wish from the heart that they come to their senses and convert: so for example I immediately sent up a prayer to heaven for the soul of Ministerial Director Roth, who died suddenly on July 5. He was a Catholic priest of the

Archdiocese of Munich, who for several years, without permission and against the will of his bishop, was an official of the Imperial Ministry for Church Affairs, and prepared and signed many documents for the Minister, Kerrl, encroaching upon the rights of the Church and insulting the honor of the Church. Now he has been involved in an accident while on a boating trip on the Inn, and he drowned in the torrent. May God be merciful to his poor soul! Thus, following the command of the savior, do we desire to pray for all who persecute and slander us! However, as long as they do not change, as long as they continue to rob the innocent, to throw them out of the province, to incarcerate them: for so long I refuse to have any kind of community with them!

No, the unity of convictions and endeavors of our nation has been, contrary to our will and despite our warnings, incurably destroyed. I cannot imagine that our old-established townspeople and farmers, artisans and laborers, our women, your fathers, brothers, and sons who now risk their lives on the front for Germany, will nurture any community of opinion with those who persecute our Religious and expel them. We will obey them, insofar as they pass on orders to us as representatives of the lawful authority. But a community of convictions, a sense of inner solidarity with these persecutors of the Church, these invaders of religious houses, who expel defenseless women and girls, the children of our best families, our sisters, from their conventual homes, many of whom have lived there for decades in work and prayer doing nothing but good for our people—that is impossible for us! I should feel ashamed before God and before you, I should feel ashamed before our noble German forefathers, before my own blessed chivalric father, who admonished, instructed, and guided my brothers and me with strict earnestness to show the most delicate respect to every woman or girl, to afford chivalrous protection to all the unjustly oppressed, particularly to those who, as women, are the images of our own mother and indeed of the beloved Mother of God herself in heaven, if I had any community with those who drive defenceless women out of house and home, and drive them out of their country without shelter and without means of support![3]

Now Bishop von Galen repeated his warning of the previous week: The actions of the Gestapo were destroying the sense of justice and any sense of trust in the leadership of the country. But this did not lead him to call for a revolution:

To be sure, we Christians do not make revolutions! We will remain loyal to our duty, in obedience to God, out of love for our German nation and fatherland. Our soldiers will fight and die for Germany: but not for those men who wound our hearts and besmirch the name of Germany before God and our fellow men by their cruel proceedings against our religious, our brothers and sisters. We will continue to fight bravely against the external enemy. But against the enemy within, who torments and strikes us, we cannot fight with weapons. There remains only one means of fighting for us: strong, stubborn, tough resistance.

"Hart werden! Fest bleiben!" exclaimed the bishop. "Be tough! Keep steadfast!" "Now we see and experience quite clearly what is behind the new doctrines that have been forced upon us for several years, for the sake of which religion has been banned from the schools, our organizations have been suppressed, and now the

---

3   Ibid.

Catholic kindergartens are being destroyed: fundamental hatred of Christianity, which wants to destroy it."

Now the idea of stubborn resistance to these attacks on Christianity led to the introduction and elaboration of von Galen's most famous and enduring image:

"Be tough!" he repeated:

> Keep steadfast! At present we are not the hammer, but the anvil. Others, most of them strangers to our way of life or rebels against it, are hammering on us, are trying by violent means to reform our nation, ourselves, our youth, to bend us away from the straightforward relationship to God.
>
> We are the anvil and not the hammer! But take a look in the blacksmith's shop! Ask the smith and let him tell you: what is formed on the anvil takes its shape not only from the hammer, but also from the anvil. The anvil cannot hit back and doesn't have to; it only has to be firm and hard. If it is sufficiently tough, firm, hard, then usually the anvil lasts longer than the hammer. No matter how vehemently the hammer strikes, the anvil stands in peaceful firmness, and will long serve to form that which is being forged.
>
> What is being forged at the moment are those unjustly imprisoned, the innocent who have been exiled and banned. God will stand by them, that they not lose the form and attitude of Christian firmness, as the hammer of persecution bitterly falls on them and unjustly inflicts wounds upon them.
>
> What is being forged at the moment are our religious, priests, brothers, and sisters. The day before yesterday I was able to visit and speak with some of the exiles in their provisional shelter. I was edified and amazed by the courageous attitude of the brave men, of the weak and defenseless women, who have been roughly and callously driven from their conventual

homes, from their chapels and their closeness to the tabernacle; by their heads, upraised in the consciousness of their innocence as they go into the uncertainty of their banishment, trusting in Him "who feeds the birds of the air and clothes the lilies of the field," even joyful, in the joy which the Savior commanded to his disciples: "Blessed are you when men hate and persecute you on my account! Rejoice and be glad, for your reward is great in heaven." Truly, these men and women are masterworks of the divine blacksmith's shop.

What is being forged at this time between the hammer and the anvil, are our youth: the growing, as yet unfinished youth, soft and still capable of being formed. We cannot protect them from the hammer strokes of unbelief, of hatred of Christendom, of false teachings and morals.

What is being preached to them and forced upon them in the club nights and service hours of the youth groups which, it is said, they have freely joined with the consent of their parents? What do they hear in the schools, to which all the children are forced to go today without consideration for the will of their parents? What do they read in the new schoolbooks? Christian parents, have a look at the books, especially the history books of the higher schools! You will be furious at how they seek to instill mistrust of Christianity and of the Church, even hatred against the Christian faith, into the minds of inexperienced children by means of a total disregard for historical truth! In the preferred state educational institutes, the Hitler schools and the new schools for future teachers, every Christian influence, every truly religious occupation is completely out of the question. And what is happening with the children who were sent to distant places last spring because of the danger of air raids? Do they have religion classes or the opportunity to practice their religion? Christian parents, you must keep an eye on all these things, or else you will be neglecting your most sacred duty; you will not be able to be justified before your conscience and before Him who entrusted those children to you so that you would show them the way to heaven!

We are the anvil, not the hammer! Sadly, you cannot spare your children, that noble but as yet unhardened and unformed raw metal, from the hammer strokes of hatred of the faith, hatred of the Church. But the anvil also does its work in forming the metal: let your parental home, your parental love and loyalty, let your exemplary Christian life be the hard, tenacious, firm, immovable anvil, which parries the weight of the enemy's blows, which continually strengthens the as yet weak power of the young people and confirms in them the holy will never to stray from the path that leads to God.

What is now being forged is, almost without exception, all of us. How many depend on pensions, government annuities, subsidies for their children, and so on. Who is there today who is still an independent and free lord in his dwelling or his business? It may happen that, at some point in the war, a strict supervision and control, or even a pooling and compulsory direction of manufacturing and industry, of production and consumption, may become necessary, and who is there who would not willingly bear that out of love for his people and his fatherland? But with this comes a dependence of each person on many persons and offices, which can curtail not only the freedom of activity, but can also bring the free independence of the conscience into serious danger and temptation, if these persons and office holders hold a world view that is at enmity with Christianity and seek to impose it on those who are under their authority. Such subordination to authority is felt first of all by all civil servants, and what courage, what heroic courage is needed by many civil

servants, to continue to show themselves and to confess themselves to be genuine Christians, true Catholics!

We are at present the anvil, not the hammer! Stay strong
and firm and unshakeable as the anvil does under all the blows
that rain down upon it; in most loyal service for people and
fatherland, but also always ready, in face of the highest sacrifices, to act according to the saying, "One must obey God
rather than men!" God speaks to every one of us through the
conscience informed by faith. Always obey unquestioningly
the voice of conscience. Take as your example and model that
Prussian Justice Minister of old times—I have spoken of him
once before—of whom King Frederick the Great demanded
that he should overturn and annul a lawful judgment in order
to satisfy the wishes of the monarch. This genuine nobleman, a
Herr von Münchhausen, gave this splendid answer to his king:
"My head is at your Majesty's disposal, but not my conscience!"
By this he meant to say: I am ready to die for my King; yes, I
will even accept death from the public executioner.

My head belongs to the King, not my conscience; that
belongs to God! Is the race of such noblemen, who think and
act in this way—are Prussian civil servants of this kind extinct?
Are there no more city-folk and farmers, artisans and workers, with that same strength of conscience and noble courage?
I cannot, I will not, believe that! And therefore once more:
Become strong! Become firm! Remain immovable! Like the
anvil under the hammer's blows! It may happen, that obedience to God, fidelity to conscience, may cost me or you our
life, our freedom, our home. However: "Better to die than to
sin!" May God's grace, without which we can do nothing, give
you and me this immovable firmness and preserve it within us![4]

4　　Ibid.

To close his sermon, the bishop spoke of some of the damage from the air raids. A monument just outside the cathedral was almost totally destroyed, except for its central figure, the statue of St. Ludger, the first Bishop of Münster. Bishop Clemens August saw this marvelous survival of his saintly predecessor, still holding up his hand in blessing, as an encouraging sign to the Catholics of Münster:

> St. Ludger exhorts you; I, his seventieth successor on the shepherd's chair of Münster, exhort you, with the words St. Peter wrote to the afflicted Christians during the first persecution of Christians: "Humble yourselves under the mighty hand of God, that in due time He may exalt you. Cast all your anxieties on him, for He cares about you. Be sober, be watchful. Your adversary, the devil, prowls around like a lion . . . Resist him, firm in your faith! . . . After you have suffered a little while, the God of all grace, who has called you to His eternal glory in Christ, will Himself restore, establish, and strengthen you. To Him be the dominion for ever and ever. Amen."[5]

He ended the sermon like his last one: "Let us pray for our exiled religious, for all who suffer injustice, for all who are suffering, for our soldiers, for Münster and its inhabitants, for our people and fatherland, and for our Führer." Someone in the church shouted out, "And for our beloved Bishop!"[6]

For the second time in eight days, the bishop lifted up his voice in protest against the injustices of the Gestapo. He revealed something of his heart to his people. The heart of a man formed in the traditions of the Catholic nobility, the traditions of Christian chivalry, refused to have anything to do with men who threw defenseless women out of their homes. He could not consider such men

---

5   1 Pet. 5:6–11.
6   Löffler, doc. 336, v. II, 855–63.

as members of the same national community as himself. He would pray for them. He would obey them insofar as they lawfully represented the power of the state. But he could not have any kind of solidarity with them. Since he believed that revolution against one's own government was not morally justified for a Christian, since he believed that those who are persecuted for the sake of Christ are blessed, his only recourse—the recourse to which he exhorted his people—was to suffer that persecution with firm tenacity, holding onto his faith. The image of the anvil, being struck by the hammer but outlasting it, fulfilled its intended purpose of encouraging and strengthening not only the Catholics of Münster but many Catholics and non-Catholics throughout Germany as well as abroad.

His indignation directed so forcefully toward the Gestapo and the Nazi leadership had taken him into dangerous territory. A police report noted that the bishop's sermon was causing great unrest among the Catholic faithful. People were saying that there was something very wrong when, in time of national need, a certain part of the population was being singled out for harsh treatment by an order of their own government. The Nazi Party was being criticized. People expressed the opinion that perhaps Hitler didn't know what was going on and that it was a case of the Gestapo and the SS getting out of control. Older people were drawing parallels to the *Kulturkampf* of Bismarck. It was clear to the person making this report that the bishop's sermon and pastoral letters, and the dissemination of these by the Catholic clergy, were aimed at leading Catholics to conflicts of conscience in regard to their duties to the state.[7]

Clearly, Bishop Clemens August knew that he was putting himself at risk. What must have been much harder for him was the knowledge that his advice could put others at risk. He had renounced the possibility of active revolution against the regime but in doing so

---

7   Löffler, v. II, 863, n. 13.

had mentioned the word revolution. He enunciated the principle of moral teaching that one must not cooperate with evil. The example of the official—who told King Frederick the Great that his head was at the king's disposal but not his conscience—was a clear application of this principle. If ordered to do something against the moral law, one must disobey the order regardless of the consequences. This was asking something more than strong, stubborn suffering under persecution. This was asking people in extreme situations to take the risk of martyrdom. But they had no doubt that the bishop himself was taking that risk, and they loved him for it.

CHAPTER 19

The Destruction of "Worthless Lives"

In 1920, long before there were Nazis, Karl Binding and Ludwig Hoche published a scholarly work entitled *Permission to Put an End to Lives not Worth Living—Die Freigabe der Vernichtung Lebensunwertes Lebens*. Binding, a legal scholar, and Hoche, a psychiatrist, argued that certain lives—for example, lives of great pain or disability or lives of severe mental illness—really were not worth living: that persons in such conditions would be better off dead and that it should not be illegal to kill them, for such would in fact be a merciful act. During the Nazi period, the concept of "lives not worth living"—or, perhaps, "worthless lives"—became the source of a murderous program of so-called euthanasia.

Much earlier than this, beginning in the 1890s, Alfred Ploetz's *Basics of Racial Hygiene—Grundlinien einer Rassenhygiene*, and the Racial Hygiene Society of which he was one of the founders, argued for racial engineering based on government control of reproduction.

They were theories that seemed to have some scientific basis— theories that originally had nothing to do with Nazism but that fit in well with the racial theories of Adolf Hitler and the Nazis. The "master race," the Nazis thought, needed to be saved from pollution, which could happen not only by the intermarriage of "Aryans" with people of "inferior" races but also by the passing on of hereditary diseases. This was also the thought of Ploetz and, in different forms, of social Darwinists in many countries. Improvements in medicine and hygiene since the nineteenth century had led to what they considered an unfortunate consequence: The "survival of the fittest" was being adversely affected, because not only the fittest were surviving. So-called unfit people now were more likely to live to adulthood and to have children, thus supposedly passing on their defects to the race. Society would inevitably have to pay the price unless those considered as unfit were prevented from having children.

Eugenic sterilization was the answer. It was a policy in several other countries, including many of the states in the United States, long before it was enacted in Germany. It was being proposed in Germany in the 1920s and early 1930s by people who had no connection with the National Socialist movement. It was, however, an idea that fit in well with the racial ideas of Nazism. Shortly after Hitler took power, a compulsory sterilization law was introduced. By 1945, more than three hundred thousand men and women had been sterilized against their will.

Forced abortion came next. Women with the "wrong" racial or physical characteristics could be forced to have the child in their womb killed, up to the seventh month of pregnancy.

Historian Anna-Maria Balbach has studied how the Sisters of Mercy of Münster, a religious order known also in Münster as the Clemens Sisters because they directed the Clemens Hospital there, came into conflict with these new laws.[1] Despite their absolute opposition, they were unable to prevent sterilizations or abortions from being performed in their hospitals. They were, of course, united in

---

1   Anna-Maria Balbach, *Die Barmherzigen Schwestern zu Münster zur Zeit des Nationalsozialismus* (Münster: Dialogverlag, 2007).

their conviction that cooperation in a grave evil such as abortion or sterilization was out of the question. Lest there be any wavering, and to help the sisters respond to any coercion, the mother superior sent a circular letter to all the communities of the order absolutely prohibiting any sister from assisting at such operations. The doctors had to find cooperative midwives or nurses from among the lay personnel.

The sterilizations and abortions prepared the way for the next stage. Persons with mental illness were among those whom the Nazis dehumanized by calling them "ballast"; they were "unproductive" persons who no longer contributed anything worthwhile to the nation and therefore had no inherent right to life. Throughout Germany, the regime began to deal with this "ballast" by cutting the rations of food and medicine to institutions where they were cared for, overcrowding the institutions, and cutting down on personnel. The Clemens Sisters looked after 1,050 mental patients at an institute known as Marienthal. The patients suffered more than hunger. The sister in charge complained to the provincial health administration that the overcrowding resulted in long lines for the toilets; when the wait was too long, patients were urinating and defecating in the corridors. The number of personnel was so reduced that, although they now had no days off, there were empty nursing stations during some shifts and never more than one caregiver per shift at any station.

Next came the so-called euthanasia. The Greek etymology of the word means "good death," but this was anything but. In October 1939, Hitler ordered that "incurably ill persons whose situation has become critical should be given a merciful death." A law entitled "An Act to End Suffering and Worthless Life" was the gateway to the murder—by poison, by gas, by shooting, or by deliberate starvation—of 230,000 people.

Following on the ideas proposed by Binding and Hoche, the Nazis had prepared people for this move by disseminating propaganda about the benefits of ending "worthless" lives. Posters exhibited photos of a disabled man being cared for by a healthy one, with a caption decrying it as a shameful waste of the talents, time, and energy of the healthy man. In his book, *Mein Kampf* (*My Struggle*), Hitler had asserted that the right to life is not absolute. It ends when the person can no longer take care of himself, when he can no longer protect and maintain his own life. Now came the time to put all these long-disseminated ideas into practice.

Beginning in 1940, health care centers, including Marienthal, were required to fill out a form giving the health status of each patient. In Berlin, officials of the "Euthanasia Program" decided on the life and death of patients based only on this form. A red plus sign in a box on the back of the form indicated that the patient was to be killed. A blue minus sign allowed the patient to live.

The purpose of the forms was kept secret from the hospitals and other institutes of care. As the program spread, however, and with the propaganda background, rumors spread too. In fact, von Galen had called Cardinal Bertram's attention to the form in July 1940, and the bishops were keeping an anxious watch. The bishops had already spoken out as early as 1934 when there was a proposal to amend the criminal code to permit the medical killing of "lives not worth living."[2]

In the summer of 1941, Marienthal was given a list of male patients who were to be made ready for transportation to a state-run center in the Black Forest. Meanwhile, a number of Party faithful had been sent to work at various jobs in Marienthal. Their presence changed the atmosphere there from one of trust and openness to one of suspicion, uncertainty, and anxiety. The order to get the patients

---

2   Peter Löffler, ed., *Bischof Clemens August Graf von Galen: Akten, Briefe und Predigten 1933–1946*, 2nd ed. (Paderborn: Ferdinand Schöningh, 1996), docs. 310, 314, v. II, 794–96, 800–801.

ready for transfer insisted on strict secrecy, warning of grave consequences for anyone who spoke of it in public and claiming that there were "spies" in Marienthal. This did nothing to ease the tense atmosphere.

Despite the threats of punishment, one of the sisters, Sister Laudeberta, tried to rescue those she could. Managing to learn from one of the lay nurses the names of the patients who were to be sent away, she spoke with their family members when they came to visit. Telling them that conditions at Marienthal were getting worse, she encouraged them to take the patients home, for at the moment, they could be better cared for by their own families.

At night, she slipped out of Marienthal to inform Bishop Clemens August Count von Galen. This was dangerous. Some of the newly placed personnel at Marienthal worked as porters, with the task of keeping a record of all comings and goings. A sister was not expected to leave the grounds. Sister Laudeberta cautiously bypassed the porters and went by back streets and alleys to the bishop's palace. Despite her heroic efforts, seventy-nine patients were taken to a train on July 31, 1941. Sometime in that night or one of the next two nights, she again made her way stealthily to the bishop's palace. She confirmed what he had also heard from Marienthal's chaplain, Heinrich Lackmann:[3] The first group of patients had been sent off to certain death, and a second transport was planned for the near future. It was time for Clemens August to lift up his voice once again.

---

3   Ludger Grevelhörster, *Kardinal Clemens August Graf von Galen in seiner Zeit* (Münster: Aschendorff, 2005), 106.

CHAPTER 20

Jesus Weeps

Sunday, August 3 found Bishop von Galen once again in the pulpit of St. Lambert's. It was three weeks since his first sermon decrying the attacks on the religious orders. The Gestapo's war of destruction against the orders was continuing, he announced, and although it was still the case that no member of those orders had been accused of a crime, rumors were spreading that they were engaging in, and would soon be indicted or arrested for, illegal activities or even treason.[1] He characterized this as base slander and encouraged his hearers to bear witness against anyone making such slanders. He had already made a complaint to the public prosecutor against a young man who had made such statements. "I expect that he will quickly be held accountable for what he has done, and that our courts still have the courage to call to account and punish slanderers who dare to steal the reputation of blameless Germans who have already had their property taken away from them." He called on his listeners and on all decent citizens to take the name of anyone making such

---

1   Peter Löffler, ed., *Bischof Clemens August Graf von Galen: Akten, Briefe und Predigten 1933–1946*, 2nd ed. (Paderborn: Ferdinand Schöningh, 1996), doc. 341, v. II, 874–83.

statements against the exiled religious, and the names of any wit-
nesses, and to have the courage to make a report to their parish priest
or to the general vicariate of the diocese. "I owe it," he said, "to the
honor of our religious, the honor of our Catholic Church, and also
the honor of our German people and our city of Münster," to see
to the prosecution of those who slander "our religious."

The sermon itself came after the reading of the gospel of the day on
the ninth Sunday after Pentecost. Taken from chapter 19 of St. Luke,
it was the passage in which Jesus came near to the city of Jerusalem
and wept over it. This gospel event provided a theme for interpreting
the current situation. Jesus wept over Jerusalem because of His love
for His people and their holy city. God had shown them the marks
of His love, but their failure to respond to His love by works of righteousness was leading them to disaster. The Old Testament prophets
had frequently given similar warnings. Von Galen was not connect-
ing the gospel account with the sad situation of the Jews in Germany
in his own time. In the tradition of Christian preaching and scrip-
tural interpretation—as when a believer responds to the question,
"Who crucified Christ?" with the answer, "I did"—he was applying
the gospel event to his own city, to its people, and to Germany as a
whole. The Son of God wept over Jerusalem because of the failure
of its people to keep the commandments of God. Now that same
failure was a characteristic of German national life. Was Jesus now
weeping over Germany? Was Germany also in danger of losing God's
favor? In his July sermons, von Galen had already prophesied a disaster for Germany if she did not change her ways. Now he repeated that
prophetic warning, illustrating it with the poignant thought of Jesus
weeping over this city, this nation.

"My dear diocesans!" he began:

> A shocking event is portrayed in today's Gospel. Jesus weeps! The
> Son of God weeps! A person weeps, who is in pain, pain of body

or pain of heart. At that time, Jesus was not yet suffering in body, and yet He wept. How great must have been the pain of soul, the sorrow of heart, of this bravest of men, that He wept!

Why did He weep? He wept over Jerusalem, over the holy city, so dear to Himself, the capital city of His people. He wept over its inhabitants, His fellow countrymen, because they did not want to recognize that which alone could prevent the punishment that He could see with His omniscience and that His divine justice had predetermined: "If only you knew the things that would serve for your peace!" Why do the inhabitants of Jerusalem not recognize this? Not long before, Jesus had said, "Jerusalem, Jerusalem! How often would I have gathered your children together, as a hen gathers her chicks under her wings, but you would not!" (Luke 13:34) You would not. I, your king, your God, I would. But you would not. How sheltered, how guarded, how protected is the chick beneath the wings of the hen! She keeps it warm, she nourishes it, she defends it. Thus would I protect you, shelter you, defend you against every kind of trouble. I would. You would not! That is why Jesus weeps, that is why this strong man weeps, that is why God weeps. Over the foolishness, the unrighteousness, the crime of this *not-willing*. And over the calamity that would come from it, which His omniscience saw coming, which His justice must decree, if man sets his *not-willing* against all the commandments of God, all the warnings of his conscience, all the loving invitations of the divine Friend, the best of Fathers: "If only you recognized, today, on this day, what would serve for your peace! But you would not." It is something frightening, something unbelievably unjust and leading to destruction, when man places his will against God's will! I would; you would not. That is why Jesus weeps over Jerusalem.

Devout Christians! In the joint pastoral letter of the German Bishops of June 26, 1941, read out on July 6th of this year in all Catholic Churches in Germany, it says among other things: "To be sure, in Catholic moral teaching there are positive commandments that do not bind when their fulfilment would be connected with great difficulties. But there are also holy obligations of conscience from which no one can exempt us, which we must fulfill at whatever cost, even at the cost of our own lives: never, under any circumstances, outside of war and justified self-defence, can someone kill an innocent person." Already on July 6th I had the occasion to add the following explanation to this joint pastoral letter:

"For several months we have heard reports that patients of hospitals and institutes for the mentally ill, patients who have been sick for a long time and perhaps seem to be incurable, have been compulsorily transferred to other locations on orders from Berlin. Regularly it happens that after a short time the relatives receive notice that the patient has died, the body has been cremated, and the ashes can be picked up. The opinion, bordering on certainty, is held everywhere, that these numerous unexpected deaths of the mentally ill are not the result of natural causes, but are deliberately brought about; that in these cases that doctrine is being followed, that one can put an end to so-called 'worthless life,' that is, can kill innocent persons, if one believes that their life is of no more value to the people and the state; a horrible doctrine, that would justify the murder of the innocent, that gives a fundamental license for the violent killing of those invalids, cripples, incurable sick, and weak old persons who are no longer able to work!"

As I have recently learned from reliable sources, there are now lists of such patients in hospitals and care centres in the Province of Westphalia, patients who are scheduled to be transported and in a short time put to death as so-called "unproductive fellow-countrymen." The first transport from the institute of Marienthal near Münster took place this week!

German men and women! Section 211 of the Reich Criminal Code still has the force of law. It states, "Anyone who intentionally kills a person, if he has done this with premeditation, is to be punished for murder by death." Perhaps in order to protect those who intentionally kill these poor persons, members of our families, from the punishment prescribed by this law, the sick who are chosen to be killed are transported from the *Heimat* to a distant institution. Then some disease or other is given as the cause of death. Since the bodies are immediately cremated, neither the relatives nor the criminal police are able to determine whether there really was such an illness and what was the true cause of death.

I have, however, been assured that there has been absolutely no concern raised either by the Reich Ministry of the Interior or by Dr. Conti in the Office of the Reich Führer of Doctors, about the fact that already a great number of mentally ill patients in Germany are being intentionally killed and will be killed in the future.

The Criminal Code states in section 139: "Anyone who has credible knowledge of a plan . . . for a crime against life . . . and fails to communicate this speedily to the authorities, is to be punished."

When I heard of the plans to transport sick persons from Marienthal in order to kill them, I bore witness to the public prosecutor and police chief of Münster by letters that read as follows:

"According to credible evidence given to me, it is planned during the course of this week (the 31st of July is spoken of) to transfer a great number of patients from the Provincial Health Centre of Marienthal near Münster to the Health Centre of

Eichberg, as so-called 'unproductive fellow-countrymen,' in order soon afterwards to have them deliberately put to death, as has happened, according to universal opinion, in the case of such transfers of patients from other institutes. As such an action violates not only the divine and natural moral law, but also is punishable by death as murder according to section 211 of the Imperial Criminal Code, I now give witness as required of me by section 139 of the Imperial Criminal Code, and ask that the threatened fellow-countrymen be given immediate protection against those who are planning the transferral and murder, and that I be informed of the actions taken."

I have received no information about the steps taken by the prosecutor or the police.

Already on the 26th of July I had made a most earnest appeal to the Provincial Administration of the Province of Westphalia, which is responsible for these institutions, to which the sick are sent for *care* and *healing*. It was no use! The first transport of innocent victims condemned to death has gone from Marienthal! And I have heard that 800 patients have been transported from the Institute for Care and Healing of Warstein.

So we must assume that these poor, defenseless sick people will sooner or later be killed. Why? Not because they have committed a capital crime; not because they have attacked their caregivers in such wise that these were left with no recourse to save their own lives in self-defence other than the use of violence against their attackers. These would be cases in which, in addition to the killing of armed enemies in a just war, use of force even to the extent of killing is allowed and, not rarely, required. No, not for such reasons do these unfortunate sick people have to die, but rather because, according to the judgment of some official, according to the opinion of some commission, they have become "unworthy of life"; because according to this opinion they belong to the category of "unproductive" fellow countrymen. It is judged that they can no longer produce goods; they are like an old machine that does not work anymore; they are like an old horse that has become incurably lame; they are like a cow that no longer gives milk. What does one do with such old machines? They are scrapped. What does one do with a lame horse or an unproductive cow?

No. I will not continue this comparison to the end, so frightful is its appropriateness and its illuminating power!

We are not dealing with machines, or horses or cows, which are created in order to serve man, to produce goods for him! One may destroy or kill such beings when they no longer fulfill this purpose. No, here we are dealing with people, our fellow human beings, our brothers and sisters! Poor people, sick people, unproductive people, granted! But does that mean they have lost the right to life? Do you, do I, have the right to life only so long as we are productive, only so long as others acknowledge that we are productive?

If that principle is accepted and made use of, that one can kill "unproductive" people, then woe to us all, when we become old and weak! If one can kill unproductive people, then woe to the disabled who have sacrificed their health or their limbs in the process of production! If unproductive people can be disposed of by violent means, then woe to our brave soldiers who return to their homeland severely wounded, as cripples, as invalids! Once it is granted that people have the right to kill "unproductive" fellow human beings—even if at the moment it affects only the poor defenceless mentally ill—then *in principle* the right has been given to *murder* all unproductive people: the incurably ill, the cripples who are unable to work, those who have become incapacitated because of work or war; then the right has been given to murder all of us, once we become weak with age and therefore unproductive. All that will be required is for some secret order to come down, that the process which has been tested on the mentally ill should now be extended to other "unproductive" people, to those with incurable lung disease, to the infirm elderly, to the severely wounded soldiers. Then the life of none of us is safe. Some commission can put him on the list of the "unproductive" who are, according to its judgment, "unworthy of life." And no policemen will protect him, and no court will take notice of his murder and subject the murderers to the prescribed punishment! Who will then be able to trust his doctor? Perhaps he will report the patient as "unproductive" and receive the order to kill him. It is unthinkable what degeneration of morals, what universal mistrust will find its way even into the family, if this frightening doctrine is tolerated, taken up, and followed. Woe to humanity, woe to our German people, if the holy commandment of God, "Thou shalt not kill," which the Lord gave on Sinai amid thunder and lightning, which God the Creator wrote into the conscience of man from the beginning, is not only broken, but if this breach is tolerated and taken up as a regular practice without punishment!

I will give you an example of what is now taking place. In Marienthal there was a man of about fifty-five years of age, a farmer from a rural community of the Münsterland—I could give you his name—who has suffered for several years from a mental illness and so was entrusted to the Provincial Health and Care Center of Marienthal for *care*. He was not totally insane; he could receive visits, and was always happy when his relatives came. Fourteen days ago he received a visit from his wife and one of his sons, a soldier on leave from the front. This son is very close to his sick father. So the goodbye was hard. Who knows whether the son will return alive from the war to see his father again?—for he could fall while fighting for his people. No, the son, the soldier, will surely not see his father again on this earth, because the father's name has in the meantime been placed on the list of the unproductive. A relative, who wanted to visit the father this week in Marienthal, was sent away with the news that the sick man, on orders from the Ministry of National Defense, has been moved. No one could answer the question, Where to? The relatives, he was told, will be given news within a few days.

What will the news be? Will it be again, as it has been in other cases? That the man has died, that his body has been cremated, that his ashes can be released in exchange for payment of a fee? Thus the soldier who is in the field putting his life on the line for his fellow Germans will not see his father again on earth because fellow Germans at home have put his father to death! . . .

"Thou shalt not kill!" God wrote this commandment in the conscience of man long before any book of criminal laws prescribed a punishment for murder, long before any prosecutor accused or any court punished someone for murder. Cain, who slew his brother Abel, was a murderer long before there were States and courts. And he confessed, under the pressure of the witness of his conscience, "My sin is so great that I cannot find forgiveness! . . . Anyone who finds me, will kill me, the murderer" (Genesis 4:13).

"Thou shalt not kill!" This commandment of God, the one Lord who has the right to decide life and death, was written into the hearts of men from the beginning, long before God gave His commandments to the children of Israel on Mount Sinai, in those brief sentences carved in stone that are written for us in holy Scripture, the commandments that we learned by heart from the Catechism as children.

"I am the Lord your God!" Thus does this unchangeable law begin. "Thou shalt not have strange gods before me!" The one, transcendent, almighty, all-knowing, eternally holy and righteous God, our Creator and our only Judge, gave us these commandments! Out of love for us He wrote them on our hearts and prescribed them for us, for they correspond to the requirements of our divinely-created nature; they are the inalienable norms of a human life and a communal life that is rational, pleasing to God, conducive to well-being, and holy.

God, our Father, desires by these commandments to gather us, His children, together, as the hen gathers her chicks beneath her wings. When we men follow these commands, these invitations, these calls of God, then we are protected, guarded, preserved from harm, saved from the threatening disaster, like the chicks beneath the wings of the hen.

"Jerusalem, Jerusalem, how often would I have gathered your children together as the hen gathers her chicks beneath her wings. But you would not!" Must that be repeated in our German Fatherland, in our Westphalian *Heimat*, in our city of Münster? How do things stand in Germany, how do things stand with us here, in regard to obedience to God's commandments?

The eighth commandment: "Thou shalt not bear false witness, thou shalt not lie!" How often is it brazenly, even publicly, broken!

The seventh commandment: "Thou shalt not take the property of another!" Whose property is now secure, after the arbitrary and ruthless appropriation of the property of our brothers and sisters who belong to Catholic religious orders? Whose property is protected, if these unjustly confiscated properties are not returned?

The sixth commandment: "Thou shalt not commit adultery!" Think of the recommendations of a liberal attitude to sexual intercourse and single motherhood contained in the famous Open Letter of Rudolf Hess—who has since disappeared—that was printed in all the newspapers.[2] What can one already see and read and experience here in Münster of shamelessness and filth! To what amount of shamelessness in dress have the young had to accustom themselves. Preparation for later adultery! For it will destroy the sense of shame, the guardian of chastity.

Now the fifth commandment, "Thou shalt not kill!" is being set aside and violated within the sight of those who are responsible for protecting the order of justice and for protecting life: for people take it upon themselves deliberately to kill innocent people, sick people granted, merely because they are "unproductive," can no longer produce wealth.

How does it stand with regard to the fourth commandment, which prescribes reverence and obedience to parents and those in authority? The authority of parents has already been greatly undermined, and will be ever more damaged by all the demands being placed upon youth against the will of their parents. Does anyone think that upright reverence and wise obedience to civil authority can be upheld if one begins by violating the commandments of the highest authority, the commandments of God, indeed, if one fights against and seeks to root out belief in the one, true, transcendent God?

---

2   Hess had written a letter in December 1939 to a fictional single mother, telling her that because there was a shortage of men on account of the war, having children outside of wedlock was a good thing. Hess had flown to Britain on May 10, 1941, without Hitler's approval, seeking on his own to negotiate a peace agreement between Germany and Britain.

The observance of the first three commandments has long since been widely discontinued in public life in Germany and also in Münster. How many no longer keep Sundays and holy days holy, and ignore the service of God! How the name of God is misused, taken irreverently, and blasphemed!

And the first commandment: "Thou shalt not have strange gods before me!" In place of the one, true, eternal God, men make their own idols to please themselves, in order to worship them: nature, or the State, or the people, or the race. And how many are there whose god is, in truth, in the words of St. Paul, their belly (Phil. 3:19), their own well-being, to which they sacrifice everything, even their honor and their conscience—the pleasures of the senses, the love of money, the love of power! This enables men to go so far as to seek divine power for themselves, to make themselves lords over the life and death of their fellow men.

When Jesus came to Jerusalem and saw the city, He wept over it and said, "If only you knew, today, on this day, what would be for your peace! But now it is hidden from your eyes. See, the days will come upon you, when your enemies will smash you to the ground, you and your children, and leave not one stone upon another within you, because you did not know the time of your visitation."

With His bodily eyes Jesus saw then only the walls and towers of the city of Jerusalem, but divine omniscience saw deeper, and knew how things stood within the city and within its inhabitants: "Jerusalem, Jerusalem, how often would I have gathered your children together, as a hen gathers her chicks beneath her wings, but you willed it not!" That is that great pain that presses on the heart of Jesus, that brings forth the tears from His eyes. *I* wanted what was best for you. But *you* would not!

Jesus sees the sinfulness, the frightfulness, the criminality, the self-destructiveness, of this *not-willing*! Little man, the frail creature, pits his created will against God's will! Foolishly and criminally defies the will of God! That is why Jesus weeps over the ghastly sin and the unavoidable punishment! God is not mocked!

Christians of Münster! Did the Son of God in his omniscience that day see only Jerusalem and its people? Did He weep only over Jerusalem? Is the people of Israel the only people whom God has embraced, protected, and gathered to Himself with a father's care and a mother's love? And that *would not*? That has rejected God's truth, thrown God's law off from itself, and thereby cast itself down to destruction? Did Jesus, the omniscient God, also see in that day our German people? Also our land of Westphalia, our Münsterland, the Lower Rhine? And did He also weep over us? Over Münster?

For a thousand years He has taught our forefathers and us with His truth, led us with His law, nourished us with His grace, gathered us together as the hen gathers her chicks beneath her wings. Did the omniscient Son of God see then that in our time He must also pronounce this judgment upon us: "You would not: behold, your house will be laid waste!"? How terrible that would be!

My Christians! I hope there is still time, but the time is urgent! Time for us to recognize, today, on this very day, that which will serve for our peace, that which alone can save us, can protect us from the punishment of divine justice. Time for us to accept without reservation and without limitation the truth revealed by God, and to bear witness to it by our lives. Time for us to make the divine commandments the guiding principles of our lives, and to do this earnestly, following the saying, death rather than sin! Time for us to call down God's pardon and mercy upon ourselves, our city, our country, our beloved German people, by prayer and sincere penance.

But whoever continues to provoke God's judgment; whoever blasphemes our faith; whoever scorns God's commandments; whoever makes common cause with those who alienate our young people from Christianity, who rob and banish our religious, who deliver innocent men and women, our brothers and sisters, to death—with all those we will avoid having any familiar relationships; we will keep ourselves and our families out of reach of their influence, so that we do not become infected by their anti-God way of thinking and acting, so that we do not become sharers in their guilt and thus liable to the judgment which a just God must and will inflict on all those who, like the ungrateful city of Jerusalem, do not will what God wills.

O God, let us all today, on this very day, before it is too late, recognize what will serve for our peace! O most Sacred Heart of Jesus, moved to tears by the blindness and misdeeds of men, help us with Your grace, that we may always strive after what pleases You and renounce that which displeases You, so that we may remain in your love and find rest for our souls! Amen.

Let us pray for the poor sick, in danger of death, for our exiled religious, for all those in need, for our soldiers, for our people and fatherland and its Führer.[3]

---

3   Löffler, doc. 341, v. II, 874–83.

CHAPTER 21

Revenge Is a Dish Best Served Cold

The sermon of August 3 against the policy of so-called euthanasia caused even more of a public stir than the sermons on the
confiscation of religious houses. Shocked German citizens discussed
with one another the possibility that their sons, having put their
lives on the line for their fatherland, could come home from the
war severely wounded and end up being murdered by their own
fatherland. Rumors spread that such murders were already taking
place or that Bishop von Galen had made such a claim. According
to his printed text, he did not, but the Gestapo report said that he
had. When the sermon was read in all the city's churches on the
following Sunday, the printed text was read.[1] The bishop's point was

---

1   Peter Löffler, ed., *Bischof Clemens August Graf von Galen: Akten, Briefe und
     Predigten 1933–1946*, 2nd ed. (Paderborn: Ferdinand Schöningh, 1996),
     doc. 341, v. II, 883–84, n. 8. Cf. the letter of Gauleiter Meyer to Bor-
     mann of August 13, ibid., doc. 343, 895: "Although the bishop certainly
     spoke thus . . . , i.e. that the wounded unproductive soldiers would be
     murdered, he expressed himself more carefully in the reprinted version of
     his talk which was read in the churches of Münster last Sunday, saying that
     if euthanasia is possible in the case of the mentally ill, then it can also be
     used in the case of wounded soldiers."

that murders *were already* taking place, and the basis on which they were justified was such that there was nothing to prevent the murder of wounded soldiers. The regime was tolerating *in principle* the doctrine that innocent people can be put to death with impunity. Once the right to life is undermined, he had argued, no one's right to life is secure.

As with the other sermons, the euthanasia sermon was secretly copied and spread throughout Germany and to soldiers on the front. The courage of Bishop Clemens August von Galen, of which the people of his diocese were well aware, soon became known throughout the country and, indeed, throughout the world. Eventually, the sermons came into the hands of the British, who printed them in leaflets in the tens of thousands and dropped them from airplanes all over Germany and read them in radio broadcasts transmitted to Germany. When the Americans came into the war, they too looked on von Galen as a hero, as an example of the "other Germany," which they hoped could be the basis of a rebuilt country after the hoped-for Allied victory.

In Münster itself, his courage inspired courage in others. Those who were not present at the sermon heard about it and wanted to read it for themselves. People were proud of their bishop, who had been able to say things in public that were not safe to say. They in turn risked their lives and freedom to copy and disseminate the sermons. A typical story was that of a sixteen-year-old girl who worked as a typist in a lawyer's office. Her employer brought copies of the sermons to the office, and she typed them onto mimeograph paper, making multiple copies. Then she would go into the streets to distribute them. Her "disguise" was collecting money for a charity. When she felt that the people she encountered were not likely to betray her to the Gestapo, she would slip them an envelope containing a copy of one or another of Bishop von Galen's sermons. Another woman typed out copies at home during the night, making six carbon copies at a time. She then delivered them to friendly homes, also by night. She told her children nothing about her activities. While the Nazis were in power, it was too dangerous for the children to know anything about this, lest they say something at school that would cause suspicion.[2]

The story illustrates the dangers of living in a totalitarian police state. No one knew whom to trust, who might betray him to the Gestapo, even unknowingly or unwillingly. One had no choice, as the woman who worked in the law office remembered more than sixty years later, about going to public demonstrations and giving the "Heil Hitler" salute; but her father and everyone in her house were opposed to Hitler from the beginning. The daughter of the woman who typed the sermons at home during the night echoed this: No one knew, she said, where his neighbors stood in regard to Hitler, so one was always discreet. But everyone knew where the Bishop of Münster stood.

The public reaction against the euthanasia project was so strong and wide-ranging that even a totalitarian state like Nazi Germany had to take it into consideration. Three weeks later, Adolf Hitler ordered a suspension of the program. The people of Münster have always said this was the second of only two cases in the twelve-year history of the Third Reich that public outcry led to a change in government policy. The first had been the "*Oldenburger Kreuzkampf*." Both took place in the Diocese of Münster, and both had their origins in the work of Clemens August von Galen.[3]

---

2   The author interviewed the first woman, and a daughter of the second, on June 5, 2008, in Münster.

3   There may have been some other cases elsewhere in Germany. Annette Dumbach and Jud Newborn say there was a Kreuzkampf in Upper Bavaria and Munich in April 1941, which resulted in a reversal of a ban on crucifixes by the gauleiter, Adolf Wagner. See their *Sophie Scholl and the White Rose* (Oxford: One World, 2006), 65.

The victory, however, was only temporary. By June 1943, the killing of the ill was begun again with more secrecy, and it continued
almost to the end of the war. And the "technology" of mass murder
by poison gas that was first used on the mentally ill was further
developed and employed in the death camps, making possible the
horror of the Holocaust.

For German opponents of Hitler, Bishop Clemens August Count
von Galen was a hero and an inspiration. At last, someone had the
courage to stand up in defense of human rights against the totalitarian dictatorship and to say in public what so many thought but were
unable to say out loud. For many, their eyes were opened for the first
time. Others were inspired in their resistance, if not to active participation in resistance movements—which all too often proved both
futile and fatal—at least to the stubborn, hard, silent resistance of the
anvil, refusing to cooperate in an evil they could do nothing to stop.

Whatever form their resistance took, copying and reading the
sermons of Bishop von Galen was part of the program. Count
Helmuth James von Moltke, after being arrested in connection with
the July 20, 1944, attempt on Hitler's life, wrote to his wife from
prison about his admiration for von Galen's sermons, telling her it
was best to read them out loud in order to appreciate their full force.
Phillip Freiherr von Boeselager, the last surviving member of the
group that plotted that assassination attempt, wrote in his memoirs
before his death in 2008 of the influence that the sermons had on
his decision to join the resistance:

> Among soldiers, there was much discussion of the sermons
> that Monsignor Clemens August von Galen, the bishop of
> Münster, had given against euthanasia . . . in the summer
> of 1941; his vehemence had led the government, contrary to
> all expectations, to put an end to the T4 program for the erad-
> ication of the handicapped. These sermons had resonated with

soldiers, who, after a wound or an amputation, were likely to be grouped with these allegedly useless people. I had not read the sermons, but I had heard many people talk about them, and I had listened all the more attentively because Monsignor Galen, in addition to being my distant cousin, was also a compatriot. The bishop was highly regarded among officers with any sense of morality, and his influence on the resistance in the military can be seen in a brief exchange I had with Colonel Hans Oster of the Abwehr toward the end of 1942. Knowing my connection to the Rhineland and Westphalia, and although he was himself a Lutheran, he asked me about the prelate:

"Are you a relative of Monsignor Galen?"

"No, not really . . ."

"Too bad. He's a man of courage and conviction. And what resolution in his sermons! There should be a handful of such people in all our churches, and at least two handfuls in the Wehrmacht! If there were, Germany would look quite different!"[4]

In far-away Munich, the sermons came into the hands of a university student named Hans Scholl. His first thought was, "We must get a duplicating machine." With other friends, including his sister Sophie, he set up a resistance group that called itself the White Rose. In 1943, their pamphlets calling for active resistance and sabotage in order to bring down the Hitler regime caused a great stir in Munich and beyond. They were eventually captured and beheaded.

---

4 Philipp Freiherr von Boeselager, *Valkyrie: The Story of the Plot to Kill Hitler, by Its Last Member* (New York: Alfred A. Knopf, 2009), 69–70. Stefania Falasca shows that von Galen met privately with the key resistance figure Carl Goerdeler in November 1943, a meeting that both men regarded with great satisfaction. Goerdeler told Hermann Pünder that von Galen was warmly sympathetic to the resistance movement. Stefania Falasca, *Un vescovo contro Hitler: Von Galen, Pio XII e la resistenza al nazismo* (Milan: Edizioni San Paolo, 2006), 68–70, 226–29.

Closer to the time of the sermons was the reaction of Father Bernhard Lichtenberg, provost of the cathedral in Berlin. On August 28, 1941, Lichtenberg wrote a letter to the Reich Führer of doctors, Leonardo Conti. He called to mind Bishop von Galen's sermon of August 3, in which the bishop charged that mentally ill patients were being deliberately killed. "If this charge were false," he wrote, "then you, Herr Reich Führer of Doctors, would have long ago publicly charged the bishop with libel and instituted legal action against him, or the Secret State Police would have taken steps to defend its honor. This has not happened. Therefore you admit that the bishop's charge is correct." Lichtenberg, who was already in the sights of the Gestapo for his public prayers on behalf of the Jewish people, was arrested in October 1941, when he was preparing to make a public statement from the pulpit denouncing an anti-Semitic poster. He was sentenced to two years in prison. Because of his age and ill health, he could not stand up to his harsh treatment and died while he was being transported to stricter punishment at the Dachau concentration camp.[5]

Why was Bishop Clemens August von Galen not arrested? Where *was* the Gestapo? What were they doing when the dissemination of his sermons was stirring up such trouble all over Germany?

What they were doing was trying to figure out what to do and seeking instructions from their superiors. After the war was over, documents were found indicating how close the bishop came to being arrested and killed.

Nine days after the sermon of August 3, Walter Tiessler, a high official in the department of propaganda, wrote to Martin Bormann, the head of the Chancellery and Hitler's right-hand man, that in his opinion, the only satisfactory measure would be to

---

5   Günter Beaugrand, *Kardinal von Galen: Der Löwe von Münster*, Freundeskreis Heimathaus Münsterland, Telgte (Münster: Ardley-Verlag, 1996), 44–45.

hang the Bishop of Münster. Any lighter punishment, whether
imprisonment or a fine, would not be enough to stop the spreading of the "lies of the bishop that the wounded will be killed
by us." On the next day, Tiessler reported to Bormann that he
had discussed the issue with Joseph Goebbels and made the
same recommendation—that the bishop should be arrested and
hanged. Goebbels replied that this was a measure that could be
decided only by the Führer. As for Goebbels himself, he feared
that if action were taken against von Galen, "the support of the
people of Münster for the rest of the war can be written off. And
you can probably add the whole of Westphalia."

To Tiessler's counterargument that it must be possible by means
of propaganda to set the people against the bishop, Goebbels replied
that in his opinion, it was best during the war to try as much as
possible to "steer" the churches in the direction of the regime rather
than to provoke them. "One should begin a fight with an opponent,"
he added, "only when one is prepared for the opponent's counterattack." This would be very difficult—indeed, almost impossible—in
the case of a counterattack by the Church during the course of the
war. Goebbels continued with a fiendish proverb: "Revenge should
be enjoyed, not hot, but cold."

It would be easy to deal with the Church after the expected victory in the war, Goebbels was convinced. In the joy of victory and
rebuilding, Hitler could announce among his great social measures
that all the property of the Church belonged to the people.

Bormann replied to Tiessler on August 13—the same day that
Tiessler gave him this report of his discussion with Goebbels—
that it was certainly the case that von Galen deserved death for his
sermon on euthanasia but that the Führer could hardly be expected
to take that step, considering the war situation.[6]

---

6   Löffler, doc. 342, v. II, 891–92, n. 4.

But Hitler himself at least considered such a step and had a plan for doing it in such a way as to win the propaganda battle. Goebbels would publicize the English radio reports about von Galen's sermon on euthanasia, and the German press would mock the British for believing that a German bishop could possibly say such outlandish things. After a time, it would be "discovered" that the English report had actually been correct, leading to a storm of anger at von Galen from the whole country. This would provide the "welcome opportunity" to bring him before the people's court for a conviction and a severe sentence.[7]

For whatever reason, this plan was not carried out. The visit from the Gestapo, for which Bishop Clemens August prepared himself, never came. The propaganda ministry sought to undo the damage done by his sermon, but as the example of Bernhard Lichtenberg made clear, Tiessler's fear was correct: A failure to arrest von Galen spread the conviction that what he had said in his sermon was true.

Nazi propaganda, of course, tried to counter the effect on the populace of von Galen's sermons. At a Party rally in Weeze, an official attacked

> the sow behind the Lambertikirche in Münster. I name this swine C. A., that is to say, Clemens August; whatever else he calls himself I do not know . . . This swine says, the Führer is murdering the war cripples. Then he says, the Führer is having the invalids of the workplace and the weak elderly murdered. This traitor against authority and against the State, this swine, goes from place to place and dares to speak against the Führer and the State; he is on the side of Churchill and Stalin. This piglet and his mob of hangers-on should be allowed to go to the front by Smolensk; let him speak there where he wills and where he can find someone to listen to him. You should also

---

7   Beaugrand, 48, citing an article by Professor Hans Günter Hockerts in *Das Parlament*.

know that this well-fed blubberball is paid 107,000 Marks by those whom he claims are murdering invalids.[8]

This speech and others like it led to a little propaganda skirmish. In late September and early October, the vicar general of the Diocese of Münster gathered together evidence, petitioned the public prosecutor to bring charges of defamation against the speakers, and informed all the priests of the diocese that he had done so. Naturally, the prosecutor found the charges to be without merit.[9] In November, the vicar general sent out another statement. In this case, someone had forged a document purporting to be a pastoral letter from Bishop von Galen, urging people to resist and sabotage with the aim of bringing down the regime. "My warnings to the Gestapo have gone unheeded," he supposedly said:

> If the Gestapo wants a battle against all upright and true Germans, then fine, we will take up the gauntlet . . . You do not have to obey an unjust and lawless regime. Our fight must be to bring down this godless system which pretends to protect the world from godlessness . . . From now on there is only one thing to do: Exercise passive resistance! Sabotage the measures of this so-called regime! Damage the war machine of the Nazis, our enemies, wherever you can! Our goal should be, not to conquer the world, but to give peace, justice and freedom to Germany once again!

The forgery seemed, said the vicar general's statement, designed to defame the bishop.[10] Never during the Nazi period did he advocate overthrowing the regime. His sermons and letters were aimed at denouncing injustice and encouraging morally upright people not to cooperate in evil and to suffer bravely if they should be persecuted.

---

8   Löffler, doc. 352, v. II, 913.
9   Ibid., doc. 352–54, v. II, 913–16.
10   Löffler, doc. 356, v. II, 919–20.

The image of the anvil standing steadfast under the blows of the
hammer but not striking back—that was the perfect illustration of
his attitude and his teaching.

Only in March 1942, seven months after the sermon, did Bishop
von Galen himself receive a direct criticism from the government. It
came in the form of a stern letter from Hermann Goering, adopting
the tone of a schoolmaster lecturing a recalcitrant pupil:[11]

Herr Bishop!

On October 19, 1933, you took an oath at my hands as the Prussian Minister-President, to be loyal to the German Reich and the
Land of Prussia. In this oath you swore and promised to obey
the constitutionally established regime and to have your clergy
do the same, and that in your dutiful concern for the good and the
interests of the German state, you would strive in the fulfillment of
your spiritual duties to guard against anything that could harm it.

In contradiction to your oath, you have, by your diatribes
and pernicious writings, sabotaged the strength of resistance
of the German people in the midst of a war. Therefore I seek
immediate clarification from you as to how you intend to
bring all your behaviour into conformity with the oath you
have sworn before the Prussian Minister President. I warn you
that there is only one option for you, which is the choice for
the State, as it is for every German citizen.

Heil Hitler!

(signed) Goering
Reich Marshall of the Greater German Reich[12]

11   Thus Löffler characterizes the tone of Goering's letter, v. I, lxxii.
12   Löffler, doc. 364, v. II, 938–39.

In his reply, von Galen recalled the "unforgettable" day on which he had made that oath and the brief remarks that he had addressed to Goering on that occasion. It was not only a duty, he had said, but a matter close to his heart, to be able to swear by oath to show loyalty to his country and to use his influence for its good. "And your Excellency's friendly greeting," he added, "gives me the confidence that I will have an understanding hearing from the leaders of the State, if I should believe myself obliged by my oath to make them aware of any danger that threatens the well-being of our people."[13]

Now, in his letter of reply to Goering, he professed by the witness of his conscience that he had never violated that oath. In any protests he had made to the Führer or other officials of the government, and in his preaching and writings, he had acted in fulfillment of his oath to guard against any danger that could threaten the well-being and the interests of the German state. He continued:

> And if, like other German bishops, I have also done this during the time of war, I saw myself obliged to do so because of the actions of certain circles that, behind the back of the German troops, carry on a battle against the Christian religion and the Catholic Church and against reverence for the inalienable fundamental rights of the human person, and endanger the inner unity and power of resistance of the German people. . . .
>
> I allow myself therefore, with the respect that I owe to your person, Herr Reichsmarshall, and to your high office, but also with the freedom and assurance that my conscience, my episcopal office and my honor demand of me, to deny the charges made against me in your letter of March 5, 1942. I am convinced that these charges can have their origin only in an inaccurate report.

---

13   Löffler, doc. 368, v. II, 947–48.

I beg most earnestly that you indicate to me in detail any of
my utterances that have led to these bitter charges being laid
against me, to give me the opportunity of giving you or some
other trusted person the true text of the incriminating sermons
and pastoral letters, so as to demonstrate that my behaviour
has always been in full accord with the obligations of my oath.

He concluded:

In the hope that I will not be denied the right as a German
man, in full freedom to defend myself against charges that
besmirch my honor, I remain, Herr Reichsmarshall, with
expressions of highest respect and the German greeting,

> Most sincerely,
>
> (signed) + Clemens August
> Count von Galen[14]

The bishop's letter brought the issue to a close. He did not hear
from Goering again. But this did not mean von Galen had been
forgotten, either by the Gestapo or by Nazis in the highest places. A
number of people were arrested and killed for the crime of copying
and disseminating von Galen's sermons. As for the bishop himself,
of course the Gestapo continued to report on every public appearance he made. But the decision had been made to deal with him
after Germany had won the war. In a dinner-table conversation on
July 4, 1942, Hitler told his associates that after the final victory, he
would have a reckoning with von Galen "down to the last penny."[15]

---

14   Ibid.
15   Adolf Hitler; Trevor-Roper, H. R., *Hitler's Table Talk 1941–1944*
      (Toronto: Oxford University Press, 1988), 555. (Eng. trans. first published
      in 1953 by Weidenfeld and Nicolson).

CHAPTER 22

Finis Germaniae

O n August 7, 1941, four days after the third of his great sermons of that summer, Bishop von Galen wrote a letter to his niece, a Clemens sister:

> Thank you for your letter of August 4th, and especially for the
> help of your faithful prayers. After everything that I have heard
> about the effects of my recent sermons, I truly believe that the
> love of the Mother of God of Good Counsel has successfully
> prayed to the Holy Spirit to put the right thoughts into my
> mind and the right words on my tongue; for I know from long
> experience that I cannot do this always, and by my own efforts.
> There are times that I am so dumb in thoughts and so unready
> in words that I would do better to keep silent. And then the
> dear God from time to time, when He thinks it is necessary,
> gives me thoughts and words that are in some way useful. But
> let us quietly entrust all success to God and be thankful when
> we are able to do something for Him.

He continued: "Thanks be to God, I have the impression that many are
now opening their eyes, and that a front of 'decent men' is beginning

to build, starting with the devout Catholics; not, to be sure, in order to make a revolution, but to help support and strengthen the 'anvil' of which I spoke on July 20th in the Überwasserkirche."[1]

Considering their worldwide distribution, it was natural that the sermons of summer 1941 would come to the attention of the pope. In September 1941, von Galen received a letter from an Austrian bishop who had had an audience with Pius XII. The pope asked him to give von Galen his personal thanks for the three sermons, which were already well known in Rome. The pope rejoiced in them so much, said von Galen's informant, that he personally read them aloud to his closest advisers with comments of high praise. The Austrian bishop added that the pope made it very clear that he treasured bishops with courage, those who were not mere "diplomats."[2]

Among the flood of letters coming to Bishop von Galen's desk thanking him for his courageous sermons was an anonymous one from a Jewish man. "I have read your telegram and your letter to the Minister in regard to the confiscation of your religious houses with the greatest admiration for your heroic courage," the writer began, "and I hope with all my heart that your appeal will be successful. We are hardly accustomed in these days to find men with the courage to stand up for justice!" Then he continued: "You at least are able to speak of 'German people' to whom injustice is being done. But the right even to *be* a German has been taken away from me!"[3]

The writer went on to say that although he had imbibed German culture since his boyhood and had fought for Germany in the First World War, since 1933 he was no longer considered a true German.

1   Heinrich Portmann, *Kardinal von Galen: Ein Gottesmann seiner Zeit*, 17th ed. (Münster: Aschendorff, 1981), 185.
2   Peter Löffler, ed., *Bischof Clemens August Graf von Galen: Akten, Briefe und Predigten 1933–1946*, 2nd ed. (Paderborn: Ferdinand Schöningh, 1996), doc. 349, v. II, 909.
3   Löffler, doc. 350, v. II, 910–11.

The situation of the Jews in Germany and in German-occupied lands was becoming worse than ever. The next step was to be the requirement that Jews wear a yellow Star of David whenever they came out of their homes. "We are at the mercy of the mobs; anyone can spit on us, and we cannot dare to defend ourselves. And—O sadism!— they have chosen the beginning of our highest holidays to do this to us! The darkest days of the Middle Ages have come to light again! No one will help us, and we will have to suffer what the poor people in the occupied lands have already had to suffer for some time!" Jews in Poland and Lithuania had long been obliged to wear the Star of David and to greet German soldiers without being greeted in return. There was hunger in the ghettos and forcible removal of Jews from some cities. "Your Excellency," the letter continued, "I wouldn't say anything if they would line us up against the wall and shoot us—but this slow martyrdom, this degradation, that is inhuman!"

The writer expressed his fear of what new miseries might come for the Jewish people after the new ordinance came into effect on September 19, 1941: "Will a helper arise for us?" he cried.

"I only hope, Your Excellency, that this letter does not cause you any discomfort. You do not know me, I do not know you. It is only the irrational wish, the foolish hope, that a helper will arise for us somewhere, that has prompted me to write this letter. God bless you!"[4]

Von Galen has been criticized for not speaking out in favor of the Jews even after receiving this heartrending letter. His defenders reply that such criticism is unfair. He always made it clear when defending human rights that they belong to every person without exception and when speaking about the fifth commandment, "*Thou Shalt Not Kill*," impressed upon his audience that the prohibition protected every innocent person, regardless of religion or any other factor. When von Galen stressed the universality of human

---

4   Ibid.

rights and obligations, his meaning would be clear to his audience whether he was writing or speaking. We will see evidence of this below. On the other hand, he was convinced that explicitly mentioning the Jews would only make their plight worse. Perhaps the author of the letter, with his phrases "irrational wish" and "foolish hope," believed the same. At any rate, he praised the bishop for his courage. We, today, might wish that von Galen had decided to wear the Star of David himself and encouraged his priests and people to do the same. There is no way of knowing whether that thought even occurred to him. The failure to take such a step, if it was a failure, was one of imagination, not courage. It is clear that when he thought it helpful to speak out, he did not lack the courage to do so. Once again, he was in a situation in which anything he did would be useless at best and might make things worse for those he desired to help. The writer of the letter himself indicated that he really did not expect that the bishop could do anything effective to help his people, and he praised von Galen for his courage, a courage made plain by the fact that when he preached his three sermons in the summer of 1941, von Galen had put his life at risk at the very moment when Germany's fortunes were at their height.

Meanwhile, in the west, England was carrying on the war effort virtually alone. This led Hitler to think that it was time to open a second front in the east. In fact, he had already opened this new front in June 1941, before von Galen's sermons. On June 22, Hitler renounced the non-aggression pact that he had made with the Soviet dictator, Joseph Stalin, and attacked the Soviet Union. Hitler believed that he could succeed where Napoleon had not and that the defeat of Russia would persuade the English to sue for peace. The time for seeking revenge on his enemies, including the Bishop of Münster, would then be at hand.

Bishop von Galen made no comment on the war against the Soviet Union until September 14, when he issued a lengthy pastoral letter on the subject.[5] Beginning with a brief reminder of the Church's repeated condemnations of communism, he lauded the Führer for renouncing the pact and for bringing to light the "dishonesty and treachery of the Bolshevists." The renunciation of the pact "delivered us from the deepest anxiety and freed us from a heavy weight," he wrote. He even went so far as to quote from the declaration Hitler made at the time: "For more than two decades the Jewish-Bolshevik power-holders in Moscow have been trying to set not only Germany, but all of Europe, on fire . . ."[6]

Why was von Galen supportive of the war against the Soviets? As we have already seen, he was convinced that communism, including Soviet communism, was a danger to the world. Among the dangers were its rejection of God and a corresponding rejection of the dignity of the human person. By the time he wrote this pastoral letter, correspondence received from soldiers at the front had confirmed his view that Germany was freeing the Russian people from a terrible slavery and enabling them once again to be able to practice their religious faith: "We have received with joy, from numerous letters of soldiers," he wrote, "the news that our soldiers in the areas that have been freed from Bolshevist control have been able to clean up churches that had been desecrated and often shamefully used, and restore them to their sacred purposes, so that our Christian soldiers could hold divine services, and could make it possible for the inhabitants—who were at first fearful and then overjoyed—to celebrate once again the divine mysteries."[7]

Convinced that the peoples under the control of communism were enslaved, von Galen was further convinced that once they overcame their fear of the invading army, they saw it as an army of

---

5   Löffler, doc. 348, v. II, 901–8.
6   Ibid.
7   Ibid.

liberation. The reports he had received so far affirmed this conviction. An example of the attitude of German soldiers at the front is the letter written to his wife on July 20, 1941, by Karl von Wendt:

> The Russian people reject this war more and more as we advance, and themselves call the Russian army "Bolsheviks," with whom they have no relationship. In many places we see people bringing their crosses and icons out of hiding places; many of the prisoners display religious medals to prove their good faith when we ask whether they are Bolsheviks . . . I think the civilian population is seventy percent on our side, especially after they have lived a few days alongside German soldiers and see that we aren't killers and brigands like the Reds, who behave in a truly crazy way within their own country . . .[8]

Regular German soldiers were *not* killers and brigands. It was not until the late spring of 1942 that Philipp Freiherr von Boeselager began to realize that the stories of atrocities in areas under the control of the SS were not isolated incidents but that gypsies and Jews were being murdered in cold blood by design.[9] If an officer at the front could find out about German atrocities only in mid-1942, and then only because he was aide-de-camp to Field Marshal Hans Günther von Kluge, a civilian hundreds of miles away had no way of knowing it a year earlier.

So Bishop von Galen prayed for the success of German arms in the battle against the Bolsheviks. But this was not the only message in his pastoral letter. He told his readers that it was crucial to fight communist ideas on the home front, lest these ideas subtly gain entry

8   Quoted in Philipp Freiherr von Boeselager, *Valkyrie: The Story of the Plot to Kill Hitler, by Its Last Member* (New York: Alfred A. Knopf, 2009), 194–95, n. 2.
9   Ibid., 71–83.

After the bombing raid of October 10, 1943, in which fifty of the Clemens Sisters were killed, workers search for survivors and bodies as two Sisters look on.

"Three cardinals on a plane." Cardinals Frings, von Galen, and von Preysing, accompanied by an American officer, leave Rome on an American military plane.

The cardinal listens to the auxiliary bishop on the occasion of his triumphant return to Münster as a cardinal, March 16, 1946. To his left (the viewer's right) is Franz Vorwerk, who had been expelled from the province by the Nazis in 1938 and had only returned in 1945. Behind him, in the top hat and with the moustache, is the cardinal's nephew, Christoph Bernhard von Galen.

In procession to the ruins of the cathedral.

In front of the bombed-out cathedral, the cardinal listens
to more addresses.

The Lion of Münster thanks his people for the support
they gave him during the Nazi days.

On Sunday, March 17, the cardinal receives the well-wishes of British officers.

Portrait photo of Cardinal Clemens August von Galen.

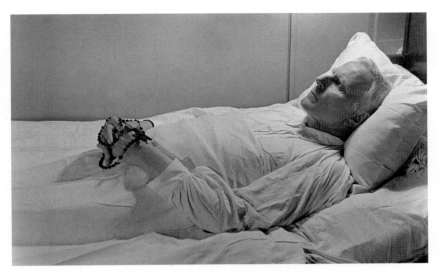

March 22, 1946, shortly after Cardinal von Galen's death.

Cardinal von Galen's funeral procession winds through the streets of Münster, March 28, 1946. On the left, carrying the cardinal's chalice, is his faithful secretary, Dr. Heinrich (sic) Portmann. Next to him, another cleric carries the cardinal's hat; ahead of them is a third cleric carrying the pastoral staff.

Cardinal von Galen's funeral procession winds through massive crowds lining the streets of Münster, March 28, 1946.

into human hearts and turn victory into defeat by bringing about a Bolshevik revolution at home. The memory of the last war and the revolutions that shook Germany after its conclusion had taught him that communist ideas at home must be fought with as much energy as communist armies were fought at the front.

Taking his guidance from Pope Pius XI's 1937 encyclical letter against communism, *Divini Redemptoris*, he laid out the basic principles of Bolshevik teaching:

- All reality is reducible to matter.
- Thus there is no room for the idea of God, for a distinction between matter and spirit, or for soul and body, and thus no survival of the soul after death and no hope of a future life.
- There are no natural rights of the human person in relation to the community.
- The community is the source of its own authority over the individual.
- Marriage and the family are expressions of a certain stage of economic development; the marriage bond has no legally or morally binding force in itself.
- The rights of parents in regard to the raising of their children are taken over by the community; any legal or moral order is a purely human construction and so is changeable and only of circumstantial importance.

These principles of communism contradicted both Divine Revelation and natural reason, said von Galen, quoting the pope, and they must be fought against if a society is to be built on sound principles. But principles like those of communism were already present in German social life. The Christian and rationally discernible moral principles of social life were being attacked in the media and rejected in practice. "No one who follows public life can doubt this," the bishop said:

For today, we will not give all the instances that illustrate this statement. For today we will recall only that the God-given *rights of the human person* are frequently not recognized and thus in practice denied. You know this: frequently today German citizens are deprived of their rights: to life; to immunity from physical harm; to freedom; to joining with others in striving for morally-permitted goals; to property and the use of one's property—without being accused of any crime before a properly-constituted court, and without these restrictions on their rights being imposed upon them as the punishment for some crime.

In the Germany of 1941, he argued, naturalism and materialism, the same basic errors of communism, were at work, so that behind the backs of the armies in the field, the way was being prepared for the spiritual reign of communist ideas at home.[10]

It was another brave and risky performance by von Galen, a pastoral letter supporting German armies and soldiers while claiming that there was an enemy behind their backs at home. Although he did not mention the Gestapo by name, as he had in the sermons of July 13 and 20, he was still saying quite clearly that *they* were the enemy, and they were the ones who this time would stab the German soldiers in the back. The Nazis were among the proponents of the stab-in-the-back legend concerning the end of the First World War. Now von Galen revived the image and made *them* the enemies on the home front. The meaning of the letter was completely clear to the Nazis. Gauleiter Meyer complained to Goebbels and Bormann. Goebbels noted bitterly in his diary that even when von Galen was attacking communism, he could not refrain from putting National Socialism on the same level.[11] Once again, however, nothing was done. The decision had already been made not to act against the

10   Löffler, doc. 348, v. II, 901–8.
11   Löffler, doc. 348, v. II, 908–9, n. 7.

bishop during the war. But this letter put one more item in the ledger against him, for which the Nazis planned to call him to account.

In the meantime, the Nazi propaganda machine was hard at work trying to counter von Galen's attacks on the Gestapo. They put out the claim that some of the religious houses that had been confiscated were hotbeds of subversive activity, possessing illegal radio transmitters that were used for traitorous purposes. It was further claimed that many of the religious refused to house people made homeless by the bombings and that the religious were given money and bus transport and had later been able to return to their homes. The office of the diocesan vicar general sent out a lengthy statement in November 1941 refuting all these claims.[12]

In the meantime, Bishop von Galen continued to protest to the government authorities on behalf of the expelled religious and to work with those bishops who were not "mere diplomats" to encourage the others to speak out more forcefully. Late in 1941, he supported a proposal to send a joint protest to the regime by Catholic and Protestant bishops together. In the end, however, Cardinal Bertram's more "diplomatic" style once again won out. Separate protests—tamer than von Galen would have liked—were sent by the Catholic bishops and the leaders of the Protestant communities.[13]

The Sisters of Perpetual Adoration in Vinnenberg were among those who had been expelled from their convent in July 1941. Christoph Bernhard von Galen, the bishop's nephew, had given them a place to live at Burg Dinklage, while the bishop sent repeated protests to the government about their unjust expulsion. Only in January 1942 did he receive a reply. It stated that the sisters had behaved as enemies of the people and of the state, and therefore the property had been expropriated to the use of the German Reich.

---

12   Löffler, doc. 357, v. II, 921–25.
13   See Löffler, docs. 358–59 and notes, v. II, 926–27.

Upon receiving this, von Galen made another vigorous protest and composed a pastoral letter to be read in all the churches on February 1. He presented it himself at the church of St. Lambert and gave another impassioned sermon.[14]

First, he noted that the sisters were strictly enclosed nuns, hence having very little contact with the outside world. The convent in which they lived their life of penance, prayer, and manual work lay in the countryside outside the hamlets of Milte, Ostbevern, and Glandorf. "Many of you," he told his listeners, "know absolutely nothing about Kloster Vinnenberg." So, he wondered, how could these poor, sweet little nuns—he used the diminutive "*Nönnchen*"—possibly be involved in any activities that could characterize them as enemies of the people and state? "Or could it be," he asked rhetorically, "that already today in the German Reich it is considered inimical to the people and the state when one takes Christianity, the following of Christ, with great seriousness, when one follows the evangelical counsels of poverty, chastity and obedience out of love for God?"

For those who thought that was the case, he continued, then all Christianity, and all those then present in the church, were enemies of the people and the state. "Against this," he shouted,

> I here openly lodge a protest! Also in your names! We feel it with bitter sorrow that we who thankfully call ourselves Christians, that we who acknowledge and defend the Christian faith which God has given us, that we who strive for the preservation of the Christian-German culture, are judged, reviled and treated as enemies of the state.
>
> As you know, I myself have been reviled as a traitor and an enemy of the state in newspaper articles and public meetings

---

14   See Löffler, doc. 362 for the sermon; 361 for the pastoral message read in all the churches; 360, n. 1, for text of the letter from the regime: v. II, 927–36.

during the last few months, because in my concern for the well-being and prosperity of the German people I have publicly stood up against arbitrariness and violence, against the "condemnation without possibility of defence" of innocent persons (as Reich Minister Dr. Frank called it), and for justice, freedom and truth. Truly I have not enjoyed having to deal with these situations. It hurts me in the depths of my soul when our enemy at war seeks to use these situations in order to influence our German people. But what other course is left to us bishops, if all of our innumerable warnings and protests are not heeded, in most cases are not even replied to, if we see that precisely the time of war is used to destroy Christianity, to undermine the foundations of German culture, freedom, truthfulness and justice, behind the lines where our Christian soldiers are fighting? Who is guilty of bringing this danger upon the German people? Not, I tell you, those who are trying to rectify these dangers, but those who bring about these situations and do not work to overcome them. I would remind those officials of the Party who dare to slander the bishops as traitors to our country because of our forthright speech, of the words of Adolf Hitler in his book *My Struggle*, page 399:

"A person who knows of a situation of genuine danger, and sees the possibility of helping, has the solemn duty and responsibility, not to work 'in silence,' but to work *in public* against the danger and for its correction. If he does not do that, he is an irresponsible lazy weakling, who refuses his duty either out of cowardice or out of sloth and incapacity."

"The German bishops," von Galen continued, "are not cowardly weaklings. When it is necessary, we act in public to correct evil."[15]

---

15   Ibid.

He went on to remind his hearers that he had tried unsuccessfully to initiate legal action against a number of high Party officials who had slandered his honor. "Is it the case that the honor of a German man can no longer find the protection of a German court if he is a bishop, if he is a Catholic?" he asked. "I do not yet want to accept that."

Now he returned to the letter from the regime announcing the expropriation of the convent at Vinnenberg. This too was an attack on his honor, and not only his. The property was taken because the sisters were accused—not convicted, he stressed, just accused—of being enemies of the people and of the state. Once again, it was a condemnation without the possibility of making a defense. But even if the sisters were guilty, he argued, the church and convent and its little bit of land were the property of the Diocese of Münster. Since they were seized in virtue of the law that allowed the confiscation of the property of enemies of the Reich, that meant that the bishop and the diocese—in effect, all Catholics of Münster—were being considered as enemies of the Reich. He thundered out his indignation:

> My fellow Christians! People say that I have good nerves, that I do not easily lose my composure and get angry. But I want to tell you a secret: when I read those words, "The property of the episcopal see of Münster in Vinnenberg has been confiscated according to the decree concerning the property of enemies of the Reich," the blood came up to my head, my heart came beating up into my throat; I jumped up from my desk and had to walk up and down in my room for ten minutes before I could get myself under control. That is how angry I was at this attack on me, on you, in principle on all German Catholics. Are we considered to be enemies of the Reich? Is that how they dare to treat us?
>
> My fellow Christians! It is beneath my dignity to defend myself against such a charge. I refuse to do so. Nor will I

defend today the members of our religious orders against this unheard-of accusation. You know them. You know that they are not enemies of the Reich.

He went on to note that the Benedictine Fathers, the Missionary Sisters, and the Jesuit Fathers had also been designated as enemies of the Reich, even though six of the Jesuits had died as soldiers, seventeen had been wounded, and about thirty had been decorated, including one who had received the Iron Cross First Class. "Is that an enemy of the Reich?" he asked. Then he added, "It is guaranteed by law to all German men who serve the Fatherland as soldiers, that when they return, their home and their work place will be there for them. But home and workplace are being taken away from members of Catholic religious orders, while they are fighting against Bolshevism and shedding their blood for Germany." Once again, he reminded his congregation of Christ's prophecy to His disciples: "If the world hates you, know that it has hated me before you."[16]

By February 1942, the bishops were discussing a joint pastoral letter as a follow-up to their December protest to the government, which had had no effect. The conference of bishops of western Germany came to an agreement on this idea on February 24. Cardinal Bertram, however, threw cold water on the plan. He thought that the time was not right for a joint action of all the bishops or for the text of the December protest to be made public. Instead, on March 22, pastoral letters referring to that protest and describing its contents were issued in various dioceses, including Münster. The letter that von Galen had prepared as a draft for the common protest had itemized the attacks on the rights of Catholics but also stressed the natural rights of the human person. The anti-Christian teaching that was being spread in Germany was "forgetting and

---

16   Ibid.

disregarding the God-given rights of each person, including those of foreign blood and of the enemy nations."[17]

In a pastoral letter that December,[18] von Galen wrote about justice, clearly and explicitly condemning the idea that might makes right. Once again, he defended the rights of the person against an authority that oversteps the bounds of justice. "The fundamental demands of justice are eternal and unalterable . . . In principle they are the same for all men and hold true across the borders of peoples and races. They also hold true for a common life with people of foreign races and nations. Thus they are the foundation for the so-called rights of peoples and for the peaceful cooperation between peoples that we hope for after the end of this war."[19] Joachim Kuropka is surely right when he says that the phrase "including those of foreign blood" was intended to mean the Jews and would have been so understood.[20] He makes the same point about a phrase used by von Galen in a pastoral letter of October 1943.

Meanwhile, the war continued, but time was no longer on Hitler's side. The United States was now in the war on the Allied side, and the victory over the Soviet Union was not in sight. In the following winter, Stalingrad would mark the end of Hitler's string of successes. Russia proved his downfall after all. With the economic and military might of the Americans behind the Allies, it was only a matter of time before Germany would be defeated. Yet Hitler's fall did not come until May 1945, by which time Germany's cities lay in ruins, six million Jews had perished in Hitler's attempt to destroy all the Jews of Europe in the Holocaust, and at least sixty million people were dead.

---

17   Löffler, docs. 366, 367, v. II, 940–46 (here 944).
18   Löffler, doc. 373, v. II, 960–64.
19   Ibid., 964.
20   Kuropka, "Bishop von Galen und die Juden," in Joachim Kuropka, *Streit-fall Galen* (Münster: Aschendorff, 2007), 159.

In 1942 and especially in 1943, the Allies increased their bombing raids on Germany, including the tactic of carpet-bombing German cities. German propaganda condemned the Allies for targeting civilians and promised new secret weapons of revenge. In Münster, there were only seven raids during 1942, with a loss of six lives, and no bombs fell between September 16 of that year and the early part of June 1943. But other cities had felt the blows, and Bishop von Galen was concerned for all those suffering from the war, both at home and on the many battle fronts. He kept up his pastoral concern for the education of the young, reminding his faithful that should their children be relocated to parts of Germany that were less likely to be bombed, the parents should take care that they continue to receive Catholic education. Indeed, this was no time for mincing words. Everyone knew that death could come at any time. Von Galen encouraged parents to make a will and to specify that their children should be raised Catholic should their parents die.[21]

On June 12, 1943, beginning at 2 a.m., over one thousand bombs were dropped on Münster, and fifty-two people lost their lives, the largest total yet.[22] Bishop von Galen consoled the bereaved and the injured and those whose property was damaged or destroyed. But he expressly rejected the talk of revenge that came from Party and government sources. On July 4, on the occasion of the diocesan pilgrimage to the shrine of the Virgin Mary at Telgte, he affirmed that "those who began the bombing war and carry it on with ever more powerful weapons bear a frightening responsibility. Nevertheless," he continued:

> I must, one time, say this publicly: I cannot and will not go along with the talk of hatred and revenge that is constantly repeated in the German press; and neither should you go along

21 Löffler, doc. 379, v. II, 973–74.
22 Stadtmuseum Münster, *Bomben auf Münster* (1983), 35.

with it. Should it truly be the desire and the will of the German people to take revenge for the suffering that we are enduring? To desire above all things to destroy churches and hospitals, and kill children and women who have nothing to do with the war, in England and the other enemy countries? Shall we Germans, we Christians, follow the old Jewish law of an eye for an eye and a tooth for a tooth, a law which Christ expressly rejected? Does it console a German mother whose child has been killed by a bomb, to be assured that we will kill the child of an English mother? No! Such a promise of revenge and retribution is in reality no consolation! It is anti-Christian, it is fundamentally anti-German, because it is unworthy, because it is ignoble, because it is unchivalrous![23]

In the midst of the terrible destruction of the Second World War, von Galen held to the principles of nobility and chivalry he had learned at Dinklage, as well as to the traditional Catholic teaching on the morality of warfare. Not only must a war be fought only for a just cause (*ius ad bellum*), it must also be fought by just means (*ius in bello*). The deliberate targeting of innocent civilians is contrary to the principles of *ius in bello*, regardless of whether or not such actions are first undertaken by the enemy. Von Galen clarified that it is morally acceptable for soldiers in war to use their weapons against the enemy, even when they know that innocent persons may also be harmed. But, he continued, "deliberately to aim at non-military targets, to strive to harm non-combatants, merely for the sake of revenge . . . , that is contrary not only to Christian thinking, it is contrary to moral thinking, to chivalrous soldiery, to noble manliness, whose pride it is, not to fall into primitive and low feelings of vengeance, but in manly self-control to fight only against the armed enemy!"[24]

---

23 Löffler, doc. 382, v. II, 983–84.
24 Ibid.

There was one more small bombing raid in Münster in July and then nothing for three months. In the meantime, the fear came to von Galen's attention that there would be more killings of the sick and disabled under the euthanasia program. Plans were being made to transport large numbers of sick people to other institutions. The bishop was skeptical of the claim that the institutes from which they were being transported were being made available to take patients from hospitals that were in danger of being bombed. These institutes were also in locations that would likely put them in the sights of a bombing raid. He would be happy, he told an official in Berlin, to dispel any unrest among the people about these moves, but the unrest had its origin in the large numbers of deaths that had occurred the last time large numbers of patients were moved, in 1941, and in the continuing propaganda for euthanasia.[25]

On September 12, 1943, the German bishops issued one of their most direct pastoral letters of the Nazi period. It dealt, in the words of Ludger Grevelhörster, with "the fundamental meaning of the ten commandments as rules of life for all peoples, and was composed without the cooperation and thus against the will of Cardinal Bertram," thus showing

> that the opinion of the body of bishops in regard to their chairman's often fruitless politics of engagement had in the meantime radically shifted and von Galen's example from the summer of 1941 had attracted numerous followers in the ranks of the German bishops. The central passage of the pastoral letter culminates in the statement, "Killing is bad in itself," even when it is done apparently for the good of the community: whether it is against the innocent and powerless mentally ill, innocent hostages and unarmed prisoners of war or convicted criminals, or "people of a foreign race or ancestry."

---

25   Löffler, docs. 383, 385–86.

The letter's defense of the rights of God and the rights of man amounted to, in Grevelhörster's words, "a moral condemnation of the ruling system which could hardly be more clearly expressed under the conditions of a totalitarian dictatorship."[26]

Other concerns about this time had to do with the spiritual welfare of the Polish workers who had been brought by force into Germany. He had received reports that doctors had been forced to perform abortions on Polish women. Another concern was that the government had decreed that German priests were forbidden to hear the Confessions of Polish workers. Clemens August urged Cardinal Bertram not only to protest this (which was done with some success) but to insist that the bishops should make it clear that all priests should disobey any such order and always be willing to hear the Confessions of those in need of the sacrament.

After the air raid in July, Münster had not come under attack for three months.

Things were quiet enough that Mother Bona, the superior of the Clemens Sisters, called in the superiors of the daughter houses for a conference in early October. It proved a tragic decision. On October 10, the United States Army Air Forces flew its first daytime bombing raid against the city of Münster. American tactics involved flying in formation over a designated target and laying down a carpet of bombs over the area. In the raid on Münster, 236 B-17 Flying Fortresses took part. Ellis B. Scripture, group navigator of the 95th US Bombardment Group, recalled his shock when he learned of the target of the mission:

> Our group had been "stood down" on the evening of October 9th. A Saturday night bash was in full swing when we were alerted about 10:00 p.m. As always, the clubs were closed

---

26   Ludger Grevelhörster, *Kardinal Clemens August Graf von Galen in seiner Zeit* (Münster: Aschendorff, 2005), 118–20.

immediately and the staff . . . immediately went to the war room. The field order was coming in on the teletype and we learned that our target was to be the front steps of the Munster [sic] Cathedral . . . I remember being shocked to learn that we were to bomb civilians as our primary target for the first time in the war. I went to Col. Gerhardt and told him that I didn't think I could fly this one. His reaction was exactly what one would expect (in retrospect) as a career officer (and a very fine commander). He said something like this: "Look, Major, this is war—spelled W-A-R. We're in an all-out fight; the Germans have been killing innocent people all over Europe for years. We're here to beat the hell out of them—and we're going to do it. Now, I'm leading this mission—and you're my navigator. You're leading the mission also! Any questions?" I said, "No, Sir."—And that ended the incident.[27]

Münster's air raid sirens began to wail at five minutes before three in the afternoon. It was a beautiful sunny Sunday afternoon, and people were out enjoying the weather or on their way to visit family or friends. Few believed that the Allies could really be launching a bombing raid out of a cloudless sky in the middle of the day, so many were still in the streets or in their houses when the bombs began to land. In fifteen minutes, more than twenty thousand bombs fell on the city. In the destruction, 473 civilians were killed, as well as nearly two hundred soldiers. For Münster, this was four times as many deaths as had occurred in all the bombing raids of the war up to that date.[28]

Some of the Clemens Sisters had family members visiting them from outside the city. Others were taking recreation in the garden of the motherhouse. Bombs fell there, and at the Hedwigsklinik, and

27   *Bomben auf Münster*, 44.
28   Ibid., 30, 17.

at the Clemens Hospital, almost as soon as the alarms were sounded. "Despite the greatest rush," wrote one of the sisters who was at the Clemens Hospital,

> many met their deaths on the way to the bombcellar. There was terrible chaos: stone was flying, windows were shattering, dust put everything into darkness. People were crying for help; this, combined with the heartfelt prayers of so many, created a unified cry to heaven for help . . . A direct hit had damaged the Barbara Wing, and the bomb had fallen through the children's area beneath it and into the cellar, without exploding. Sister Coleta was calling for help from within the ruins caused by this bomb . . . Sister Regina and Dr. Jolta, with superhuman strength, pulled her free of the wreckage. She was unrecogniz- able because of the dust and dirt, but her mind was clear and she was able to identify herself. Her right arm and her left leg were wounded in many places, and she also had many internal injuries, so Rector Brandkamp gave her the holy anointing. The next day she died of her injuries.[29]

This was one of many deaths. Other sisters, some after being freed from being trapped in fallen buildings, went frantically to work seeking other survivors—and the bodies of the dead. By the end of the day, twenty-seven bodies of sisters had been found, includ- ing that of Mother Bona, the general superior. Twenty-five were still missing. The damage was so great that a week later, despite con- stant searching, nine sisters were still missing. Some fifty sisters were killed, including Mother Bona, her assistant, two provincial superi- ors, and fourteen local superiors.[30]

---

29   Anna-Maria Balbach, *Die Barmherzigen Schwestern zu Münster zur Zeit des Nationalsozialismus* (Münster: Dialogverlag, 2007), 109–23.

30   Ibid.

The cathedral and the episcopal palace were among the many buildings destroyed or terribly damaged by the bombs and the fires that they caused. Professor Alois Schröer described how the bishop survived:

His Excellency, the Most Reverend Lord Bishop Clemens August Count von Galen, was upstairs in his palace when the air raid sirens gave the alarm. He was vested in choir dress, waiting for his chaplain to accompany him to Vespers (in the cathedral). Laying the vestments aside, he remained in his study. When the planes flew over Münster and the flak began, he realized the danger of the situation, but it was already too late to go down for shelter. Only a few seconds later the first wave of bombers released their carpet of bombs. Four or five bombs landed on the palace. At that moment, the Bishop had the presence of mind to move to the doorway between his study and his bedroom, a place that could provide some shelter in the middle of the house. Within seconds, the bombs exploded and reduced the main buildings of the stylish old monument to a pile of ruins. One of the bombs shattered the staircase of the palace's left wing, three others destroyed the rear wall of the central section, and a last one fell into the rear part of the right wing. The roof of the central building broke into pieces. The beams and the floor of the first story lost their support when the rear wall was destroyed. They collapsed, producing an inclined plane of ruins and broken beams extending down from the floor of the Bishop's study to the bomb crater at the back of the palace. The study and bedroom of the Bishop collapsed into nothingness, but the inner wall between them remained, giving the bishop a secure place to stand and protection from falling rubble. The chimney also served to protect him from the explosive power of the three bombs that destroyed the rear

wall of the central part of the palace. Eventually the Bishop was
able to reach the anteroom to his study, part of which was still
intact. There he saw, while the air raid was still in progress, that
a fire was starting, but he could not put it out, as all the water
pipes were destroyed.

As the flak continued and the enemy airplanes were still cir-
cling the city, the Bishop's chaplain, Dr. Portmann, rushed to
the scene, and saw the most reverend Bishop standing high up
in the ruins in the open air. The Bishop seemed to be unhurt.
In order to be more free to move, he had removed his cassock,
and he made a strange impression in his unusual apparel—
shorts to his knees, long violet stockings and a leather vest.
When Dr. Portmann asked if he was all right, the most reverend Bishop was peaceful and calm. The chaplain offered to help
him come down, but the Bishop said that was not necessary;
he would come right down, but what was more important was
to find water to put out the fire in the anteroom. Water, however, was not available. The Bishop slowly came down through
the leaning beams, supported by Dr. Portmann. Exhausted
by the horrible fears of the air raid and the tiring climb down
from the ruins—the Bishop had received a small injury to his
lower leg—the most reverend bishop sat down at the edge of a
bomb crater and rested a short while. Then he went immediately to the cathedral.[31]

There he tried, unsuccessfully, to fight the fire that eventually
destroyed the cathedral's roof. Firefighting and rescue efforts were
desperately needed throughout the center of the city. The air raid
of October 10, 1943, was the worst Münster had suffered so far.
In terms of lives lost, it was to be the city's worst in the entire war.

---

31   *Bomben auf Münster*, 53–54.

But it was only the 46th of 102 air raids that would target Münster, and there were to be several that were much larger in terms
of the number and weight of bombs dropped and in the physical
damage caused.[32] By the end of the war, over 680,000 bombs had
been dropped, and the historic center of the city was a pile of ruins,
almost 90 percent destroyed.[33]

Despite the fact that his palace and diocesan curia were destroyed,
Bishop von Galen desired to stay in the city. He took lodgings and
set up the diocesan offices in the seminary. From here, he sent out
notices to his clergy, the other bishops, the apostolic nuncio, and
Pope Pius XII. He even petitioned the government to allow the
return of his exiled cathedral canons Vorwerk and Echelmeyer, considering that two other canons had been killed in the bombing raid
of October 10. The petition, of course, was denied. The two priests
could return to live in Münster only if the bishop withdrew their
nomination as canons. This he would not do.

In November 1943, he was able to hold a conference of deans.
The bishop gave the names of the four priests who were killed in
the bombing raid of October 10, asking for prayers for their souls.
In addition, he gave the names of fourteen priests and one deacon
who were in concentration camps; seven priests in prison and one
in a penitentiary; three who had died in the concentration camp;
eighteen who died in the war; one taken as a prisoner of war; four
missing in Stalingrad, and five others missing in action. Two of the
priests in prison had been arrested from the high school where they
taught religion classes. In the summer of 1943, after the fall from
power of Benito Mussolini in Italy, some students in one of the class-
rooms turned over the photo of Adolf Hitler on the wall, saying,
"Now it's over with Hitler." As a result, five of the staff members of

---

32   Table in *Bomben auf Münster*, 35–36.
33   Ibid., 39.

the school, including the two priests, were arrested. Subsequently, they were sent to concentration camps.[34]

More and more, Bishop von Galen's time was taken up with pastoral concerns raised by the continuing devastation of the war. His pastoral letters dealt with finding a spiritual message behind all the death and destruction. Much of his correspondence was a catalog of the damage and deaths caused by the bombings and letters of consolation to priests whose parishes had been struck or whose people were being evacuated. He thanked them for their fortitude as good shepherds to their flocks and encouraged them to do the best they could in ministering to their people. He urged them when possible to send a priest to accompany groups of their people who were being evacuated, so that they could continue to have Mass and the sacraments and religious instruction. With so many priests on military duty, or in prison or concentration camps, he had to deal with a shortage of priests. This was exacerbated by the fact that he had almost no new priests available—almost all the seminarians had been called to military duty. With the difficulties of communication and travel added to this, von Galen and his chancery officials could not make provision for all the pastoral needs but had to content themselves with words of encouragement and advice to the priests, who then had to figure out as best they could how to serve their people.

Of course, von Galen was not exempted from the kind of personal sorrows and anxieties that affected practically everyone in Germany. His brother Franz, his closest friend since childhood, was arrested in August 1944. One month after the July 20 assassination attempt on Hitler, the Gestapo rounded up all the old Centre Party politicians they could find. On November 22, "Strick" was sent to the Sachsenhausen concentration camp. For a month, the bishop

---

34   Löffler, docs. 397, 403.

had no idea where he was, until Strick's wife received a letter from him a few days before Christmas. Franz had already lost a son in battle and had two others at the front. He had suffered frequent health problems since being in a severe automobile accident ten years earlier, and his brother did not expect to see him alive again. Fortunately, he did survive and was released after the Allies liberated the camp in April 1945.

On September 12, September 30, and October 5, Münster again was the target of massive Allied air raids. It was no longer possible to keep the diocesan general vicariate in the city. On the fourteenth, it was relocated to a hospital at Sendenhorst, about twenty kilometers away. For a time, the bishop continued to live at what was left of the seminary in Münster, spending a few days each week at Sendenhorst. Then came further air raids, on October 22, 25, 26, and 28. The inner city was by now a pile of ruins. The bishop had hoped to celebrate the feast of Christ the King, as he had done every year, in the church of St. Servatius on October 29. It was destroyed, as was the city's famous city hall, on the twenty-eighth. He had to content himself with a pastoral letter reminding his people that after all the sufferings of this life, those who are faithful and who show Christian love to their neighbors in need will rejoice in eternal life with God.[35]

Now he had to stay in Sendenhorst; there it was that a young Count Fritz von Loë, who was hospitalized after being severely wounded, woke one day to find the bishop standing by his bedside.[36] Occasionally, Clemens August was able to travel to Münster by car. In a letter to a friend, he regretted that he had not ridden a bicycle in forty years and could no longer do so—this was now the most reliable form of transportation.

---

35   Löffler, doc. 428.
36   Conversation with the author, August 2010.

On Holy Thursday, March 29, 1945, priests who were able to travel to Sendenhorst for the Mass of Chrism brought rumors that Allied forces were near. Dispirited German troops passed through the city in retreat. On Holy Saturday, American tanks rolled into Sendenhorst. Two days later, Allied troops were in Münster. According to Heinrich Portmann, when England and France had declared war on Germany in 1939, Bishop von Galen had uttered the words *"Finis Germaniae."* Now, with foreign tanks in the bombed-out streets, the end of Germany was at hand. For the Bishop of Münster, the task was now to do what he could to ease suffering and hardship and offer his contribution to the building of a new Germany on Christian foundations.

CHAPTER 23

Under Occupation

The Allies assumed that Bishop von Galen, having been a firm opponent of Nazism, would welcome them as liberators of Germany from the dictatorial regime. It was true, of course, that he was happy to see the end of Nazism. But it was still, as he expressed it on Easter Sunday, "an unnerving experience" to see the march of enemy troops through the German Heimat, which would always be a "sad memory." "This is not the time or the place," he continued, "to speak of how bitterly we feel this event and how our hearts bleed for the needs of our people."[1] There was one thing he wanted to make clear. Although Sendenhorst and much of Westphalia had now surrendered, the war was still on, and the Allies were still Germany's enemies. Although he did not mention this at the time, it must not be forgotten that the Allies were the nations that had reduced Münster to rubble by their bombing. Furthermore, they were the nations that had, in his judgment, subjected Germany to an unjust treaty at Versailles in 1919, leading to the situations that

---

1   Peter Löffler, ed., *Bischof Clemens August Graf von Galen: Akten, Briefe und Predigten 1933–1946*, 2nd ed. (Paderborn: Ferdinand Schöningh, 1996), doc. 446, v. II, 1102.

had made the Hitler phenomenon possible. Bishop von Galen was upset at rumors that he had entered into discussions with the foreign troops, rumors which he indignantly denied. Another rumor, which made it all the way to Hitler's bunker in Berlin, had it that the Bishop of Münster had surrendered the city to the Allied forces. Hitler fumed, "If I could get my hands on that fellow, I would have him hanged!"[2]

So far from entering into negotiations with the Allies as though he had the authority to do so, he issued a public statement on April 9: "I have explained to the gentlemen of the English and American press who have called on me, that as a German bishop I feel and suffer with my German people; that as long as the war continues I refuse to speak with them about political matters or make any declarations of any kind; that it is my strong wish not to be mentioned in the press or on the radio."[3] He continued by denying the truth of an article that had appeared in the Reuters dispatches a few days earlier. According to the article, the purpose of which was to praise him as an example of the "other Germany" that did not approve of Nazism:

> When Himmler once sent his agents to arrest him, Msgr. von Galen asked to be excused while he changed his clothes. He reappeared in his episcopal vestments, wearing his mitre and carrying his crook. "You cannot come into the streets with us like that," said the Gestapo agents, to which the Bishop replied, "Only in my official robes will I go to jail with you. All I have done here I have done as a servant of the Church."
>
> The Gestapo left without their prisoner.[4]

2   Heinrich Portmann, *Kardinal von Galen: Ein Gottesmann seiner Zeit*, 17th ed. (Münster: Aschendorff, 1981), 244.
3   Löffler, doc. 448, v. II, 1104.
4   Ibid., 1105, n. 2.

It would be a great story, and it so well expressed his character that it was widely believed,[5] but there was not a word of truth to it. "The story about an attempt to arrest me," von Galen wrote, "is a complete invention and not true."[6]

Now Westphalia, and soon all of Germany, was under the military rule of those who a short while before were the enemy in a gruesome war. True to his principles, von Galen recognized the legitimacy of the new military government. But to the consternation of those now in charge, he proved to be as difficult for them to deal with as he had been for the Nazis. He considered himself responsible to speak up for those who were suffering, and as usual, he brought to the situation the principled way of thinking he had learned from his father and from the writings of Bishop von Ketteler.

On the fifth of April, von Galen wrote a short note to the British Colonel Ledingham, now in charge of the military regime in Münster. After assuring the colonel that the populace would respect the fact that the occupying powers were now in authority and would obey their ordinances, he continued:

> In the Christian understanding which I represent as a Catholic bishop, you have undertaken not only the power and the right of command, but also the duty and the task of procuring public order and protecting life and property insofar as this is possible and not deleterious to the continued prosecution of the war. As is well known, there are now in our region a great number of now-unemployed foreign workers from the east.

5   Indeed, I heard a version of the story in Toronto in 2011, told as truth by a man who had been a boy in the diocese of Münster at the time. In this version, the bishop asked the Gestapo men whether they had come to arrest Count von Galen or the Bishop of Münster; it was when they replied that they were arresting him because of what he had done as the bishop that he supposedly changed into his pontifical vestments.

6   Löffler, doc. 448, v. II, 1105 and n. 2.

The civil authorities whom you have appointed have no means of protecting lives and property. Therefore I request that comprehensive orders and measures be put into place immediately to hinder and punish wanton acts of violence, destruction, and plundering.[7]

A week later, he made his first visit to Münster since the occupation and spoke with Colonel Ledingham. The next day, he wrote a memorandum for himself of the points he had covered in the conversation.[8] "I presume that my name is known," his memorandum begins:

It has been used in English leaflets and on the radio. Since I confronted the German regime with the demands of truth, freedom and justice, I now do the same in regard to the occupying power.

You have come to a Christian land. We will be obedient to authority. But along with power, authority has also taken on the duty and task of procuring public order and protecting life and property from wanton violence, destruction, and plundering.

It was not only the foreign workers, he complained, who were engaged in pillaging and looting. American soldiers were also stealing. In regard to the foreign workers, von Galen recognized that they stole because they were needy and that providing food and shelter for them was a difficult problem. But he proposed that at least a curfew be imposed on them, confining them to their lodgings at night. Later, he would learn that the Allies saw the situation of the foreign workers from an entirely different perspective and regarded with consternation what they saw as von Galen's blindness to the fact

---

7   Löffler, doc. 447, v. II, 1103.
8   Löffler, doc. 449, v. II, 1105–6.

that these foreign workers were in Germany only because they had been forcibly brought in as slave labor. As for the soldiers, he boldly insisted that they too should be kept under proper military discipline. Four girls in Sendenhorst had been raped during the night of April 10, he said, and churches had been desecrated.[9]

The bishop told the colonel that toward the end of the war, the German populace had believed Allied propaganda rather than German propaganda. Nazi propaganda had claimed that on both the eastern and western fronts, the Allies tolerated or even promoted rape and pillage, whereas the English radio broadcasts had promised that the Allies were coming in order to restore justice and freedom to Germany. Now, unless immediate steps were taken to control the situation, he warned, "we will have to believe what was said by our own propaganda." He feared this would lead to hatred and retaliation and open the door to Bolshevist agitation.[10]

Again and again, von Galen had to complain to the governing authorities. In early June, a priest was robbed at knifepoint and wounded. A Belgian lieutenant was able to report to him that the Russian thieves had been apprehended. The bishop thanked the officer, a devout Catholic who showed him great respect, and went on to urge that all weapons be confiscated from the Russians. When the lieutenant replied that their camps had been searched and no weapons had been found, von Galen gave way to his temper: "If Germans possessed a single child's toy pistol," he thundered, "you would find it. With the Russians, you can't find submachine guns!"[11]

In addition to begging the military regime for justice and security, and trying to help his needy people in whatever ways he could, Bishop von Galen encouraged his people to keep their trust in God

---

9   Ibid.
10   Ibid.
11   Portmann, 247.

during these trying times. On April 18, he issued a pastoral letter expressing his deep compassion for all the sufferings and anxieties they were experiencing and recommending that they bring them all to the feet of the Blessed Virgin Mary, the Mother of Mercy.[12] A deep devotion to Mary had marked him since his childhood. He loved to make pilgrimages to Marian shrines and particularly during his time as bishop to the shrine of the Sorrowful Virgin at Telgte. He would walk the pilgrim route from Münster in the early morning hours and pray before the small wooden pietà, dating from the late fourteenth century. Along the pilgrim route are five double-sided images, erected by his predecessor and relative, Bishop Christoph Bernhard von Galen. On the way to Telgte, the images show the sorrows of Mary during the suffering of her Son. On the return, the reverse sides show her joys. Von Galen's solitary pilgrimages to Telgte had helped him to face the struggles with the Nazis. Now they gave him courage in dealing with the sorrows of the war's end. He communicated his deep devotion to his people in his pastoral letter: "I would like to lead each one of you, without exception, to Mary beneath the Cross," he wrote. He knew what kinds of anxieties and struggles they faced: uncertainty whether their sons or husbands were missing, or prisoners, or dead; homes and businesses and churches destroyed; an economy and a social order in ruins; shortage of food; anxiety for the future. God, he told his people, has allowed all this. Let us accept and bless His holy will. "Like the beloved Mother of God, let us willingly accept the sorrows that God has sent us as our share in the atonement for the disobedience to God's will, as our share in the atonement for sin, which is the source of all the sorrows that come upon the children of Adam. Yes, come with me to Mary, the Sorrowful Mother beneath the Cross. Contemplate her sorrow in the

---

12   Löffler, doc. 450, v. II, 1107–11.

face of the deadly peril of her divine Son who hangs on that Cross, dying." Reflecting on the *Stabat Mater*, the pious hymn of Jacopone da Todi that so often accompanies Catholics as they meditate on the Stations of the Cross, the bishop recalled the sufferings that Mary had to endure in union with her Son. "She sees His scourged body, the horrible wounds in His hands and feet by which He hangs on the Cross, His thorn-crowned head, His lips parched with thirst, the look of death in His eyes, the blood pouring down— and she cannot help Him; she cannot provide the tiniest amount of relief to His sufferings."[13]

By beginning his reflection on the sufferings of Mary, and on those of her divine Son, the bishop was able to remind his people of the Christian understanding of suffering. It is not only a punishment for sinners. The most holy Son of God and His Mother underwent the worst of sufferings, although they were without sin. This introduces us, he told his readers, to the mystery of vicarious atonement. Jesus suffered for the sins of the world. His Mother united her sufferings to His. And every Christian can do the same. "For us," he told them,

> all these sufferings are not only the punishment for sin; above all, they are an opportunity and an invitation to participate, with the dear sorrowful Mother, in the atoning sacrifice of the Son of God, to make in truth our contribution to the glorification of God and the salvation of the world . . . We must take the sorrows of the time upon ourselves, bear our cross. We have no choice about it. But we do not want to make this useless and fruitless by rejecting what God has permitted; rather, we want to make it fruitful for our salvation and that of our brothers by uniting it with the Way of the Cross of the Lord.[14]

13 Ibid.
14 Ibid.

As the Allied armies continued their rush toward Berlin from both east and west, more sufferings came to the German people. They received little sympathy. By the time the war ended in early May, and Allied troops had liberated the concentration camps and death camps, there was a widespread sentiment that the Germans were now only getting what they deserved for putting the Nazis into power, for plunging the world into the most destructive war ever seen, and for the terrible atrocities and mass murders perpetrated by their leaders. In the opinion of a shocked world, all Germans were guilty of these crimes against humanity. Bishop von Galen was one of the first to protest against the thesis of the collective guilt of all Germans. Preaching on July 1, 1945, at the diocesan pilgrimage to Telgte, he reminded his listeners that just two years earlier, at the same place, he had preached against hatred and revenge:

> Two years ago during the Münster pilgrimage I publicly protested against the destruction of the divine order, the violations of justice and of love, that were being proposed and carried out by those who then had power in our nation. At that time, in speeches and on the radio, the talk was that the entire German people were filled with hatred against our enemy in the war, and longed for vengeance and retribution for the sufferings that were brought upon our cities and homes by the bombing war. At that time I said here in Telgte: We reject that! In the name of the Catholics of my diocese I said: That is not our opinion and our conviction. I said: Our soldiers will continue to do their duty as long as the war continues; they will use their weapons against armed opponents in order to achieve peace. But to seek revenge, deliberately to even the score by seeking destruction, or killing women, children and the unarmed—that we reject; that is unchivalrous, that is unchristian, that destroys justice and love . . .

I was criticized for those words. It was said that I was a traitor to my country. I had to bear that. But those words, which I spoke two years ago against the hate and vengefulness of my German countrymen, give me the right this year to express a rejection of some expressions and deeds that can only be explained by the hatred and desire for revenge of our former opponents in the war.

If today things are depicted in such a way that the entire German people and every one of us is guilty because of the horrible things that were done by *some* of our German people in the war: that is unjust. If people say that the entire German people and each one of us is guilty of the crimes that were done in foreign lands and in Germany, above all in the concentration camps: that is an untrue and unjust condemnation of many of us.

The concentration camps themselves show, with their numerous German prisoners and victims, by what means every opposition against the crimes of those in power, indeed every free expression of opinion, was suppressed, punished, and truly made almost impossible. It is a violation of justice and of love to say that all of us, every German, is guilty of these crimes and therefore should be punished for them.

We will accept, and with God's help we will bear with patience, the unavoidable accompaniments of war: the sorrow over our dead; our destroyed cities, homes and churches. But we will not accept unjust condemnation and punishment for arbitrary injustices and horrors the likes of which we have ourselves already wept for and severely suffered under for years.

In years past, words that I have spoken have sometimes, without my leave, been heard, respected, repeated, and made known. I hope that also today my words will press upon the ears of our former enemies in the war, of the peoples beyond the German border, and will find a hearing and be understood. Formerly I spoke up for the divine order of justice and charity against the sayings and doings of those in power in Germany. Today I speak for the same principles and make the same demands to those who now have power in Germany, and to those in lands beyond the German borders who give them their orders, and to the peoples of those lands.

People talk of peace, and want a lasting peace. If they truly want that, let them remember that only justice can secure a path for peace, can push roadblocks to peace out of the way. And only true brotherly love, the rejection of revenge and hatred, can build that peace in hearts which alone can guarantee the peace that is implied by the laying aside of weapons.

So, away with the untrue condemnation which claims that all Germans are guilty of the evil deeds that were done during the war, that all Germans share responsibility for the horrors of the concentration camps . . .

Let those who are truly guilty and responsible be arrested and justly punished by fair legal processes. But for the others, the truly innocent great majority here in our country, who together with me before the war and during the war rejected and condemned injustice, hatred, and revenge, for them let justice and love be the path to "tranquility of order" according to the holy will of God, to a true peace among peace-loving peoples.

Mary, Queen of Peace, pray for us! Gain for us and for all men the insight and the will to bring about God's order of justice and charity and never to damage that order![15]

Like his famous sermons of 1941, the text of this sermon spread quickly throughout Germany. Germans found encouragement

---

15   Löffler, doc. 484, v. II, 1172–77.

and hope in the bishop's words. The occupying military government, however, feared that they would lead to unrest. Three weeks after the sermon, Colonel J. Spottiswoode, then in charge of the military regime in the Münster area, sent Bishop von Galen a message requesting a meeting to discuss the topics of the sermon. Spottiswoode had already corresponded with von Galen in June, in reply to one of the bishop's many letters of complaint. Von Galen had written,

> Once again I urgently request that an end finally be put to the murders, plunderings, and rapes by the Russians and other foreign workers. The German populace cannot believe that the military regime is too weak to take the weapons away from these men and to keep them in their camps. I call to your attention that the deliberate killing of livestock and destruction of foodstuffs, furniture and farming tools will make it completely impossible for the German people to feed themselves. A continued toleration of these acts is equivalent to an acceleration of what is feared will be a serious problem of hunger, leading to a reign of communism and anarchy.[16]

In his reply, Spottiswoode had promised, "Such steps are being taken to reduce the trouble as are consistent with fair treatment of the large bulk of (the foreign workers) who are behaving themselves. You will understand," he continued archly, "that we cannot keep closely confined Allied subjects, who were brought into Germany against their will for forced labor to help prosecute the war against their own countries, and control of isolated parties can never be complete. We are naturally repatriating them as quickly as possible starting with the Western nations and the U.S.S.R. nationals."[17]

---

16   Löffler, doc. 479, v. II, 1166.
17   Löffler, doc. 480, v. II, 1166–67.

Spottiswoode then took the opportunity to introduce another topic. The Allies had a policy of arresting all prominent Nazis. It was happening too frequently, he wrote, "that appeals are made for release, supported by the local clergy, on the grounds that (the arrested man) was a good Catholic. We take good care that there are very sound reasons for these arrests and I regret that I cannot accept previous religious observance as mitigation of Nazi practices. We have as yet had no instance, as far as I can discover, of any Nazis being reported to us by the Church."[18]

The letter indicates the frostiness that was coming over the relationship between von Galen and the British authorities. They respected him for the great courage he had shown in standing up for justice and human rights. Officers, soldiers, and journalists all wanted to see and meet the famous opponent of Nazism. Allied soldiers who had converted to Catholicism rejoiced to be able to receive the Sacrament of Confirmation at his hands. But the authorities hoped for greater cooperation from him and understanding of the difficulties of their task. Now Spottiswoode wanted to discuss the Telgte sermon. They met for two and a half hours at Spottiswoode's office in Warendorf on July 24. Present were the colonel, the bishop, the bishop's secretary, Dr. Portmann[19]—who described the meeting as tense but "correct"—and a Polish officer acting as translator. Colonel Spottiswoode did not want the presence of the German woman who was the usual translator. Several topics were discussed, but the main theme was the Telgte sermon. The colonel produced a copy of the sermon with many passages underlined in red.

The first topic was the question of collective guilt. Spottiswoode insisted that a people as a whole is indeed responsible for the evils done by the government that it chooses. Only those who took part

---

18   Ibid.
19   His careful notes on the discussion are in Löffler, doc. 490, v. II, 1189–93.

in active resistance could be exempted from this judgment, and the numbers were far too few. Only about one hundred thousand people of a population of eighty million were put in concentration camps, and this number included Jews, foreigners, and communists. The occupying powers nevertheless had no hatred for or desire for revenge against the German people. They stressed the collective guilt of the Germans, not as a punishment but as an educational measure, so that in rebuilding their society and government, the Germans would never again stand by and do nothing while an evil government committed atrocities. He was concerned that the bishop's denial of the universal guilt of the German people would hinder this necessary educational work.

Bishop von Galen, for his part, noted that Colonel Spottiswoode's description of the Allied position on the question of German guilt corresponded with what he had said in his sermon. Nevertheless, he insisted, although many people bore responsibility for the evils of the Nazi regime, it was not the entire German people and certainly not the people of Westphalia. The colonel, he said, who did not live under the Nazi terror, did not know from experience what it was like. Everyone knew that open resistance led to the concentration camp or to death. He himself was ripe for such a fate. The only thing that spared him was the conviction of the regime that an attack on the bishop would be bad for "public opinion." That fact itself proved that the Nazi Party and the regime knew that a large segment of the population was in agreement with the bishop. In addition, he reminded the colonel that the *New Westphalian Newspaper* had recently uncovered examples of electoral fraud in the election that first brought the Nazis to power. They had not, in fact, been elected in a fair and secret ballot. The colonel nevertheless stuck to his position that a more active opposition would have made these things impossible.

The two men understood each other better, but neither changed his position on the key question. They turned to the next issues:

plundering and crime and the danger of a hunger crisis. The colonel insisted that hatred and revenge were not part of the policy of the occupying powers. They were working hard to bring peace and order and had no intention of having people go hungry. The task of bringing order was not easy, particularly as there were not enough soldiers; British soldiers were needed in places all over the world. He reminded the bishop that many of the foreigners had been brought to Germany against their will, and he also let it be known that many of those who had caused trouble had been placed under arrest and were being returned to Russia. Portmann noted that Colonel Spottiswoode gave no clear answer to the question of how many had been arrested but that he seemed to think it desirable that the bishop should make it public that such arrests and deportations were taking place.

On his part, Bishop von Galen made it clear that his sermon had not blamed the military regime for talk of hatred and revenge. Rather, the propaganda in the foreign press and radio was spreading such ideas, and these ideas seemed to justify the plundering and robbery that were causing such misery. He accepted gladly the colonel's assertion that the regime was doing whatever it could to put a stop to such crimes, and he recognized the difficulty of doing so. He saw, too, that this was an international problem, which he hoped would be alleviated by the deportation of the foreigners.[20]

The desire of the colonel was that Bishop von Galen would issue a clarification of some of his statements in the Telgte sermon. The next day, von Galen sent Spottiswoode the text he planned to publish in the diocesan newsletter: "The English Military Regime," he wrote, "has assured me that it is far from desiring that its measures lead to hatred or the desire of revenge, and that it does not approve or tolerate the disorders and crimes against which I have spoken, nor will

20   Ibid.

they stand by and do nothing to prevent a hunger catastrophe from occurring. I am glad to share this declaration with the people of my diocese, in order to alleviate any possible misunderstandings."[21]

On the same day, Colonel Spottiswoode wrote von Galen a private letter in English, wishing to explain in more detail his thoughts on the foreigners, whom he referred to, using an English plural to a German word, as "Auslanders."[22] "I am sure that Your Grace, with your natural deep feelings at seeing your people suffering hardships which at first sight appear to be largely preventable, does not realise fully the other side of the picture," he wrote. He then proceeded to describe the other side of the picture:

> There are some hundreds of thousands of men in your diocese who have been brought to this country against their will and have already spent here some years being compelled to work for the country which forced them to come and which was fighting against their own. Many of them have been very badly treated while here. They have imbibed the doctrine, by example, that might is right. They have lost, many of them, their own homes, and many of them have nothing to look forward to when, if ever, they do get home. They have heard, and maybe seen, many frightful deeds committed by Germans against themselves, their countrymen, and allies. Is it then surprising that *some* of them still look on the Germans as their enemies and consider that they should take any opportunity to pay back part of the score? Is it surprising that they have lost any Christian ideas and civilised inhibitions which they may have previously possessed?

---

21 Löffler, doc. 492/I, v. II, 1197. In the end, publication of the statement did not take place for several months, after which permission was finally given for the diocesan newsletter to resume printing.
22 Löffler, doc. 491, v. II, 1193–95.

However, these men who now only respond to force . . . are only a part of the Auslanders here, and the greater number of them still behave well. Is it therefore to be wondered at that we do not feel justified in keeping all these men, who are still our allies, in concentration camps behind barbed wire? That we give them that liberty which they have so long been denied? That we do not confine the many for the lack of discipline of the few? Consider then the thousands of scattered farms and small villages in the area. Consider the fact that we still have as our first responsibility the fighting of a major war against the Japanese. Consider that we have as our second responsibility the rebuilding and restoration of our own country after the ravages . . . consequent on that war. Is it therefore surprising that we keep here as small an army as is necessary to preserve only such order as is required to avoid any threat to our first two responsibilities? The preservation of order is the first duty of our army, be it threatened by Germans or others. We deplore all crimes committed here now, as we deplored the far worse and more wholesale ones committed in the past few years by Germans. We have, we hope, stopped the latter for ever. We hope that soon a term will be put to the former, and are taking all practicable methods to do so. To have expected that they would not occur or that they will be stopped at once is vain. To restore these unfortunate people to the homes from which they were forcibly reft and which are in many cases now destroyed or damaged by war is the earnest hope of us all.[23]

Spottiswoode continued with a pointed contrast between von Galen's temper and the self-control of the Polish interpreter during their meeting:

---

23   Ibid.

Your Grace, I fully understood the heat which you showed at times during our talk. I admired still more the restraint of our interpreter, Lt. Klink, who has himself, as a captured Polish officer, suffered far more in the last few years in physical and mental torture than any unfortunate German in the recent affairs of which we were speaking. I myself took him out of Belsen where the horrors would not have been noticeably increased had all the crimes committed in Münster in the last two months been added. He can be well understood to feel all Germans guilty of the failure to control the leaders who acted in such an inhuman way in their name.

But, I repeat, we deplore all violations of the laws of humanity, and do all the circumstances permit to prevent and punish them, and these circumstances I ask Your Grace to keep in mind.[24]

Father Portmann confirmed that Bishop von Galen had difficulty hiding his anger at times during the meeting but that the conference proceeded with perfect correctness. Despite the difficulties the English continued to have in understanding him, they persisted in receiving him respectfully whenever he came to petition for the needs of the many people who contacted him for help. They always rose to greet him and did so again at the end of their meetings. Von Galen now saw himself as a father to a large and needy family, and he trudged through the ruins of the city to the Allied military headquarters as often as six times a week to bring their needs to the ears of the British officers. He was, Portmann relates, much more a fighter than a negotiator, and although this did not lead him to forget the proper forms of etiquette, it did lead him frequently to use what Portmann delicately calls "picturesque images" in his speech

---

24   Ibid.

that were difficult for the translators, who were unfamiliar with the ways of Münsterlanders, to render into English.

Thus the bishop who had been such a thorn in the side of the Nazis was now a thorn in the side of the Allied military regime. Obviously, there were differences. Only at the very beginning of their reign did the Nazis treat him with respect. But he began to feel that with the English, too, although they listened to his complaints, he was not able to improve the situation of his people. In early 1946, he wrote in his pastoral letter for Lent, "Believe me that it is bitterly painful and often makes me deeply weary, that I am able to offer so little, indeed practically no help; that over and over I must write or say, 'I have no power; I have no influence on those in power; it is simply not possible for me to bring our needs and our requests to those who have the power to make decisions.'"[25]

Nevertheless, the Allies continued to respect him, and one of the very clear differences between them and the Nazis was that they did not try to prevent his complaints from becoming public. Indeed, although he was still hesitant to talk to journalists—Portmann says that the reporters from all over the world clamoring for interviews were a plague—he did receive two reporters from a Swiss magazine for a lengthy interview. Before beginning, he asked the English officers whether he could tell the reporters openly his criticisms of the military regime. Because they knew that his criticisms were not irresponsible fault-finding but based on a sense of justice, they allowed him to speak frankly.[26]

And speak frankly he did. The article appeared in the October 26, 1945, issue of the weekly magazine *Die Tat*, under the title

25   Löffler, doc. 540, v. II, 1280.
26   Portmann, 252–54. In a film that was made dramatizing his life, the bishop is depicted wearily refusing to speak to a journalist until he finds out that the man is Swiss, not English or American.

"German Balance 1945."[27] The author, Fritz Allemann, began by noting that of all the criticisms of the methods of the British regime in Germany, none was more sharp and uncompromising than that of Count von Galen. The Bishop of Münster was highly regarded by the English, the article continues. His criticisms of the Nazi regime in 1941, before the war took a turn against the Nazis, gave him a moral authority in their eyes similar to that enjoyed by the Protestant pastor Niemöller. Now he was criticizing them with the same recklessness with which he had criticized the Hitler regime—or perhaps, the author suggested, with more recklessness, because now his words did not have to be so carefully weighed.

Nevertheless, Allemann wrote, Bishop von Galen "at first showed himself unwilling to speak to neutrals over the things that lay so close to his heart, not out of fear, but because he thought that criticisms of the English should be made in a British forum, not a foreign one (and I have been told by the English themselves that when speaking to them von Galen takes no trouble to stifle what he desires to say). It was only the encouragement of the British liaison officer to speak freely and openly that loosened his tongue."[28]

The defeat of the war and the consequent sufferings of the German people, von Galen told his interviewer, were very painful to bear after the years of bearing the yoke of what he called the foreign rule of National Socialism, perhaps referring to the fact that the Nazi program was antithetical to Germany's Christian culture. Now the Germans realized that their great desire to be freed from Nazism could only be at the price of suffering, which they would have to bear patiently. Still, they felt extremely bitter to be considered responsible for the deeds of those who had enslaved and oppressed them.

---

27   Ibid., 254–56.
28   Ibid.

He was quick to assert that much had grown better under the British occupation. In the religious sphere, there was freedom once again, although he still found too many unnecessary restrictions; not enough had been done to reintroduce Catholic schools, for instance, and the Corpus Christi procession was forbidden that year. Also he saw no reason to justify major church feasts having been transferred to the nearest Sunday. This reminded him of the methods of the National Socialists.

And here he came to the nub of his complaints. In some ways, the British seemed to have been infected by their enemies, so that von Galen had complaints against them similar to those he had made against the Nazis—for example, in their way of dealing with people suspected of the wrong political views. "Certainly I am in favour of punishing those who were responsible for the National Socialist regime and keeping them out of public office," he told the journalist:

> But that hundreds of people who simply took on a Party title and Party functions in order to prevent worse things from happening have been arrested and are in concentration camps, where they languish for weeks, months without the possibility of defending themselves—these are unjust methods which we do not understand in the English. The poison of National Socialist ideology has clearly infected other peoples, including those who pride themselves on their democracy. And even the National Socialists gave the people in concentration camps the opportunity to exchange letters with their relatives twice a month, and to receive packages from them. The English make no such provisions. And when I say this to them and they answer that the Nazis didn't have such provisions in all of their concentration camps, I can only ask them, "Must you then copy the worst of the Nazi prisons, if indeed you have to copy them at all?"[29]

---

29   Ibid.

The magazine printed this section of the interview under the provocative heading "Concentration camps worse than those of the Nazis!" Von Galen had not said that the conditions in the camps were worse than those of the Nazis.[30] He had simply compared the methods. Imprisonment without trial and refusal to allow any communication with family were injustices of the Nazis that the English had copied. He found a similar situation with regard to those who were not imprisoned but removed from their jobs because of suspected Nazi leanings. The Nazis had done the same with regard to their opponents at the beginning of their reign, but again the comparison was not good for the English. At least the Nazis had given pensions to such men or provided some means of their finding another job. This the English had not done.

His greatest concern was that the methods of the occupiers would combine with material poverty to lead to a radicalization of many people. Nihilism and Bolshevism could easily be the result. Von Galen could not understand why the English had, as yet, done nothing to provide the people with heating material for the upcoming winter, when there were plenty of coal supplies available in the Ruhr area. When the journalist pointed out that in the previous winter, the French were also without coal, the bishop was astounded: "That too was unjust! The English and the Americans should have helped them."

A final point that Germans found impossible to understand was the changing of borders in the east and the removal of Germans from areas where they had lived for centuries. This, he said, "is

---

30   Later in 1945, he learned more details about the terrible conditions of
      some of the camps. A letter from a priest (Löffler, doc. 514, v. II, 1246–49)
      tells of a camp where the prisoners were undernourished, where it was
      constantly wet and always so cold that despite their two blankets,
      they would get up in the middle of the night and move around to warm
      themselves.

a novelty in history that has not taken place since the coming of Christendom into the world, until it was begun by the Allies and the National Socialists. It didn't surprise us in the National Socialists. What astonishes us is that the Christian peoples of the west give their approval to such methods, that they remain silent about them or in some cases accept the responsibility for them."

"The Bishop," Allemann wrote,

> rejected the idea that as a priest, he should not speak about such things, because they are of a material nature. "I am not only a bishop, I am also a German man, a Christian who has compassion for the poor, and a pastor of souls, who knows how his work will be made difficult if people live in terrible material need and are led thereby to have doubts about heaven, about God, about religion. That is why I feel obligated, precisely as a priest, to lift up my voice. To be sure, my primary responsibility is to see that people find their way to the one true God, but they must also have the right, as children of the heavenly Father, to their share in the cultural and material goods of this world."

"The Bishop conceded," continued Allemann, "that perhaps there is no remedy for the poverty and injustice, but if that were the case, it would still be poverty and injustice. But he protested (and he is not alone in this protest) that the English refused to give any explanation as to why their way of doing things is necessary. 'If it really is impossible to do things in any other way, why does no one explain this to us?'"[31]

The article in the Swiss magazine caused something of a sensation and, like the sermons of 1941 and the Telgte sermon, was passed on from hand to hand by Germans. One key difference, of course, was that

---

31   Ibid.

this time the article could be distributed openly. The Allies were clearly far from perfect, but they believed in giving a man like Clemens August von Galen freedom of speech. Despite their differences with him, they still greatly respected him as a courageous opponent of the Nazis.

In January 1946, the bishops in the British zone were invited to a meeting with General Templer, the deputy chief of staff to the then military governor. The general impressed the bishops greatly, giving them an overview of the many difficulties of the European situation in a wide-ranging discussion. He spoke for two hours without notes and gave the bishops an opportunity to ask whatever questions they wished. By this time, Pope Pius XII had announced that von Galen was to be made a cardinal, and it was clear that the other bishops deferred to him as their leader, even though Archbishop Frings of Cologne, who was also to be made a cardinal the next month, out-ranked him as the metropolitan archbishop.

Over lunch, when the only Englishman present was Brigadier R. L. Sedgwick, a German-speaking convert to Catholicism who was in charge of relations with the churches, von Galen acknowledged that the general had handled them very adroitly. Another bishop remarked that he now understood firsthand the meaning of the English words "fair play," and the bishops agreed that they had an obligation to tell their people to respect the authority of the military government. For his part, General Templer confided to another general that he was impressed with von Galen. He had expected to be confronted with a "fire-breathing dragon" and was pleased to have found instead an honest and forthright interlocutor. As for Brigadier Sedgwick, he wrote that von Galen was the greatest German that he ever met. He kept two photographs of him on the walls of his study and translated Portmann's biography into English.[32]

---

32   Portmann, 256–57, and Sedgwick in Heinrich Portmann, *Cardinal von Galen*, trans. R. L. Sedgwick (London: Jarrolds, 1957), 28–29.

Sedgwick was asked by his superiors on several occasions to try to extract from von Galen some statement of collective guilt. "Such requests drove him into a frenzy of anger," Sedgwick wrote of von Galen, "and were soon abandoned."[33] The bishop was severely critical, Sedgwick continued, "of what he called our 'spirit of compromise and vacillation.'" He reported a conversation in which von Galen said to him: "You promised us in your propaganda that you would come as liberators, and the first thing you do is to throw innocent people into concentration camps without preferment of charge and without trial. My own cousin, Count Max von Galen, is now in one at Corvey near Hoexter. He was never a member of the Party, and when he protested at his imprisonment, he was told, 'You have been in the Army and that's enough for us.'" Sedgwick managed to get him released. The bishop continued his criticism of the English:

> At one moment you order non-fraternization, at the next you cancel it and complain if we are cold and hostile. You make us tear down or dismantle our factories, and ere the dust has settled you order us to build them up again. You take away our weapons even down to an airgun, and I prophesy that before much time is out you will ask us to arm again, so that we may be a bulwark between you and Russia. You are inconsistent, tough in the wrong way, and this softness mixed with your sensitiveness at what I and others say in criticism of your actions increases our humiliation at the thought that you have twice conquered us.[34]

Another officer in the English forces who was greatly impressed with von Galen was Jesuit Father Murphy, a chaplain who frequently

---

33   Portmann (Eng. trans.), 17.
34   Ibid.

helped the bishop in his dealings with the military government. After seeing, on practically a daily basis, the enormous amount of work von Galen was taking upon himself, Father Murphy decided to give him a gift of what he called "medicine"—a flask of whisky. Greatly moved, the bishop asked Father Murphy to drink the first glass with him. When the priest refused, von Galen had to resort to a humorous subterfuge: "Father," he said with a smile, "I cannot accept your medicine unless you drink the first glass; since you are my 'enemy,' you must first convince me that this drink is safe and not poisonous." With a laugh, the two men shared the first glass of whisky.[35]

---

35   Portmann, 257–58.

CHAPTER 24

Cardinal

O n December 18, 1945, Bishop Clemens August von Galen was
able to return to his episcopal city, where a temporary residence
had been prepared for him in the Borromäum, the seminary of the diocese. Five days later, Father Portmann and another priest were listening
to the radio when the news came on that Pope Pius XII had announced
his intention to create the astonishing number of thirty-two new cardinals from twenty different nations. It was to be the first consistory of his
pontificate, which had begun shortly before the outbreak of the war in
1939, and the largest consistory in history up to that time. As the long
list of names was read out, suddenly they heard the name of their own
bishop. Both jumped up, Portmann reported, as if they had been given
an electrical shock. Off they rushed to the Borromäum to give him the
news, for they knew he did not have a radio. They greeted him as one
greets a cardinal, with "Your Eminence," hoping to surprise him, but he
had already heard the news via a telephone call from another priest. And
he did not trust it. "The radio has lied before, and today it is not much
better," he told the two priests.[1]

---

1   Heinrich Portmann, *Kardinal von Galen: Ein Gottesmann seiner Zeit*, 17th
     ed. (Münster: Aschendorff, 1981), 262.

But the news was true, although he did not receive official confirmation of it until well into the new year. Soon, heartfelt congratulations were coming daily in the mail from all over Germany and abroad. The people of Münster, who had never had a cardinal, were overjoyed at the honor paid to their bishop. The pope had given the names of three German bishops whom he intended to raise to the cardinalate. Not only was Archbishop Frings of Cologne named, as would have been expected, but also two bishops from dioceses that had no history of having cardinals, two bishops who were well known for their struggles against the Nazis—the noblemen Konrad von Preysing, Bishop of Berlin, and Clemens August von Galen, Bishop of Münster.

On December 28, von Galen wrote to Frings:

Excellency! Eminence!

Is it true, what the radio and the English newspapers are reporting: that you are to be made a cardinal? I happily believe it, for it is something I have hoped for and expected, and I send you my most humble congratulations!

But that my name also stands on the list of those called to such an honor? I still cannot fully believe it, as long as there is no official confirmation, and I also cannot wish it in the slightest, for many reasons! But the whole world believes it, so I must get used to the idea.[2]

He wrote von Preysing on January 3, 1946: "I rejoice in, and am moved by, the goodness and love of the Holy Father; and the joy of the people of my diocese is great and almost overwhelming.

---

2   Peter Löffler, ed., *Bischof Clemens August Graf von Galen: Akten, Briefe und Predigten 1933–1946*, 2nd ed. (Paderborn: Ferdinand Schöningh, 1996), doc. 523, v. II, 1258.

Personally I still cannot get fully used to the idea, and I feel ashamed that I have been undeservedly placed ahead of others who have worked longer and better. In cases like this the Pope is not infallible; I find that has now been confirmed in the strongest way."[3]

With both of his fellow cardinals-elect, von Galen wished to discuss practical details: how they were to get to Rome, where they would stay, how they would pay for all the things they would need to purchase, not least the clothing they would need as cardinals. He was quite concerned about all the customary visits he would have to make and guests he would have to receive, especially considering, as he confessed to Preysing, that he spoke no Italian, and his French and Latin were not good.

By the feast of the Epiphany, January 6, 1946, when he wrote a letter of thanks to the Holy Father, he had still heard the news only by radio and newspaper. The official letter from the papal nuncio was written only on January 9, and with the vagaries of postwar postal service, not received until the twenty-sixth. By then, however, he could not doubt its truth. Von Galen's letter thanked the pope for his goodness to the German people:

> That our poor German people, left in ruins by the war, humbled by defeat, hated and vengefully treated on all sides, have not been overlooked, but rather shown great respect by the calling of three German bishops to the College of Cardinals: for this the German Catholics with their bishops and priests, and also many non-Catholic Germans, thank the Vicar of Christ on earth from hearts that have been deeply moved.
>
> But if Your Holiness has also decided that my insignificant person should also be one of these who should be brought into the College of Cardinals, then I can only say that this unexpected

---

3   Löffler, doc. 526, v. II, 1261.

and undeserved honor and call has humbled and oppressed me, so that I must say with St. Peter, *Exi a me, quia homo peccator sum, Domine*. It is only that fundamental principle that I have held to with all my strength throughout my life, to consider every wish of the Pope as a command of Him who has made the Pope the shepherd of the entire flock, that makes me pronounce my *Adsum* as I did on the day of my priestly ordination, and so take on this heavy office and honor. Besides this, I am consoled that I can see in this a recognition of the brave stance of the majority of the Catholics in the diocese entrusted to me, who kept their fidelity to Christ, to His holy Church, and to the Holy Father during the years of persecution and oppression, and also made it possible for me by their convictions and their stance to stand up publicly for the rights of God and the Church and for the God-given rights of the human person. The unbounded expressions of joy on the part of my diocesans on the news of my nomination, the innumerable congratulations from the diocese and from all parts of Germany, give me the right to interpret the gracious decision of Your Holiness in this way.[4]

In letters to friends and relatives, von Galen repeatedly expressed his humble surprise at being named a cardinal and his conviction that it was really an honor to the people and clergy of his Diocese of Münster. In the weeks before his departure for Rome—the consistory was scheduled for February 18, 1946—he continued to work for the needs of his people. On January 6, the same day that he drafted his letter of thanks to the pope, he preached in the Church of the Holy Cross in Münster. He read to the congregation excerpts of the pope's Christmas message, in which the Holy Father stressed the need for a real peace based on justice. Von Galen thanked Pius XII

---

4   Löffler, doc. 528, v. II, 1262–63.

for mentioning the injustice to the Germans who were being exiled from their homes in eastern Europe, the prisoners of war who had not yet been released, and those who had been imprisoned because of their political activity but who had not committed any crimes. "I believe," the bishop said,

> that not many in other countries can imagine, and do not understand, the kind of terror and almost unbearable pressure under which many of our fellow citizens labored—particularly civil servants, officials, and teachers—so that they took out party membership in order to earn their daily bread for themselves and their families, but without professing the false beliefs of National Socialism. They kept away from evils and crimes, and were able to do much good and to hinder much evil. It would be unjust to punish all these men without distinction, and thus to hinder them from getting work and an income and a well-deserved old age pension. On this topic the Pope has said, "We believe that we express the thinking of all right-thinking people when we say that harmony and peace cannot be better begun than by freeing and rehabilitating them."[5]

Von Galen noted the pope's frequent use of the saying, *Opus iustitiae pax*: Peace is the work of justice. How often in the past, he continued, had the Germans suffered under a system of might going before right, before justice. He recalled his own protest, in his sermon of July 13, 1941, on behalf of Queen Justice, and the old saying, *Justitia est fundamentum regnorum* (Justice is the foundation of states):

> I gave the warning: if the reign of justice is not restored, then despite the heroic bravery of our soldiers, the German Reich will fall into ruins. My warning was not heeded; and so today

---

5   Löffler, doc. 529, v. II, 1264–65.

we stand in the ruins not only of our cities and homes, but also of our independence as a people! O, may those who now have the fate of peoples in their hands listen to the voice of the Pope, who once again teaches that justice is the way to peace, who is the advocate for justice also for a conquered and powerless people, and who warns that the innocent should not be punished together with the guilty![6]

He continued to urge the British to release political prisoners and prisoners of war and to give them better treatment in the meantime. He had a great concern for the spiritual care of the exiled Germans from eastern Europe, many of whom were being relocated to predominantly Protestant areas where there were no churches or priests to care for them. He struggled for the rights of parents to send their children to Catholic schools. This issue, for which he had fought so long against the Nazis, came to the fore again under the military government. The British wanted the people to decide whether they wanted denominational or non-denominational schools by filling out a complicated survey. Von Galen protested against the injustice of this. The survey would be difficult for many parents to fill out. Apart from its length and difficulty, it was required that it be filled out in block capitals, a form of writing with which the Germans were unfamiliar. Further, it would be assumed in principle that anyone who did *not* fill out a form was not interested in having denominational schools or was actually in favor of non-denominational schools. Bishop von Galen went to great steps to ensure that his people would understand the importance of filling out the forms and would be helped to fill them out correctly.

The journey to Rome would not be possible in the immediate postwar period without the permission and the help of the military regime. Travel was very difficult anyway. A crazy adventure was to

---

6   Ibid.

show him and the other new cardinals just how difficult it was. He would also need money while in Rome—the currency then being used in Germany was useless anywhere else. For himself, he asked for only one person to accompany him: his secretary, Dr. Portmann. In normal cases, a cardinal would bring a much bigger retinue, and a large contingent from his diocese would make the pilgrimage to Rome. A group of laymen asked the military government for permission for a delegation of just seven notable Catholics to travel to Rome for the consistory. The group included von Galen's brother, Count Franz von Galen, and Baron Rudolf von Twickel, the mayor of Havixbeck—both of whom were honorary chamberlains of the pope—and Dr. Karl Zuhorn, the mayor of Münster. All were people who should have been considered acceptable to the military regime. The request was transmitted to the British at the end of January. Only on February 18, the day the consistory took place, was a reply sent, stating that the difficulties of travel made the request impossible to fulfill.[7]

By the middle of January, it was still unclear whether von Galen himself would be able to get to Rome to receive the red hat of a cardinal. Brigadier Sedgwick, the Catholic convert who was head of the religious section of the military government, took on the task of obtaining the passports and accompanying the cardinals-elect Frings and von Galen on their journey.[8] Although he did not tell this to the Germans, Sedgwick had a great deal of difficulty getting the Foreign Office to realize the importance of cooperating to make the trip easy for the new cardinals. He did receive permission for each cardinal to have two attendants for the pilgrimage. Everything

---

7   Löffler, doc. 543, v. II, 1286–87.
8   Details of the journey to Rome are given by Portmann, 274–87, with additional notes by Sedgwick in the introduction to his English translation of Portmann's book: Heinrich Portmann, *Cardinal von Galen*, trans. R. L. Sedgwick (London: Jarrolds, 1957), 23–28.

else seemed to fluctuate. Although the army wanted to help, they were dependent on the Foreign Office, which for some reason was against allowing the cardinals to fly to Rome. Sedgwick managed to get permission for a plane, but the specific plans were changed twice. To make matters worse, the Foreign Office absolutely refused to provide facilities for exchanging money. Finally, General Sir Brian Robinson put his own plane at their disposal, and the departure date was set for Thursday, February 7. They would fly from an airfield near Münster, with the flight to go via Frankfurt and Vienna. On the day before the scheduled flight, Archbishop Frings was driven from Cologne to Münster. Car troubles delayed the journey so that when he arrived in the city, it was nearly midnight. His driver could not find his way through the ruins to the Borromäum, and because of the curfew, there was no one on the streets to ask for directions. So the crazy adventure began. Frings and his entourage spent the night at a convent of sisters and found their way to the Borromäum the next morning.

The group of travelers expected to find a four-engined aircraft at the airfield but discovered only a two-engined plane. The chief of the airfield announced that there were two problems: Bad weather over Austria would require a different route to be flown; more seriously, there was the question whether the airplane could carry all the persons and baggage. On seeing it, von Galen said, "That bird isn't big enough even to carry me. We want an eagle, not a swallow." The passengers and their baggage would have to be weighed. This settled it—the plane was far too small, and they would have to make other plans. Sedgwick tried to contact headquarters, but the storm had damaged the telegraph lines. He thought perhaps the group could drive to Frankfurt and fly on an American plane, but they would have to return to Münster while Sedgwick went off for further instructions. The two bishops altered that plan by making a stop in Telgte, where they knelt together in prayer before the image of the sorrowful Virgin. Sedgwick's superior was exasperated: "I don't care how you do it, Sedgwick, even if you take 'em in a wheelbarrow; but get them there. That's an order."

The next day at noon, they departed Münster in two cars, bound for Frankfurt. It had rained for twenty-four hours straight and continued to rain as they drove. Flooding was starting to affect the low-lying areas, and in places, water stood in the roads. In a flooded part of the road in a small town en route, the car in which the two cardinals were riding became stuck, and its engine died. It was an old Daimler that had once belonged to the late Queen Mary. Sedgwick shouted to the locals, who were watching the storm from the windows of their houses, that the car contained two German cardinals and an English general and asked them to help push the car to higher ground. There was no garage nearby, so the car was attached to the other vehicle with a chain and towed. This was no easy task. As they were now in hilly country, the chain kept breaking. After the third time, Sedgwick sprang angrily out of the car and told Portmann, in the other car, to switch places with him, and he would drive off to the next larger town to find help. The cardinals sat in their motionless car in the streaming rain for an hour until a mechanic was brought to get the vehicle back into operation. For a few hours, they were able to drive on, until again the cardinals' car came to a sudden stop in deep water. Sedgwick told the other car to drive on and test the road, but soon they heard shouts from the windows of the nearby houses: "Stop, or you will be drowned! There's a washout ahead!" Saved just in time, they had to retrace part of their route and found another way to Marburg, where the Americans provided them with more fuel and showed them the way through the city. At 10:30 that night, the cardinals' car again came to a stop at a little place called Sichardshausen, between Marburg and Giessen. No one could get the motor started again. Again Sedgwick had Portmann switch into the vehicle with the two prelates. "Are we there already?"

an astonished von Galen asked his secretary. Portmann replied that
Sedgwick was going on to Frankfurt in the other car to get help from
the Americans. Von Galen's patience was wearing thin. "Without
asking us? Without saying goodby? And with our luggage?" It was
eleven o'clock at night. The locals pushed the car to the side of the
intersection and went home. The bishops, priests, and driver tried
to sleep in the car with the rain still pouring down. At seven the
next morning, they woke the driver, who looked under the hood,
returned to the car, tried the starter—and the engine started. Now
what to do? If they drove on to Frankfurt, they might miss Sedgwick
in the other car. They decided to drive on nevertheless and signal
every car they saw coming the other way. Fortunately, they met, and
Sedgwick recounted how he had not reached his goal in Frankfurt
until 3 a.m.

So it was that they arrived in Frankfurt on Saturday morning. There
they remained for a day, and on Sunday morning, von Galen preached
in the Frankfurt Cathedral. He told the faithful that the damage to
their cities was symbolic of the nihilistic aim of Satan over the past few
centuries to destroy Christianity in Germany. Now they had the noble
task of rebuilding Germany on Christian principles. It was a time for
decisive, bold Christians who would be 100 percent Catholic. There
was no room for halfhearted Christians who would appear in church
on Sunday and live by the standards of the world during the week.
After the service, the people gave him a rousing ovation.

At noon, they were in cars once again. A British furlough train was
to pass through Karlsruhe at 6 p.m., on its way to Villach in Austria.
Six places were reserved on the train. At Villach, they would board
an American plane that would take them to Rome. They arrived in
Karlsruhe at 4 p.m. and waited for two hours in the car. Then Sedgwick received more bad news. The train was not coming. The furlough ship from England to Calais had been unable to sail because
of the weather, so there was no reason to set the train in motion.

It was no longer funny. They had planned to fly from Münster on Thursday. Now it was Sunday evening, and they were only in Karlsruhe, with no means in sight for continuing their journey to Rome. The two cardinals-to-be thanked Brigadier Sedgwick for his heroic efforts. Day and night, he had been telephoning and telegraphing on their behalf. "It is not your fault," von Galen told him. "You must now take us back to Frankfurt, and if by tomorrow morning something concrete is not forthcoming we must return home, and I shall make a formal protest to the Commander-in-Chief. This is the revenge of your Foreign Office for my having stood up for what I believed was just and right." Poor Sedgwick was unable to persuade von Galen and Frings that this was not the case.

The first step was to return that night to Frankfurt, where the possibilities for communication were much better than in Karlsruhe. The sisters at the hospital where they had stayed the previous night were surprised to find the bishops ringing the night bell nearly at midnight on Sunday. They had heard on the radio during the afternoon that the bishops had safely landed in Rome!

During the night, the industrious Sedgwick considered what to do. He recalled that there was an American colonel in Frankfurt who had a position in the American zone parallel to his own position in the British zone. The colonel was away, but the captain who was left in his place, a young Catholic, was very helpful. They made calls through the night but got nowhere. Sedgwick said a prayer to Our Lady of Telgte, snatched an hour or two of sleep, and woke with another plan. They would try the French, who had a small mission in Frankfurt. At 6 a.m., he and the American captain found an elderly major still on night duty, and Sedgwick explained the situation. "*Mon Général*," responded the major, "I am appalled at what you have to tell me. One does not treat Princes of the Church in this cavalier way. As members of the Sacred College they are supranational, and France will accord them every facility for reaching the

Eternal City. If the captain here will reserve them a compartment on the officers' leave-train for Paris tonight, I will guarantee the rest." The American furlough train could take them to Paris, and from there, the Orient Express would take them through Switzerland and on to Rome. The Quai d'Orsay would provide accommodations in a Paris hotel and defray all their costs, including the tickets to Rome. When Sedgwick brought the plan to the German bishops, they were dubious until he showed them the tickets to Paris and the French and American visas. He assured them that von Preysing had traveled by this route and had been in Rome now for several days.

It sounded too good to be true. After all that had happened, it seemed only normal when the radio reported that all the railway bridges over the Rhine were in danger because of the high waters. Fortunately, this time the news was wrong, and they were able to board the train for Paris. Or rather, trains. The cardinals-elect and Colonel Sedgwick took places on a train that was reserved for higher officers. The priest attendants were placed on a second train for lower-ranking officers. The second train departed fifteen minutes later than the first. Naturally, Portmann was anxious that they would not find each other again in Paris.

But all was well. After a good night's sleep on the train, they arrived in Paris on Tuesday morning, where they were brought to the Grand Hotel. There, von Galen embraced Sedgwick: "You have performed a miracle, Herr General!" he exclaimed. "How did you do it?" "You must ask Our Lady of Telgte," Sedgwick replied, to the cardinal's great delight. The entire group was invited to lunch at the papal nunciature, where the nuncio was Archbishop Angelo Roncalli, later Pope John XXIII. Other guests included the Archbishops of Paris and Rouen, who also were traveling to Rome to be made cardinals. In this friendly meeting of prelates from countries that had been at enmity in the terrible war, the German travelers began to learn how highly Clemens August von Galen was esteemed in other countries for his heroic stance against the Nazis. They were to experience this much more in Rome. Von Galen entertained everyone with the story of their journey, ending with the only English expression Sedgwick ever heard him use: "All's well that ends well, as your Shakespeare says; but we are not at the end yet!"

On the same evening, after seeing some of the sights of Paris, the pilgrims boarded the Orient Express. Before departing, Sedgwick told them that he would not accompany them; for some reason, the Foreign Office would not allow it, to his great dismay.

The French archbishops and their entourage were booked through to Rome. The Germans, having booked at the last moment, found places on another car that was going only as far as Milan. The French government saw more clearly than the British one the importance of showing the greatest honor and respect to the new cardinals. As the major in Frankfurt had promised, the foreign ministry paid the fares for the entire group, and two officials of the ministry accompanied the group as far as the Swiss border. These officials contacted both the Swiss and the Italian border guards, who gave diplomatic treatment to the cardinals and their retinue, allowing their luggage through without inspection.

On Wednesday evening, nearly a week since Archbishop Frings had arrived in Münster, the train carrying the German prelates pulled into the station in Milan. On the next platform stood a train bound for Rome. The sleeping car on which the French bishops were traveling was quickly attached to it. After a brief visit on the platform with a Milanese prelate and a group of German sisters, the Germans decided to try their luck in boarding the Rome-bound train. The railway official would not allow it: It would not be fitting, he said, for German cardinals to board a train for which they did not have reserved seats and to risk having to stand in the corridor. Bishop von Galen joked that the Roman tailors might not have enough time to make the "red things" the new cardinals would need, but this time their bad luck did not hurt them. The train with the French cardinals would spend seven hours sitting in the station in Bologna, where the Germans caught up with it. In the meantime, the Germans had an opportunity to see the sights of Milan and visit with its Cardinal Schuster.

Before the war, the train journey from Milan via Bologna to Rome took about twelve hours. With the damage caused by the war, it took twenty-six hours for the German group to make the trip. When they caught up with the French cardinals in Bologna, the Frenchmen invited Frings and von Galen to share their sleeping compartment, which had now become empty of other travelers. The four priests had to take a different train, leaving Bologna an hour later, but with the goal so near, there was no longer anxiety. On Friday morning, a week after they departed Münster, the pilgrims arrived in Rome. The ceremonies of the consistory were set to begin on the following Monday.

From the time of his arrival in Rome, von Galen was busy with visits and the receiving of visitors and well-wishers. Naturally, the first order of business was to inform the Vatican of their arrival, after which an invitation soon came for a private audience with Pius XII on Saturday morning. As he passed the Swiss guards on his way to the audience, von Galen pleased them by giving them a friendly greeting in German. Pope Pius XII knew the German bishops well, having been the nuncio in Germany under Pius XI and then his secretary of state during the discussions with von Galen and the other German bishops in 1937 that led to the encyclical *Mit brennender Sorge*. Since the start of the war, it had not been possible for these old friends, who had first met when von Galen was a pastor in Berlin, to see one another. Now the pope could express personally his thanks to von Galen for his courage during the Nazi period. He took great interest in the photographs and documents von Galen brought showing the ruins that had been left by the war and detailing the sufferings of the exiled Germans of eastern Europe.

Soon it became clear to the German travelers that their cardinal-elect von Galen was regarded as a hero by everyone in Rome, including the cardinals from other nations. And the friendly visits paid to him and his fellow German cardinals soon put an end to any worries they had about expenses while in Rome. The American cardinals, particularly, showed their generosity. A cardinal would pay a call at the residence of the German church in Rome, Santa Maria dell'Anima, and on departing would leave a thick envelope on a table containing plenty of dollars, for which the banks gave very favorable exchange rates for Italian lire.

On Sunday, February 17, von Galen preached in the German national church. He thanked the Holy Father, on behalf of all Germans, for the sign of respect he showed to Germany by naming three German cardinals and also for his Christmas message. He returned to his frequent theme that peace had to be built on justice but ultimately on love. At the end of the sermon, he recalled a statement of Pope Pius XI, which he had once heard in a sermon of the then-cardinal Pacelli: "I thank God every day that He has allowed me to live in these times. Good and evil are ranged against each other in a gigantic struggle. We can be proud to take part in this battle. Now no one has a right to mediocrity." Focusing on this passage, von Galen made a call to everyone to a serious life of Christian charity. In the struggle for true peace, no one had a right to be a mediocre Christian.[9]

In this sermon, he acknowledged that terrible evils had been committed by many Germans during the last twelve years. These evils, he asserted, were not based on an error that affected Germany alone. They were a consequence of the rejection of the law of God, a rejection that had been taking place for centuries in many places. "The fate of Germany," he said, "should be a warning to

---

9   Löffler, doc. 548, v. II, 1300–1304.

all peoples, that only a return to Christ and to the divine law can bring peace."[10]

During his stay in Rome, Cardinal von Galen found the time to work on a statement of principles for the rebuilding of society, which he planned to offer for discussion at the meeting of west German bishops that was scheduled for March 22.[11] He did not know that that was to be the day of his death. The document, which he worked on with the assistance of the Jesuit social thinker Gustav Gundlach, is thus Cardinal von Galen's last statement of what he referred to as "Catholic Principles" for social life. The first of these was that religion must be the foundation of communal life. Without the correct idea of the human being as made in the image of God, he asserted, one loses the true sense of the value of the person. From this follows a disintegration of the family, the state, and the meaning of authority in the state. The family would be reduced to merely a group of people who lived together as long as they found it in their interests to do so. The state would be simply a mass of people, each also serving his own interests and self-will. State power would be in the hands of whatever groups could wield it for their own interests. As he had argued so often, a theory that did not anchor state authority in the authority of God would give absolute value to some earthly community, whether it be the people, the nation, the race, or the proletariat. The human person would be reduced to slavery to this community. The German people had experienced more than enough slavery to a self-idolizing government. It was time to rebuild on Christian principles, and von Galen wished to make his contribution to this by clarifying what those principles were and why they were necessary. The rights of the human person had been subordinated to the community under National Socialism, leading to such evils as the eugenic killing of innocent persons. The false ideas that led to

---

10   Ibid.
11   Löffler, doc. 549, v. II, 1304–13.

the evils needed to be battled, and the truth needed to be clearly taught that the human person is the goal of all communal life, and so the community is at the service of the person. The essential and proper roles of the family and the state needed to be rediscovered. It would take years, von Galen predicted, for the soul of the German people to free itself completely from the "passivity, emptiness, and apathy" that years of living under Nazism had engendered.

This brought him to the question of education and the young. The principle of compulsory education by the state was shown by the Nazi period to be an extremely dangerous principle, so much so that von Galen wondered at the prescience of the nineteenth-century thinkers who opposed it when it was gaining popularity. Quite apart from its attack on the Church's rights in education, the Nazi state's compulsory education and compulsory youth camps had produced a uniformity that destroyed all independence and inculcated a sense of self-consciousness and self-respect that was in reality a slavery to those in power in a totalitarian state—all with the ultimate goal of leading the country into war.[12]

Von Galen's document of Catholic principles included a discussion of the importance of the right to private property. In defending this, he said, the Church was not taking the reactionary standpoint that holds onto whatever exists merely because it exists. Rather, the right to private property is necessary for two principal reasons. First, it provides the material security for a family, which is crucial for the development of the human person. Second, without the right to the earnings one gains from his property, the incentive to work would be lacking. The postwar situation in Germany perfectly illustrated the need for private property. The German people had lost an enormous amount of capital and had for the most part only their ability to work as a source of wealth. They would have

---

12   Ibid.

to work very hard and save very carefully. Without the right of private property, the human person would be robbed of the hope and the right to acquire something of his own by means of his work. Here von Galen drew a sharp distinction between the Catholic position and the Marxist position on "de-proletarianization." Both sides saw a problem in the fact that large numbers of people possessed nothing but their strength to work and were forced to ask the owners of the means of production for a job. Marxism, whether socialism or communism, says that the problem lies in the right of private property, and so private property must be outlawed. "But we say," von Galen wrote, "that the oppression lies in the fact that the proletarian sees his situation as unworthy of himself and of his children, to whom he cannot leave any inheritance except the same situation." The solution lies not in overthrowing the private possession of the means of production but in broadening it to include more and more people. The war economy had already shown the negative effects of handing over all the means of production to the community or the state.[13]

All these ideas were in the tradition of Catholic social teaching that von Galen had continued to study from the time of his first acquaintance with the work of his great-uncle Bishop Wilhelm Emmanuel von Ketteler. To the end of his life, he kept the habit he had learned from his father, of tracing social, political, and economic questions back to first principles. In the plan of Providence, his effort in rebuilding a just social order in Europe was ended by his sudden death just a month after he was raised to the cardinalate.

During the days of the consistory, Cardinal von Galen became one of the favorites of the Italian press and the Roman people. The story of his resistance to Nazism was told and retold, and when he preached in the church of Santa Maria dell'Anima, many

---

13   Ibid.

non-Germans crowded into the church to get a glimpse of the
man people were starting to call the "Lion of Münster." The press
enthused over his enormous size. The people saw his humanity and
came to love him. Portmann writes:

> They had expected a dignified Prince of the Church, a man of
> knightly bearing, a stubborn-looking fighter, a man to whom
> respect and awe was due; and now a totally different picture.
> True a giant in stature, but so homely, unaffected, and natural,
> with the expression of a gentle father, and having the eyes of a
> good shepherd. And so it was that folk in a foreign land went
> into raptures of enthusiasm and cried out, *"Uomo simpatico!"* It
> was an enthusiasm and attachment that mounted daily.[14]

The ceremonies of the consistory took several steps over the next
week. Monday, February 18, was the day for the Secret Consistory,
at which the pope solemnly informed the old cardinals of the names
of those he was choosing to add to their ranks. At the end of this
ceremony, the briefs of appointment were handed over to papal couriers, who were monsignors, to be delivered to the new cardinals.
These couriers, accompanied by laymen, Privy Chamberlains of
the Sword and Cape, fanned about from the Vatican to make their
deliveries. To make things go smoothly, there were designated places
where the new cardinals were waiting. Frings, von Preysing, and
von Galen were at the monastery of the Salvatorian fathers. When
the chamberlains arrived, von Galen recognized them as nephews
of the pope and was much moved by Pius's kindness in sending
his relatives to the German cardinals. The couriers were announced.
To each cardinal-elect, beginning with Frings, who had seniority as
Archbishop of Cologne, the couriers presented their briefs, which
were opened and read aloud. Cardinal Frings made a short speech of

---

14   Portmann (Eng. trans.), 202.

gratitude to the Holy Father on behalf of all three, and the couriers withdrew. After this came visits of congratulation, known as the *visita di calore*, and then filming by an American film crew.

On Wednesday evening came the semi-public consistory for the receiving of the red biretta. As the cardinals prepared for the ceremony in the Sistine Chapel, donning the long red cloak, the *cappa magna*, the new American cardinals came over to give a friendly greeting to the German ones. Cardinal Spellman of New York had learned about their adventurous journey to Rome. After joking about it, he promised to procure an American plane for their return to Germany. Brigadier Sedgwick had met Spellman at a reception in Paris and told him about the adventure and about the fact that the German cardinals had no money. Spellman promised to take care of both difficulties and was able to do so.

During the procession of the new cardinals into the Hall of Benedictions, a whisper passed through the crowd as Cardinal von Galen came into view. "*Conte di Galen—Vescovo di Münster!*" people said to one another. The cardinal whispered to his secretary that he found it painful to have everyone staring at him.

On Friday morning came the public consistory for the receiving of the red hat. For the first time in history, it was held in the central nave of St. Peter's Basilica. Again, the people in the crowd—much larger than at the abovementioned consistory—began to say to one another with excitement, "*Il Conte Galen! Il Conte Galen!*" The applause that greeted each cardinal grew to what the newspapers called an *applauso trionfale* as Cardinal von Galen approached the papal throne. The red hat was placed on his head, and as the Holy Father embraced him, he whispered, "God bless you. God bless Germany." As von Galen descended the steps, Portmann writes,

> with the spotlights, the cameras, and the eyes of the tens of
> thousands focussed on him, a storm of applause broke out,

continuing for minutes on end, with cardinals and diplomats themselves taking part . . . On the same day a former high official in the diplomatic service wrote, "As Bishop von Galen came down from the papal throne, it seemed to me that at that moment the German name, covered for the last decade in so much shame and infamy in the whole world, recovered some of its lustre in the person of this great bishop."

The Americans who were there to celebrate with Cardinal Spellman said quite simply, without a trace of envy, "He was the star."[15]

The new cardinal did not return to Germany right away after receiving the red hat. On Monday, February 25, he began a journey by car to southern Italy. It had been more than nine months since the end of the war in Europe, and tens of thousands of Germans were still languishing in prisoner of war camps there—as in many other places. They had no communication with their families and no idea when they would be released. Cardinal von Galen and the other German cardinals sought and received the permission of the Allied authorities for each to visit several camps.

His visits were far in the south. A two-day drive took him to Taranto, where on Wednesday, he visited three camps and a hospital. The next day, he visited two more camps and, after a drive to Bari, another hospital. At each camp, the prisoners were gathered, and the cardinal spoke words of encouragement to them. He would ask who was from Westphalia and Münsterland, to an enthusiastic show of hands. After the address, he and the priests accompanying him mingled with the prisoners. "I have a good memory," he would tell those who were from Münsterland. "Give me your name and

15   Portmann, 295–301; Eng. trans., 198–205; memoir of Konstantin Prinz von Bayern in Joachim Kuropka, *Clemens August Graf von Galen: Sein Leben und Wirken in Bildern und Dokumenten*, 3rd ed. (Cloppenburg: Runge, 1997), 275.

the address of your relatives, and I will pass on a greeting to them."
Fathers Portmann and Bierbaum also became couriers of information. The prisoners asked them if they were able to carry letters with
them. Strictly speaking, Portmann replied, it was forbidden, but he
held up his arms so that the pockets of his overcoat were clearly visible and accessible. Small scraps of paper were pressed in, with simple
messages: name, address, name of camp, a simple "I'm all right."
Portmann noted that the British officers were very carefully looking
the other way. He and Bierbaum, after a few qualms of conscience at
breaking the rules, which had a certain justification, concluded that
they were free to consider the notes as equivalent to the contents of
a diplomatic bag.[16]

At the end of his visits to the camps, Cardinal von Galen would
take his leave with an *Auf Wiedersehen*, "Until we meet again," adding, "in heaven at least, if not sooner," a long-standing custom of
his when on pastoral visits. "May the first one to get to heaven,"
he continued, "pray for those who remain." A few weeks later, the
prisoners were shocked to learn of his sudden death. Soon after this,
they received other news—they were finally to be released. "He kept
his promise!" thought one prisoner to himself, recalling those part-
ing words. Portmann, in fact, believed that this loving visit to the
prisoners was the source of the infection that ultimately led to von
Galen's death. During the long drive south, with the car windows
open as he liked, he developed a toothache and eventually a swell-
ing of the jaw. Although urged to by his companions, he did not
seek any medical attention, and eventually the inflammation disappeared. After his death, the doctors said that it was likely because of
this that his cecum, kidneys, and heart were infected.

At Bari, the new cardinal and his entourage visited the relics of
St. Nicholas, and on the drive back to Rome, they made a stop at

---

16   Portmann (Eng. trans.), 211.

Monte Cassino. On Saturday, March 2, 1946, they climbed through the bombed-out ruins of the ancient monastery to visit the tomb of St. Benedict. Later that day, they were back in Rome, where on Sunday, von Galen took ceremonial possession of his titular church as a cardinal, the church of St. Bernard. After a few more days in Rome and a final visit to Pope Pius XII, it was time to return to Germany.

Cardinal Spellman of New York had fulfilled his promise. An American military plane was made available to fly the three new German cardinals to Paris, with a German-speaking American officer assigned to accompany them. The officer, Theobald Dengler, clearly relished his assignment. In a photo taken of the cardinals and their entourages at the steps of the plane before boarding, he is enthusiastically gesticulating to the photographer. A second photo shows the three cardinals inside the door of the plane. The giant Cardinal von Galen is a step behind Frings and von Preysing, the top of his head not visible because of the height of the doorway, and his face in shadow while the other cardinals are in the light—and in the corner of the doorway is the smiling face of Dengler above the shoulder of von Preysing. Dengler also created a souvenir from a thousand-lire note, which he asked the three cardinals to autograph. On the lower margin of the bill, he printed the words: "For first time in history 3 cardinals in one plane." The bill was turned sideways for the autographs, including Dengler's own. Above them, Dengler wrote "3 cardinals"; in the center of the bill, in large letters, "Rome to Paris"; and at the bottom, "7 March '46 over Mediterranean sea." The pilot very kindly gave the cardinals a nice aerial view of the Vatican and Rome and then flew the four hours to Paris. Thick clouds over Paris delayed the landing for an hour, causing some anxiety to several of the passengers who had never flown before, but all was well, and cars took them to the familiar Grand Hotel. The plan was to fly the next day to Frankfurt—1,500 dollars had already been paid for the flight—but the snowy weather made it impossible, and they were put on an overnight train. When they arrived in Frank-furt on the morning of Saturday, March 9, three cars were waiting for each cardinal and his entourage. Cardinal von Galen enjoyed, for the third time, the hospitality of the sisters at the Marian Hospital and was taken the next day to Haus Merfeld near Dülmen, about twenty miles southwest of Münster. He wanted to spend a week there with his brother Franz before taking part in a public ceremony of return to Münster.

Thanks to Cardinal Spellman, the return journey to Münster-land had certainly been much easier than the journey to Rome had been. The kindness of the American and other cardinals had also removed all the financial anxieties regarding the journey and the stay in Rome. Upon arriving at his brother's house, Cardinal von Galen gave his secretary 150 Reichsmarks to give to the three English driv-ers. It was, Portmann relates, the first time in the entire journey that he had had occasion to pay for something out of his own funds. Grinning, the cardinal said to Portmann, "I believe no one has ever become a cardinal as cheaply as we German bishops."[17]

---

17   Portmann, 316.

CHAPTER 25

Two Homecomings

Saturday, March 16, 1946, was set as the date for Cardinal von Galen's homecoming reception in Münster. It was his sixty-eighth birthday. Early on that cold winter day, he traveled by car from his brother's house southwest of Münster, through the side streets of the city, to the pilgrimage town of Telgte, east of the city. There—where he had so often prayed in private before the Sorrowful Virgin, had led so many large pilgrimages, and had preached some of his most important sermons—the day of celebration began. The whole town was filled with flags and banners; the struggles of the 1930s with the Nazi regime over the display of church banners were over, and the people wanted to show their overwhelming joy that Pope Pius had honored their beloved bishop, and honored the German people, by making him a cardinal. The church and the market square were overflowing with people. Cardinal von Galen celebrated Mass and gave Communion to a large number of people. When he was coming down from the altar to distribute Communion, he lost his footing and stumbled, bumping against the Communion rail with his elbows. Father Portmann remembered this weeks later and wondered whether this accident added to the damage that must have already affected his appendix.

A procession to the nearby rectory through the jubilant crowd was followed by a breakfast with the clergy and the mayor, and then the cardinal was able to retire for a few hours of rest. In the room that was set aside for his use, he wrote down an outline of the topics he wished to cover in his address in Münster later that afternoon.

About two o'clock in the afternoon, he came out of the house and boarded a coach drawn by four beautiful horses—the Münsterland has a great tradition of horse breeding and training. Standing in the coach, the cardinal waved to the cheering crowd. As the coach went on its stately pace toward Münster, he frequently adjusted the blanket over his knees. Again, in retrospect, Portmann suspected that he was feeling a chill that portended his coming mortal illness. For that matter, many people noted that despite his joy and liveliness, he looked unusually pale that day—it is clear to see in many of the photographs—but no one suspected that he would die within the week.[1]

Fifty thousand people were waiting in the ruins of the episcopal city for the arrival of the great man. In the eleven months since the Allied tanks had rolled into Münster, there had been almost no reconstruction or repairs. Debris had been piled up so that one could tell where the streets were, but almost all the buildings in the old city center were still in ruins. In order to have a better view of their cardinal, many people climbed onto the piles of ruins or what was still standing of the buildings.

The first point of meeting was the principal market. There the Catholic young people stood in two rows, making an aisle for

---

1   Detailed reports of the day and numerous photographs in Bernd Haunfelder and Axel Schollmeier, *Kardinal von Galen: Triumph und Tod. Fotos seiner letzten Lebenstage* (Münster: Aschendorff, 2005).

the procession of the coach. A triumphal arch was made by clothing two pillars with greenery and extending a garland between them. Of all the buildings surrounding the market, only the church of St. Lambert, the cardinal's former parish church, was standing in nearly its full form, but it had no roof or windows, and there was bomb damage to the tower. Nevertheless, trumpeters from the city orchestra had a place there from which to play a fanfare as the cardinal's coach came into view. Upon arriving, he stood in the coach smiling, waving, and blessing the people and then was helped down by Father Portmann. Two altar boys took hold of the fifteen-meter-long train of the *cappa magna*, the ceremonial cardinal's cape with its ermine hood, and marched well behind him as he blessed the clergy who were assembled to greet him.

The city officials and the Cathedral Chapter had worked out the program for the day. The principal market, with the "city and market church" of St. Lambert, was the traditional site for official city activities, so it was here that the mayor was to pay Münster's respects to the new cardinal. A balcony decorated with greenery stood before the south portal of the Lambertikirche. The cardinal mounted the steps and stood alone there, to a storm of applause. A chronogram with a play on his name decorated the front of the balcony: a sign with the Latin phrase, "CARDINAL CLEMENS UBIQUE SIT AUGUSTUS FIATQUE LARGE FELIX"—"May Cardinal Clemens be everywhere exalted and abundantly happy." Certain letters were printed in a lighter color. When given their value in Roman numerals, they added up to mark the year, 1946.

The mayor ascended to the balcony and came to the microphone. Public officials had been appointed by the military government from among those deemed not to be tainted with Nazism. Karl Zuhorn had been mayor in 1933, before the Nazi seizure of power, and had been deposed by them; the British had given him the position once again. The city council had unanimously agreed to grant Cardinal von Galen the title of honored citizen of Münster. Zuhorn read aloud the letter conferring this honor on the cardinal:

"The citizens are proud," it said,

> to see within their walls, on the venerable bishop's seat of St Ludger, a man from an ancient Münsterland family, who in the years of the recent tyranny stood in the foremost place as a fighter for the ideals of religious and human freedom.
>
> Your Eminence: Faithful to your motto *Nec laudibus Nec timore*, you have fought for twelve years against the violations of justice and of conscience, making use of the spoken and written word, at the risk of your freedom and your life, to the amazed approval of all right-thinking people throughout the world . . . You have consoled and comforted millions of Germans by your manly words.

The cardinal now came to the microphone. "Deeply moved," reported the *Neue Westfälische Zeitung*, "the Cardinal gave thanks for the great honor, and declared that since his childhood Münster had always been his *Heimat*. He begged God's richest blessings for the city, so that it would recover as soon as possible from the terrible wounds of the war."

Now he came down from the balcony and began a procession on foot toward the cathedral square. Four seminarians held a baldachin above him. Others carried symbols of his episcopal authority: mitre, crozier, pontifical book of ceremonies, and bougie, the candle held by an assistant so that a bishop could read prayers during liturgical ceremonies.

When the procession reached the square of St. Michael, the medieval dividing line between the realm where city officials held authority and the so-called freedom of the cathedral, it was met by the Cathedral Chapter, led by the auxiliary bishop and including Canons Vorwerk and Echelmeyer—the canons who had been exiled from Münster by the Nazis—and Friedrichs, who had spent four years in the concentration camp at Dachau. The two groups of clergy faced each other at the dividing line, while the auxiliary bishop gave a speech of welcome on behalf of the chapter. Then the procession continued, with the canons leading the cardinal to the cathedral. The Knights of Malta acted as an honor guard on either side of von Galen. The British had forbidden them to carry their ceremonial swords, so they decided not to wear their uniforms either, instead opting for dark suits and overcoats and top hats.

The procession came to the side entrance of the cathedral known as the paradise. Part of the building inside that entrance was still usable, and the Blessed Sacrament had been exposed on an altar there. Cardinal von Galen went in and knelt in adoration of his Savior, after which the procession continued. To make viewing easier, a small hill had been built in front of what had been the west portal between the two great towers of the cathedral. On it was a raised platform with a throne. There, with the backdrop of a screen covered with greenery, the Cathedral Chapter stood around their bishop. Behind the backdrop of evergreen branches was open space where the portal had been and a view into the empty, roofless cathedral. Fifty thousand people, according to police estimates, crowded into the cathedral square. Many had climbed onto the pillars and gateposts supporting the fence of the ruined episcopal palace across the square. A couple of young men had climbed a pile of ruins directly behind and above the throne on which von Galen was sitting.

Now several more speeches were made. The high president of Westphalia, Rudolf Amelunxen, praised the cardinal's courage during the Nazi regime. Further addresses were made by the mayor, a priest, and a representative of young Catholics.

Finally, it was the cardinal's turn to rise and approach the microphone. He had made notes for himself that morning at Telgte, but that was simply to exercise his memory. He did not have any papers in his hand while he gave his speech, which turned out to be the last great address of his life. Speaking from the heart, he left a profound effect on his listeners.[2]

He began by giving thanks to all present for the wonderful, joyful welcome they had prepared for him. The great crowd of people, he said, had gathered in a joyous atmosphere and in the conviction that even though their cathedral was terribly wounded, their churches destroyed, their houses smashed to pieces, their city a city of ruins—nevertheless, they all had reason to face the future with cheerful optimism, because they knew the foundation on which they must rebuild: God's holy law. "What our ancestors achieved as Christian Catholic people," he said, "so too you, your children and your children's children can achieve, if the same Christian Catholic spirit lives in you which once enabled them to accomplish such noble works, including works of culture."

He repeated his thanks to the city of Münster and all its people for honoring him on his return to his beloved *Heimat* after the Holy Father had given him what he called the greatest honor that he could receive on earth. "I have come home from Rome. There the Holy Father has received me into the Senate of the Holy Roman Catholic—catholic, universal, world-spanning—Church. He has called me into the group of his closest advisors, and marked me with the honor of the cardinalate and with the vesture that indicates the

---

2   Peter Löffler, ed., *Bischof Clemens August Graf von Galen: Akten, Briefe und Predigten 1933–1946*, 2nd ed. (Paderborn: Ferdinand Schöningh, 1996), doc. 557, v. II, 1324–27; about fifteen minutes of audio from a tape recording of the speech is available on an audio CD from a two-CD set, "Nachgehört und nachgefragt: Clemens August Graf von Galen," LWL-Medienzentrum für Westfalen, 2007.

determination to defend the truth of God and the holy rights of
God even to the shedding of blood."[3]

A shout of approval greeted his assertion that he was overwhelmed
at the honor that Pope Pius had shown to him personally. But, he
added, the pope's action should not simply be interpreted as an
honor paid to an individual person:

> The dear God placed me in a position in which I had a duty
> to call black "black" and white "white," as it says in the rite of
> consecrating a bishop. He gave me a position that made me
> the leader and responsible guide of hundreds and thousands,
> who, like me, found it hard, who suffered it only with virtue
> and with the greatest pain, when God's truth and justice, the
> value of the human being and the rights of the human being,
> were set aside, rejected, and thrown on the ground; who,
> like me and with me, found it a bitter injustice against the true
> good of our people when the religion and truth of Christ were
> ever more constricted and pushed aside. I knew that I could
> speak for thousands who, like me, were strongly convinced
> that our German people could find happiness, true unity, and
> a blessed future only on the foundation of Christianity.
>
> I knew that many suffered more, much more than I person-
> ally had to suffer, from the attacks on truth and justice that we
> experienced. They could not speak. They could only suffer. It
> may be that in God's sight, in which suffering has more value
> than actions and words; it may be that despite their suffering,
> even many of those who are standing here have truly merited
> much more in the holy eyes of God, because they have suffered
> more than I have. But it was my right and my duty to speak,
> and I spoke, for you, for countless people who are gathered

3   Löffler, doc. 557, v. II, 1324–27.

here, for countless people in our dear German fatherland; and God gave it His blessing. And your love and loyalty, my dear diocesans, also kept far from me what might have been my fate, but also might have been my greatest reward, the crown of martyrdom.

His voice broke with emotion as he spoke these words, perhaps thinking of the many who had been martyred, perhaps regretting that he had not received that blessing. He went on: "It was your loyalty that prevented it. The fact that you stood behind me, and that those who were then in power knew that the people and the Bishop in the Diocese of Münster were an unbreakable unity"—loud cheering from the crowd interrupted him at this remark—"and that if they struck the Bishop, all the people would feel as if they had been struck—that was what protected me from external harm; but it was also what gave me inner strength and confidence."[4]

By this time, some of the Nazi archives from 1941 had been discovered. The public knew about the Gestapo's desire to hang the Bishop of Münster and Goebbels's pragmatic reply that if any action were taken at that point, Münster would have to be written off for the war effort. Indeed, the loyalty of the people of Münster had saved their bishop's life. In 1941, he could only speculate on that, but he certainly experienced their great loyalty on countless occasions, and it was a source of his strength. Now in 1946, he was convinced that Pope Pius XII had made him a cardinal to honor not only him but them. It was their loyalty that the pope wanted to honor, he said: "It was the loyalty of the people of Münster, it was the loyalty of the overwhelming majority of the diocesans of Münster, who despite all allurements and

---

4   Ibid.

pressure maintained their fidelity to Christ the Lord and His holy Church. If today, people have so frequently and always expressed their thanks to me, then I must also give each of you, and each of those whom you represent from the large diocese of Münster, my heartfelt thanks, on behalf of a German bishop, on behalf of three German bishops."

He added that when the bishops and the Catholic community had criticized those in authority, when they had said, "We are not allowed to do that," or "You, you in authority, are not allowed to do that," it was not because they were against the *Volk* or fatherland; it was in order to protect the people and fatherland from the destruction that would be brought upon them by doing evil. God had allowed frightful ruin to come upon Germany, he said, because his warnings were not heeded. This showed that Germany had been on the wrong path. "*We* were on the right path when we warned that . . . as I once expressed it, if things continued in this way, our German fatherland would fall into ruin despite the heroic bravery of our soldiers. Sadly, that is what has happened." Nevertheless, he insisted that the German soldiers had been heroic in fulfillment of their duty. Their service to the fatherland, he said to vigorous shouts of approval, was meritorious before God and should be acknowledged as such by everyone.[5]

This point was crucial to von Galen's entire worldview, and he held it consistently to the end of his life. To serve one's country in the military is, he believed, a noble act, and one does not do evil in obeying evil men who have authority, unless one obeys them when they give evil orders. This was why he constantly denied the thesis of the collective guilt of all Germans. He saw the pope's act in naming him a cardinal as a confirmation of his stand. The Holy Father, he continued,

---

5   Ibid.

has called three German bishops into the College of Cardinals, and thereby has indicated to the whole world—a world that, to a large extent, at least if one judges by the expressions of public opinion, seems inclined to see in Germany only the end of a criminal and anti-Christian regime, that seems inclined today to despise and reject every German, that seems inclined to consider the entire German people to be a gang of criminals—the Holy Father has indicated to the entire world that he does not think like that.

Again he was interrupted by strong applause. He continued by claiming that the pope knew the German people better than most:

He has shown that in spite of the injustice and criminality of many Germans, which we bitterly mourn, and the consequences of which we have had to suffer in the destruction of our cities and in other consequences of the war, that a large portion of our people did not embrace those destructive heathen principles, and that there are many, thousands, millions of Germans who truly deserve, as honorable people, to have freedom and justice like all other peoples of the world, all other children of God on this earth.

When he came to conclude his address, Cardinal von Galen asserted that the creation of three German cardinals had been applauded by the entire Catholic world. He once again expressed his thanks to the Holy Father but also to the Catholics of his diocese, "whose stance during this entire time," he said, "made it possible for me to fight for God and His kingdom. I must close, and in doing so tell you that the Holy Father greets all of you from the heart, and—I must say this here—at the moment when he placed the famous red hat on my head in St Peter's Basilica, he said to me, 'I bless you and I bless Germany!'"[6]

---

6   Ibid.

Again came boisterous shouts of approval, and the cardinal ended by asking the enthusiastic crowd to join him in a resounding three cheers for "our gloriously reigning Pope Pius XII."

A final bit of sweetness capped the unforgettable day. After the ceremonies at the cathedral square, the chapter and the Knights of Malta accompanied Cardinal von Galen in procession to his lodgings at the Borromäum. At the entrance, he was greeted by two four-year-old girls dressed as angels. Together they recited a poem of welcome, telling him that he was loved also by the little ones. The poem included a prayer that God reward him with a beautiful crown in heaven and ended with the girls ringing little bells to announce that Cardinal Clemens August was now coming into his home. He had been away for just over five weeks, since February 7, and now he was ready to settle back into the work of helping to rebuild his diocese and his country on Christian principles. It was a work in which he was not to have a part.

The next morning, Sunday, March 17, Clemens August celebrated his first pontifical Mass as a cardinal. It was also, although no one knew it, his last. A horse-drawn carriage returned him to the Borromäum, where he smilingly blessed the onlookers before having his first bite to eat at about noon. For an hour, standing in one of the small rooms that were available to him, he received the congratulations of a number of well-wishers, including many of the British officers. By the end of this time, his exhaustion was evident. He had to be called to lunch twice before coming, and eating was painful to him. Nevertheless, there was a theological colloquium prepared for later in the afternoon, and he managed to attend and to give a short address. His attendants noted that he was very pale, and there was a bit of trembling in his hands. After he returned to his room at the Borromäum, his secretary came to ask how he was feeling. He admitted to suffering from abdominal pains, but the clergy took the view that he was just exhausted from all the events of the previous weeks.

The next morning, he offered a less public Mass, at which a young relative received her first Holy Communion. At the end of the Mass, he led the congregation in praying an Our Father for the restoration of Catholic schools. After spending some time with his family members, he went up to his room, more exhausted than ever, but he refused to go to bed. It was enough, unusual as it was, that he rest at his writing desk or lie down on the sofa. It was a matter of pride to him that, as he had told the other cardinals while in Rome, he had never gone back to bed in the daytime since 1890, when he was a boy of twelve.

Finally, on Tuesday morning, he consented that a doctor be called. The two doctors agreed that his condition was very serious, and he should undergo an operation on that very day. At two o'clock in the afternoon, when the ambulance came, there could be no doubt that he was seriously ill. Still, it was a terrible shock to Father Portmann when the cardinal pointed toward the windowsill and said, "Over there you will find the red book. You know the one I mean; we brought it from Rome. In it you can read how a cardinal is to be buried."[7]

It took some doing to carry this giant of a man down the stairs to the ambulance. A couple of bricklayers who were doing repair work in the seminary gave a helping hand, but despite their care, it was a painful journey for the cardinal. In the ambulance, he gave further instructions to Portmann in regard to his burial.

The Cathedral Chapter and other priests were waiting at the hospital. One of the hospital chaplains heard von Galen's last Confession, and the others came into the room to join in prayer as he

---

7   Heinrich Portmann, *Kardinal von Galen: Ein Gottesmann seiner Zeit*,
       17th ed. (Münster: Aschendorff, 1981), 323.

received his Lord in Holy Communion. Again, the cardinal indicated his awareness of how serious his condition was. Before the auxiliary bishop came into the room with the Blessed Sacrament, he remarked that it was the anniversary of his Baptism, the feast of St. Joseph, the patron of the dying. Everyone there noted the childlike piety with which he then recited the prayers and received Communion. When all had left the room, he called back one of the priests, who had been his contemporary in the seminary. "If it ends in my death tonight," he said to him, "you must come. I would not want to be completely alone."

It was, as he had said, the feast of St. Joseph, March 19, 1946. He died not that evening but three days later, on Friday the twenty-second. The British had brought in a specialist from Bonn to assist in the operation, but peritonitis, resulting from a ruptured appendix, proved in the end too much for his system to overcome. For three days, in full consciousness, he patiently endured the various interventions of the doctors and thanked them and the nurses for all their efforts to save his life. General Sedgwick pulled strings to acquire hard-to-get penicillin for him, but it was too late.

On Friday, March 22, the Cathedral Chapter and the cardinal's relatives and friends gathered at the hospital. From time to time, nurses came to the waiting room to report that he had prayed for the diocese, the fatherland, children, and the young. In delirium, he asked for a horse-drawn carriage to take him to the cathedral square. There he would give a blessing in all directions over the city and the diocese, and then they could return him to the hospital to die. His last words were: "God's will be done. May God reward you. God protect the dear fatherland. Continue to work for Him. O, dear Savior!"

At the end, the doctors published the following report:

> Given the lack of consideration His Eminence often gave to matters of a personal nature, it was not until the morning of

March 19th that he first presented for medical evaluation. At the time of this examination it was noted that peritonitis had already developed along with small bowel paralysis. Surgery performed the same day at Franziskus Hospital in Münster proceeded without complication. By March 22nd His Eminence's cardiac function and general condition had worsened substantially. The decline in cardiac and circulatory function observed earlier that morning continued to worsen inexorably over the course of the day, despite intensive intervention.[8]

At five o'clock in the afternoon, he peacefully breathed his last. Four weeks earlier, he had humbly lain prostrate in St. Peter's Basilica with the other new cardinals and then knelt before Pope Pius XII to receive the red hat, with triumphant applause ringing through the basilica. Just six days earlier, he had greeted the jubilant crowd of fifty thousand in his episcopal city. Now his body lay still on a bed in the Franziskus Hospital. After his face was washed, his hair combed, and a rosary entwined in his hands, a photograph was taken showing a wondrous peace and beauty in his face.

Soon after his death, those church bells that had survived the war began to toll the death knell. The suddenness of his death brought an enormous shock to the Catholic community of Münster. So soon after celebrating his triumphal return in the scarlet robes of a cardinal, they would be taking part in his funeral. There were some, unfortunately, who believed and spread rumors that the British had poisoned him because of his outspokenness. Brigadier Sedgwick thought that his efforts in bringing penicillin to Münster may have contributed to the rumors. The next week, walking in the funeral

---

8   Max Bierbaum, *Nicht Lob, Nicht Furcht: Das Leben des Kardinals von Galen* (Münster: Regensberg, 1946), 288–89. Thanks to Dr. Glenn Whitted for assistance in the translation.

procession, he saw an inscription in chalk on one of the ruined walls of the city: "Clemens August, victim of the English Secret Service."[9] Father Portmann took pains when writing his biography of the cardinal to show that the British had in fact done all they could to save von Galen's life.

The cathedral, of course, could not be used for the funeral Mass. Nor, for that matter, could the church of St. Lambert, or the Überwasserkirche, or any of the churches in the old city center. The cardinal's body therefore was laid out for visitation in the church of St. Maurice, the Mauritzkirche, just to the east of the city center. Over four days, from Sunday, March 24 until Wednesday afternoon, thousands of the faithful filed by the body of their great cardinal, in stunned sorrow at his sudden death. On Wednesday evening, the body was taken in procession to the Kreuzkirche, the church of the Holy Cross, where the funeral Mass took place on Thursday morning at ten o'clock. Cardinal von Preysing was the celebrant of the Mass, and Cardinal Frings preached. Another of the new cardinals, the Archbishop of Westminster, Cardinal Edward Griffin, was also in attendance.

In his funeral sermon,[10] Cardinal Frings tried to portray in words what everyone was feeling about the dramatic situation: the sudden end of the great man at the height of his powers and fame, a giant of a man brought to his death by something apparently small. Frings recalled the journey to Rome, when von Galen was in the peak of health. He had seemed, of all the cardinals at the consistory, not only the tallest but the strongest. The strains of the journey did not seem to bother him. He seemed never to get cold or tired but kept busy from morn to night. He took on, said Frings, the most grueling of the itineraries for visits to the prisoners of war.

---

9   Heinrich Portmann, *Cardinal von Galen*, trans. R. L. Sedgwick (London: Jarrolds, 1957), footnotes on 208, 225.

10   Löffler, v. II, 1335–38.

The Catholics of Münster learned from Frings what a great impression their cardinal had made in Rome. "Wherever he appeared, there was a storm of applause, be it on the streets, be it in the palaces, be it in the churches themselves. Every word he spoke was passed on to the whole world by press and radio. He himself jokingly said, 'I have been in mortal danger twice in my life: once when enemy bombs rained upon my palace; the second time in Rome, when the students of the Gregorian University surrounded me with such enthusiasm that I feared for my life.' In fact," Frings continued, "Cardinal Galen was the lion of the day. They called him 'The Lion of Münster.'"[11]

It was the first time many of the people of his city heard of this title, and the joy it brought helped them bear the sorrow of their loss.

Frings praised his fellow cardinal for the simplicity and straightforwardness of his character. He lived up to his motto, *Nec laudibus Nec timore*, in such a way that everyone marveled at his heroic courage. He was able to stand up, practically alone, against a power that sought to put an end to Christianity in Germany. "He was probably at his greatest," Frings said, "in 1941, when he preached the three sermons. The theme to which he continually returned was the freedom of the Church and the religious communities, and the preservation of the Catholic schools. He was the protector of the weak and those suffering injustice and the so-called undeserving of life." Recalling the desire of the Gestapo to arrest and execute von Galen, Frings said that they did not arrest him because they feared him, the Lion of Münster.

He added that perhaps von Galen showed his greatness even more after the war when, instead of resting on his laurels, he spoke to the new rulers with the same freedom and courage he had shown to the Nazis. "Where he thought he saw injustice, he said so openly and honestly to their faces: what was going on in the east, what was

---

11   Ibid.

going on with our prisoners of war, what was going on with regard to prisoners in camps."

Frings characterized von Galen as a man who combined courageous heroism with the simple faith of a child:

> He was a hero before God, a hero before men, and at the same time a child in the presence of God. A deep faith ruled his very being. He believed in the triune God, in the savior who became man for us, in the real presence of Christ in the Blessed Sacrament. And he revered the Mother of God like a child. It is just a month since I knelt behind him in Telgte. He, that giant of a man, knelt down like a child and prayed like a child for Mary's protection for the journey to Rome.

To these two characteristics, Frings added a third. Von Galen had a genuine goodness, transfigured by Christian charity—he was a good man, a good bishop, a man of kindness and good deeds, as, Frings was sure, many people could testify. He encouraged his listeners to show, by their lives, that with Cardinal von Galen, "the race of upright men has not died out; that there are still people who have the heart of a man, combined with the faith of a child and the tenderness of a mother."[12]

The great cardinal's body lay in a stately wooden casket on which wood-carvers had engraved his coat of arms, including the stylized cardinal's hat and his motto, *Nec laudibus Nec timore.* When they brought the coffin from the church, the Knights of Malta placed it on a wagon covered with greenery, to which a team of four black horses was attached. The three cardinals, numerous bishops, the Cathedral Chapter, priests of the diocese, and representatives of the military regime walked in the long procession to the cathedral. All along the route, the streets were lined with spectators and mourners—perhaps

---

12   Ibid.

the overall crowd was even larger than the estimated fifty thousand who had greeted Cardinal von Galen on his triumphal return to Münster just twelve days before. Seminarians accompanied the coffin, escorted by the Knights of Malta, who again wore their dark suits and top hats. The cardinal's beloved brother Franz, "Strick," his closest friend since his childhood, took his place in the funeral procession just behind his brother's body.

A grave had been prepared in the ambulatory chapel, which Christoph Bernhard von Galen had built centuries earlier for his own resting place. There was no question of going into the cathedral from the bombed-out western portal. An entrance was available leading directly to the chapel, which is at the farthest eastern point of the church. There his mortal remains were laid to rest. Since then, pilgrims have come constantly to venerate the Lion of Münster, including, in 1987, Pope John Paul II.

Cardinal Frings described him well in his funeral homily. Bishop von Galen was a man of great courage and of great and simple faith. He was a good man with a good heart, a giant with the soul of a child. He was not a great scholar, but he had what great scholars often lack: a clarity of vision and a grounding in the principles he had learned in his childhood from the Catechism lessons of his mother and deepened in the conversations with his father and in the study of the writings of his great-uncle, Bishop Wilhelm Emmanuel von Ketteler. This clarity of vision, his knowledge and love of the Catholic faith, combined with his courage and his devotion to the Virgin Mother of God, gave him the ability to speak out when others were silent and to give courage, hope, and guidance to countless people trying to live rightly in evil times.

Cardinal Clemens August von Galen's time in office as Bishop of Münster coincided almost exactly with the twelve years of Adolf Hitler's rule over Germany. Von Galen had been named bishop in the autumn of 1933, just a few months after the National Socialists had taken power. He died on March 22, 1946, just over nine months after Hitler's fall. Von Galen's place in history is thus defined by his principled opposition to the Third Reich. Having chosen as his episcopal motto *"Nec laudibus Nec timore,"* he lived that motto to the end. Neither the praises of men nor fear of what they might do to him hindered him from preaching the gospel and the moral teachings of the gospel, from speaking up for the rights of the Church and the fundamental rights of the human person. In God's plan, because he did not live long enough to take part in the rebuilding of Germany on a Christian foundation, he is remembered primarily for speaking up heroically, at the risk of imprisonment or death, against the arbitrary power of the Gestapo, the unjust confiscation of the property of the religious orders, and the murder of the handicapped. He should, however, be remembered not only for his courage but for the clarity of his teaching. He knew that preaching the truth and teaching his people how to live a Christian life were central to his task as a bishop. He used whatever means were at his disposal to do so: Sermons, pastoral letters, pastoral visits, processions, pilgrimages, and the printed word were all crucial to his work. So was his tireless work of encouraging his priests and seminarians, Catholic teachers and parents, and leaders of Catholic organizations. Their cooperation with his work made it successful, to the degree that it could be successful in the times in which he lived. It truly was the case that there was an unbreakable unity between the bishop and the faithful in the Diocese of Münster.

On October 9, 2005, the Catholic Church acknowledged his sanctity. He was beatified—that is, named as one of the blessed, the last step before canonization as a saint—in a ceremony at St. Peter's Basilica in Rome. The miracle required for the beatification involved the sudden cure of a twelve-year-old boy in Indonesia who was close to death in 1991 from a ruptured appendix. A German missionary sister prayed for the intercession of Cardinal von Galen, knowing that he had died from a similar ailment.[13] In anticipation of the beat-ification, his grave was opened in the spring of 2005, as required by church law, for what is called the recognition of the mortal remains and the removal of some relics. Perhaps because the coffin was lined with lead, the body and the vestments in which it was clothed were found to be in an excellent condition, with his features still recognizable.

At the conclusion of the beatification in St. Peter's Basilica, Pope Benedict XVI asserted that everyone, and "particularly we Germans," should be thankful to the Lord for "this great witness of faith who made the light of truth shine out in dark times and had the courage to oppose the power of tyranny."[14]

"However," the pope continued,

> we must also ask ourselves: Where did this insight come from in a period when intelligent people seemed as if they were blind? And where did he find the strength to oppose [tyranny] at a time when even the strong proved weak and cowardly? He drew insight and courage from the faith that showed him the truth and opened his heart and eyes.
>
> He feared God more than men, and it was God who granted him the courage to do and say what others did not dare to say and do. Thus, he gives us courage, he urges us to live the faith anew today, and he also shows us how this is possible in things that are simple and humble, yet great and profound.
>
> Let us remember that he often used to make pilgrimages on foot to the Mother of God in Telgte, that he introduced per-petual adoration at St. Servatius and that he frequently asked

---

13   http://kirchensite.de/index.php?myELEMENT=100884.
14   http://w2.vatican.va/content/benedict-xvi/en/speeches/2005/october/documents/hf_ben_xvi_spe_20051009_beatif-von-galen.html.

for and obtained the grace of forgiveness in the Sacrament of Penance.

He therefore shows us this simple Catholicity in which the Lord meets us, in which He opens our hearts and gives us spiritual discernment, the courage of faith and the joy of being saved. Let us give thanks to God for this great witness of faith and pray to him that he will enlighten and guide us.

Blessed Cardinal von Galen, at this very moment, pray for us and for the Church in Germany and throughout the world. Amen.[15]

---

15   Ibid.

ACKNOWLEDGMENTS

My dear friend Paula von Ketteler, without whom this book never would have been started, did not live to see its completion. May she rest in peace.

It was she who introduced me, in 1991, to Christoph Bernhard von Galen and later to his daughter Johanna von Westphalen. They, too, are no longer with us to see the result of my fascination with his uncle, her grand-uncle.

A look at the footnotes to this book will demonstrate the debt that a non-historian owes to all those who have gathered the materials and worked in this field before me. Almost all the diocesan archives and bishop's archives in Münster were destroyed by American bombs on October 10, 1943. Thanks to work that began soon after the war was over, we now have the invaluable collection of documents published by the Kommission für Zeitgeschichte under the editorship of Peter Löffler. All researchers owe an enormous debt of thanks for this work. I owe thanks as well to all the earlier biographers of Cardinal von Galen, from Portmann and Bierbaum to Beaugrand, Heitmann, Grevelhörster, Trautmann, Wolf, and Falasca, among others. A recent discovery on YouTube of a 2005 television interview with Joachim Kuropka reminded me how much I owe to his historical judgment.

I owe more thanks than I can properly express to Clemens von Ketteler; Wilderich and Elisabeth von Ketteler; and Philipp and Caroline von Ketteler, authors of a wonderful children's book on the cardinal. Fritz von Loë gave me crucial help by sharing both his memories and his research. Special thanks to Dietrich Graf Spee, through whom I met the Kettelers and Graf Loë, and who long ago made a gift of Löffler's book to the Toronto Oratory. Thanks also to Sister Monica Lewis, O.S.B., and Sister Ulrike, O.S.B., of Kloster Dinklage; and to Peter Sieve of the Offizialatsarchiv Vechta of the Bischöflich Münstersches Offizialat and Pfr. Clemens Heitmann, both of whom kindly answered several questions forwarded by Sister Monica. Thanks to Frau Hilber and Frau Horst for their recollections. To Provost Hans-Bernd Serries and Ingrid Lueb, I have expressed my thanks in the appendix. Also to Heinz Mestrup and his colleagues and Birte Koch. Now I know why researchers are so grateful to archivists and librarians. I learned some things I did not previously know through an e-mail correspondence with Beth Griech-Polelle. Since I have had occasion in these pages to express a gentle disagreement with her, it is a pleasure here to acknowledge her graciousness and kindness.

During this long project, I have had help and encouragement from Fran Baldner, Andrew Blake, Maggie Gibson, Timothy Hambor, the late Father Karl Hoeppe, C.Ss.R., and the German community at St. Patrick's Parish, Toronto, Thea Lamshoeft, Donna Lasecki, Kathleen McGinnis, Karin Morse, Douglas Peck, David Warren, Hilary White, Dr. Glenn Whitted, and many others.

The final impetus to write this book came in 2005, when our Oratory group for World Youth Day in Cologne spent a week in Westphalia. At the Heimatmuseum in Telgte, when I told some of our pilgrims about Cardinal von Galen, Elena Repka said, "Why have I never heard of this guy? Someone should write a book about him." If you don't like the book, blame her.

Thanks to Christian Tappe of Saint Benedict Press for accepting this book for publication, and thanks to my editor John Moorehouse, as well as the entire team at Saint Benedict Press.

Finally, to Father Jonathan Robinson and my confreres in the Oratory, and especially to Father Juvenal Merriell and Father Philip Cleevely, abundant thanks.

APPENDIX

On the Trail of a Mysterious Document

After this book was in the hands of the publishers, I learned of a book critical of the German bishops during and after the Nazi era—Michael Phayer's *The Catholic Church and the Holocaust, 1930–1965* (Indiana University Press, 2000). I was surprised to read there the following passage:

> While the debate over Holocaust guilt and responsibility persisted, the bishops changed their minds about the punishment of individual perpetrators of atrocities. In spite of the fact that in 1945 their Fulda statement had unequivocally said that those who engaged in atrocities must be brought to justice and must pay for their crimes, only months later German bishops began to plead for leniency for those who had engaged personally in the Holocaust. The reason for their reversal can be traced to Rome. Just months after the Fulda statement, Bishop Clemens August Graf von Galen—the "Lion of Münster" who had dared to challenge the Nazis on euthanasia—published an address in which he sharply attacked the Nuremberg "show trials" (the International Military Tribunal at Nuremberg). The

trials, Galen said, were not about justice but about the defamation of the German people. In one passage of Galen's statement, the bishop made the outrageous claim that the prisons of
the occupational authority were worse than the Nazi concentration camps in eastern Europe.

As recently as one month before the publication of von
Galen's statement, an OMGUS[1] report indicated that the
Catholic clergy were "pleased with [Nuremberg prosecu-
tor] Justice Jackson's determination to convict those guilty of
crimes against natural law and the law of conscience." Abruptly
after Church leaders found out about von Galen's attack, they
distanced themselves from OMGUS authorities, who would
not have allowed Galen to publish in Germany. Of course, the
fact that von Galen's tract came out in Rome signaled the bishops that the Holy See opposed punishment of German war
criminals. Given the green light from Rome, German bishops
began a long and largely successful campaign to free imprisoned criminals and have the sentences of those condemned to
death commuted to incarceration. (138–39)

A little further on in his book, Phayer adds this:

It was not only ordinary Germans whom Pius wished to exon-
erate. The pope was also anxious to see that convicted war criminals be given clemency, and in all likelihood he opposed the
Nuremberg Trials. This became evident in the spring of 1946,
when Bishop von Galen penned a diatribe against the trials
that was published in Rome. Von Galen's tract illustrates the
Vatican's postwar strategy. The bishop's objection that the Allies
had agreed to Germany's postwar boundaries without any German input echoed Pius's wartime efforts for a negotiated peace

---

1   Occupational Military Government–United States.

that would leave Germany intact and vigorous. Since that did not happen, von Galen warned that Europe was falling prey to socialism, as Italy was demonstrating. Von Galen implied that a restored, strong Germany could stop the socialist erosion.

As we have seen, von Galen's tract initiated the reversal of the policy of the German bishops toward war criminals.

This was exciting material but also humbling and disconcerting. Had Cardinal von Galen in fact made the "outrageous" claim that the Allied prisons were worse than the Nazi concentration camps? Consulting again Beth Griech-Polelle's critical book on von Galen, I saw that she had cited Phayer's book, whereas I had not noticed her citation. How had I overlooked the existence of this publication by von Galen, which must have been one of the last things that he wrote? The monumental collection of documents published by the Kommission für Zeitgeschichte under the editorship of Peter Löffler—*Bischof Clemens August Graf von Galen: Akten, Briefe und Predigten 1933–1946* (1996)—on which I, as an amateur historian, have leaned so much in writing this book, had not carried the document. Nor could I recall von Galen's first biographers, Heinrich Portmann and Max Bierbaum, having said anything about it. Phayer, it seemed, had made the exciting discovery of a hitherto-unknown document, which might require me to adjust my assessment of the great cardinal. Where was this document to be found, and why was it not in Löffler's collection? Perhaps it was discovered after the collection had been printed. But why did Portmann, the cardinal's secretary, seemingly not know of it? Why could I recall no discussion of it in the more recent biographies of Wolf, Grevelhörster, and Trautmann or in any of the many historical studies of Joachim Kuropka and others?

I can only be grateful to Michael Phayer for setting me on the trail of this mysterious document. What I learned, it turns out, was known by some experts in Germany, but many people who have seen copies of the document have no idea that it, in fact, was not authored by Cardinal von Galen. The first thing I learned was that it was not "published" in the sense of being a printed document but distributed hand to hand in typewritten form. The six versions of it I have seen are neither from a common duplicating machine nor carbon copies from one typewriter, but all come from different typewriters with various changes and errors made by the copyists.

Already in 1946, many of the people into whose hands it came were suspicious of its authenticity. The Diocese of Münster issued a statement in June 1946 categorically denying that von Galen had anything to do with the document. Nevertheless, many people continued to believe in its authenticity, and so it could have influenced their thinking, not only on its own merits but because they thought it was by the late Lion of Münster. It can also be said that it is a fascinating document expressing what many Germans must have thought about the governing methods of the Allies. Incidentally, the claim that it does make about the concentration camps run by the Allies is not as "outrageous" as Phayer suggests. As to whether the document influenced Pope Pius XII or the German bishops in their attitude to the Nuremberg trials, or that Pius "in all likelihood" opposed the trials, Phayer gives no evidence beyond his assertion. Further study would be necessary to see whether this document found its way to other diocesan offices (certainly it was circulating widely in Germany); whether it fooled the bishops into thinking it was by von Galen; whether it is to be found in Rome; and whether it influenced the thought of Pius XII.

My first step on the trail of this mysterious document was to consult the endnotes of Phayer's book, where I learned that he had found it in the Munich city library, Stadtbibliothek München. An e-mail inquiry to that library produced an extremely helpful reply from reference librarian Birte Koch. Presuming that it would not be easy for me to visit Munich, she scanned the document for me and sent the image as an attachment to her reply e-mail. The document turned out not to be a published document in the sense of a printed text but a typescript of twenty numbered pages, of which page 18 is missing. The title given is:

ADDRESS OF CARDINAL COUNT V. GALEN IN ROME
MARCH 1946
RECHTSBEWUSSTSEIN UND RECHTSUNSICHERHEIT

The capacity of the German language for the creation of compound words is one of the factors that makes it almost impossible to give a concise translation of this title into English. The layers of meaning in the words themselves add to this difficulty. *Recht* can mean justice, or right, or law, or jurisprudence. *Bewusstsein* is consciousness or awareness. *Unsicherheit* means uncertainty or insecurity. So the first word of the title can mean consciousness (or awareness) of justice (or right, or law), which is then compared or contrasted with uncertainty (or insecurity) in regard to justice (or right, or law). These layers of meaning are reflected in the content of the document.

Beginning with a reference to Pope Pius XII's encyclical *Mit brennender Sorge*, which it characterizes as "perhaps the sharpest attack on National Socialism and the best refutation of its theories," the document cites the pope's stress on the principle that justice (*Gerechtigkeit*) is the foundation of states. *Rechtsbewusstsein und Rechtsunsicherheit* cites the Latin formulation of the principle, *Justitia fundamentum regnorum*, noting that the pope was calling attention to its corollary: States that ignore this principle, by undermining their own foundations, are setting themselves up for their own collapse.

National Socialism, it goes on to say, did just this. It cited the concept "Right and Justice" (or, perhaps, "Law and Justice," *Recht und*

Gerechtigkeit), but it deliberately created uncertainty or insecurity about the law in the people. This *Rechtsunsicherheit*, the document goes on to say, "belongs to the methods by which authoritarian states rule"—namely, through terror. All the authoritarian states of the postwar (i.e., post–World War I) period—Russia, Italy, Germany, and Spain—put fear into the hearts of the citizens by establishing order in society through violence.

Before the war, such methods had been rare in European countries. The methods occasionally used by the state police in czarist Russia were opposed to the legal principles that European states were proud of. European citizens had a sense of security of their lives and property under the law that fostered a peaceful public order, which in turn made possible the economic growth of the nineteenth century. But there was a fundamental flaw in legal theory—a refusal to admit a metaphysical foundation to law:

> The 19th century wanted to give value only to positive law, but not to a natural law. If the head of state or a law-making body or the People is the sole source of law, and if only the positive law has value, then it must be the case that the State or the head of state or the People can arbitrarily change this system of law on which the order in Europe rested. The legal theorists were firmly convinced that justice (or right) would remain, that like a free-floating iron curtain it would have enough solidity and inner consistency that a shaking of the fundamental rights of the person was out of the question. Important law professors in all countries of Europe spoke as ever about the value and majesty of justice, but refused just as energetically to acknowledge any metaphysical grounding of justice . . . Napoleon I in his memoirs casually remarked that the authentic and final meaning of the French Revolution consisted in the equality of all under the law. This equality under the law was demanded by

everyone in the 19th century by invoking the rights with which each human being is born. But why in fact every human being has these rights was of no interest to legal positivism.

The author of *Rechtsbewusstsein und Rechtsunsicherheit* saw Adolf Hitler as drawing the logical consequences from this state of legal theory. If the state is the sole source of law, then the state or the ruler in the state can arbitrarily decide what the laws should be. Law and justice are under the power of the state. Might goes before Right. "If all the legal theory of an entire century continually taught that right is subject to the power of the State and is not founded in fundamental moral principles, one can only be astounded that today's statesmen are surprised at the consequences that uneducated and brutal politicians drew from these teachings," the author writes. And again: "At any rate it was one of Hitler's foundational theses, which he repeated in every possible variation, that every right that is not protected by a strong power will be abused." So for National Socialism, since the Führer "was the sole representative of the People, and the People the sole source of rights, the Führer as the highest law in the State did not need to bow before the demands of justice, but was above justice."

Having set forth the kind of thinking that led Hitler to conclude that might comes before right, the author of *Rechtsbewusstsein und Rechtsunsicherheit* then detailed the systematic ways in which the National Socialist regime undermined the order of justice in Germany and thereby eroded the sense of security under the law in the German people. By punishing political opponents for their beliefs, by undermining the fundamental rights of the individual, by creating a police power that was not answerable to the ordinary functioning of the judicial system, by creating a system of concentration camps, by inventing new and undefined legal concepts such as "the will of the people," by punishing not only the regime's enemies but also their families, by declaring entire groups of people—indeed, an entire race—as criminal, and in many other ways, the Nazis undermined the morale of the people. There was no security about the law but only the anxiety of being under an arbitrary power.

This led to the criticism of the Allied occupational authority. Despite their propaganda during the war and their promises to restore a just order in Germany, the Allies, argued the author, were doing some of the same *kinds* of things the Nazis had done. The thesis of collective guilt, for example, blamed all Germans for the crimes of their rulers, even though the Allies had always stated their awareness that the National Socialists, before invading any foreign countries, had first enslaved Germany itself and treated it as a conquered land. Officials were removed from their posts because they were suspected of being Nazis, just as after 1933, officials had been removed from their posts because they were not Nazis.

The discussion of the concentration camps and of the Nuremberg war crimes tribunal require a lengthy treatment. Phayer had accused the author, whom he thought to have been von Galen, of making the "outrageous" claim that the prisons of the occupational authority were worse than the Nazi concentration camps in eastern Europe. It is unfortunate that Indiana University Press followed the practice of using endnotes rather than footnotes in printing Phayer's book, for in this case, the endnote on page 256 gives some evidence for qualifying the assertions on page 139. Regarding the "outrageous claim" about the prisons of the occupational authority, Phayer writes in his endnote: "To provide an 'out' for this assertion, Galen referred to an anonymous English newspaper writer who had made the comparison." Fairness might suggest that if an English newspaper writer had actually made this comparison so that it was not regarded as "outrageous" by his editor, a German author could hardly be criticized for reporting it. In fact, Phayer misread the text. The claim of the author of the text, which Phayer attributes to von Galen, was that conditions in the prisons of the occupying authority *in the east* (i.e., those run by the Soviet Union) were worse than the conditions both of those in the west and of those same camps when they had been run as concentration camps by the Nazis. The entire text is:

> The National Socialist regime consciously created concentration camps by law. At the beginning, it was German citizens who were imprisoned in these camps, citizens whose only offence was having political opinions different from those desired by the regime. If these men and women had committed crimes, they could have been tried before an ordinary court. There were enough judges to have been able to hear and judge these cases. But they had not committed any crimes; they seemed sufficiently suspected by the regime solely of having dangerous thoughts or were overheard to have expressed such thoughts. What sufferings they then endured were better known to people in the Allied countries than to the German people. From reports in English newspapers, there are now about ½ million prisoners, men and women, in the former concentration camps. It is not only criminals who find themselves in these camps, but also those who are suspected of having been National Socialists. In these concentration camps, to be sure, there are no more torture chambers, but to allow these prisoners *en masse* to hunger and freeze, so that they face certain death, is not a method that is in keeping with humanity. One can wonder whether it is worse to kill people, or to maintain their lives in such a way that they do not completely die of hunger, but become so weakened in the passage of time that they stand on the edge of the grave. It is deplorable that the military regime makes use of such a method which makes a mockery of the consciousness of justice.

> The horrors of these concentration camps, and even of the National Socialist concentration camps, are nevertheless massively surpassed by what is now taking place in the east of Germany. Considering that an English correspondent has declared that the concentration camps are overshadowed by what is taking place in the east, we need to add no further words . . .

Perhaps this claim is not as outrageous as Professor Phayer says. Perhaps also it is fortunate that Phayer saw the version of the text that is found in the Munich city library. In all the other versions of the document that I have seen, the final sentence is longer: "Considering that an English correspondent has declared the evils of the concentration camps, if they in fact took place, are overshadowed by what is taking place in the east, we need to add no further words." Anyone thinking this was by von Galen would have rightly been appalled.

Now to the Nuremberg trials. The author of *Rechtsbewusstsein und Rechtsunsicherheit* expressed no antipathy to the idea of trying war criminals and making them pay for their crimes. Like the genuine von Galen, he conceded that many crimes were committed by Germans and that the perpetrators should be brought to justice. Probably 90 percent of Germans, he claimed, would be in favor of such prosecution, but he raised several difficulties with the way this prosecution was taking place at Nuremberg. Among them was the introduction of a new concept in law, "crimes against humanity," without sufficient definition of that concept. The author was especially incensed that judges representing the Soviet Union, which invented concentration camps, would be judging Germans based on the concept of humanity. This was what led him to think that the trials would end up being show trials, with the object of defaming the German people as a whole. Another bone of contention was the aspect of the trial that involved seeking to brand various organizations in the Third Reich as criminal organizations. If a person is

guilty simply by being a member of an organization, without knowing or approving of the criminal plans of the leaders of the organization, how, the author asked, is that different from the Nazis' own
policy of thinking that a person is a criminal simply because he is
Jewish? The author suggested that Germans would have a better
sense that justice was being done if the accused were tried for crimes
against laws that were already on the books at the time, and in the
places where the crimes were committed, and by judges from those
countries. Even making use of judges from neutral countries such
as Switzerland and Sweden would be an assurance to the German
people that they were not being subjected to victor's justice:

> Besides this, these newly-constructed laws will be used in a
> one-sided way against German war criminals, and among the
> crimes which have been created is the superfluous destruction
> of cities and human dwelling-places. Who will decide which
> acts of destruction were necessary and which were superfluous?
> Will the generals of the Allied armies, who recommended the
> destruction in Germany, themselves declare that such destruc-
> tion was necessary? Does the International Court of Justice
> believe that any German could be convinced that the destruc-
> tion done by the allied air forces in small German cities, such
> as in Würzburg and Paderborn, was necessary? If however the
> destruction of an entire city and the death of thousands of
> women was militarily necessary in order to put an anti-aircraft
> battery out of operation, then truly the war was a dishonour-
> able slaughter and every soldier merely an instrument of anni-
> hilation. Are there educated Englishmen and Frenchmen who
> think that the destruction of the artistic inner city of Dresden
> was a military necessity in the ebb and flow of war? Will the
> generals who commanded this destruction be brought before
> the court?

The author went on to predict terrifying consequences if the Allies did not change their ways. The German people would conclude that the Nuremberg trials were indeed the greatest show trials in history, following upon the greatest and most terrible war in history and the greatest defeat in history. They would conclude that the trials had nothing to do with right and justice but were a theatrical production before the world, designed to give the masses in the Allied countries a satisfying feeling of revenge, to give the politicians material for propaganda against Germany, and to provide a pretext for confiscating German property in order to ease the postwar difficulties in their own countries:

> And then the German people will be led to the conclusion that Hitler was right when he always said there was no such thing as justice in this world, there was only power, and the one who has power decides what is just and unjust. His foundational saying, "Justice is what serves the German people" will have been taken over by the victors, who declare to us that justice is what enables the victors to take revenge on the defeated, and in a few decades, based on this notion of justice, the yellow race will destroy the Europeans.
>
> The Allies have the ability to treat the war criminals with the true sense of justice. . . . [If they do,] then the German people will know that the Allies are truly determined to give justice its true worth, and by this they will once again establish and strengthen the consciousness of justice in the German people . . . [If not,] then one day this people, terrified first by the Nazis and then by the victors, will be led into the greatest self-destructive war the world has ever seen, taking thousands, perhaps millions, into the abyss.

At first, it did not occur to me to consider that *Rechtsbewusstsein und Rechtsunsicherheit* might have been a forgery. Thinking that it was an expansion of Cardinal von Galen's thought, addressed to foreigners sympathetic to Germany's postwar plight, my desire was to find out just when and where in his busy schedule in Rome he had delivered this address. Further, since the text in the Munich library was only a typescript, were there other copies, and how had they been distributed? A partial answer to the second question came when I contacted Sister Monica Lewis, O.S.B., at Kloster Dinklage. The Benedictine Sisters who now live at the cardinal's birthplace have an archive of material related to him, and Sister Monica was able to send me a photocopy of a version of *Rechtsbewusstsein und Rechtsunsicherheit* that is in their possession.[2] Much later, in January 2016, I was able to visit the diocesan archive in Münster, Bistumsarchiv Münster, where I found four more versions of the document.[3]

To answer the first question, I began by going back to the early biographers of von Galen, Heinrich Portmann and Max Bierbaum. These two men, both priests of the Diocese of Münster, were the only persons permitted by the British occupying authority to travel with von Galen to Rome. Portmann seems to hold the key to *Rechtsbewusstsein und Rechtsunsicherheit*. In his *Kardinal von Galen: Ein Gottesmann seiner Zeit* ([Münster: Aschendorff, 17. Auflage, 1981], 294, n. 1), he discusses the sermon given by the cardinal at the German church of Santa Maria dell'Anima on February 17, 1946, and adds: "In the following weeks, a text of about ten typewritten pages, with the title, 'Rechtsbewusstsein und Rechtsunsicherheit— sermon of Cardinal von Galen at the Church of the Anima in Rome'

---

2   For convenience, I will call the Munich document #1 and the Dinklage document #2.

3   Bistumsarchiv Münster, D103Sammlung von Galen, A73, A80, and A110, and Bistumsarchiv Münster, Generalvikariat, 011, 101–34. I am extremely grateful to Dr. Heinz Mestrup and his colleagues at the Bistumsarchiv Münster for finding these documents for me and providing me with copies. Let these be #3–6.

circulated throughout Germany. These remarks by an unknown author were a sharp critique of the methods of the Allies in Germany. To gain authoritative weight for these opinions, the author had not hesitated to misuse the name of the great bishop."

Bierbaum says nothing in his biography[4] about any other discourse than the sermon of February 17. But I was able to acquire a copy of his earlier, long out-of-print book, *Die letzte Romfahrt des Kardinals von Galen* (Münster: Aschendorff, 1946).[5] After describing the contents of the sermon at the Church of the Anima, he writes,

> This sermon, which has been reproduced here from the manuscript of the bishop, was misused for political ends by an unknown party. A document with the heading "Sermon of Cardinal von Galen in Rome," 14 pages in size, was put into circulation; it is a forgery and had nothing to do with the bishop's sermon. For this reason the Capitular Vicar of the Diocese of Münster found himself obliged to issue the following clarification in the Church Newsletter of the Diocese of Münster on June 14, 1946:
>
> "In these days a document has been distributed in areas of our diocese and elsewhere under the title 'Rechtsbewusstsein und Rechtsunsicherheit' (sometimes with the subtitle 'Address of Cardinal von Galen in the Anima Church of Rome'). It consists of a commentary on the current situation in regard to justice in Germany. We hereby declare that the deceased Cardinal did not deliver such an address or anything like it in Rome or anywhere else. We further declare that the above-named document was not composed by him or at his instructions. It appears that this commentary was intended to receive a greater

---

4   Max Bierbaum, *Nicht Lob, Nicht Furcht: Das Leben des Kardinals von Galen* (Münster: Regensberg, 1946.)

5   The book has recently been reprinted.

importance by the claimed authorship of Cardinal von Galen. We beg the clergy to make these facts known from the pulpit wherever it seems necessary."[6]

The clarification by the vicariate is not totally satisfactory, as none of the versions of the text that I have seen has the words "Address of Cardinal von Galen in the Anima Church of Rome." Only #6 mentions the Anima church. At the very end of the document are the words, "Kardinal Graf von Galen (Anima Rom)." This document, however, has the advantage of being the first one received by the diocesan office. The others all say "Address of Cardinal Graf von Galen in Rome, March 1946." This does not fit the descriptions of Bierbaum and Portmann, either. It is clear that we are dealing with the same document, but it does not claim to be a sermon and certainly—since its date is given as March 1946—not the sermon given at the Animakirche on February 17.

It was puzzling that the documents did not give more detail as to the place and circumstances of the address supposedly given by the cardinal. Further, Portmann and Bierbaum would presumably have known if the cardinal had delivered such an address. On the other hand, was it possible that he had given such an address but not prepared it for publication, and that after his untimely death, his secretary and associates for some reason felt it necessary to disavow a document that was being widely disseminated and stirring up much attention?

On my visit to the Bistumsarchiv Münster in January 2016, Dr. Heinz Mestrup acquired for my perusal (and copied for me) the correspondence on the topic in the archive of the general vicariate.[7]

---

6   The actual date of the Kirchlichen Amtsblatt in which the denial appeared was June 26, 1946.

7   Bistumsarchiv Münster, Generalvikariat, 011, 101–34.

From this we can see how the diocesan officials came to be aware of the existence of *Rechtsbewusstsein und Rechtsunsicherheit*, how little they knew at first about what Cardinal von Galen had done in Rome, and how they grew in their conviction that the document was a forgery. We learn also that many people doubted its authenticity from the start.

Cardinal von Galen died on March 22, 1946. His funeral was on March 28. Two weeks later, on April 11, the diocesan general vicariate in Münster received a letter from a priest in Dortmund, dated April 8. The priest asked whether the vicariate knew whether Cardinal von Galen had given a talk under the title "Rechtsbewusstsein und Rechtsunsicherheit." "Lay people," he wrote, were distributing the supposed talk in typewritten form. Having read one of the documents, the priest expressed serious doubts that it was genuine. A reply was composed to the effect that the officials at the vicariate did not know whether the cardinal had given a talk under that title.

A letter dated April 16 came from a layman in Neuenkirchen bei Rheine. He was hearing rumors that in his last sermon, the cardinal had said that every child knows that a war with Russia is coming. The correspondent was strongly convinced that the cardinal would not have made such a statement about foreign political questions. The vicariate assured him that the cardinal had not made such a statement, but they did not have a copy of the cardinal's last sermon to send him.

In early May, another priest wrote and sent them, along with a second letter, a copy of *Rechtsbewusstsein und Rechtsunsicherheit* (the one I have designated as #6). In replying to his first letter, the vicariate had professed not to have seen the document but expressed suspicion that it was a forgery. This priest's reverence for the late cardinal was such that he regretted that texts were being distributed under his name that perhaps were simply not written by him.

By the first week in July, at least sixteen more letters came in on the same topic from various parts of Germany. A number of the writers doubted its authenticity. All of them wrote because they wanted to be certain, an indication that at that time in Germany, much propaganda was going around, including, as some of the writers stated, some distributed by Nazis. There were other writers who wished that it was genuine but wanted to be sure before distributing it further.

Interestingly, one of the earliest correspondents was a lawyer, Dr. Walter Ballas, writing from Nuremberg, where he was on the defense team for Admiral Erich Raeder. He had received a photocopy of a text that was described to him as an excerpt from a speech given by Cardinal von Galen in Rome. He was not sure whether he would use it in court, or indeed whether the rules of the court would allow him to do so, but in any case, he would do so only if he first had official assurance of its authenticity and had an authentic text to work with. Unfortunately, the vicariate returned the photocopy to him, apparently without making a copy for their files. By this time (May 23), they were more certain: His Eminence never gave such an address: "The author presumably wanted to give his work greater importance by ascribing it to the deceased warrior for truth and justice."

By the fourteenth of June, when the diocesan newsletter carried the published denial of its authenticity, diocesan authorities had no doubt that the document was a forgery from start to finish. They added in writing to one correspondent that there were no written or spoken comments by von Galen that had been worked on or expanded by others to make this text. After this, the standard answer included sending a copy of the published statement of denial.

The letter from Heinrich Dietz in Wuppertal indicates the points for and against the authenticity of the document and also gives some insight into the historical situation. After describing the document that has come into his hands from an unknown source, "that is, anonymously," he continues:

Some of the reasoning recalls earlier sermons of the late Cardinal and could actually have come from him. On the other hand, the attacks on definite positions are sometimes so massive that doubts have come into my mind about the authenticity of the address. These doubts of mine have been increased by men who also have received the document anonymously. If the address were genuine, the one distributing it would have no need to fear the publicity. Merely the fact that the distribution is happening anonymously tends to justify the opinion that it is a forgery. Were it genuine, in my opinion it could be distributed with no problems, as, so far as I can tell, even the English occupying authorities have never suppressed the expression of opinion, even when it was somewhat uncomfortable.

In these circumstances it is greatly wished by me as an historian to have an authentic declaration from you as to whether the late Cardinal gave an address in Rome in March 1946 under the given title.

In my own case, I confess that there were times that I doubted the official denial of the document's authenticity. As the first sentence from Dietz's letter indicates, many passages of the document pass the smell test. A discussion of the foundations of law would not be unexpected from Cardinal von Galen. Nor would a discussion of how an unjust regime damages human morale and the sense of security under law that leads to social peace. He had already made many of the criticisms of the Allies that appear in this document, including his firm rejection of the thesis of collective guilt. And, as I have indicated, his sudden death could have given Portmann and Bierbaum reason to deny the authenticity of a text that perhaps the cardinal would have wanted to rework before publishing or not publish at all.

On the other hand, as one of the correspondents wrote to the vicariate general, the document almost completely lacks a theological section. It is hard to picture von Galen predicting the Germans rising up in a war of revenge without adding that he and his fellow bishops would of course do all in their power to prevent such an unChristian thing from happening.

A final piece of information, which put an end to the thought that Portmann was being disingenuous when he denied that the text came from von Galen, came to me through meeting Provost HansBernd Serries in Billerbeck. Serries had kindly contacted Dr. Ingrid Lueb, who was preparing Portmann's private diaries for publication. Dr. Lueb made available to me Portmann's diary entry for June 22, 1946. Writing only for himself, Portmann wrote, "The false address of the Cardinal, Rechtsbewusstsein und Rechtsunsicherheit, is spreading further. The Kirchliche Amtsblatt will bring clarification. Questions still coming in."

Clearly, Portmann was convinced that the cardinal had nothing to do with *Rechtsbewusstsein und Rechtsunsicherheit*. The wide circulation of the document, in Lueb's judgment, was due to its similarity with the criticisms Cardinal von Galen had already made of the Allied authorities. There is no doubt that many people thought that it was genuine and were encouraged by the thought that the great man was once again defending them. So it is, Lueb added, that many people who have copies of the text today still are unaware that it is not in fact by von Galen. This was certainly the case with regard to the librarians in Munich and Sister Monica at Dinklage. At Münster, the archivists and historians I consulted were aware of its inauthenticity, and there is a copy of the official denial in the archive. But on the other hand, the three typescripts in the von Galen collection are not marked as forgeries, and it is easy to understand how a researcher could be fooled. Dr. Mestrup also pointed out to me a footnote in the Löffler collection that I had overlooked, giving a brief description of the text, noting that several exemplars are in the Münster archive, and citing the denial of its authenticity.[8]

To the above evidence that the document is not by Cardinal von Galen, let me add one more crucial piece of internal evidence, based on the very first sentence of the document. As noted above, *Rechtsbewusstsein und Rechtsunsicherheit* begins with a reference to the encyclical letter of Pope Pius XI, *Mit brennender Sorge*. It states that the pope's encyclical was "perhaps the sharpest attack on National Socialism and the best refutation of its theories," and states that the pope cited the ancient principle, *Justitia fundamentum regnorum*, "justice is the foundation of states." In fact, neither of these statements is true. The encyclical was not intended as a refutation of National Socialist theory. It criticized the *practices* of the regime in regard to the Church—such as the repeated violations of the provisions of the Concordat and the attack on confessional schools—and the deliberate misuse of religious terminology in favor of a new racially based paganism but not the overall political theory.

The citation of the ancient principle that justice is the foundation of states, and the corollary that unjust regimes are destined to collapse, was of course, a familiar theme to von Galen. He himself had stressed this theme at great length in his sermon of July 13, 1941, the first of his three great sermons of that summer. But the principle was not cited by Pope Pius XI in his 1936 encyclical letter. It is possible that someone forging a document in 1946 in Germany, without easy access to a copy of *Mit brennender Sorge*, could make this mistake. But Cardinal von Galen himself—who knew well his own use of the principle and who was in Rome when he supposedly worked on

---

8   Peter Löffler, ed., *Bischof Clemens August Graf von Galen: Akten, Briefe und Predigten 1933–1946,* 2nd ed. (Paderborn: Ferdinand Schöningh, 1996), 1305, n. 7.

this text and therefore could easily have had access to a copy of the encyclical—would not have made such a mistake.

In summary, then, *Rechtsbewusstsein und Rechtsunsicherheit* was not by Cardinal Clemens August von Galen, although its author knew enough about von Galen's way of thinking to make a pretty good forgery. The specific arguments it makes about the Nuremberg trials cannot be attributed to him but would, however, likely have occurred to many Germans. Many people suspected that the work was a forgery, and any German bishop who thought the document was by him would have been able to get the facts from the Münster diocesan administration. Further, like the many people who wrote to the diocese, they would have been suspicious of a typewritten document passing anonymously into their hands, or at least would have wanted to verify its authenticity. The theory of the diocesan officials, that the author wanted to make use of von Galen in order to get greater circulation for his ideas, is plausible. Since the document was not by von Galen, it was not approved by the pope. It was not published in Rome. Indeed, it was not published in a proper sense of the word anywhere. It was not presented by von Galen to the German bishops. If the document indeed had any impact on the attitude of the German bishops to the Nuremberg trials, it was not because of Cardinal von Galen.

When I first put a draft of this appendix into the hands of Saint Benedict Press, I wrote, "The mystery of who the actual author was remains open." As of May 10, 2016, I learned that there is another candidate named in the literature. On that date, I received an e-mail from Dr. Andreas Freiträger, archivist at the University of Cologne. Dr. Freiträger told me that he was preparing an exhibit of documents in regard to the Nuremberg Trials, and one of the documents he was working on was *Rechtsbewusstsein und Rechtsunsicherheit*. Dr. Freiträger had consulted Dr. Mestrup in Münster, who suggested he contact me as having an interest in the document, which he described as "wrongly attributed to the cardinal Graf von Galen, as it seems to have been written by the provost of Paderborn cathedral, Paul Simon (according to Dieter Riesenberger's Simon-biography 1992)." Leave it to mystery!

Finally, although Professor Phayer's general thesis is beyond the scope of my competence, I can still ask: Is it nevertheless likely that *Rechtsbewusstsein und Rechtsunsicherheit* did have an impact on the attitude of the German bishops to the Nuremberg trials? I suspect not. I note once again that the article explicitly approved of the idea of prosecuting criminals. I note, too, that if the bishops wanted to get some guidance from Rome on the issue, they already had this from Pope Pius XII himself. Robert A. Ventresca notes in his biography of Pius (*Soldier of Christ: The Life of Pope Pius XII* [Belknap: Harvard, 2013]) that the pope was seeking commutation of death sentences of war criminals *before the end of 1945*: "It was out of a similar concern for the effect on public opinion of so many death sentences being meted out to former German and Italian generals, along with the logic of Christian compassion and forgiveness, that Pius XII could appeal to Allied authorities all the way to Truman to commute the sentences of convicted war criminals" (260). Did the German bishops need any more than the "logic of Christian compassion and forgiveness" to agree that the prosecution of war criminals was justified and to combine this with a plea for the commutation or lessening of the sentences of those who had been tried and found guilty? Perhaps they did not really make a reversal of policy at all.

BIBLIOGRAPHY

Books

Adolph, Walter. *Geheime Aufzeichnungen aus dem nationalsozialistischen Kirchenkampf 1935–1943*. 2nd ed. Mainz: Matthias-Grünewald Verlag, 1980.

Balbach, Anna-Maria. *Die Barmherzigen Schwestern zu Münster zur Zeit der Nationalsozialismus*. Münster: Dialogverlag, 2007.

Beaugrand, Gunter. *Ein Leben im XX. Jahrhundert: Begegnungen und Gespräche mit Christoph Bernhard von Galen auf Haus Assen / Lippetal*. Werl: Boerde-Verlag, 2004.

———. *Kardinal von Galen: Der Löwe von Münster*. Freundeskreis Heimathaus Münsterland, Telgte. 4th ed. Münster: Ardey-Verlag, 1996.

Bierbaum, Max. *Die letzte Romfahrt des Kardinals von Galen*. Münster: Aschendorff, 1946.

———. *Nicht Lob, Nicht Furcht: Das Leben des Kardinals von Galen*. Münster: Regensberg, 1946.

Conway, John S. *The Nazi Persecution of the Churches 1933–1945*. Vancouver: Regent College Publishing, 1997.

Dumbach, Annette, and Jud Newborn. *Sophie Scholl and the White Rose*. Oxford: One World, 2006.

Evans, Richard J. *The Coming of the Third Reich*. New York: Penguin, 2003.

———. *The Third Reich in Power*. New York: Penguin, 2005.

Falasca, Stefania. *Un vescovo contro Hitler: Von Galen, Pio XII e la resistenza al nazismo*. Milan: Edizioni San Paolo, 2006.

Grevelhörster, Ludger. *Kardinal Clemens August Graf von Galen in seiner Zeit*. Münster: Aschendorff, 2005.

Griech-Polelle, Beth A. *Bishop von Galen: German Catholicism and National Socialism*. New Haven: Yale University Press, 2002.

Haunfelder, Bernd, and Axel Schollmeier. *Kardinal von Galen: Triumph und Tod. Fotos seiner letzten Lebenstage*. Münster: Aschendorff, 2005.

Heitmann, Clemens. *Clemens August Kardinal von Galen 1878–1946*. 2nd ed. Dinklage: B. Heimann, 2005.

Hitler, Adolf, (Trevor-Roper, H.R.). *Hitler's Table Talk: 1941–1944*. Oxford/Toronto: Oxford University Press, 1988. (English translation first published 1953 by Weidenfeld and Nicolson).

Kershaw, Ian. *Hitler*. London: Penguin, 2009.

Kuropka, Joachim (Hg.). *Clemens August Graf von Galen: Sein Leben und Wirken in Bildern und Dokumenten*. 3rd ed. Cloppenburg: Runge, 1997.

———. *Streitfall Galen*. Münster: Aschendorff, 2007.

Löffler, Peter (ed.). *Bischof Clemens August Graf von Galen: Akten, Briefe und Predigten 1933–1946*. 2nd ed. Paderborn: Ferdinand Schöningh, 1996.

Phayer, Michael. *The Catholic Church and the Holocaust, 1930–1965*. Bloomington: Indiana University Press, 2000.

Portmann, Heinrich. *Cardinal von Galen*. Translated and with an introduction by R. L. Sedgwick. London: Jarrolds, 1957.

———. *Kardinal von Galen: Ein Gottesmann seiner Zeit*. 17th ed. Münster: Aschendorff, 1981.

Stadtmuseum Münster. *Bomben auf Münster*. 1983.

Trautmann, Markus. *Clemens August von Galen: Ich erhebe meine Stimme.* Kevelaer: Topos Plus (Lahn-Verlag), 2005.

Trautmann, Markus, Christiane Daldrup, and Verona Marliani-Eyll. *Endlich hat einer den Mut zu sprechen: Clemens August von Galen und die Predigten vom Sommer 1941—kommentiert und illustriert.* 2nd ed. Münster: Dialogverlag, 2013.

Trost, Ralph. *Eine gänzlich zerstörte Stadt: Nationalsozialismus, Krieg und Kriegsende in Xanten.* Münster: Waxmann Verlag, 2004.

Ventresca, Robert A. *Soldier of Christ: The Life of Pope Pius XII.* Cambridge: Belknap (Harvard University Press), 2013.

von Boeselager, Philipp Freiherr. *Valkyrie: The Story of the Plot to Kill Hitler, by Its Last Member.* New York: Alfred A. Knopf, 2009.

Wolf, Hubert. *Clemens August Graf von Galen: Gehorsam und Gewissen.* Freiburg: Herder, 2006.

Pamphlets and Articles

Balbach, Anna-Maria. "Schwestern kämpften für das Leben." *Aufroter Erde: Heimatblatter für Munster und das Munsterland.* April 2008.

Conrad, Horst. "Stand und Konfession. Der Verein der katholischen Edelleute. Teil 2: Die Jahre 1918–1949." *Westphälische Zeitschrift*, Band 159, Jahrgang 2009: 91–154.

"Heute bist Du, morgen bin ich dran. Kardinal von Galen warnt die jüdische Familie Jonas aus Borken—Emigration in die USA." *Borkener Zeitung*, September 11, 2005.

Hughes, John Jay. Review of *Bishop von Galen: German Catholicism and National Socialism* by Griech-Polelle. *Catholic Historical Review* 89, no. 2 (April 2003): 321–25.

Kleyboldt, Norbert. *Seligsprechung Clemens August Kardinal von Galen.* Pamphlet issued by the Diocese of Münster, n.d., 2005.

Kuropka, Joachim. "Franz von Galen und das Ende der Zentrum-spartei." *Westfälische Nachrichten*, May 10, 2008.

Lothar Groppe, S. J. "Zur Seligsprechung von Kardinal Graf von Galen (1878–1946) am 9. Oktober 2005." *Katholische Bildung*, October 10, 2005.

Loy, Johannes. "Mütiger Bischof in schwerer Zeit." *Westfälische Nachrichten*, March 22, 2006.

Patch, William. "The Catholic Church, the Third Reich, and the Origins of the Cold War: On the Utility and Limitations of Historical Evidence." *Journal of Modern History* 82, no. 2 (June 2010): 396–433.

Archival Materials Cited in Appendix
from Bischöfliches Archiv Münster
Stadtbibiliothek München

Internet Sites
Foerderverein in der St. Clemens-Kirche Berlin e.V.:
http://www.st-clemens-berlin.de

http://w2.vatican.va/content/vatican/en.html

http://kirchensite.de/index.php?myELEMENT=100884

INDEX

A

Abitur, 10

Acts of the Apostles, St. Paul's exhortations in, 44, 113

"Act to End Suffering and Worthless Life, An," 231–33

Address of Cardinal Count v. Galen in Rome, March 1946, *Rechtsbewusstsein und Rechtsunsicherheit*, 367–84

Against the Obscurantists of Our Time (Rosenberg), 77

air raids on Münster, 197–202, 225–27, 275–79, 285–86

Allemann, Fritz, 304–8

Allgemeine Rundschau, 20–21

Allied forces: advance in Germany of, 294–95; management of concentration camps by, 307, 310–11, 364–84; pillaging and looting by, 290–91, 300; von Galen's interaction with and criticism of, 287–90, 297–311, 352–53, 370–84. *See also* Great Britain; United States

Amelunxen, Rudolf, 341

Anabaptists, 86–87

anti-Semitism: acceleration of, 262–63; *Kristallnacht* and, 171–78; von Galen's silence on, 51–53, 263–66, 274–86

Aryanism, evolution of, 229–33

atrocities by Nazis, revelations concerning, 266–86

Augustinus, Father, 10

Austria, Nazi annexation of, 162

authority, von Galen on limits of, 85–92, 103–9, 112–13

B

Balbach, Anna-Maria, 230–33
Ballas, Walter (Dr.), 379
Basics of Racial Hygiene (*Grundlinien einer Rassenhygiene*), 229–30
Benedictine Abbey in Gerleve, 216
Benedictine Monastery of Maria Laach, 11
Benedictine Sisters of Perpetual Adoration (Vinnenberg), 216
Benedict XVI (Pope), 356–57
Berlin, von Galen in, 14–30
Berning (Bishop), 195–96
Bertram, Cardinal Adolf: birthday telegram to Hitler, 187–88; Catholic division over resistance to Nazism and, 98–99, 102, 123–24, 130–32, 141, 187, 273–74, 277–78; on Nazi euthanasia policy, 232–33; Polish workers confessions and, 278; suppression of religious education and, 155, 160, 162–63, 179–80, 187
Bierbaum, Max, 365, 375–77, 380–81
Binding, Karl, 229, 231–32
Bischof Clemens August Graf von Galen: Akten, Briefe und Predigten 1933–1946 (1996) (Löffler), 365
Bismarck, Otto von, 5, 193–94
bombing raids: in Münster, x–xii, 197–202, 225–27, 275–86; von Galen's discussion of, 197–202, 225–27
Bona, Mother (Sisters of Mercy Superior), 278–81
Bormann, Martin, 254–55
Braun, Fr., 196–97
Breslau, Archdiocese of, 14–15
Brinkmann, Johann Bernhard, ix, 5, 83–84, 88–89, 193–94

C

Camillians in St. Mauritz-Sudmühle, 216
Caritate Christi encyclical, 55
Castle Dinklage, von Galen's childhood at, 1–8
Catholic Action, 107
Catholic Church: Allied forces restrictions on, 297–99, 306–11; anti-Semitism and, 174–77; compulsory sterilization opposed by, 69, 230–33; Concordat with Nazis and, 65–69; Concordat with Prussia, 33–34; division over resistance to Nazism in, 98, 123–33; German

state and, 23–24; Germany and role of, 30–32, 142–43; Gestapo confiscation of religious houses and orders, 192n233, 195–214; Nazi attacks on, 80–81, 85–90, 99–102, 155–69, 192–93, 273–74; Nazi conciliation with, 192–93; Night of the Long Knives and, 106–7; paganism as threat to, 77–84; Prussian suppression of, 5, 15; resistance to Nazism by, 36–40, 46–48, 59–60, 68, 73–74, 85–92, 97–102, 251–60, 269–70; sexuality morality charges by Nazis against, 138; Spanish Civil War opposed by, 135–37

Catholic Church and the Holocaust, The, 1930–1965, 363–84

Catholic organizations, Nazi suppression of, 68–69, 96, 98, 190

Catholic press, Nazi suppression of, 69–70, 137–41

Catholic schools: Allied forces lack of support for, 318; Nazi suppression of, 52–53, 68–69, 95–96, 100, 115–21, 127–33, 147–69, 179–80; von Galen's effort to save, 183–86. *See also* school curriculum

Catholic Working Men's Clubs, 16–17, 69–70, 96, 137

Catholic Youth Sports Association, 107

censorship: of Catholic press, 69, 139–41; of newspapers, 136–41; of Pius XI's *Mit brennender Sorge*, 124–33, 138–39; of von Galen's pastoral letters, 53–61, 137–38

Centre Party (Germany): Catholic loyalty to, 30–31, 37, 73–74; Nazi arrests of members of, 284–85; Nazi promises to, 65

Christianity: in Germany, 15, 30–32, 142–45, 189–90; Nazi subversion of, 57–58, 66–67, 71, 80–84, 131, 140–45, 189–92; resistance to Nazism and, 270–74

church bells, von Galen's decree concerning, 110

"church colors," Nazi ban on display of, 165–67

Clemens Sisters. *See* Sisters of Mercy of Münster

collective guilt thesis, von Galen's denial of, 294–304, 309–11, 345–46, 370–84 communism: Catholic opposition to, 46, 59–60, 136–37, 182–83, 265–67; Nazi attacks on, 64, 156; in postwar Germany, 307–8; von Galen's rejection of, 27–28, 160–61, 265–86

community schools, Nazi promotion of, 149–69, 187–88

compulsory sterilization, Nazi policy of, 69, 230–33

concentration camps: Allied management of, 307, 310–11, 364–84; German citizens in, 116, 121, 164, 195, 209, 211; international outrage over, x, 294–304; Jews sent to, 171–72; priests sent to, 135, 176, 254, 283–84; as security apparatus, 211; von Galen's silence on, 51–53, 263–66, 274–86, 370–84; wartime growth of, 195. *See also* anti-Semitism; Holocaust

Concordat: Nazis' agreement to, 65–69, 72; Nazi violations of, 95–96, 100, 121, 125, 137–40, 152, 190; Prussian signing of, 33–34, 37, 39, 46; religious education curriculum and, 52–53, 95–96, 156–57, 185–86

Conference of the Deans, 66–68, 95

Congress of Vienna, 15

Conti, Leonardo, 254

cross, Nazi orders for removal of, 115–21, 168–69, 192–93, 251–52. See also *Oldenburger Kreuzkampf* (Battle for the Cross in Oldenburg)

D

Darré, Walther, 142

da Todi, Jacopone, 293

democracy: death in Germany of, 33; von Galen's perspective on, 21–25

Dengler, Theobold, 335

Die letzte Romfahrt des Kardinals von Galen (Biermon), 376–77

Die Tat magazine, von Galen interview in, 304–8

Dietz, Heinrich, 379–80

Dingelstadt, Hermann (Bishop), 12

diocesan priests: Nazi imprisonment of, 69, 97; resistance to Nazism by, 97–102

Divini Illius Magistri (Pius XI encyclical), 184

Divini Redemptoris encyclical, 267

Donders, Adolf, 34–35, 75

Droste zu Vischering, Clemens August, 5, 8, 39

Droste zu Vischering, Maria, 2

E

Echelmeyer (Canon), 283, 341

educational system: Nazi overhaul of, 149–69. *See also* Catholic schools; community schools; Protestantism; school curriculum

Enabling Act (Germany), 36–37, 65

Essen National Newspaper, 136–37

eugenics, Nazi embrace of, 230–33

euthanasia: Nazi program of, 195, 197–98, 229–33, 277–86; public reaction to Nazi policy of, 249–60

Evans, Richard J., 64, 107, 171–72

F

Falasca, Stefania, 253n270

Faulhaber, von (Cardinal), 123, 177–78

Fire Procession. *See* Great Procession of Münster

(First) Vatican Council, 8, 78

forced abortion, Nazi policy of, 230–33

Franks, Hans (Dr.), 206–9

Frederick the Great (King of Prussia), 113

Freemasonry, Marxism linked with, 31

Freiträger, Andreas (Dr.), 383

Fribourg University, 11

Frick, William, 72–74, 110

Friedrichs (Canon), 341

Frings (Archbishop), 309, 314–15, 320, 323, 331–34, 351–54

G

Galen Chapels, 13

German Bishop's Conference, 123, 130, 363–64

German Episcopal Conference, 98

German Faith Movement, 118

German Labor Front, 69

German National Church, 78, 80–81

German National Party, 31

Germany: Allied occupation of, 287–311; appropriation of Church property by, 192n233; Christianity in, 15, 30–32, 142–45, 189–90; collective guilt of, von Galen's sermon on, 294–304, 309–11; Nazism and destruction of, 262–86; political culture in, 175–78; postwar borders of, 307–8; postwar conditions in, 316–17; revolution in, 20–24; as World War I victim, 188–89

Gestapo: censorship by, 137–39; confiscation of religious houses and orders by, 195–214, 216–27, 235–36, 269–74; religious organizations suppressed by, 155–69; surveillance of von Galen by, 110–11, 142, 191, 202, 211–14, 226–27, 249–50, 254, 256, 268–69, 344–45; threats to Catholic Church by, 92–93; von Galen's criticism of, xii–xiii, 139–40, 199–214, 268–69

Goebbels, Joseph, xiii, 65; on arrest of von Galen, 255–56, 344; Catholic Church attacked by, 141–42; propaganda campaign against Poles, 189; von Galen's correspondence with, 139

Goerdeler, Carl, 253n270

Goering, Hermann, 39, 61, 64, 81, 213, 258–60

Götting, Heinrich, 117, 121

government, von Galen's perspective on, 20–25

Great Britain: air raids in Germany by, 197–98; German occupation by, 290–91, 294–95, 300, 341; von Galen's illness and death and, 349–51; von Galen's ordination as cardinal and, 318–36; von Galen's relations with, 289–91, 296–311, 318; war against Hitler by, 264

Great Procession of Münster, 83–92

Grevelhörster, Ludger, 277–78, 365

Griech-Polelle, Beth A., 172–73, 365

Griffin, Cardinal Edward, 351

Gundlach, Gustav, 328

gypsies, Nazi atrocities against, 266

H

Hakenkreuz ("bent cross"), as Nazi symbol, 48

Hess, Rudolf, 142, 245n265

Heufers, Heinrich, 35

Himmler, Heinrich, 213

Hindenburg, Paul von, 33, 39, 47, 64, 156

Hitler, Adolf, ix, 2, 20; on
    arrest of von Galen, 256,
    288; assassination attempt
    on, 284–85; attack on Soviet
    Union by, 264–65; bish-
    ops' birthday telegram to,
    187–88; Catholic Church
    opposition to, 38–39, 124; as
    chancellor, 33, 36, 63–64; on
    Christianity and paganism,
    82, 84, 99, 190–92; dictator-
    ship of, 36–37, 65, 354–55;
    euthanasia policy of, 231–33,
    251–52; legal theory of, 367–
    70; Lüninck's praise of, 47–
    49; Night of the Long Knives
    and, 106–7, 111–12; pagan
    propaganda and, 96–97;
    personality cult of, 125, 186;
    protests against, 283–84;
    racial theories of, 229–33;
    state absolutism under, 30;
    Sudetenland crisis and, 187;
    von Galen's correspondence
    with, 70, 81, 156, 159, 186;
    von Galen's reservations con-
    cerning, 46–47, 56–57, 74
Hitler Youth, 58, 70–71, 85,
    90, 136–37
Hoche, Ludwig, 229, 231–32
Holocaust: Catholic inaction
    during, 51–53, 263–66,
    274–86; von Galen's silence
    on, 51–53, 263–66, 274–86
Horten, Titus, 107

J
Jesuit order: opposition to Hit-
    ler from, 38–39; von Galen
    and, 10–12
Jewish persecution, 51–53,
    263–66, 274–86
John Paul II (Pope), 354
Jonas, Leo, 176n213
Journal for the Academy for Ger-
    man Law, 206–9
Judaism: Marxism linked with,
    31. See also anti-Semitism
Justitia est fundamentum regnorum
    (Justice is the foundation of
    states), 382; von Galen's ser-
    mon on principle of, 317–18
just war, von Galen's discussion
    of, 188–89

K
Kardinal von Galen: Ein Gottes-
    mann seiner Zeit (Portmann),
    375–76
Kerrl, Hans, 110–13
Klausener, Erich, 107, 111–12
Klemm, Kurt, 93, 166
Knights of Malta, 92, 341, 347,
    352, 354

Koch, Birte, 366–67

Kolping, Adolph, 16–17, 70

Kolping House, 16–17

Kristallnacht (Nights of Broken Glass), 171–78

Kulturkampf (culture war), 5, 36, 57, 93, 96, 99, 158–59, 193–94

Kuropka, Joachim, 274, 365

L

Lackmann, Heinrich, 233

Lambertikirche, 200–14, 339–40

Lammers, Hans, 213, 218

Lateran Treaty of 1929, 182

Laudeberta (Sister), 233

League of Catholic Nobles, 31–32, 90

Ledingham (Col.), 289–91

Legge, Peter (Bishop), 97

Leo XIII (Pope), 1–2, 11, 23, 136

Lewis, Sister Monica, 375, 381

Ley, Robert (Dr.), 69

Liberal Party (Germany), 31

Lichtenberg, Bernhard (Father), 254, 256

Löffler, Peter, 68, 365, 381–82

loyalty oath, von Galen's swearing of, 39, 47, 61–62, 81

Lucas, Bernhard (Dr.), 128–30

Lueb, Ingrid, 381

Lüninck, Ferdinand von, 31–32, 46–49, 49n53, 66, 84, 89–90, 93, 110, 142

Lüninck, Hermann von, 31–32, 90

M

Marienthal institution, euthanasia of patients from, 230–33, 239–48

martyrdom, von Galen's comparison of Catholic resistance to, 103–9

Marxism: Catholic resistance to, 16, 330–36; German politics and, 31

materialism, von Galen's critique of, 268

Mein Kampf (Hitler), 74, 232

mentally disabled: Catholic institutions for, 230–33; euthanasia of, Nazi policy for, 195, 197–98, 229–33, 235–48, 252–60

Mestrup, Heinz (Dr.), 377–78, 381–83

Meyer, Alfred, 82, 135

Mit brennender Sorge encyclical, 124–33, 326–27, 367–68, 381–82 mixed marriages (Protestant and Catholic), 5

Moench, Antonius (Auxiliary Bishop), 35

monarchy, von Galen's perspective on, 21–23

Monte Cassino monastery, 335

Münster: air raids on, 197–202, 225–27, 275, 278–86; Allied occupation of, 286–311; bomb damage in, x–xii, 338–39; Catholic identity in, 4–5; episcopal election in, 33–35; hunger crisis in, 300–301; von Galen's pastoral career in, 30–31

Murphy, Father, 310–11

Mussolini, Benito, 283

Myth of the 20th Century, The (Rosenberg), 53, 75–77

N

nationalism, German embrace of, 189

National Socialist party (Nazi party), 2; attacks on Catholic Church by, 69–70, 80–81, 85–86, 89–90, 95–96, 99–102, 191–93; Catholic resistance to, 36–40, 46–48, 59–60, 74, 85–92, 252–60; conciliation with Catholic church, 192–93; destruction of Germany and, 262–86; division in Catholic Church over resistance to, 98, 123–24; growing power of, 33, 36; imprisonment of priests by, 69, 97; in Münster, 30–31; Night of the Long Knives purge of, 106–7, 111–12; paganism in, 82–86; propaganda against von Galen by, 256–58; racial theories of, 229–33; subversion of law by, 367–70; suicide and extramarital relations and, 190; totalitarian regime of, 65

National Socialist Teachers' League, 178

naturalism, von Galen's critique of, 268

Nec laudibus Nec timore, as von Galen's motto, 353–55

Neuss, Father Wilhelm, 75–77

New Westphalian Newspaper, 299, 340

Night of the Long Knives, 106–7, 111–12, 175

Nights of Broken Glass. See *Kristallnacht* (Nights of Broken Glass)

Nuremberg war crimes tribunal, 366–84

O

Oldenburger Kreuzkampf (Battle for the Cross in Oldenburg), 115–21, 168–69, 251–52

Oldenburger Münsterland, 3–4

Oldenburg Grand-ducal *Gymnasium* Antonianum, 10

"On the Situation of the Catholic Church in the German Reich" (papal encyclical), 124–33

Opus iustitiae pax (Peace is the work of justice), Catholic principle, 317

Orsenigo, Cesare, 34–35

P

Pacelli, Cardinal Eugenio, 35, 84, 98–99, 123–24, 163–64, 327

pagan ideology: anti-Semitism and, 174; history in Germany of, 143–45; Nazi revival of, 53, 67, 96–97, 125–33; von Galen's opposition to, 53–61, 67, 71, 73, 75–84, 143, 174

Pauly, Julius, 114–15, 121, 152–53, 192

Permission to Put an End to Lives not Worth Living—Die Freigabe der Vernichtung

Lebensunwertes Lebens (Binding and Hoche), 229

Phayer, Michael, 363–84

Pius IX (Pope), 8

Pius X (Pope), 9

Pius XI (Pope), 49, 55, 267; death of, 180–83; *Mit brennender Sorge* encyclical of, 124–33, 326–27, 381–82

Pius XII (Pope), ix, xii, 98–99; Nuremburg Trials opposed by, 366, 384; von Galen and, 262, 283–86, 309, 313–37, 343–45, 350

Ploetz, Alfred, 229–30

Poggenburg, Johannes (Bishop), 30–31, 33, 36

Polish workers in Germany, von Galen's support for, 278

political prisoners in Germany, British release of, 307, 310–11, 318

politics, von Galen's involvement in, 6, 20–22, 30–32

Portmann, Heinrich (Fr.): on Allied presence in Münster, 298, 300, 303–4; biography of von Galen by, 212–16, 365, 375–76, 380–81; diary of, 381–84; on von Galen's criticism of euthanasia, 198–200; on von Galen's illness

and death, 337–38, 348–51;
on von Galen's ordination
as Cardinal, 309, 313, 319,
321–22, 324, 331–36
positivist school of law, 27–28
power, von Galen's perspective
on, 20–29
press coverage of von Galen:
censorship of, 136–41; false
reports in, 289; pastoral
letters in newspapers, 53–61,
137–38
prisoners of war: British release
of, 307, 310–11, 318; von
Galen's visit to, 333–34
Privy Chamberlains of the
Sword and Cape, 331
Probst, Adalbert, 107
Protestantism: in Germany, 5,
27, 31, 86–87; Nazi "Ger-
man National Church" and,
80; Nazi suppression of
religious schools of, 147–69;
opposition to Nazism in,
37–38, 85, 132, 269–70;
in Prussia, 5, 15; religious
schools under, 69, 115,
184–86
Prussia: Catholic Church and,
33–34, 39–40; Münster as
part of, 5, 15
Pünder, Hermann, 253n270

R

racial superiority, Nazi doctrine
of: evolution of, 229–33; von
Galen's opposition to, 51–53,
71–72
Raeder, Erich (Adm.), 379
Reich Ministry for People's
Enlightenment and Propa-
ganda, 138–39
Reichstag, burning of, 64
Reisenberger, Dieter, 383–84
religion: Nazi subordination of,
147; von Galen's compari-
son of paganism to, 53–58.
See also specific religions, e.g.,
Catholic Church
religious houses and orders,
Gestapo attacks and confiscation of, 195–214, 216–27,
235–36, 269–74
religious instruction: history in
Germany of, 184–86; Nazi
suppression of, 52–53, 68–69,
95–96, 100, 115–21, 127–
33, 147–69. See also Catholic
schools; Protestantism
religious symbols: Nazi order
for removal of, 115–21, 155–
56, 165–69; Oldenburger
Kreuzkampf (Battle for the
Cross in Oldenburg) and,
115–21, 168–69, 192–93

Rerum Novarum encyclical, 1–2

"Right to Vote—The Duty to Vote, The" (von Galen), 20–24

Robinson, Brian (Sir), 320

Röhm, Ernst, 106–7

Roncalli, Angelo (Archbishop), 324

Rosenberg, Alfred: anti-Semitism and, 174; Catholic Church attacked by, 81–85, 142; German Faith Movement and, 118–19; pagan ideology of, 53, 60, 66–67; von Galen's criticism of, 73, 75–76, 179–80

Röver, Carl, 59–60, 116–19, 192–93

Russian forces in Münster, von Galen's complaints concerning, 291–92

Rust, Bernhard, 178

S

Sacred Heart, von Galen's devotion to, 192–94

Saint Anthony of Egypt, 9

Saint Boniface, 123

Saint Elizabeth of Thuringia, 71

Saint Hubert, 9

Saint Ludger, x, 42

saints, von Galen on inspiration of, 103–6

Saint Stanislaus, 196

Saint Thomas Becket, 196

Saint Victor, 104–5, 112–13

Schirach, Baldur von, 70, 81

Scholl, Hans, 253–54

Scholl, Sophie, 253–54

school curriculum: anti-Semitism in, 174–78; von Galen's criticism of, 51–53, 179–80

Schröer, Alois, 281

Schulte, Cardinal, 34–35, 75–76, 123, 186

Scripture, Ellis B., 278–79

Secret Consistory ceremony, 331

Sedgwick, R. L., 63n68, 309–10, 319–25, 332, 349–51

self-love, von Galen's discussion of, 25–27

Serries, Hans-Bernd, 381

Simon, Paul, 383–84

Sisters of Mercy of Münster, 230–33, 239–48, 278–86

Sisters of Our Lady of Lourdes, 216

Sisters of Perpetual Adoration, 269–74

Sisters of the Cross in Haus Aspel, 216

Sisters of the Good Shepherd, 2

slave labor in Germany, 290–91, 297–98, 300

social Darwinism, 230

Social Democrats (Germany), 31

socialism: Catholic resistance to, 15–16, 136; von Galen's rejection of, 27–28

social life, von Galen's Catholic Principles for, 328–36

Soldier of Christ: The Life of Pope Pius XII (Ventresca), 384

Sorrowful Virgin, shrine of (Telgte), von Galen's pilgrimages to, xi, 14, 197–98, 275–76, 292–93, 298–99, 320–21, 337–38

Soviet Union: German attack on, 264–65; Nuremberg war crimes trials and, 370–84; Spanish Civil War and, 136

Spanish Civil War, 135–37, 161

Spellman (Cardinal), 332–33, 335–36

Spottiswoode, J. (Col.), 297–304

Sproll, Joannes Baptista (Bishop), 162, 164–65

Stabat Mater (da Todi), 293

Stalin, Joseph, 264

state-absolutism, von Galen's critique of, 23–30, 95–96

Stella Matutina (boarding school), 10

Studies on The Myth of the Twentieth Century, 75–77

Sudetenland crisis, 187–88

suffering, von Galen's pastoral letter on, 292–93

T

Templer (General), 309

ten Hompel, Adolf, 38

theology, Nazi suppression of, 68–69

Tiessler, Walter, 254–55

Timothy, Second Epistle of, St. Paul's command in (4:1–5), 54

Trautmann, Markus, 365

Treaty of Versailles, 20

U

United States: air raids by, 274–75, 278–79; cardinals from, 327, 332, 335

University of Innsbruck, theological college at, 12

Uppenkamp (Fr.), 212

V

Ventresca, Robert A., 384

Virgin Mary, von Galen's devotion to, ix, 9, 14

von Bayern, Clemens August (Duke), 8

von Boeselager, Phillip Freiherr,
252–53, 266

von Galen, Anna, 1–2, 7, 14

von Galen, Cardinal Clemens
August: Allied occupation
and, 287–311, 352–53;
arrest considered for, 254–56;
attacks on Oldenburg palace
of, 177–78; beatification of,
355–56; birthday telegram
to Hitler and, 187–88; birth
of, 8; Catholic Principles for
social life of, 328–36; Catholic workers and, 16–17,
69–70; communism opposed
by, 27–28, 160–61, 265–86;
Concordat with Nazis and,
66–68, 72–73; consecration
as bishop, 40–49; death of
Pius XI, address concerning,
180–83; Die Tat magazine
interview with, 304–8; diocesan decree issued by, 109–10;
division in Catholic Church
over Nazism and, 98–99; early
life of, 2–9; early pastoral
ministry of, 13–33; education of, 10–11; efforts to save
Catholic schools, 183–86;
election as Bishop of Münster, 33–39; enrollment in
priesthood, 11–12; euthanasia
opposed by, 232–33, 277–78;
euthanasia sermon of, 235–
51; final sermon by, 342–47;
First Communion of, 9;
on German collective guilt,
294–96, 327–28; on German
invasion of Soviet Union,
265; on Gestapo confiscation
of religious houses and orders,
196–214, 216–27, 235–
36, 269–74; Goering and,
258–60; Great Procession of
Münster and, 85–92; illness
and death of, 337–38, 347–
54; as inspiration to German
resistance, 252–60; international reputation of, 262–86;
journey to Rome for ordination, 318–36; on Klausner's
murder as martyrdom, 107;
Kristallnacht, silence on,
172–78; martyrdom com-
pared to Nazi resistance by,
103–11; Mit brennender Sorge
encyclical and, 124–33; Nazi
attacks on Catholic Church
and, 139–42, 159–69; Nazi
campaign against, 63, 87–
89; Nazi regime opposed
by, xii–xiii, 2, 38, 66–68,
71–72; Nazi reprimands of,
256–60; Nazi suppression of

religious schools opposed by, 149–69; *Oldenburger Kreuz-kampf* (Battle for the Cross in Oldenburg) and, 118–21; ordination as Cardinal, 309, 313–36; paganism opposed by, 53–61, 67, 71, 73, 75–84; pastoral letter of 1933, 42–46, 53–61; pastoral letter of 1941, 192–94; pastoral letter of 1945, 292–93; Pius XI encyclical and, 123–24; political activities of, 6, 20–22, 30–32; postwar return to Münster by, ix–xii, 337–47; resistance tactics outlined by, 97–102; seminarians' conversations with, 58–59; silence on Jewish persecution, 51–53, 263–86, 274; on Spanish Civil War, 135–36; on Sudetenland crisis, 188; survival of air raids by, 281–86; Telgte sermon of, 294–304; on wartime devastation, 188–90, 276–86

von Galen, Christoph Bernhard (Bishop), 4, 13, 269–70, 292, 354

von Galen, Ferdinand Heribert, 2, 4, 6, 8, 11, 14

von Galen, Franz, 3, 9–12, 31, 37, 46, 284–85, 319, 354

von Galen, Matthias (Count), 1–2

von Galen, Max Gereon, 13–14

von Ketteler, Wilhelm Emmanuel (Bishop), 1, 5, 8, 13, 16, 25, 29–30, 330

von Kluge, Hans Günther, 266

von Loë, Fritz (Count), 285–86

von Moltke, Helmuth James (Count), 252

von Preysing, Count Konrad (Bishop of Berlin): Catholic resistance to Nazis and, 98–99, 123–24, 187–88; funeral mass for von Galen and, 351; Nazi suppression of Catholic schools and, 133; ordination as Cardinal, 314–15, 324, 331, 335

von Schleicher, Kurt, 112

von Spee, Elisabeth, 2, 4

von Spee, Friedrich, 13

von Spee, Placidus (Father), 10

von Twickel, Rudolf (Baron), 319

von Wendt, Karl, 266

Vorwerk, Franz (Monsignor), 115–16, 121, 164, 169, 192, 195, 283, 341

W

Weimar Republic, 20, 30, 36, 63–64, 136

White Rose resistance group,
253–54
Wolf, Hubert, 98, 365
women: Nazi policy of forced
abortion for, 230–33; von
Galen's awkwardness with,
15–16
workers: German Labor Front
restrictions on, 69–70; German slave labor and, 290–91,
297–98; von Galen's support
for, 16–18, 278
World War I (1914–18), 17,
20; Germany portrayed as
victim of, 188–89, 268

X
Xanten, Germany, von Galen's
consecration of the martyrs
of, 103–4, 109–13, 174–75

Y
youth organizations: in Catholic
Church, 58, 68, 81, 85–86,
138, 155–69; Nazi suppression of, 58, 70–71, 96

Z
Zuhorn, Karl (Dr.), 319,
339–40

 TAN·BOOKS

TAN Books is the Publisher You Can Trust With Your Faith.

TAN Books was founded in 1967 to preserve the spiritual, intellectual, and liturgical traditions of the Catholic Church. At a critical moment in history TAN kept alive the great classics of the Faith and drew many to the Church. In 2008 TAN was acquired by Saint Benedict Press. Today TAN continues to teach and defend the Faith to a new generation of readers.

TAN publishes more than 600 booklets, Bibles, and books. Popular subject areas include theology and doctrine, prayer and the supernatural, history, biography, and the lives of the saints. TAN's line of educational and homeschooling resources is featured at TANHomeschool.com.

TAN publishes under several imprints, including TAN, Neumann Press, ACS Books, and the Confraternity of the Precious Blood. Sister imprints include Saint Benedict Press, Catholic Courses, and Catholic Scripture Study.

For more information about TAN,
or to request a free catalog, visit
TANBooks.com

Or call us toll-free at
(800) 437-5876

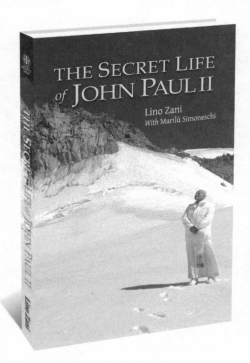
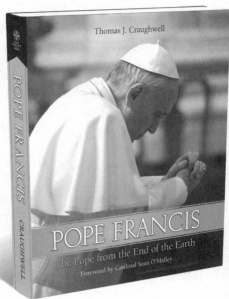

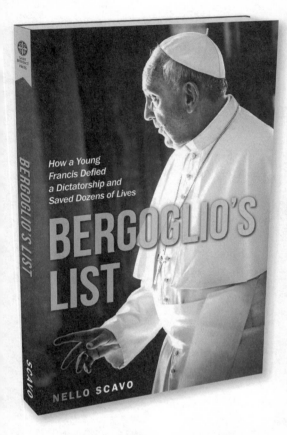

TAN · CLASSICS

*A collection of the finest literature
in the Catholic tradition.*

978-0-89555-227-3

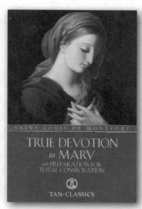

978-0-89555-154-2

978-0-89555-155-9

Our TAN Classics collection is a well-balanced sampling
of the finest literature in the Catholic tradition.

978-0-89555-230-3

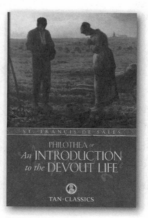

978-0-89555-228-0

978-0-89555-151-1

TAN · BOOKS

978-0-89555-153-5

978-0-89555-149-8

978-0-89555-199-3

The collection includes distinguished spiritual works of the saints, philosophical treatises and famous biographies.

978-0-89555-226-6

978-0-89555-152-8

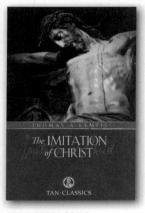

978-0-89555-225-9

Visit us at TANBooks.com

Spread the Faith with . . .

TAN·BOOKS

A Division of Saint Benedict Press, LLC

TAN books are powerful tools for evangelization. They lift the mind to God and change lives. Millions of readers have found in TAN books and booklets an effective way to teach and defend the Faith, soften hearts, and grow in prayer and holiness of life.

Throughout history the faithful have distributed Catholic literature and sacramentals to save souls. St. Francis de Sales passed out his own pamphlets to win back those who had abandoned the Faith. Countless others have distributed the Miraculous Medal to prompt conversions and inspire deeper devotion to God. Our customers use TAN books in that same spirit.

If you have been helped by this or another TAN title, share it with others. Become a TAN Missionary and share our life changing books and booklets with your family, friends and community. We'll help by providing special discounts for books and booklets purchased in quantity for purposes of evangelization. Write or call us for additional details.

TAN Books
Attn: TAN Missionaries Department
PO Box 410487
Charlotte, NC 28241

Toll-free (800) 437-5876
missionaries@TANBooks.com